SO-ACP-719

# HOW TO MAKE YOUR DREAMS COME TRUE STARTING TODAY!

 4 Ways to Evaluate a New Idea
10 Commandments of Possibility Thinking
 5 Principles for Putting Problems in a Proper Perspective
12 Principles for Managing Problems Positively
 3 Characteristics of an Emotionally-Free "Game Attitude"
 5 Ways to Overcome a "Brownout" and Prevent a Burnout
 5 Phases Necessary for the Faith that Can Move Mountains
26 Action Words to Get You Started and Never Let You Quit
366 Messages, Making Every Year a Leap Year, a Leap from
    Self-Doubt to Self-Fulfillment through Faith

# The INSPIRATIONAL WRITINGS of ROBERT H. SCHULLER

*Tough Times Never Last, But Tough People Do*

*Tough Minded Faith for Tender Hearted People*

Copyright © 1983 by Robert Harold Schuller
Originally published in two volumes as *Tough Times Never Last,*
*But Tough People Do* and *Tough Minded Faith for Tender Hearted People*

All rights reserved. No part of this work may be
reproduced or transmitted in any form or by any means,
electronic or mechanical, including photocopying,
recording, or any information storage and retrieval
system, without permission in writing from the publisher.

Published in 1986 by

Inspirational Press
166 Fifth Avenue
New York, New York 10010


By arrangement with Thomas Nelson, Inc.


Library of Congress Catalog Card Number: 86-81447

ISBN: 0-88486-008-6

Printed in The United States of America

# Acknowledgments

## Tough Times Never Last, But Tough People Do

This book would not have been possible without the help of Sheila Schuller Coleman who organized and edited the manuscript. I also want to thank Barbara Hagler for typing the manuscript and Marjorie Kelley for her careful assistance.

## Tough Minded Faith For Tender Hearted People

It is with profound gratitude that I acknowledge the editorial help of my wife, Arvella. Somehow she managed to take 2,000 of my written pages and condense them into 366 pages! I cannot count the number of days she arose in the dark of the early morning to tackle this editorial project. Then additional thanks goes to my daughters Sheila Coleman and Jeanne Dunn, both of whom worked so closely and creatively with Mrs. Schuller in improving my work.

This book has been a joyful family project. Both my wife and daughters understand this subject so well. We are one in heart and mind, because we have walked this walk of faith as a successful family for so many years.

# Tough Times Never Last, But Tough People Do!

To my grandchildren:
Angie Rae Schuller
Robert Vernon Schuller
Jason James Coleman
Christopher John Coleman

# CONTENTS

# PREFACE

*Lord,*
*give me the guidance*
*to know*
*when to hold on*
*and*
*when to let go*
*and the grace*
*to make the right decision*
*with dignity.*

This could be the most important prayer you've ever prayed, and this book could be the answer to that prayer.
For this book will provoke you to tough action: (a) To hold on until the light breaks, the tide turns, and the times change for the better; to tenaciously dig in and bloom where you are planted; to inspire people with your cheerful attitude while you are going through such obviously difficult times. In the process you will inspire others to choose the noble and positive outlook.

Or (b) this book will inspire you to take action to make a bold and daring move; to make a creative transition, recognizing an era has come to an end. The factory will never reopen. The steam engines are never going to be manufac-tured again. Sometimes the cup has fallen. It is broken. "All the king's horses and all the king's men couldn't put Humpty Dumpty together again." Now you may need to absorb the spills and develop new skills. This book will get you started on the path to success once again.

# PART
## I

*Tough Times Never Last,*
*But Tough People Do!*

# 1

## *Tough Times Never Last . . .*

It was a harsh summer, the summer of '82. For many, it was as if the clocks had rolled back to the thirties and the time of the Great Depression. Company upon company declared bankruptcy. Unemployment soared. The "severe and prolonged recession," as it was dubbed by the media, sent ripples of depression across America.

Politicians used the depressed state of the country to their advantage. It provided a great opportunity to highlight the failures, shortcomings, and faults of the opposite political party. Democrats found in it an opportunity to blame the Republican administration which was in charge. Predictably, the Republicans, in turn, blamed the "Democratic administration that created the problem" which the Republicans had inherited.

*Everybody was fixing the blame—nobody was fixing the problem!*

The problems persisted. They grew. The recession ran rampant across the country until nearly everyone was affected by it. No one was immune.

I, personally, felt it as pastor of the Crystal Cathedral congregation and head of a national television ministry, which was broadcast on 169 television stations every week. With five hundred people on the payroll, we were operating on a budget of well over twenty million dollars a year. The cost of operations continued to increase dramatically. Like the rest of America, we too were faced with tough economic times.

No one could deny that the country had problems. But the biggest problem we had was our *attitude* toward the economic problem. Negative thinking spread like a plague through all levels of society. It was not easy to protect oneself from the infection of negative thinking, which spread by word of mouth, by conversations with friends as well as strangers, by television screens, and by radio news reports.

It spread quickly because in recessive times the tendency is to react negatively. Once an organism, a business, a life, or a country is infected with negative thinking, the infection attacks the mind, the heart, and the soul like termites that secretly gnaw away at the emotional support system.

It was in the midst of this national mood that I arrived at the Hilton Hotel in downtown Chicago. I was there to present a motivational lecture at a major convention.

Delivering lectures of inspiration as well as on successful management principles was nothing new to me. Each year I travel from coast to coast, giving nearly one hundred talks to doctors, executives, educators, you name it.

However, I was particularly fascinated by this engagement. My audience would be members of the Ag-Industry. ("Ag" is, of course, the abbreviation for *agriculture*.) This industry represents those who are involved in the farming enterprises of the Midwest states of Iowa, Michigan, Illinois, and Minnesota. Having been born and reared on an Iowa farm, I looked upon this as an opportunity to touch base with some of the people that came from the same soil I left forty years before.

My anticipation of a warm, inspirational evening was quickly doused by a couple of somber-looking gentlemen. The convention badges pinned to their dark lapels identified them as the men for whom I was looking. They greeted me with restrained enthusiasm. "Dr. Schuller? Thank you for coming."

Their words reminded me of the thousands of times I have arrived at some scene of tragedy. In hospitals, mortuaries, courtrooms, and cemeteries, I have heard those words: "Thank you for coming." I couldn't help feeling that I had

[14]

arrived at the scene of some tragedy, rather than at a motivational convention.

The younger man spoke: "There are thirty-five hundred people in there waiting to hear you speak."

His companion interrupted. "These people are going through tough times. They don't want to hear your funny stories. They don't want to see you grinning from ear to ear like you do on television. They don't want a pat on the back with a hollow promise that 'Everything is going to be okay.'"

At that point, both men moved shoulder to shoulder to face me as if they meant to block me from entering the platform. The first man spoke up, "That's right, Dr. Schuller. These people are losing their farms. Their businesses are going bankrupt. Terrible pressures are being placed on their marriages and families. They need help. And more than anything else they need hope. Give it to them."

With that admonishment they nodded to the sound man, who pinned the microphone to my suit. As he did, I heard through the thin wall that separated the backstage area from the speaker's platform, the master of ceremonies' introduction: "Ladies and gentlemen, it is my pleasure now to introduce our keynote speaker. His name is Dr. Robert Schuller. He is the pastor of the world-famous Crystal Cathedral. This beautiful building was built at a cost of over twenty million dollars and was dedicated virtually debt-free. No minister or priest or rabbi speaks to more people every week in the world or in the United States of America than does Dr. Robert Schuller from Garden Grove, California. It's our pleasure now to welcome one of the world's most successful men—Dr. Robert Schuller. Let's give him a great welcome!"

The sound of enthusiastic applause surrounded me as I stepped onstage to face this collection of depressed souls. Thirty-five hundred people were on their feet, applauding me. The grand ballroom was packed to capacity.

Inwardly I shuddered. My carefully planned speech had just gone out the window. The three jokes I was prepared to tell for my own pleasure and for the purpose of "warming up my audience" now seemed out of place.

I found myself walking across the stage without the faintest idea of what I would tell these troubled people. I paced quietly from one end of the platform to the other, trying to collect my thoughts. I searched the eyes of the audience. I recalled the words of the stern welcoming committee. I decided to recover my position by asking a question.

"They tell me that you are having tough times. Is that right?"

The question gave me time to embrace a dramatic pause. Such a pause can be a lifesaver to a public speaker.

I continued to pace back and forth, pretending to exude the confidence of a well-prepared lecturer.

I could tell that my opening question had grabbed their attention—probably more effectively than the three funny stories I had carefully placed in my front pocket.

From that point on I delivered a spontaneous lecture that at times erupted with new insights. Wanting desperately to help these people and give them hope, I decided to address myself specifically to the pressing problems of these men and women who represented an industry vital to the health and welfare of our country. They represented the core of the breadbasket of America. The food in the markets and on the tables of our country comes from the labor and the leadership of these agriculture businessmen and women.

I remembered years ago what I was taught in my undergraduate studies in public speaking, lecturing, debating, and oratorical work in Hope College, Holland, Michigan, and again in my training at Western Theological Seminary in preparation for delivering sermons and talks from pulpits: the most effective speech is not a sermon but a witness. Essentially the principle is this: If you don't have any advice to give, you can always share your own story.

If there has been any excitement, challenge, crisis, and resolution in your life, then share it! Everybody likes a good story.

Drawing on this principle, I decided to share with the farmers how I handled the tough times in my life.

I suspected that my audience was not aware of the fact that

[16]

I, too, had tough times. My introduction portrayed me only as a very successful man, senior minister, founder and builder of a twenty-million-dollar, internationally acclaimed work of art called the Crystal Cathedral. They could only perceive me as very successful. They had not been told that I, too, had walked a path similar to the one they were now walking.

Should I tell them about the time a twenty-below-zero blizzard raged through the lonely blackness of an Iowa night?

Should I tell them how the wind whistled around the fragile country house, successfully penetrating the cracks between the window frame in the northwest corner of my bedroom, leaving fresh drifts of snow on the floor beside my bed?

Should I tell them how we didn't have the money to buy coal to warm the house?

Should I tell them how we raced to escape with our lives from a tornado?

Should I tell them how we survived the great drought, when the shortage of natural rainfall parched the earth and proved more devastating and destructive than the shortage of cash flow that had already hit all of the Americans in the Great Depression?

Should I tell them about my struggles to get through college?

Should I tell them about the fire in my rooming house in which I lost the few possessions I had?

Should I tell them how I had to struggle to start a church with only five hundred dollars, in a strange state without friends, contacts, property, or community support?

Should I tell them about my wife's bout with cancer? The near-loss of my daughter's life in a motorcycle accident? The amputation of her leg?

Should I share with them our struggles of the past three years, as we have tried to help her accommodate effectively to life as a young teen-ager with a disfigured, left stump of a leg?

Should I tell them how I was forced by circumstances beyond my control to build the Crystal Cathedral when I didn't want to build it, didn't have the money, and knew well enough that I would be criticized for building a "monument"?

I decided not to pour out my whole life story. But I did decide to begin with the realities of the tough times I had been through and how they had been handled successfully through a faith based on possibility thinking.

"Farming life has never been easy. My boyhood farm was a typical Midwestern farm. That meant it was small. The industry was not simple crop farming. The crops were harvested and fed to livestock. Chickens laid the eggs, which we traded for groceries. Cows grazed the grassland along the river that was too difficult to plow. We milked the cows and sold the milk. When the hogs reached their prime weight, they were sold at market. It was a one-crop-a-year farm. That meant that we planted the oats and the corn in the springtime and harvested it in the fall, to be gathered into barns and saved for feed for the hogs. The winter season was merely a time of survival—waiting and hoping for spring."

My father purchased our farm when prices were at their peak. Real estate had been climbing steadily. I was born only a few years later, September 16, 1926.

How my father saved enough to buy our farm is a story in itself. Because he lost his parents as a teen-ager, Dad was forced to drop out of school in the sixth grade and to find the only job he could—as a hired hand for the local farmers. One could always husk corn: Rip each single golden ear from its nest of leaves, crack off the six-foot stem, and throw it into the wagon. My father was a thrifty young man and was able to save a few nickels and dimes that he earned for each ear of corn he picked.

Finally he had saved enough to purchase a 160-acre farm. Unfortunately he bought it at the top of the price cycle. When I was three years old the Great Depression hit. Real estate prices plummeted along with the stocks. While internationally famed corporate chiefs were committing suicide in Wall Street, lonely farmers—America's original small businessmen—were clinging with broken fingernails to the earth, hoping to survive.

My father was one of those tough, tenacious farmers. Winter was the worst. I shall never forget the times when we did not have money to buy coal. The trees that surrounded the house were considered precious living creatures that could not be sacrificed for fuel. So we never considered cutting them down and sawing them up for the wood-burning stove.

Instead it became my job, as a child, to step over the three-foot high splintered wooden fence and climb into the hog yard among the one hundred squirming, squealing hogs. With an empty basket I maneuvered my way through the excrement, picking up every corncob left after the hogs had consumed the kernels.

Not a single cob was left uncollected. Every single one was considered of real value. When the basket was filled, I would carefully carry it to the tiny two-story, white sideboard home where my mother, father, brother, and sisters lived. The corncobs would fuel the stove in the kitchen. They would also be used in the potbelly stove in the little living room. These were the only two sources of heat in the house. Little grills in the ceilings allowed some of the heat to pass from the downstairs kitchen and living room to the upstairs bedrooms. But cracks in the walls let in just as much freezing air.

"Do you want to hear about my experience with poverty?" I said to the struggling thirty-five hundred businessmen, seated in the carpeted ballroom of the plush Hilton Hotel. "Let me tell you about poverty. I was so poor we had to use corncobs to heat our homes to keep from freezing to death in the subzero winters. We used corncobs because we could not afford coal."

*"Those were tough times!"* I bellowed.

Then I recalled the years of the great drought. Even as the economic depression ravaged the country, the Iowa farmers fought a far tougher battle. For reasons we never understood, the normal spring rainfall never came to moisten the newly planted corn and oats. The few precious dollars that my father was able to save had to be spent on seed corn.

I always wondered how he dared to risk throwing seed in the ground where it might rot and die, when he could safely bring it to town and convert it to cash. "Why take a chance?" I once asked my father. "Why don't you play it safe and sell it?"

"People who never take a chance," he taught me wisely, "never get ahead."

Of course, there is no success without the application of the multiplication principle. It was a natural, native, basic principle that every farmer understood. So in the springs of 1931, 1932, and 1933 my father took all that he had left—the last kernels of corn, the last cups of oats—and planted them in the ground of his small Iowa farm, expecting that the rains would fall. He hoped that the seeds would become wet and bloated until they erupted with new life, sending their tender little sprouts up through the softened spring soil. Light-green rows of corn would begin to grow and stand out against the black background of the dark Iowa ground.

Rainfall is essential to a farmer's success. And Iowa farmers can expect rain to fall at least once every other week.

If, for some reason, the rains did not fall for three or four weeks, one inch of the topsoil would dry out first. Then, if rain still did not come, the soil would gradually grow dry at two, three, four, five inches deep, until the hair-like tentacles of the roots of the new corn plants would die.

The first evidence of the death of the roots would be a wilted leaf.

When the rains did not fall for two weeks, my father was worried. When the third and fourth weeks passed with no rain I saw his face grow very grave. Not once did he become angry. Never did he miss praying with bowed head at the table before our morning, noon, or nighttime meals.

The only thing my father did about the drought was pray. That was the only thing he could do. Farmers gathered from miles around, at special prayer meetings, filling the little white churches that dotted the rolling landscapes. Out of respect and reverence to the almighty God, each farmer came, not in his overalls, but in his one and only suit and tie.

They called upon God Almighty to save their land and their crops. They asked Him to send rain.

Then all they could do was to go home and wait for His answer. For a whole year the Lord was silent. Day after day, the sun bore down on the crops. Every day we thirstily scanned the scorching sky for a sign of a cloud. More than once I ran into the house, calling out, "I've seen a cloud! God may be answering our prayer!" But the clouds always dissipated.

Finally, as if in fact our prayers were being answered, there was a gathering of clouds. Hopes began to rise again. The desperately needed rainfall was moving in from the west! Flashes of lightning slashed through the black sky. Thunder cracked. The trees trembled with fright as the wind whipped through their branches. It rained!

I was jubilant, but my father did not share my enthusiasm. Neither did my mother. For they knew what I did not know: the rain was totally inadequate. When the last thunder clap echoed in the distance, signaling the passing of the storm, the sun came out bright and hot again. We walked outdoors. My father scooped up a handful of the wet, moistened surface soil. Only the top quarter-inch was wet and black. Below that the earth was powdery dry.

Then the winds began to blow—from where we did not know. The sky turned from bright blue to a drab gray to a dirty brown. And the clean bright air that I enjoyed breathing as a child suddenly became polluted with dust. "That's South Dakota land you are breathing, Son," my father said. South Dakota, the state that bordered Iowa on the northwest, was suffering a worse drought than Iowa. It did not even enjoy the sporadic showers that moistened the surface soil. The barren land, devoid of any vegetation, lay helpless before the gathering winds. They swept the feathery particles of earth high into the sky, carrying them hundreds of miles to the east. Like drifts of snow the dust settled on our farm. When the winds blew harder, the dust sandblasted the few rows of corn that had managed to survive the drought. The fragile young plants, wilted and weakened for want of refreshing

*Nobody is a
total failure
if he dares
to try
to do something
worthwhile.*

water, were no match for the grit driven by the hot winds. There was total devastation. Here and there, like bones of a dead animal, dead corn stalks protruded above the drift of dry sand.

Still the winds did not cease. It became a common procedure for my brother, sisters, and me to cover our faces with wet cloths as we walked the short distance from our house to the outdoor toilet. When we walked to the well, where we hoped we would be able to pump water from the forty-foot reservoir, we would have to protect ourselves from the suffocating dust with our moistened masks.

Our water became more and more scarce as the meandering snake of a river dried up. The Floyd River had been my closest childhood friend. On its green banks, near open pastures, I would lie, watching the clouds change shape in the blue sky. It was there that I felt closest to my Creator.

I became incurably addicted to God's natural green gardens. Years later, I would hope and dream of a place where I could worship and see the sky above me, day and night. Years later I would dream of a church that could allow all of the sky to permeate our troubled minds with its peace, bringing healing from worry and anxiety. Years later I would find that dream fulfilled in a Crystal Cathedral.

But during the summer of the great drought, I watched the river dry up. Little pools of water became mud holes where squirming bullhead catfish died. We were surrounded by death—the river was dead, the fish were dead, and most importantly, the crops were dead.

Summer finally gave way to fall. Newspapers nationwide proclaimed the Midwest farm belt to be in "total disaster." Even the New York bankers and corporate chiefs became concerned about a plague that was as great, if not greater, than their own economic depression. The breadbasket of America was in ruins.

If it had been a normal year, my father would have expected to harvest corn that would fill dozens of wagons. That year, my father harvested barely a half a wagon of corn, grown on a half-acre of ground. In a normal year, this swampy lot, fed by some mysterious underground spring, was too wet to produce any fruit at all.

My father had often thought about digging deep into that plot to drain the subsurface water away. Now in the year of the drought this small plot of ground was the only parcel out of 160 acres where the corn had survived. Here the corn lived, drawing moisture from a subterranean source. Here the corn grew nearly six feet tall. And here we harvested the minuscule crop.

It was but half a wagon of corn.

A total disaster? Not quite. For a half a wagon of corn was better than none at all. In fact, it was equal to the amount of seed that had been sowed earlier that year. A total loss? No. We gained nothing. But more importantly we lost nothing!

I shall never forget my father's dinnertime prayer that night.

"Dear Lord. I thank You that I have lost nothing this year. You have given me my seed back. Thank You!"

Not all farmers had as much faith as my father did.

"For sale" signs began to appear on farm after farm. Discouraged farmers who could not imagine that things would get better packed up and abandoned their land. Other farmers simply threw their hands up in despair and allowed the bank to foreclose. More than one piece of property sold on the courthouse steps.

Years later I asked my father how he had survived. After all, he had had no cash reserves. He had had no rich relatives.

"I went to the bank," my father said, "and I promised them that if they would help me, somehow I'd return their money. I pleaded with them to refinance, rearrange the mortgage, postpone the due date. For some reason, the bank believed in me and it helped."

I remember that bank! I have early childhood memories of going there, in patched overalls, with my father. I recall seeing this slogan on a calendar in that bank: *Great people are ordinary people with extraordinary amounts of determination.*

I'm convinced that that slogan exemplified the positive attitude of my father and inspired the bankers to go along with him and give him an extension on his mortgage payment.

That slogan was an explanation of my father's success and an inspiration to me to attempt the impossible too! For I had dreams of my own—to go to college and seminary.

Some years later, on a quiet June afternoon, the tornado struck. I had not unpacked my suitcases, having returned only a few days before for the summer recess from my college studies. Throughout the afternoon, my dad and I could hear an awesome roar reverberating like the hum of a mighty organ. The eerie sound was like many freight trains rumbling above the threatening and gathering clouds.

"Sounds like we're in for a hailstorm," my dad murmured.

In a desperate attempt to protect his prize roses, we rounded up empty pails and wooden boxes to cover every treasured bush. It was six o'clock now. We had finished our evening meal in haste. From the vantage point of our front lawn we could see more than a mile across the rolling farm land. The sun was lost now, seemingly swallowed by the black monstrous storm that was prowling the western sky.

Slowly, with alarming stillness like a tiger crawling up on a sleeping prey, the storm crept closer. Gusts of hot wind blew the dry dust of the country road. The old box elder bent before the mounting winds.

Out in the pasture a cow bellowed frantically, calling her little calf to come to her side for safety.

My riding horse seemed to sense impending disaster. He cut a commanding picture, standing erect, with head held high, graceful neck arched. His tail, lifted slightly, fanned in the wind; his ears searched the air for sounds of danger.

Suddenly a black lump, about the size of the sun, bulged out of the black sky. In an instant it telescoped to the ground in a long gray funnel. For a moment it hung suspended—like a slithering serpent, about to strike death to helpless victims below. Dad called to Mom: "It's a tornado, Jennie!"

I asked excitedly, "Are you sure it's a real tornado, Dad?" My first emotion was delightful excitement. This would be something to tell the fellows when I returned to Hope Col-

[25]

lege in the fall. The funnel seemed so small I couldn't imagine the fury that could be unleashed from such a funny cloud.

"Call Mother, Son, and tell her to take whatever she can grab and come to the car. We've got to get out of here—right away!"

A moment later we were driving crazily down the road. We lived on the east end of a dead-end road and had to drive a mile west, directly into the path of the oncoming tornado in order to reach a side road that led south, away from the path of the storm. We made it.

Two miles south, we parked our car on the crest of the hill and watched the wicked twister spend its killing power. As quickly and quietly as it had dropped, it lifted and disappeared. It was all over. The storm was gone. The air was deathly still, but the danger was past. Gentle raindrops now began to fall. The tail end of the dark sky dropped a soothing shower of cool rain, as if heaven were pouring a soothing balm on fresh wounds.

We could go home now. "Oh, God, will we find our house?" We reached the crossroads, only to find a long line of cars. Curious sightseers, sensing that something terrible had happened, already were gathering. They were looking at the complete destruction of a neighboring farm.

Wondering if our house had been spared, we drove down the lonely road, crisscrossed by wires from broken telephone poles, toward our secluded farm. We came to the base of the hill that hid the view of our house. Before, we had been able to see the peak of our barn. But not now. We knew before we went over the hill that our barn was gone.

Now we were on the top of the hill. We saw it. Everything was gone. Where only a half hour before there had been nine buildings, freshly painted, now there were none. Where there had been life, there was the silence of death. It was all gone—all dead.

Only white foundations remained, lying on a clean patch of black ground. There was no debris. Everything had simply been sucked up and carried away. Three little pigs, still liv-

*When
you've exhausted
all possibilities,
remember this:
You haven't!*

ing, suckled the breasts of their dead mother, lying in the driveway. We could hear the sickening moan of dying cattle, the hiss of gas escaping from a portable tank of butane used to provide fuel for our stove. Then I saw my riding horse—lying dead with a fourteen-foot-long two-by-four piercing his belly.

Dazed, our brains reeling, we sat in our car. My father was past sixty and had worked hard for twenty-six years to try to win this farm. The mortgage was about due. This seemed to kill all chances of ever saving the place from the creditors. I looked at my dad, sitting horror-stricken, white-haired, underweight from overwork, his hands blue, desperately gripping the steering wheel.

Suddenly those calloused hands with their bulging blood vessels began hitting the steering wheel of the car, and Dad cried, "It's all gone! Jennie! Jennie, it's all gone! Twenty-six years, Jennie, and it's all gone in ten minutes."

Dad got out of the car, ordering us to wait, and walked with his cane around the clean-swept, tornado-vacuumed farmyard.

We later found out that our house had been dropped, in one smashed piece, a half-mile out in the pasture. We had had a little sign on the kitchen wall—a little molded plaster motto. Its simple verse was: "Keep looking to Jesus." My dad found and carried to the car the broken top half: "Keep looking. . . ." Well, this was God's message to Dad—Keep looking! Keep looking!

Don't quit now. Don't sell out. Dig in and hold on. And he did! People thought my dad was finished, but he was not. He was not finished because he would not give up. He had faith with hanging-on power! There's one ingredient that mountain-moving faith, miracle-generating faith, earth-shaking faith, problem-solving faith, and situation-changing faith must have, and that ingredient is *holding* power. So Dad didn't quit.

Two weeks later we found in a nearby town an old house that was being torn down. A section of it was available for sale for fifty dollars. So we bought this remnant and took it apart, piece by piece. We saved every nail and every shingle. And from these pieces we built a new little house on the old home farm! One by one, additional farm buildings were built. Nine farms were demolished in that tornado but my father was the only farmer to rebuild a completely demolished farm. A few years later prices rose sharply. Farm products prospered. Within five years the mortgage was paid off. My father died a successful man![1]

"So you're having tough times! Are they tougher times than my father experienced?" I looked deep into the eyes and the hearts of the new generation of Iowa farmers. "Are you burning corncobs for fuel? Have you lost everything in a tornado? Is the mortgage due and the cash not there? Are you tempted to walk away and put the place up for sale? Then let me tell you something about tough times. I believe I have walked the path and have earned the right to comment on tough times. Let me tell you something about tough times!"

I hadn't the foggiest idea *what* I was going to tell them about tough times! I had painted myself into a corner. I prayed silently. I prolonged the dramatic pause as I paced like a tiger in a cage back and forth across the empty stage, returning the stares of a very attentive audience.

I was stunned to hear this sentence come out of my mouth. I was shocked. I was inspired! I am convinced it came directly from God. It was a sentence that would not only inspire me and my audience but many others. It would even give birth to a book. Like a thunderclap, this sentence filled every corner of the huge ballroom:

**Tough times never last, but tough people do!**

The place broke up with applause. Those thirty-five hundred farmers who had lost hope and had battled depres-

---

[1]The tornado story is an excerpt from *Move Ahead With Possibility Thinking*. Copyright © 1967 by Robert H. Schuller. Reprinted by permission of Doubleday and Company, Inc.

sion found that hope. They caught a new vision and began to dream again.

Are you facing tough times today? Overwhelmed? I invite you to take a walk with me. Let me tell you about survivors— and how *you* can be one too! In the process your life will become a light for someone else's pathway.

The path is called "The Possibility Thinking Path." I've been preaching it for years. It has never let me down. It has never let anybody down. It never quits on us. We may quit the path, but the path keeps right on going on to happiness, health, and prosperity.

# 2

## . . . But Tough People Do!

**K**nute Rockne said it: "When the going gets tough, the tough get going." When the roads are rough, the tough rise to the occasion. They win. They survive. They come out on top!

People are like potatoes. After potatoes have been harvested they have to be spread out and sorted in order to get the maximum market dollar. They are divided according to size—big, medium, and small. It is only after potatoes have been sorted and bagged that they are loaded onto trucks. This is the method that all Idaho potato farmers use—all but one.

One farmer never bothered to sort the potatoes at all. Yet he seemed to be making the most money. A puzzled neighbor finally asked him, "What is your secret?" He said, "It's simple. I just load up the wagon with potatoes and take the roughest road to town. During the eight-mile trip, the little potatoes always fall to the bottom. The medium potatoes land in the middle, while the big potatoes rise to the top." That's not only true of potatoes. It is a law of life. Big potatoes rise to the top on rough roads, and tough people rise to the top in rough times.

Tough times never last, but tough people do.

Possibility thinking works. It worked for my father, it has worked for me, and I've seen it work for men and women who heard me preach it. I preached it, they practiced it, and here is what happened.

## Mary Martin

As I was working on this book, I received a beautiful letter from a person I had never met but had admired from a distance. Six times Mary Martin's picture has appeared on the cover of *Life* magazine. America loved her as Peter Pan, flying across the stage on Broadway, as Nellie Forbush in "South Pacific," and as Maria Von Trapp in the original Broadway production of the "Sound of Music."

I saw her as a person who was always positive, joyous, optimistic, and happy.

I never understood or knew the personal tragic paths she has walked quietly and has faced prayerfully. Then an unexpected letter from her arrived.

"Three times in the past nine years your ministry has deeply changed my life," she wrote, adding, "I'd like a chance to tell the world about it sometime."

I responded. She invited me to lunch and told me her story. I asked her if she would mind if I shared it in this book. Here it is:

"The principles of possibility thinking that I heard from your television ministry helped me accept the loss of my beloved husband, Richard Halliday, nine years ago. That was a tough time, believe me!

"Then I lost my voice and was unable to sing. That was like losing my life. Then one morning a possibility-thinking message inspired an idea that led me to health again. My singing voice returned!"

Sparkling with joy as she shared the event, she looked as young and attractive at sixty-nine as she must have looked when she was a bright, young starlet beginning her career. I could hardly believe that she had come out of the hospital only weeks before, following a car crash that had claimed one life and almost two others.

I had seen her interview on the "Today" show not long before, and she had walked with a walker. After all, she had broken her pelvis in two places and had come dangerously close to death. Now, having celebrated her sixty-ninth birth-

*Tough
times never
last . . .
but tough
people do!*

day, she had not only recovered, she walked without a limp!

"Of course, I have some trouble with arthritis and cataracts," she laughed heartily. Her eyes twinkled and flashed with exuberance and youthfulness, almost belying her confession.

Then she told me the terrible story of the accident as it had happened a few months before. She, along with her dearest female friend, Janet Gaynor, and her dearest male companion and manager, Ben Washer, had stepped into a cab in San Francisco.

"Ben insisted, 'Please get in first, Mary.' I obliged. 'You're next,' Ben said to Janet, who slipped in the middle of the back seat. Then Ben, like a gentleman, followed and closed the door behind him. Because of this seating arrangement, Ben bore the immediate impact of the speeding car, driven by a drunken driver who ran a red light. The impact was horrible! Ben was killed and Janet spent month after torturing month lingering near death, finally recovering enough to be able to return home to Palm Springs for Christmas.

"I think maybe that was one of my toughest times," Mary Martin said. Without losing the twinkle, she continued, "But as you say, tough times never last, but tough people do. And I'm a tough Texan, you know!"

What gives some persons the power to fight on after the loss of a precious loved one, after experiencing torturing physical pain day after day? There is no substitute for deep abiding faith. If we hold on, we will win out! Unquestionably the profound faith and the beautiful providence of God produce a strong and unquenchable optimistic mental attitude.

"Richard Rodgers told me that he wrote the song, 'Cockeyed Optimist' for me!" Mary spoke softly, humbly; yet she was very pleased. She continued, "He was writing the play, 'South Pacific' and he said to me, 'Mary, when I knew you'd be playing the part of Nellie, I simply thought about you and wrote the words. And he was right, you know. I *am* 'stuck like a dope with a thing called hope.'"

That's the spirit that heals all diseases, redeems lives from destruction, and brings sunshine back after the rain: Tough people have it. And they can weather the worst storm. They can rough out the toughest times. They win! They come out on top.

### Benno Fischer

I met Benno Fischer in 1960, in the Richard Neutra architectural office where he served the prestigious Los Angeles firm as one of the associate architects. Richard Neutra, Benno Fischer, and I spent many days together, sketching the architectural dream church.

I noticed "KL" tattooed in bluish letters, one inch high, on Benno's left hand. Beneath it were tattooed eight numbers, each approximately one-quarter inch high.

"What does the *KL* stand for, Benno?" I asked.

Surprised, he looked at me: "You mean you don't know?"

I said, "No, really. What does the *KL* stand for?"

"Oh," he said. "It stands for *Konzentrationslager*. That's German for *concentration camp*."

And then he unfolded his story!

It took place in Warsaw, Poland, in 1939. Benno Fischer and his sweetheart, Ann, were in love and were planning their marriage when the German army took the city. In the terrible confusion that followed, Benno was loaded on a truck and was taken, along with other Jews, to a concentration camp where he would be confined until 1945.

"Where's my Ann?" he wondered those first days—which eventually stretched into tormenting weeks and horrifying months.

Unknown to him, Ann, hearing of the impending disaster that was falling upon her city, had slipped through dark alleys. In disguise, she managed to slip out of Germany by successfully passing herself off as a non-Jew. She assumed Benno was dead.

But Benno was one of four thousand Jews in the concentration camp, each of whom was offered a daily cube of bread and a bowl of soup. The soup, of course, was far more satisfying. It extended the stomach and relieved the painful empty feeling that a cube of bread hardly satisfied. Trading bread for soup became, for many inmates, a major activity of the day. Benno was offered cubes of bread by more than one fellow inmate. He always agreed to the transaction.

As the time of the liberation approached, the camp's population dwindled from four thousand to four hundred. In a desperate effort, the Nazi Gestapo tied the feet of the remaining prisoners to each other and led them off on a long, cold march through the snow of the late winter season. Emaciated and disease-ridden, many dropped from exhaustion and were left to freeze in the snow.

Then came that unforgettable morning! A rumble of heavy engines was heard from over the hill. Then on the horizon there appeared  tanks, approaching quickly through the melting snow. GI's with American flags overtook the pitiful, tragic cordon of surviving Jews. Benno Fischer was set free!

Freedom! Benno's first act was to search for his beloved Ann. Was she dead? Was she alive? "I heard someone say he thought he saw her in Stuttgart," he was told by another survivor.

On a long shot, he went to Stuttgart. While riding a bus through the city, he suddenly recognized a lovely young lady standing on the corner. He jumped off and whirled her around. He looked at her. She stared at him. In the depth of their eyes, they recognized the love that would not die.

"Ann?" Benno said.

"Benno!"

They embraced; they cried; they laughed; they loved; they survived. And they came to America! *Tough times never last, but tough people do!*

## Judy Hall

In July 1980, Judy Hall, mother of two young teen-age daughters, found herself unemployed. Divorced and without steady income, Judy wondered how she would possibly survive. She had no formal education and no skill that she could call upon.

She was living in Minneapolis, Minnesota, listening to our television program as we urged her week after week to be a possibility thinker. She heard such suggestions as: "Open your mind to God. Ideas will flow in. One of these will be the idea that God means for you to grab hold of."

Judy believed what she heard. So, she decided to try real estate. But she couldn't have picked a worse time to enter the business. As a result, she failed. She could have easily gotten discouraged, but she didn't.

Her next idea was to "take the girls back to their birthplace where they can get acquainted with their heritage." She scraped together enough dollars to pack up herself and her two daughters and return to the state of their birth—Hawaii.

After returning to Hawaii, she wanted the comfort of a muumuu, the loose-fitting dress of the Islands, but also a garment with enough style to be worn to non-Hawaiian events. As she shopped for such a muumuu, she discovered that all of them were sold "off the rack" in one size. All had a similar Hawaiian print, and none really had any distinctive design. And because they were made of the Hawaiian printed fabrics, they really didn't fit any social occasions that were not Hawaiian in tone and spirit.

She suddenly remembered hearing the lesson taught in all the possibility-thinking literature: "The secret of success is to find a need and fill it." Judy saw a need and decided to fill it. She purchased some fabric in a "mainland" print and proceeded to make for herself a muumuu with a decorative border at the hem. She customized the fit so that it was comfortable but not so loose-fitting as to lose all sense of line and design. The final result was something very distinctive.

Her landlord's wife loved Judy's muumuu.

"Can you make me one?" she asked.

"Of course," Judy said, "I'd love to. When can I take your measurements?"

"Measurements?" she said. "You mean it's tailored to fit me? A muumuu tailored to fit me?" the wife asked.

"Of course," Judy said, "I specialize in custom-made, hand-tailored muumuus. The sleeves should match the length of your arms. The length and the width of the shoulders should be tailored for you."

Beyond a doubt, this was a totally new concept in manufacture and design of muumuus.

As Judy thought about the muumuus she had made, she remembered what we teach in our possibility-thinking lectures: You can test an idea to see if it will be successful or not by asking four questions.

The first question is: Is it practical and will it fill a vital human need? Judy realized a muumuu is exceptionally practical because it fits any lady, of any shape. Anyone with weight problems can easily hide bulges under the full and flowing style of the muumuu.

The second question: Can it be done beautifully? Judy thought, *Yes, the muumuu can have a greater fashion flare. It can be done with more sophisticated draping and tapering and with a layered look like formal dresses on the mainland.*

The third question: Can it be done differently enough so that it will stand out from all the others? She decided that it could if she didn't use Hawaiian prints. If she used fabrics that are popular on the mainland, the muumuu would not be restricted to wear at Hawaiian parties.

She asked the fourth question: Can it receive the stamp of excellence and be a little better than anything else that is being offered? Her answer was immediate to the fourth question also. Yes! This muumuu would not only be practical, beautiful, and different, but it would excel in value, quality, and style compared to the muumuus currently marketed in Hawaii! With one hundred dollars and this confidence she decided to start.

"Dr. Schuller," Judy Hall told me recently, "I made my first muumuu ten months ago. Today I'm turning out 123 dresses a month!"

"But are you really making money? I know you need to!"

"You bet I am!" she answered. "I'm doing it by keeping my overhead down to almost nothing. I take the measurements. I buy the fabrics—only three basic ones, so I'm not stuck with a lot of fabric and inventory that isn't being sold. I deliver the fabric and the measurements to a lady who cuts the entire dress in her house. She works as an independent contractor. Therefore, I don't have to have a payroll. I don't have to make the payroll deductions and have all of the expensive accounting that goes along with it.

"I pick up the cut-out pieces and deliver them to one of several women who do the sewing in their homes. Because they, too, are independent contractors, I don't have the problem of overhead.

"As a result, I've been able to run this entire business, manufacturing 123 dresses a month, without any office at all. I operate out of my little apartment.

"However," she added, "my business has grown so much that we are moving to a new office next week. It will be one hundred seventeen square feet!"

I couldn't believe it. "One hundred seventeen square feet? But that's only one room, less than ten feet by twelve feet."

"Yes," she said to me, "that's all I need. Because all of the cutters and all of the seamstresses work out of their homes, I don't have the overhead or expense that go along with maintaining a factory building. I don't have the expenses of a payroll. My overhead is virtually nothing."

"But you still needed cash to finance the beginning of your operation, didn't you?" I asked.

"No," she said. "I really started with only one hundred dollars and the idea. The idea was that if people were having a muumuu tailor-made for them, then I could expect and ask for an advance payment along with their order. The deposit made with the order covers the upfront capital outlay.

"Guess what, Dr. Schuller?" she said. "You're right! Anything is possible if you have faith. And I'll tell you something else. The biggest problem any of us ever face is our own negative thinking.

"When my friends saw me with my two children and no income, they really worried about how we were going to survive. When I told them I was going to go into the dressmaking business, with my own brand and design of muumuus, they laughed at me. They said, 'You're going to try to sell muumuus to Hawaiians? Why don't you go to Alaska and sell snow to the Eskimos? Don't you know that there are tens of thousands of muumuus hanging on the racks of all of the hotel shops, dress shops, and tour centers in Hawaii today? Don't you know there is a recession going on?'

"Those were the comments I heard, but guess what?" she said enthusiastically. "I just received an order to make all of the muumuus for the two hundred girls in the graduating class of one of the largest high schools in Honolulu. It is customary for the senior girls to wear muumuus on their graduation day. For years and years and years, the muumuus have been ordered from another old Hawaiian dressmaking firm. But they were so impressed with my fashions and style and distinctive quality of manufacturing that they have placed their entire order with my firm.

"My next step is to start selling them on the mainland," she said. "After all, the mainland hasn't really discovered the muumuu because the design and the fabric haven't been correct. But I've learned what works and how to do it and I'll be selling them all over the United States of America. And do you know what, Dr. Schuller? They won't call them muumuus; they'll call them 'Judi-muu's!'"

"But, Judy," I said, "didn't you have special training for this somewhere along the line? Where did you study dress designing?"

"Oh, no, I never studied dress designing. I never studied any kind of designing. I just designed it to fit myself. You see, Dr. Schuller, I was once very heavy. I've lost sixty-five pounds! I decided I wanted a dress that would fit me and fit me well! I designed it according to my own needs."

If a single, divorced mother of two children, with no money and no special training, is able to invade a surplus market with a new product and a new concept and develop a super successful enterprise, then it's probably possible for you to create employment opportunities for yourself.

*It works! Believe me! Tough times never last, but tough people do!*

## BUT TOUGH PEOPLE DO

### John Prunty

John Prunty was known throughout his community as "the roadrunner man," for in 1965, running had not become the popular endeavor it is today. There were the usual guffaws and good-natured chiding during his early morning jaunts. On June 6, 1973, John took his usual twenty-one-minute run, not knowing it would be his last.

Later that morning, John, along with the rest of the five-member construction crew, scrambled onto the roof of a small home. It was one of those hot, oppressive days, and the work was difficult. John was atop a scaffold when his foreman called to him for a tool. In reaching for it, John stepped forward, and instantly a cinder block pulled loose and gave way under his weight.

John fought the impulse to jump, thinking that he could regain his balance and avoid breaking an ankle on the uneven turf some ten feet below. But it was too late. John was already airborne and out of control from his momentum. He seemed to float, as if in a suspended weightless state, similar to flying in outer space.

His flight ended with terrible finality. His 160 pounds landed with full force upon his head, and as John tells it:

"I still shudder when I recall the sickening, grinding sound of crunching vertebrae as they snapped under the strain. My body's trajectory, coupled with its momentum, tried to force my forehead against my chest in pretzel-like fashion. Instantly I was aware I had lost feeling in my legs.

"Waves of fear, anger, and utter frustration assaulted me in those first seconds, as my immediate efforts to get up proved futile. Only my head would respond to my brain's commands. I heard a yell from above: 'Hey, John's fallen!' I alternately cursed and prayed. I turned my head to the left and saw, a few inches away, a pair of booted feet, toes facing me, which looked grotesquely like my own. 'That's strange,' I thought, 'my legs are outstretched!' But they weren't, and the subsequent realization was terrifying.

"I felt no pain until someone lifted my head slightly to place a pillow under it. Then the pain was so severe that I had to request him to remove the pillow. I felt as if my head were suspended only by a thread. Every time I rotated it, even slightly, the pain increased and gave me the weird idea that the thread would break and my head would detach. I struggled to stay conscious.

"Surprisingly soon, the rescue squad arrived and efficiently went about preparing to place a stretcher beneath me. I dreaded the move, for by now the pain had become quite severe. I was comforted, however, by the squad's professionalism as they reassured me and tried to minimize the effects of my trauma.

"Once inside the ambulance, I began to feel a little better, comforted by the belief that I would soon be in the care of experts who would set everything straight.

"At the hospital, the neurosurgeon who took my case had me lifted onto an X-ray table. He then climbed up on hands and knees to pull and tug at my head to achieve the needed angles for pictures. Though I had known pain before, I was sure I had never experienced anything like this. A short time later the doctor brought me the unhappy confirmation that my neck was indeed broken, between the fifth and sixth cervical vertebrae. I had learned to pray as a child, so now once again I turned to God and prayed for strength to endure whatever was ahead in life's uncertain road.

"The night seemed interminable, and I spent agonizing hours reliving the outrageous events of the day, over and over again.

"But through the pain and confusion of a traumatic, potentially mortal, and life-changing injury came the memory of the words from our wheelchair president, Franklin D. Roosevelt: 'All we have to fear is fear itself.' Following that was a positive reaction—a rededication and reaffirmation of love. There were prayers of supplication to God, whose master plan undoubtedly was to unfold in the coming days; and there were prayers of thanksgiving for life that had been preserved for another endeavor.

"But the real battle was yet to come!

"I was abruptly reminded, when I awoke, of the 'tongs' which protruded from both sides of my head. The more quietly I lay, I soon discovered, the less the pain. I felt as if I were wrapped like a mummy from the chest down. That was frightening because it meant the feeling was gone. There were gadgets and meters all around me. A nurse, whom I assumed to be virtually omniscient and omnipotent, seemed to have the power to intervene at a moment's notice if anything went awry. I had never before been hospitalized, and the entire environment was foreign to me. It was like living out a novel I must have read at some time or another."

During the following weeks, it became more apparent that the major effects of John's injury would be permanent. He continued to hold out hope, though, that a miracle would occur and mend the spinal cord to the extent that it could again process messages—any message—from the brain.

With this in mind, John began to concentrate on recovery. He became interested in discovering as much as possible about just what it was he needed to recover from. He didn't even have to ask, for one day John overheard one of the nurses commenting to an aide, in reference to him, "That's the way quadraplegics are!" John had never before seen a quadraplegic. In fact, he could not spell the word, though suddenly he was one!

In that moment of truth this young husband and father knew he was a quadraplegic, a victim of a broken neck, paralyzed from the neck down for life!

But he was alive! It was a tough time . . . but no one's tougher than John.

He said, "I decided to be a survivor. In fact, three D's became my guiding theme . . . desire, dedication and determination. I knew I needed to generate and sustain the *desire* to live, to heal, and to recognize my true potential. Then I had to *dedicate* myself to that concept. *Determination* alone would give me the victory. I resolved never to surrender!"

Today, after more than eight years in a wheelchair, John claims that life is every bit as good as ever.

[43]

He says, "I know there is no place in my life for recrimination, bitterness, or hate. I fervently believe that to hate is to destroy. I want instead to love and, in so doing, to demonstrate that, regardless of body impairment, the heart retains its divinely ordained function. I recognize now that the truly handicapped are those who measure beauty by the sole prerequisite of physical perfection.

"I decided my accident was something I could never escape from. It would become a millstone around my neck, or if I practiced possibility thinking, I could turn my millstone into a milestone! I decided to do just that! I have accepted *me* as I *am* rather than as I *wish* I were. I need but to smile or wink at a wide-eyed child in the supermarket, as I buzz down the aisles in my electric wheelchair, to elicit a comment like one youngster made recently: 'Gosh, you're lucky!'"

John does more than wink or smile at children. Today he manages his own business, serving surrounding hotels and his community with a professional baby-sitter placement service. He also gives many hours as a volunteer counselor in the NEW HOPE crisis telephone counseling center in the Crystal Cathedral. Because of the new hope he has found, he is able to give new hope to the discouraged people he counsels.

John Prunty's a winner. He's a survivor, because he knows that *"Tough times never last, but tough people do!"*

## Sundo Kim

I met him here in California, though his home was in Korea. My first visit to that country was right after the Korean War. Never have I seen such a bleak, barren, and defeated land. Not a single tree, shrub, or other greenery graced the landscape.

All living vegetation had been consumed in order to preserve human life. Even the trees had been stripped and cut down. The leaves were eaten as a vegetable. The bark was boiled until it became a thick, black soup. Then the bare stems and trunks were burned to provide warmth in the subzero weather. Those were tough times in Korea!

[44]

Among the crowd of impoverished refugees who fled from the North were throngs of Christians. These Christians believed in a God who would never forsake those who never forsook Him. So they held on to their hope in God. One young Korean minister from that impoverished land received a scholarship to Fuller Seminary in California. While he was studying there, we invited him to be our guest at an institute held at our church.

Imagine how impressed this young man must have been when he walked onto these church grounds with the thirteen-story tower and saw the large modern sanctuary with fountains! He heard and believed what we taught at our institute: "Believe it and you can achieve it." So he took pictures of the tower and pictures of the church. He began to dream that someday he could build a church like that in Korea.

Four years ago, I returned to Korea. When this minister heard I was going to be there, he asked me to speak in his church. All he had was a tent, but he and his people were excited. I said I'd be honored to preach for him in his tent on Saturday night.

But Saturday morning, the telephone call came. My daughter, Carol, had been seriously injured in a motorcycle accident. My wife and I got on the first plane, so I wasn't able to keep my commitment. My friend had to tell about a thousand people that I would not be able to be there as they had thought.

Just a few weeks ago, I returned to Seoul, Korea, to receive an honorary degree from Hangyang University. When my young minister friend heard that I would be in Korea, he said, "Dr. Schuller, four years ago you promised to speak at my church. You broke the promise—for a good reason—but this time you must stop and see my church." Although I was scheduled to be in Korea for only forty-eight hours, I promised him that somehow I would make it to his church.

I was amazed when I arrived in Korea. The difference the past four years has made is incredible. We flew into a beautiful airport that is a spectacular piece of architecture. Surrounding the whole airport is a glorious park of lawns, trees,

[45]

and waterfalls. In downtown Seoul, a beautiful hotel has been reconstructed. It is so elegant that the sidewalks in front are of polished granite and the circular driveway is veneered in ceramic tile. As we drove down the magnificent new freeway that slices through Seoul, I saw it! Looming in the sky was a replica of our Garden Grove, California, Tower of Hope—fourteen stories tall, with a cross on top! And next to it was a glorious church building with four thousand seats. This was the Methodist minister's church!

The young pastor greeted me and must have seen how shocked and thrilled I was. He showed me through his church, introduced me to his elders and deacons, and shared with me that he has over twelve thousand members. I said, "That's amazing! That's wonderful!"

He had learned this lesson too: *"Tough times never last, but tough people always do!"*

It is amazing what God can do if we will give Him a little time to work His plan out!

In four years' time (1978–1982) a band of one thousand poor Christians moved from a tent on an abandoned acre of ground in Seoul, Korea, to a four-thousand-seat cathedral. Today they are the world's largest United Methodist church!

## Carol Schuller

In the same four-year period we watched our daughter, Carol, move from a hospital bed to the ski slopes.

When we arrived from Korea to Carol's bedside in Sioux City, Iowa, after her motorcycle accident, I was shocked. She lay in her bed in intensive care. Her body was bruised, broken, and disfigured. But her spirits were whole and healthy.

On the long trip back, I had searched for my opening line. What would my first words to her be? She solved the problem by speaking first: "I know why it happened, Dad. God wants to use me to help others who have been hurt."

It was this spirit, this positive attitude, that carried her through seven months of hospitalization, intravenous feed-ings, and consequent collapsed veins. This positive attitude gave her the courage to fight a raging infection that threatened her limb and her life. She hung on until a new drug was released by the FDA. It was the right drug at the right time—a real miracle.

It was that same positive attitude that helped Carol make the transition from hospital patient to a "handicapped" member of a family and school. It helped her feel normal and whole again.

She refused to allow the inconvenience of an artificial limb to keep her from pursuing the active life she loved, including softball. The last picture we have of Carol with both legs is one taken when she was in her softball uniform. The athlete of the family, Carol loves to play softball.

The summer after her accident, she shocked me by saying, "Dad, I'm going to sign up for softball again this year."

"That's great!" I responded, not wanting to discourage her.

At that time, Carol's artificial leg was attached just below the knee. She was plagued by a stiff knee that could barely bend at a thirty-degree angle. She walked very stiffly. Running was out of the question.

However, I took her to the local school where all the parents were lining up with their girls to sign up for the girls' softball team. Carol signed up and went to check out her uniform.

As she swung her stiff plastic leg into the car and rested her jersey, socks, and cap in her lap, I turned to her and said, "Carol, how do you expect to play ball if you can't run?" With flashing eyes, she snapped back at me, "I've got that all figured out, Dad! When you hit home runs you don't have to run."

My daughter is tough. She's a survivor. I want you to know that she hit enough home runs that season to justify her presence on the team!

Carol has learned the lesson too. *Tough times never last, but tough people do.* She has had six surgeries since that first amputation. Today she is skiing and has met her goal, which was to win a gold medal in the qualifying races that, in turn, admitted her to that elite corps of skiers participating in the

National Ski Championships! In March 1983, she pulled her goggles on and took her place among the champions in the country—at the young age of eighteen years! Yes, she still walks with a limp. She draws curious looks from strangers. But her positive attitude helps her even with that.

Last summer my family and I were privileged to be the guests of the American-Hawaiian Steamship Company on a one-week cruise of the Hawaiian Islands. It was absolutely beautiful! On this cruise, it is customary on the last night to have a talent show in which any of the passengers can participate. Carol, then seventeen years old, surprised us one day by saying, "I'm going to be in the talent show tonight."

Now Carol doesn't sing, and of course she doesn't dance. So, naturally, I was curious as to what she would do that night. Carol is not in the least ashamed to be seen in shorts or swimming attire, although her present artificial left leg covers her stump to just below the hip. But she is very conscious of the fact that people look at her out of the corners of their eyes and wonder what happened to her.

On Friday evening, the night of the talent show, my wife and I sat in the lounge along with six hundred other people. The talent show was scheduled to take place on the stage in the big, glorified cocktail lounge. As you can imagine, it's a very secular scene. The acts that were performed that night were typical of amateur talent shows. Then it was Carol's turn.

She came on stage wearing neither shorts nor Hawaiian garb, but a full-length dress. She looked beautiful. She walked up to the microphone and said, "I really don't know what my talent is, but I thought this would be a good chance for me to give what I think I owe you all, and that is an explanation. I know you've been looking at me all week, wondering about my fake leg. I thought I should tell you what happened. I was in a motorcycle accident. I almost died, but they kept giving me blood, and my pulse came back. They amputed my leg below the knee and later they amputed through the knee. I spent seven months in the hospital—seven months with intravenous antibiotics to fight infection."

[48]

She paused a moment, and then continued, "If I've one talent, it is this: I can tell you that during that time my faith became very real to me."

Suddenly a hush swept over the lounge. The waitresses stopped serving drinks. The glasses stopped tinkling. Every eye was focused on this tall seventeen-year-old blonde.

She said, "I look at you girls who walk without a limp, and I wish I could walk that way. I can't, but this is what I've learned, and I want to leave it with you: It's not how you walk that counts, but who walks with you and who you walk with."

At that point she paused and said, "I'd like to sing a song about my friend, my Lord." And she sang,

> And He walks with me,
>     and He talks with me
> And He tells me I am His own,
> And the joy we share
>     in our time of prayer
> [originally, "as we tarry there"]
> None other has ever known.[1]

"Thank you."

There was not a dry eye, not a life that wasn't touched that night. *Tough times never last, but tough people always do!* Because tough people know that with men it may appear impossible, but with God *all things are possible!*

What makes a person survive and thrive? Why are some people tough enough to win over their tough times? These questions have never before been as important as they are today because we are going through some of the toughest times that our country has ever faced. We cannot merely talk about strategies for success. We have to get down to hardcore principles that will work. And the only principles that we can believe in are principles that are tested, tried, and proven.

[1]Copyright © 1912 by Hall Mack Co. © Copyright renewal 1940 (extended). The Rodeheaver Co., owner. All rights reserved. Used by permission.

*It's impossible
to fail totally
if you dare
to try.*

## BUT TOUGH PEOPLE DO

Many of you who are reading these words do not have time to experiment. Your energies and your resources are running out. You have to be assured that the next thing you try will not be some wild and reckless whim.

Possibility thinking works. It has helped countless people survive really tough times. It can help you too! Because possibility thinking is not just a vague attitude. It is a hard-core principle. In this book I will show you specifically how possibility thinking can get you through the hard time you are going through. Your life can also be the portrait of a survivor. You can make it. You can win, if you carefully follow the possibility-thinking plan outlined in the following chapters. The first step will be to put your problems in proper perspective. Sure, you have problems. They may be the worst you've ever faced. But chances are, they are not the worst thing that could possibly have happened. No matter how bad it is, it could always be worse. Be glad it's not. Put your problem in proper perspective. Stop making a mountain out of a mole hill.

Everybody has problems. No life is problem-free.

Now you must learn to solve and manage problems. And there is not necessarily a solution for every problem; however, every problem can be managed positively. In Chapter 4 of this book are specific guidelines on how to manage your problems creatively. To do so, it is necessary to take charge and control of your problems.

Now "to manage" means "to control." Too many people lose control of their life by surrendering leadership to outside factors. We will discuss the many factors that can inadvertently take over the leadership spot in your life.

Who is in control of your life? You can be in control yourself if you will follow the Ten Commandments of Possibility Thinking. Many suggested solutions to our problems may appear impossible. Consequently too many solutions are thrown away and never given a chance. The Ten Commandments of Possibility Thinking can show how you can make the most of the ideas that God will give you.

[51]

How does God give ideas? I've received most of the ideas that have solved my seemingly unsolvable problems through a game I call, "Count to ten and win." It's amazingly simple, but it can change your life! I will share how in Chapter 7.

Next, after you've explored and applied these principles, then you'll need to put faith to work. I'll outline for you faith's five phases to get you going. People who win over tough times are people who never stop believing. They have faith in themselves and their Lord and in the ideas that God gives them. These winners, survivors, pray for God's guidance and when they know what it is they have to do, then they take action. They do something about it. To help you get going, the entire last part of this book is dedicated to an Alphabet for Action. These times we're going through are tough, but if you are going to get through them, it's up to you. You must begin to act.

You say, "But that's easy for you to say, Dr. Schuller; these ideas, these principles work for others. They have education. They have alternatives. They have capital. They are not in my situation."

I say to you: you can do anything you want to do. You can be anything you want to be. You can go anywhere from where you are—*if* you are willing to dream big and work hard.

Have you ever heard of the story of the three negative women who lived in the bayou? They complained every day, "We've got it bad living in this bayou. No opportunity here. Others are living in the city where they have unlimited opportunities. Us, we got nothing." This is the complaint they lived their lives by, until one day a positive-thinking woman came along. After listening to the complaints, she said, "Nonsense! Opportunity? You want opportunity? You got opportunity. You live on the bayou. The bayou leads to the river. The river leads to the gulf. The gulf leads to the ocean. You can go anywhere from where you are!"

## BUT TOUGH PEOPLE DO

These are tough times you're going through, but if you're going to get through, it's up to you. Ready to go? Get ready to make your dreams come true!

# PART
## II

*Here's How You
Can Be Tough Too!*

# 3

## *Put Your Problem in Proper Perspective*

**W**hat is the secret ingredient of tough people that enables them to succeed? Why do they survive the tough times when others are overcome by them? Why do they win when others lose? Why do they soar when others sink?

The answer is very simple. It's all in how they perceive their problems. They look at problems realistically and practically. They understand the six principles that pertain to *all* problems.

What are these principles? If you knew them, understood them, and practiced them, would you, too, be a winner, a survivor? You bet! Here they are. Listen carefully, and adopt them as your own.

**1  Every living human being has problems.**

What is your problem? Are you unemployed? If you're an impossibility thinker you probably think that a job would solve all your problems. The truth is that employed people have problems too. Most people who have jobs complain about the fact that they have to go to work on Monday morning.

And countless people have jobs they don't like. They are giving five days a week to unhappiness. They work to live rather than live to work. They hate their jobs. They drag their feet getting to the office or factory. And once they're there they devote a great deal of their time to negative thoughts. They focus on the unenjoyable aspects of their jobs.

Some people think their problems stem from the fact that they have to report to a boss. They falsely assume that they would be happy if they could be self-employed. It's true that they might find more enjoyment in such a working arrangement, but many self-employed people have more problems than those who work for others. They have to be concerned about employee relationships and managing personnel for maximum productivity. So you work for a boss? You may think so, but in reality you're probably not. Chances are he's working for you. Everybody's got problems—the employer as well as the employee.

Well then, what is the answer? Retirement? How many people long to reach sixty-five, planning for the day they can lie in the sun, take each day as it comes, be accountable to no one, and still have money to live comfortably? Sound like bliss? It's not, really. Retired people also have their problems. Many are bored. Not a few become very depressed soon after retiring because they no longer feel productive or useful. Many actually wish they could be back at work.

Successful people! Surely they are exempt from problems. Right? Wrong! Actually the contrary is true, for success doesn't eliminate problems, it creates new ones. Imagine you are rich enough to hire cleaning people and custodians to do all the jobs you hate. Sound wonderful? Not really.

I have friends who are super wealthy. With two hundred fifty dollars, they started a business in a little garage, manufacturing Venetian blinds for house trailers. After a year they had saved a few thousand dollars from their small profits. After a couple of years, they had parlayed that into ten thousand dollars, which they used as capital to build their first little house trailer, complete with their own custom-made Venetian blinds. Sales continued to grow, netting them a handsome sum and swelling their assets to nearly fifty thousand dollars. As the years passed, their business continued to grow solidly and expand strongly.

They moved from their simple little trailer to a larger

*If it's*
*going to be,*
*it's up to*
*me!*

house. A few years later they moved to the ocean-front, and then to a ninety-acre ranch where they enjoyed the comfort of many to do their housework.

Now with their fortunes nearing the hundred-million-dollar mark, they have built a home in Beverly Hills, California. And guess what! They have no servants' quarters in their new luxurious home. Why not? They are tired of the loss of privacy that comes with having servants. They are weary of the problems that come with managing hired help. They're sick of servants. They've found them to be more trouble than they're worth. And so they are now cooking their own meals and cleaning their house themselves.

Yes, every living person has problems. Even the nonstriving person has the problem of inertia. This, in turn, produces a lack of zest and enthusiasm. He lives life on a low level of physical energy, becoming bored. Boredom is hardly a state of happiness or contentment. The nonstriving person who elects to avoid problems actually creates new ones.

How about the striver? The student who is knocking himself out to get an *A* average? The mountain climber who is clawing the side of the cliff, risking life and limb, for the joy of overcoming an enormous challenge? How about the handicapped person who spends hours every day in painful exercises and rehabilitation therapy? Problems? Of course! They run the risk of failure. There is always the enormous possibility of heart-wrenching disappointment if they should lose the prize after years of training.

How about the arriver—the person who reaches the mountaintop? Doesn't this person enjoy a sense of freedom and relief from all problems? Is he not free from the problem of the boredom that plagues the nondreamer? And is he not free from the fear of failing that annoys the striver? Is it not heaven on earth to come in, in first place? To reach the top of the mountain? To be elected president of the United States?

I have had a little personal experience as an achiever. My testimony is that the arriver often has greater problems than the striver.

Certainly, it is wonderful to be an arriver, an achiever. But saying that the arriver leaves all problems behind would be an error. In my experience, I have found that the arriver has greater problems than the striver.

You could not have convinced me of that back in 1955, when I was twenty-eight. I had received a call from the Reformed Church in America to begin a new church in California. We were promised five hundred dollars in cash. We had no money, no connections, no open doors. All we had was a dream. But I learned that if you have a dream, you have everything—including an awful lot of problems! I dreamed of the day when I would reach my goals, when I would be an achiever, when I would find self-satisfaction in winning and witnessing the realization of a dream come true. I dreamed of the day I would trade my problems for a prize.

I proceeded to establish a forty-year plan. I wanted to build one of the greatest churches in the world. I believed then, and still do today, that the church is the only institution in human society that is totally committed to keeping faith alive in the hearts of men and women. Without this dynamic faith the human race is doomed.

I felt that a successful church would consist of about six thousand members. I divided forty years into six thousand members and concluded I could succeed in forty years. All I would have to do was gain one hundred fifty members a year.

I worked hard and poured my life into my church. As a result I learned that great dreams of great dreamers are never fulfilled: They are always transcended. After only fifteen years, my church reached the six-thousand-member mark. We were successful. Richard Neutra designed a beautiful church that seated fifteen hundred persons at each of the two morning services.

Doors to a television ministry opened. We began to reach more people than I had ever dared to dream possible. My goals were not only reached, they were eclipsed.

I had arrived. I was a success. Was I happy with my prize, the satisfaction that comes with a job well done? Was my life free from problems? No! The more successful we became, the more problems I had.

For one thing, success attracts people. We had more people than we could handle. Our sanctuary, which seated fifteen hundred at each service, could not accommodate everyone who wanted to come. Week after week people came, saw the crowds, grew frustrated as they looked for a parking place, and left, never even having gotten out of their cars. My heart ached for them.

We decided to handle the problem with an overflow seating section outside the church. Because Neutra had designed the building with one all-glass side overlooking a beautiful grass lawn, it was natural to set up chairs outside in sunny California. The plan worked splendidly. Many worshipers opted to sit outdoors in what we called the "garden sanctuary." Until it rained.

It was disastrous. Hundreds of people were sitting outside, with no awning, and no covering for their heads. Suddenly, in the middle of my message, a cloud came from nowhere and it began to rain—not a sprinkle, but a torrential downpour. People leaped from their seats to run for cover. But there was none. The church building was packed, and fire codes prevented us from letting them join the worshipers in the dry, sheltered church building. They had no choice. They ran for their cars. They drove away. For me it was a black day.

Meanwhile, I had reached all of my goals. I tried to sit back and enjoy my success, but soon I began to die inside. I soon discovered that the only joy of living is the joy of giving. When I didn't have any goals, I was miserable.

So I focused on human beings who were empty and hurting inside—people who needed healing. The more I focused on such human predicaments and torturing sorrows, the more we came to the inevitable conclusion that we needed a larger facility. I began to contemplate how we could increase the seating of our sanctuary. We engaged an architect and instructed him to draw up plans for knocking out the wall of our fifteen-hundred-foot auditorium. In so doing we could enlarge it to three thousand seats.

We spent two years and twenty thousand dollars pursuing that idea, only to conclude it would destroy the garden environment we had created. It would cost over a million dollars and it would be a horrendous development. Everybody agreed that this was not the solution. Over the next three years, we spent another thirty thousand dollars with another architectural firm that created a model of a building that could seat three to four thousand people and would cost four to five million dollars. We engaged professional fund-raisers, but the campaign fizzled. We failed.

After five years, fifty thousand dollars, and two architectural firms, our problem was still unresolved. One day I picked up a magazine and read an article about Philip Johnson. Somehow, I felt that he was the key to solving our predicament. I called him and asked him if he could design a building to seat three to four thousand persons. I said to him, "My only request, sir, is that it be all glass."

He was shocked. He said, "All glass?"

"Yes. *All* glass." My dream for an all-glass church stemmed from a childhood loneliness to return to the river banks of Iowa. I wanted to worship under the open sky again.

"How much money can you afford to spend on the project?" he asked.

I said, "We have a four-million-dollar corporate debt which we are amortizing responsibly over twenty years. But our cash flow allows no surplus whereby we can handle any additional corporate debt," I told him. "We have borrowed an additional two hundred thousand dollars from the bank to retain you. You'll have to come up with the kind of building that will attract its own financial support."

Three months later he delivered a six-inch plastic model of an all-glass, four-pointed, star-shaped structure that was 414 feet from one point to the other. The glass roof, which was 100 feet longer than a football field seemed to float in space. At its peak it soared twelve stories above the ground! It was stunning! Unbelievable!

Today the building is a reality. It was a solution to a problem. Of course, with the creation of the Crystal Cathedral, we inherited a whole new generation of problems.

We have encountered acoustical difficulties. All-glass

structures are a nightmare for sound technicians. It is a problem we have completely solved. But it was tough! Maintenance of the cathedral is also a monumental challenge. Do you know how many window washers it takes to keep it clean? (I hear that stock in Windex soared after the cathedral was completed.) The budget to keep a building like the cathedral operational was much more than we expected. Raising the money to keep the cathedral open and in tiptop shape is a new problem we have had to solve—and we have!

These are the problems I inherited when I solved my problem of overflow seating. Naturally, the trade-off is acceptable. I would much rather deal with maintenance and budget problems than deny people the right to worship God and find spiritual and emotional healing.

However, when the cathedral was built, and my goal reached, I once more faced the problem of a lack of goal.

What do you do to top a Crystal Cathedral? How do you handle emotional stimulation produced by the mountain peak which taunts you to scale it? If you have climbed Mt. Everest, where do you go from there? How does the president of the United States maintain purpose and excitement after he has had to step down from the lofty office?

*The point is clear: Nobody is free from problems. A problem-free life is an illusion—a mirage in the desert. It is a dangerously deceptive perception, which can mislead, blind, and distract.* To pursue a problem-free life is to run after an elusive fantasy; it is a waste of mental and physical energies. Every living human person has problems. Accept that fact and move on to the second principle.

## 2 Every problem has a limited life span.

Every mountain has a peak. Every valley has its low point. Life has its ups and downs, its peaks and its valleys. No one is up all the time, nor are they down all the time. Problems do end. They do go away. They are all resolved in time.

This principle is evident when you look carefully at history, for the history of humanity is a study in peaks and valleys. Humanity peaks at times when societies rise from decadence to a highly sophisticated state of civilization. Eventually, however, most cultures allow decay to set in. Rather than rooting out the negative influences, the human institutions adjust to the downward movement. The decline continues and accelerates until it reaches a low ebb at which point it begins the long, slow ascent once more.

History teaches us that every problem has a life span. No problem is permanent. Do you have problems? They will pass; they will not last. Your problem will not live forever, but you will! Storms always give way to the sun. Winter always thaws into springtime. Your storm will pass. Your winter will thaw. Your problem will be resolved.

 **Every problem holds positive possibilities.**

"It is the glory of God to conceal a thing" (Prov. 25:2). Every problem contains secret ingredients of some creative potential either for yourself or someone else.

There are two sides to every coin. What may be a problem to someone can be a profitable business for others. For instance, rats and mice are plagues to the human world. However, the presence of rats and mice in America alone results in tens of millions of dollars in our economy. Rats and mice are responsible for thousands of jobs! Factories make mousetraps. Families are supported from the income of exterminators of such pests.

Similarly, every human problem holds possibilities for someone willing to look for them.

Bankruptcy was such a horrible experience for one man that he decided to help others who were going through it. Today he is a counselor to those who are having to declare bankruptcy.

One man's problem is another man's opportunity. Consequently, hospitals exist because people are sick. Lawyers are in business because people violate laws in a moment of weakness or ignorance. Mortuaries, cemeteries, colleges, churches, and universities all exist for the purpose of helping people through their problem times.

## 4 Every problem will change you.

Problems never leave us the way they found us. Every person is affected by the tough times. No one emerges from a problem untouched by tough times.

Recently I was talking to a supersuccessful salesperson. His income is in the six-figure bracket. When I inquired about his training, I was surprised to learn that his degree is in history and education.

"Dr. Schuller, the truth is that I was a very boring teacher. Because I was boring, my students were restless and I failed to communicate to them. I was a boring teacher because I was a bored teacher. My boredom rubbed off on the students. It was not a good situation. Because I had a problem with students, my contract was not renewed—actually I was fired. When the school fired me I became so angry I decided to go out and make something of myself. I went out and landed a better job."

And then he shared a gem of a line. He looked at me with flashing eyes and said, "I had to get fired before I got fired up!" He went on to explain. "Basically, I was too lethargic. My contract cancellation jolted me out of a lazy rut. I'll always be grateful that I was fired, for it made me angry enough at myself to get up and get going."

## 5 You can choose what your problem will do to you.

You may not be able to control the times, but you can compose your response. You can turn your pain into profanity—or into poetry. The choice is up to you. You may not have chosen your tough time, but you can choose how you will react to it.

*Never*
*let a problem*
*become an excuse.*

I remember hearing Dr. Norman Vincent Peale interviewed on national television many years ago. The interviewer asked him: "Dr. Peale, how far do you apply positive thinking?"

Dr. Peale answered: "I apply it in the areas over which I have control." He continued, "If I buy a plane and the plane crashes, I have no control over that." I thought about that for a long time.

In a subsequent meeting with Dr. Peale, I said to him, "I apply possibility thinking not only in the areas of life over which I have control but over every area of life." He looked puzzled. I explained. "Actually, Dr. Peale, we can control our reaction even when we cannot control the problem."

When you control your reaction to the seemingly uncontrollable problems of life, then in fact you do control the problem's effect on you. Your reaction to the problem is the last word! That's the bottom line. What will you let this problem do to you?

It can make you tender or tough. It can make you better or bitter. It all depends on you.

## 6 There is a negative and a positive reaction to every problem.

In the final analysis the tough people who survive the tough times do so because they've chosen to react positively to their predicament. This is not always as easy as it sounds.

Consider, for example, the problem of an unwanted pregnancy.

What are the options? What are the alternatives? Which "solutions" are really solutions? How do you determine which reactions are positive and which are negative?

Let me answer the last question first. The positive reaction is the one that would contribute most to the collective self-esteem of the human family. Of my options, I must choose the one that would diminish any shame that could fall upon the human family. I must choose the reaction that will ultimately make me more proud of myself as a person. Furthermore, a positive reaction would be that which would bring the greatest joy to the most people. In addition, a positive reaction would be the reaction that holds the greatest possibility of making a constructive contribution to society.

By contrast, the negative reaction would be the reaction that would be most embarrassing to myself or to the human family and would prevent any good from coming from the problem that I am facing. Based upon these positive principles of choosing the most positive reaction to a problem, I have long advocated that an unwanted pregnancy should be allowed to go full term and the child should be allowed to be offered as an answer to the prayers of a childless family. Abortion is a negative solution to a problem.

How do these principles for choosing the most positive reaction to a problem apply to other problems?

For instance, what is the positive reaction to a terrible financial setback? In this situation would it be the positive reaction to cop out? Run away? Escape through alcohol, drugs, or suicide?

No! Such negative reactions only produce greater problems by promising a temporary "solution" to the pressing problem.

Stealing money in order to pay your bills is a negative solution because it will (a) generate a whole new set of problems, (b) fill you with the fear of exposure and detection, (c) haunt you with shame and rob you of your self-dignity, and (d) lower the collective self-esteem of the human family.

The positive solution to a problem may require courage to initiate it. It takes courage to face up to your creditors and to deal with them honestly and forthrightly. If they insist on pressing for payment and refuse to give time for you to resolve your position more favorably, then choose the legal and honorable route of filing for bankruptcy. This will provide the breathing space to work out your solutions without committing a crime.

Next, let's consider the problem of a troubled, quarrelsome marriage. For years it has been assumed that it is better for a child to live in peace with one parent than to live in a home with father and mother who argue frequently. Based on that unstudied, unscientific, generally accepted assumption, hundreds of thousands of married couples have chosen divorce as a swift and immediate solution to their problems of marital unhappiness. Many have sincerely believed that this is better for the children.

However, recent studies indicate that this may be, in fact, the more negative solution.

"If children ruled, there would be no divorce." So Dr. Albert A. Solnit reported to the American Academy of Pediatrics recently. This Yale University psychiatrist continued, "We do not in any sense know what the long-term effect of divorce is on children. If we were living in a world governed by children's wishes, there would be no divorce."[1]

Another child psychiatrist said there is no way he could be convinced that children were better off when parents divorce.

Dr. Derek Miller, a Northwestern University professor of psychiatry and head of the adolescent unit at Northwestern Memorial Hospital in Chicago, said there is no proof a child brought up by a single parent feels more secure and is better off than a child brought up by two parents.

He took note of a rise in suicides among adolescents, drug abuse, teen-age pregnancies, alcoholism, and even murders—problems that emerged in the sixties and grew in the seventies.

Such research indicates that it might be more positive to stay together despite the tension and arguments.

My own father and mother had quarrels. I have vivid, childhood recollections of some strong verbal arguments in our home life. But divorce was never considered. Because of this, I grew up believing that solutions are never found by running away from a tough problem.

I believe that because my parents kept their marriage intact despite problems, I am a better person and a more tenacious achiever. Their overriding, ever-recurring love taught me to believe in the importance of commitment.

[1]*Honolulu Advertiser,* Oct. 29, 1982, p. C–8.

If you know that divorce is not an option, it is amazing how you can learn to love again.

*Tough times never last, but tough people do.* Tough people stick it out. They have learned to choose the most positive reaction in managing problems. And that's the real key: "Managing problems." For in spite of all of our possibility thinking, there are after all some problems that defy solutions.

If your leg is amputated, you can't grow it back. You can manage this problem, however, by considering all the possible ways in which a prosthesis can be developed, improved, and refined. You can manage it by determining to walk better, more smoothly, more quickly than anybody else could imagine. In the process you will become an inspiration to everyone whose life touches yours.

Possibility thinking—I do not claim that it can solve every problem. But I have no doubt that the vast majority of problems can be solved if we only believe. "With men this is impossible; but with God all things are possible" (Matt. 19:26).

But if a problem defies solution, then what?

*When you can't solve the problem, manage it.*

Survivors. How do they do it? When they can't solve the problem, they manage it creatively. And how do you do this? By following twelve principles for managing problems creatively and constructively! We will take a look at these in the next chapter.

# 4

## *Twelve Principles For Managing Problems Positively*

The month was October. The year was 1982. Unemployment problems in America were peaking, with Flint, Michigan, hit hardest. My good friend, Tom Tipton, wanted to help the unemployed of Flint, and he asked me to conduct a two-day seminar, applying possibility thinking principles to the problem of unemployment.

Facing my audience of nearly five thousand citizens, gathered in the city's largest convention center, I asked this rhetorical question: "Are you unemployed today? Then consider this: Is your problem of unemployment really any different from any other problem? Or are there universal principles that we can apply to unemployment as to almost every other serious problem?"

I say that, yes, there are universal principles that can help manage any problem, including the problem of unemployment, that seems to defy solution. Every living human being has problems. You do too. Learn to manage them.

Are you overweight? Have you tried all kinds of diets, losing the weight only to gain it again? Have you lost a loved one through divorce or death? Have you been told that you have cancer? Do you have a problem with alcoholism? Are you facing possible bankruptcy?

If you have a problem today—any problem—I can help you if you'll let me. I offer to you the principles that I shared with my audience in Flint. They'll work if you use them.

# 1 Don't underestimate.

Don't underestimate the problem—or your potential power to cope with it creatively! Unquestionably, many problems are never resolved or managed effectively because they are not taken seriously enough. Have you ever been guilty of one of these thoughts?

"I'm not too fat. I don't have to worry about losing weight yet."

"I'm not getting A's or B's, but I'm passing."

"I haven't been exercising as much as I should, but I'll be O.K."

"I probably should cut down on my smoking, but I don't need to worry. Lung cancer may hit others, but I won't get it."

Such thinking is dangerous! We must avoid the temptation to underestimate the seriousness of problems that on the surface may appear slight. Problems are like a pregnancy. They will grow until their presence is obvious. No one is just a little pregnant. And no problem is unimportant enough to ignore.

Never underestimate a problem or your power to cope with it. Realize that the problem you are facing has been faced by millions of human beings. You have untapped potential for dealing with a problem if you will take the problem and your own undeveloped, unchanneled powers seriously. Your reaction to the problem, as much as the problem itself, will determine the outcome.

I have seen people face the most catastrophic problems with a positive mental attitude, turning their problems into creative experiences. They turned their scars into stars.

# 2 Don't exaggerate.

Instead of underestimating the problem, your instinctive (and often, first) reaction is to exaggerate it.

Are you closing your business? That isn't the end of the world. You can start over again.

Are you unemployed? It doesn't mean you can *never* get another job.

Flying back on the lonely, torturing trip from Korea to America, after Carol's motorcycle accident, I was overwhelmed with grief. I wept. I prayed.

Out of this time of deep prayer, a sentence, as clear as if it were skywriting against the clouds, passed through my mind: *Play it down and pray it up.* I took that as a direct message from God.

To me it meant this: "Don't exaggerate the problem. You're playing it up too much. She didn't lose *both* legs. She has had no head injury. She suffered no brain damage. No vital organs are permanently impaired. She is not in a life-threatening situation. You are totally exaggerating the impact of the accident. Play it down. Then pray it up. Give it to God and give God a chance to show how the scars can be turned into stars."

Are you unemployed? Are you depressed to the point that you want to stop the world and get off? Maybe you are exaggerating your problem.

Would you rather have your left leg amputated? Would you like to trade places with my daughter? My wife had her left breast removed because of cancer. Would you rather have her problem?

In my experience as a pastor, *I have never met anyone who wanted to exchange his problem for someone else's.* Put your problem in its proper perspective. The seriousness of it will pass.

Ask yourself these questions: What is the worst that will happen to me? Can I handle that?

If you will play it down and pray it up, God will give you

[74]

The one battle
most people lose
is the battle
over the fear of failure...
try...
start...
begin...
and you'll be assured
you won the first round.

the ability to cope with the worst that will happen. Stop exaggerating the depth, the length, and the breadth of the problem.

 **Don't
wait.**

There is a time and place for patience—after you have tried every avenue possible and have planted as many seeds of solutions as you can. Patience is not a virtue if you sit back and wait for your problem to solve itself.

If you are unemployed, don't expect the phone to ring or a letter to miraculously show up in your mailbox with job offers. Don't expect the government to telephone you and offer you a job. Don't expect the union to call you and offer you a job. Don't expect the company to call you and rehire you.

If such should be the case, wonderful. But merely waiting for it to happen could be the worst thing to do. And many problems have the built-in capability to grow more serious with the passing of time. To wait quietly for God to do something or for someone to come to your rescue could give the problem time to multiply its negative fallout.

During President Lyndon Johnson's administration, the federal government purchased several blocks in the South Bronx in New York City. The president announced that the many multistoried structures in this slum area would be demolished, and through government financing, a new model city would rise.

Several years after the federal government purchased the property, I visited the area. I saw the buildings still empty; windows, still shattered; the area, totally dilapidated. The situation has not changed. The South Bronx is still waiting!

To wait is to waste time and opportunity. And to wait may be to surrender leadership to forces that may never materialize.

If you want to solve your problem, don't wait for somebody else to help you. Tackle it yourself. I'll show you how in Chapter 7. *Right now, understand that you alone are personally responsible for managing your problem. Don't expect anybody else to do it for you.*

Look to God and to your own capabilities. If you expect others to rescue you, you will only be disappointed. Worse than that, you may also become cynical and bitter.

 ## Don't aggravate.

We have the power to make any problem better or worse. We do this when we react positively or negatively. The normal reaction would be to feel threatened by the problem. Threatened people become angry people. Fearful people reflect hatred. Hatred and anger only aggravate the problem. They are not positive reactions. They will not help solve the problem.

So you are overweight? Don't hate yourself for eating so much. That will not help you one bit.

Unemployed? Don't hate your company for laying you off. Likewise, don't hate your country for not coming through with a job offer, or your community for having an I-don't-care attitude about the unemployed people.

Coach John Wooden chalked up a string of victories while he coached the famed University of California at Los Angeles basketball team. I once heard him say, "Nobody is defeated until he starts blaming somebody else."

My advice is, "Don't fix the blame; fix the problem." You begin fixing the problem when you begin to control your negative emotions.

One of the first pieces of advice I gave to my daughter after arriving at her wounded side was: "Carol, there is one thing you'll have to be careful of. And that is feeling sorry for yourself. Self-pity will only lead you into hell on earth."

"Don't worry about that, Dad," she replied quickly, adding, "I've got enough problems without that one."

If you've got a problem, don't add to it. Don't make your problem worse by aggravating it with self-pity, jealousy, cynicism, hatred, anger, or lack of positive faith in the future.

# 5 Illuminate.

Illuminate your mind. Get smart and then get smarter. Ask yourself some questions:

"Has any other person faced my problem and overcome it?"

"What really is my problem anyway?"

"Is my problem unemployment or is it early retirement?"

"Is it a lack of money to meet my needs, or is it boredom?"

"Could I solve the problem of boredom by volunteering to work in my church or community organizations?" My own father enjoyed his retirement because he was always volunteering to repair things in the houses of people who lived in his town.

If you think your problem is finances, think again. Is it really finances, or is it a problem of managing what you have? You probably need to pare down some of the expenses that you have taken for granted. Remember: Nobody has a money problem; it is always an idea problem.

My youngest daughter, Gretchen, is taking driving lessons. She will soon be sixteen and will have her driver's license. Her teacher tells her that she has to learn to drive with the IPDE method: *I*dentify, *P*redict, *D*ecide, *E*xecute. Her teacher explained: "As you are driving down the street, *identify* the other moving vehicles. *Predict* what they are going to do and when they are going to do it. *Decide* how you will respond and react to their behavior. *Execute* your response decisively and forthrightly."

The IPDE prescription can help you face a variety of problems. *Identify* the problem. *Predict* what this problem will do to you if you don't do anything about it. *Decide* on your response from all of the options and alternatives. Then, *execute* and act on the most positive option that you can imagine.

**Motivate.**

When you consider all of the positive reactions, you will be motivated to positive action. "It take guts to leave the ruts," I said to someone whose only solution to his problem was a major alteration in his life-style. His drinking problem was connected with a group of friends with whom he had been associating for years. "You've got to separate yourself from this crowd," I said. He followed my advice, and his problem went away.

"You don't have a problem to solve—you just have a decision to make" was my advice to another person. He had been laboring under the illusion that he had a problem, when in fact he only lacked the courage to make the right decision. Once I gave him this advice, he made the tough decision. Some wonderful people who worked for him in his company were not contributing to the company's profit. In fact, they were unnecessary drains on the payroll. It was a tough and painful decision. But when the employer realized he didn't have a problem to solve, but a decision to make, he was on his way to creative problem management.

"Every obstacle can be an opportunity" was my advice to still another person who was unemployed. "Think about that," I said, "and come back to see me in one week and give me a list of all the new opportunities that face you today that wouldn't have been yours if you were still employed." One week later he came back with this list of exciting opportunities: (1) I do have the opportunity to start my own business; (2) I do have the opportunity to travel; (3) I do have the opportunity to go back to school; (4) I do have the opportunity to give more time to my church and to my children and grandchildren.

The list was long enough to lift my friend from depression to real enthusiasm. It's not surprising that from this list emerged an idea that since has given him meaningful employment.

## 7 Bait.

"How do I get a job when I'm unemployed?" one person asked me.

My answer was a question: "How do you catch a moose?"

"What do you mean by that?" he asked, almost irritated.

I told him this story: "Your problem with unemployment really isn't that much different from the problem I faced a few years ago when I had to raise ten million dollars to build a new church, the Crystal Cathedral. At that time I had heard about a friend, Dr. Milton Englebretson, who successfully solicited a million-dollar donation from one individual. I went to my friend and asked, 'How do you raise a million-dollar donation from one person?' He answered me with the same question I threw at you.

"'How do you catch a moose?' He smiled at me. He stared at me. His eyes unflinchingly met mine, in a steady, twinkling gaze.

"'What kind of an answer is that?' I asked.

"'You're smart,' he answered. Turning to walk away, he threw a parting comment to me, 'Think about it—that's all the advice you need.'

"I couldn't get his comment out of my mind. I didn't want his riddle to get the best of me. I thought, *Well, if I wanted to catch a moose I would go to Canada. I'd never catch one in Orange County, California. Then I would have to find out what paths they take and where they find their water. I'd have to bring the kind of food that would attract them to me. And I'd have to be able to close in.*

"So, prayerfully I made a list of persons who had the potential of giving a million-dollar gift. And as a result of that advice, we successfully collected several contributions in the million-dollar bracket.

"Now when others ask me, 'Dr. Schuller, how do you raise a million-dollar gift?' my answer is, 'How do you catch a marlin?'"

I was born and raised in Iowa, where the largest fish I ever caught was a five-pound walleyed pike. But when I came to California I learned that California fishermen caught glamorous, flying marlin, which could weigh more than three hundred pounds!

I decided that I wanted to catch a marlin sometime in my life. And I have! In the process, I learned something about catching marlins. First of all, you don't stay in Iowa; you go to where the marlin are—probably off Catalina Island in southern California or off Kona Coast in Hawaii, or in Cabo San Lucas in Baja California, Mexico. Then you get into a boat. You'll never catch a marlin from the shore or on the pier. You have to head out for the open waters, cruise, and throw out bait.

Need a job? Go to where the jobs are. And then throw out the bait. Put in your application. Put ads in the paper. Let people know you are available.

 **Date.**

If you are unemployed, find a job the way you found a wife or husband. Discover the many different kinds of jobs there are. Look them over. Play the field. Don't let age be a factor; a change of career at forty may be just what you need. And don't tell yourself, "There aren't many jobs. The few that are available will be snatched up by other people who are unemployed. I don't stand a chance."

Don't get discouraged. You do have a chance. You can find the job that's best for you. Even if you called last week, call again. Every day somebody retires or quits because he is fed up with his job. And every week people decide to pack up and move to Florida, Hawaii, or California, leaving a job behind. Every month somebody burns out. So every day, every week, and every month there are brand-new job openings where there weren't any before. The person who knocks at the door, telephones, dates, and plays the field is the person who is going to get that job.

"Dating" is a principle of problem management that applies to many areas other than unemployment. It applies to loneliness, and to the problem of finding people you need to help make your company a success.

# 9 Sublimate.

Every problem, even yours, is loaded with possibilities. You can turn your mountain into a gold mine. Try "possibilitizing." Believe that every time one door closes, another will open. Sublimate your problem. That means believing that every adversity holds within it the seeds of an undeveloped possibility.

A young lady had been hurt deeply. Her boyfriend had treated her shabbily, then had dumped her. "God uses life's bruises if we surrender them to Him," I promised her. "In love's service only broken hearts will do." A person who is hurt can become bitter and calloused, or one can react positively and prayerfully, becoming tender, compassionate, sensitive, and profoundly caring for others who are hurt. *God uses life's bruises!* When you can't eliminate the problem, sublimate it. Turn the stumbling block into a stepping stone.

# 10 Now dedicate.

Most people fail, not because they lack intelligence, ability, opportunity, or talent, but because they haven't given their problem all they've got!

Anyone can succeed if he can get enthusiastic about life even when life seems empty. Doors will open to the enthusiastic person first!

I was in a hotel in Los Angeles when I ordered room service. The waiter was Mexican and spoke halting English: "Good morning! Good morning! Good morning!" Strangely enough, his repeating the greeting three times did not seem overdone, but very sincere.

"You seem enthusiastic," I offered.

"Oh, yes," he said, grinning from ear to ear. "I've got a good job. And I'm in America. May I pour your coffee for you?"

"Yes, of course," I replied.

"The weather is going to be beautiful today," he said.

"I heard they were predicting rain today."

"Yes, but the rain will be nice. It will make the lawns green. And the flowers and trees need it, don't they?"

By the time he left the room I was enormously impressed by him. *I know why he has a job,* I told myself.

The smartest and the most enthusiastic people will get the jobs that are going to be opening up in the next thirty days. Get enthusiastic. Dedicate yourself to enthusiastic living, and you'll be surprised how people will want to hire you.

I didn't say it was easy. It's not always been easy for me to step in front of the television cameras and smile enthusiastically. It's a commitment I've made to dedicate myself to being positive always—especially if I don't feel like it. And it has never failed me. The positive approach has always attracted positive support, from friends I've known a long time as well as from people I never knew before.

So your problem is not unemployment? Remember this: Unexpected sources of help come from unpredictable quarters to the person who remains positive and enthusiastic and cheerful! That's my promise.

 **Communicate.**

Manage your problem by remembering that oftentimes the solution lies in help from some other source. Do you need help? Then ask for it. Don't be too proud to tell people you need help.

Our television ministry is one of the most successful in America today. At one time we were on the verge of terminating the program for lack of financial support. My advisors said, "Dr. Schuller, you have to go on national television and tell the people the truth. Tell them that you need money. You have to tell them that if you don't get the money needed that you'll have to discontinue the program."

Frankly, that hurt my pride. I had to make a decision. Did I want to be successful? Or did I want to be proud? I chose to be successful. I humbled myself by honestly telling my national television audience, "I need help." And they responded.

Every alcoholic will agree that the three hardest words to say are, "I need help!" More than one "impossible" marital problem has moved from an impasse to a creative resolution when a husband or wife has said, "Honey, you have to help me work out the negative feelings I have toward our situation. I should not have these negative feelings. I know they are wrong, but I have them. I don't want them; they hurt me and they are going to ruin both of us. Please help me."

Do you need help? Do you need hope? Are you discouraged? Depressed? Has enthusiasm waned? Do you want to quit, pack up, and run away from life? Then ask for help. Seek it out. There is hope waiting for you. Whatever else you do, *communicate*. Don't *ex*communicate yourself from the help that is available.

Proud people are inclined to withdraw. Don't reject or neglect the free hope and help that is available. Start listening to positive thinking messages. Try praying. Ask God questions. And listen for His answers. Be brutally honest when you ask Him for advice.

Do you need wisdom? Counsel? Guidance? *Go for it!* But isolating yourself from all available help will ultimately defeat you.

Try linking-thinking. Visit a church. Join a club. Get into a community group. But discipline yourself to share your dreams, your hopes, and your needs with others. You'll be surprised at how help will come to you and your problem will be managed.

# 12 Insulate.

Don't isolate yourself from help, but do insulate yourself from negative forces and negative personalities.

Maintaining a positive mental attitude becomes a near-impossible task if we allow ourselves to be bombarded by the negative thoughts that constantly surround us.

Check out the positive or negative content of your own conversations and the advice that people give you. Become sensitive to the widespread, taken-for-granted, negative sentences that are pumped into your brain daily by well-meaning friends. Insulate yourself from the following phrases:

1. *"Take care."* In the next chapter we teach: "People who take care never get anywhere." Managing problems requires that we take control.

2. *"Take it easy."* Of course it is important to maintain poise and calm rather than give in to panic and hysteria. What I object to is the advice that would urge us to take it easy and wait. I repeat: Don't expect somebody to just hand you the solution. Resourcefulness and creative initiative can be stifled by the take-it-easy attitude.

3. *"Thank God, it's Friday."* It is impossible to determine the extent to which productivity has declined in America because of the more than one hundred million workers that have allowed themselves to say or think, "TGIF." Obviously, enough people have thought this thought and have repeated these words to contribute to a collective reduction of enthusiasm. Enthusiasm is energy. Therefore, if you reduce the collective level of enthusiasm, you reduce energy. The work pace slows, and output per hour is unquestionably going to suffer.

4. *"I've got to see it before I believe it."* The trouble with this negative statement is that it is inside out, upside down, and backward. The truth is, "You've got to believe it before you see it!"

5. *"No way."* How many times has a positive idea been

[85]

slaughtered, strangled, or sunk with these two torpedoing words. Never repeat them. Never allow anybody to use them in your presence. There is *always* a way if people are willing to pay the price in time, energy, or effort!

6. *"Not too bad."* How many times have you asked a person how they were, only to have them answer with "Not too bad"? Basically this is a negative statement. It may appear an innocent and harmless comment, but it programs persons for emotional mediocrity. That adds up to lack of enthusiasm.

We need to insulate ourselves from such statements, as well as from a negative climate, if we are going to keep our enthusiasm at a peak.

You cannot live in a bubble. Many, many people that you meet each day will threaten to pop your bubble and drain your enthusiasm with their so-so, not-too-bad, pretty-good attitudes. I face them too. But I insulate myself by sharing with them "Schuller's Scale of Spirit."

When I ask someone, "How are you today?" their answer falls somewhere on my scale from one to ten:

1. Silence, trembly lips, eyes filled with tears.
2. Profane anger; a torrent of swear words.
3. "Awful. You would be too if you had the problems I face."
4. "Not too bad." (That's just one step above awful!)
5. "Pretty good." (That's just one step above "not too bad" and two steps above "awful.")
6. "Good."
7. "Great."
8. "Terrific."
9. "Fantastic."
10. "Sensational!"

Remember, you can control your mood. Tell yourself you *are* great. For nothing great ever happens on the "O.K." level.

7. *"I've heard that before."* This is another one of those negative cynical remarks. Avoid cynical people like a plague.

8. *"Never." "Can't." "None."* Any negative absolute is destructive. Insulate yourself from negative absolutes.

9. *"The case is closed."* So? Maybe the case can be reopened.

*God's delays
are not
God's denials.*

Maybe it can be appealed. Just because the case is closed doesn't mean you need to accept defeat.

10. *"It's terminal."* Nothing is terminal. Everything is transitional. Every end is a new beginning. Don't let phases faze you. Phases are passages. And passages are never dead ends. What looks like the end of the road will turn out to be a bend.

Tune your positive antennae to hear the difference between positive and negative statements. And insulate your mind from the negative, for solutions always lie in the positive.

Consider the following article by Barry Siegel. It shows in a light-hearted way how ridiculous it is to give in to negative arguments.

PALO ALTO, CALIFORNIA. Alarmists, worrying about such matters as nuclear holocaust and pesticide poisoning, may be overlooking much more dire catastrophes. Consider what some scientists predict: If everyone keeps stacking *National Geographics* in garages and attics instead of throwing them away, the magazine's weight will sink the continent 100 feet some time soon and we will all be inundated by the oceans.

If the number of microscope specimen slides submitted to one St. Louis Hospital laboratory continues to increase at its current rate, that metropolis will be buried under 3 feet of glass by the year 2024. If beachgoers keep returning home with as much sand clinging to them as they do now, 80 percent of the country's coastline will disappear in 10 years. Hard to believe? Scientists have the statistics and formulas to prove all this. They have even published them. Welcome to the *Journal of Irreproducible Results,* the official publication of the Society for Basic Irreproducible Results. The general public may not know about the journal but many scientists do. Published for 26 years, written and edited by scientists, the journal now has 40,000 subscribers in 52 countries. The *Journal* spoofs, parodies, and satirizes what its editor calls "the verbosity, pompous obscurantism, and sheer stupidity encountered in scientific publications and projects." Some items in the quotes are real reprints from legitimate journals to illustrate their factuality. But most articles are parodies written in technical scientific language complete with diagrams, tables, formulas, mathematical calculations and nonsensical conclusions. Far-reaching conclusions extrapolated from limited data are a favorite target of the journal. Several articles over the years have achieved the status of legend.

In "Pickle and Humbug" the journal reported the striking discovery that pickles cause cancer, communism, airline tragedies, auto accidents and crime waves. About 99.9% of cancer victims had eaten pickles some time in their lives, the article pointed out. So have 100% of all soldiers, 96.8% of Communist sympathizers and 99.7% of those involved in car and air accidents. Moreover those born in 1839 who ate pickles have suffered 100% mortality rate and rats force-fed 20 pounds of pickles a day for a month ended up with bulging abdomens and loss of appetite.

By far the most famous article the journal has carried is "*National Geographic* Doomsday Machine," written by one George H. Kaub. Kaub pointed out that more than 6.8 million issues of the *National Geographic*, each weighing two pounds, are sent to subscribers monthly and that not one copy has been thrown away since publication began 141 years ago. Instead copies are relentlessly accumulating in basements, attics, in public and private institutions of learning, the Library of Congress, the Smithsonian Institute, Goodwill, Salvation Army . . . soon the geologic substructure of the country will no longer support the load, Kaub predicted. Some subsidence will occur. Rock formations will compress, then become plastic and begin to flow. Great faults will appear. The continent will begin to sink and be inundated by the seas. In fact the increased earthquake activity in California along the San Andreas Fault that has already occurred was triggered by population growth in the state, the article said, and the subsequent increase in *National Geographic* subscriptions. Kaub ended by calling for nothing less than the immediate halt to publication of the *National Geographic* by Congressional action or Presidential edict if necessary.[1]

[1]"World May End With a Splash," *Los Angeles Times*, Oct. 9, 1982. Copyright © 1982, *Los Angeles Times*. Reprinted by permission.

The point of it all? The point is that negative thinking can easily produce exaggerated conclusions that are most irresponsible.

Be positive. You can solve your problems. When a problem seems to defy solution, you can manage it. You manage it when you work the twelve principles that I've shared with you. But none of this will work effectively unless you take positive control of your life and your thoughts. Let's see how to do that.

# 5

## *Take Charge and Take Control*

There's a seemingly harmless phrase that has swept the country. People no longer just say, "Good-bye." They inevitably add, "Take care."

But I contend it's wrong to say, "Take care." Instead say, "Take a chance; take charge; take control!" Why? Because people who take care never get anywhere! If you want to manage your problem successfully, you need to "take a chance, take charge, take control!" Taking a chance by itself is a reckless risk. But when you take charge, you manage that risk. When you take control, you manage your problems.

Take charge, take control, and never surrender leadership. What do I mean by leadership? I'll give it to you in a sentence: Leadership is the force that selects your dreams and sets your goals. It is the force that propels your endeavors to success.

Abraham Lincoln told a marvelous story about a blacksmith who stuck a long, round iron bar in the coals until it was red-hot. Then he put it on the anvil, where he hammered it flat to make a sword. When he was finished, he was most unhappy with it. So he put it back into the red-hot coals and decided to broaden the flat part out a bit and make a garden tool. That didn't please his fancy either. He put the bar back into the coals, rounded it a bit, and then shaped it into a horseshoe. This effort also failed miserably. As a last resort, he put the bar into the coals one more time. He removed it from the hot fire, wondering if there was anything else he could make from it. Deciding that there was nothing, he merely stuck it into a barrel of water. At the resulting hiss, he said, "Well, at least I made a fizzle out of it!"

Your dreams don't have to fizzle. Your life can sizzle, and your problems can be overcome if you will take charge and take control by learning and following the dynamic leadership principles outlined in this chapter.

You would be amazed how many "leaders" are unaware of these principles. Before they know it, they lose control and are defeated by problems they should have been able to manage successfully.

 ## Don't surrender leadership to outside forces.

In a corporate structure, leadership is not always at the desk of the president or the chairman of the board. Too often people in top positions surrender their power to outside forces.

I know this to be true. Some years ago, my congregation met in a smaller church building. Like so many other churches and corporations, we surrendered leadership to our property and our buildings. The church board was not in command. The pastor was not in command. People said, "We can't do that. We don't have enough parking. We don't have a large enough auditorium."

Then this thought came to me: The shoe doesn't tell the foot how big to grow. The body doesn't surrender leadership to the garment.

Don't surrender leadership to forces such as property, buildings, location. If you need to rebuild or relocate, take charge and take control.

Never surrender leadership to such forces as poverty. Don't allow lack of money to determine your dreams or your goals. There is always a way to raise the capital you need. You may have to save and count your pennies, but somehow the money will come. There is a universal principle that al-

*Today's
decisions
are
tomorrow's
realities.*

ways manifests itself: Money flows to good ideas; good ideas spawn other good ideas; dreams inspire creativity in money management.

There are many things we can't control. We can't control inflation. We cannot control a recession. But we can control our ideas and what we do with them.

I have a dear friend who, like many others, was caught in the depression of the thirties. He was broke, penniless. He couldn't control his poverty, but he didn't surrender leadership to the forces of the depression.

He was a salesman and not doing too well. One night, one of his fellow salesmen said, "Hey, did you hear about the guy who made so much money with Coca-Cola? You know, it used to be that the only way you could get a glass of soda was from a soda fountain. But then this guy came up with a way to bottle it. He told the Coca-Cola company that they could use his idea if they would give him a fraction of 1 percent of their increased sales. That minute percentage made him a millionaire."

That day my friend had been to the gas station because he needed oil in his car. In those days, the only way you could get oil was to go to a gas station where they pumped it out of huge drums and poured it into your car. Later that night he thought to himself, "I wonder if I could bottle oil?" Then he thought, "No, if the bottle broke, there would be a mess. But cans would work!"

So he went to a can company and said, "Can you sell me cans?" He went to a friend who owned a Pennsylvania oil well that produced so much oil he couldn't market it.

Then he went to a grocery chain and said, "I've got an idea how you can vastly increase your retail sales. I'll tell you how if you'll give me just seventy-five dollars for every freight car load of oil you sell."

They said, "O.K., what's your idea?"

"Sell automobile oil in cans. I'll provide them to you."

"Canned car oil?"

"Yes."

At only seventy-five dollars per freight car of cans, he

became a multimillionaire during the Great Depression. He used it as the base of his now-enormous financial empire.

## 2 Don't surrender leadership to faces.

Lots of people do that. I've seen it happen. I've done it myself. You read an audience. You see an eyebrow raise or hear a throat being cleared. Through body language, someone suggests that he may not support you. You read on his face that he's going to criticize you. He's not going to back you. He's against you. Before you know it, you have been intimidated by body language into silence and retreat. At that point you have surrendered leadership to a face.

## 3 Don't surrender leadership to farces.

Farces are lies, masks. Often people of Asian, African, and Spanish minority groups have been taught that they are genetically and intellectually inferior. Now that's a farce, a mask, a lie! If people say that one race is superior or inferior to another, don't you believe it!

A good friend of mine, a black man named George Johnson, has experienced racism. He grew up in Chicago, polishing shoes in a barber shop. George used to hear his black friends say, "I wish I could straighten my hair."

One day while George was shining a man's shoes, he asked him, "What do you do?"

"I'm a chemist," the man replied.

"What do chemists do?" George asked.

"I mix things," the man explained.

"Do you think you could mix something that would straighten my hair?"

The chemist said, "Maybe I can put something together."

He did. George tried it on his hair and it worked. He bottled the product and sold it to some of his friends and a few stores. Soon he built a sales force to sell "Ultra-Sheen."

Today, George Johnson's personal fortune is over several million dollars. That's not bad for someone who was once a shoeshine boy.

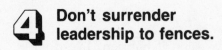

## Don't surrender leadership to fences.

Fences are limiting concepts that you allow to influence your goals and dreams. Because of these concepts, we throw away ideas and dreams that we are sure we'll never be able to realize. They also cause us to lower our goals, with the result that we strive for and achieve far less than our capabilities.

These fences are negative self-image perceptions such as:

"I don't have an education."

"I don't know the right people."

"I don't have enough money."

"I'm not a member of the right organization."

Never surrender leadership to fences or locked-in thinking. Locked-in thinking is the thought process that says, "It's never worked before. Why should it now?"

Or, "This is the way it's always been done, so it must be the best." Nobody is more guilty of locked-in thinking than trained, educated professionals. They have been so disciplined, so trained, that as they develop a discipline, an expertise, they also develop locked-in thinking.

The elevator at the El Cortez Hotel in San Diego couldn't handle the traffic. The experts—engineers and architects—were called in. They concluded that they could put another elevator in by cutting a hole in each floor and installing the motor for the new elevator in the basement. The plans were drawn up. Everything was in order. The architect and the engineer came into the lobby discussing it. The janitor, who was there with his mop, heard them say they were going to chop holes in the floors.

The janitor said, "That's going to make a mess."

The engineer said, "Of course. But we'll get help for you, don't worry."

The janitor replied, "You'll have to close the hotel for a while."

"Well, if we have to close the hotel for a while, we'll close the hotel. We can't possibly survive without another elevator."

The janitor held the mop in his hands and said, "Do you know what I would do if I were you?"

The architect arrogantly asked, "What?"

"I'd build the elevator on the outside."

The architect and the engineer just looked at each other.

They built the elevator on the outside—the first time in the history of architecture that an elevator was built on the outside of a building.

## 5 Don't surrender leadership to frustrations.

There are people who reach a point where they just can't handle people any more. They can't handle government regulations any more. They can't handle cash-flow problems any more. Anyone who has dreams and goals also has frustrations: lack of time and money, high interest rates, disappointments when your best people let you down. Such frustrations can mount up, and if you surrender leadership to them, you'll soon cash in, give up, throw in the towel, quit. Don't give in to such temptations.

## 6 Don't surrender leadership to your fantasies.

It's amazing. God gives you a brilliantly exciting idea, and you soon give in to negative fantasies: "I might try it and be rejected"; "People might laugh at me."

My dear friends, let me tell you something very honestly. I am not immune to such negative thoughts.

When we dreamed of the Tower of Hope and the Crystal Cathedral, two major building projects on our church campus, I wondered, "What will people say? What if we try it and it fails? We'll be the laughingstock of the country."

Let me tell you, if your dreams are bigger than most, if your ideas are more creative, there will be criticism. There will probably be some ridicule. But don't create more condemnation than is really there. Don't allow yourself to indulge in negative fantasies that limit the size of your goals and stifle your creativity.

## 7 Don't surrender leadership to fears.

The Bible says, "God has not given us a spirit of fear, but of power and of love and of a sound mind" (2 Tim. 1:7). That means when you surrender to fears, you can be sure the fears did not come from God. God does not give us the spirit of fear. God gives us the spirit of power and love and a sound mind.

If you have many fears, all you have to do is cure yourself of one fear, and that's the fear of failure. This will help: "I'd rather attempt something great and fail than attempt nothing and succeed."

I admire people who make a commitment, and stick their neck out. I admire a person who tries to reach the top and doesn't make it. Perhaps he is someone who declares his candidacy for public office in a sincere desire to be a public servant for community good. He can be sure that he will be criticized and condemned, and probably misinterpreted and distorted. His ego will surely take an awful beating. What does he get out of it? Even if he loses the race, he is a winner because he has conquered his fear of trying. In doing so, he has won his biggest battle. Every loser who tries to do something great is really a winner.

There is no need to fear failure. As I said in *You Can Become the Person You Want to Be:*

Failure doesn't mean you are a failure . . . it does mean you haven't succeeded yet.

Failure doesn't mean you have accomplished nothing . . . it
does mean you have learned something.

Failure doesn't mean you have been a fool . . . it does mean
you had a lot of faith.

Failure doesn't mean you've been disgraced . . . it does mean
you were willing to try.

Failure doesn't mean you don't have it . . . it does mean you
have to do something in a different way.

Failure doesn't mean you are inferior . . . it does mean you are
not perfect.

Failure doesn't mean you've wasted your life . . . it does mean
you have a reason to start afresh.

Failure doesn't mean you should give up . . . it does mean you
must try harder.

Failure doesn't mean you'll never make it . . . it does mean it
will take a little longer.

Failure doesn't mean God has abandoned you . . . it does
mean God has a better idea![1]

 ## Don't surrender leadership to fatigue.

Everybody runs tired once in a while. You better be able to
know when you're running tired and then back off. Because
if you don't, you're going to make some bad decisions.

I'm not one who likes to give in or slow down when I'm
tired. But even Jesus retreated occasionally. Do you remember the time when the multitudes pressed upon Him and He
got into a boat? While they were calling to Him and reaching
to Him, He left them. He just pulled away, escaped, and
went to the mountains to pray.

History will long ask the question: "Did Franklin D. Roosevelt surrender leadership to his fatigue at Yalta?" He was a
very sick man. The wisdom of his decisions that affected the
present-day Eastern bloc countries is still being debated by
historians.

There are times when you should not see people or make

---

[1]From *You Can Become the Person You Want to Be*. Copyright © 1973 by Robert H.
Schuller. Reprinted by permission of the publisher, E. P. Dutton, Inc.

decisions. When I'm tired, I often do not see people. I owe a great deal to my dear wife. She knows me very well, and she has arranged my calendar very carefully. She knows when my energies are taxed, and she blocks off time for renewal. Each year she plans mini-vacations for me immediately after busy times of the year. That way I never get burned out.

## 9 Don't surrender leadership to faults.

A lot of people do that. Somebody comes along with a good idea only to have someone else say, "Oh, but it will take too long, or it will cost too much." Or "Somebody else is doing it." They find fault with a good idea and annihilate it. They surrender leadership to the faults instead of to the potential. There are problems with every idea. But problems call for polishing, not for demolition. It's amazing how faults can control our lives if we let them.

I once counseled with a young person who had a problem. She said, "Everything is going wrong with my life. I'll never be able to amount to anything. It's all my parents' fault, really. They broke up. My family fell apart. Dr. Schuller, if you had my problems, you'd be where I am too."

I said to this young person, "Listen, I understand you have had problems. But let me tell you something. Never let a problem become an excuse."

When you let the problem become an excuse, you've surrendered leadership. Accept the faults, the shortcomings, and the imperfections. And then rise above them. You can if you have the right attitude. That leads me to the next principle.

## 10 Don't surrender leadership to facts.

The problems you are facing today may be fact, not just theory. The unemployment statistics are factual. You may recognize this truth when you collect your unemployment check. But don't surrender leadership to it. Facts, statistics, interest rates can definitely influence your life, but you can choose whether or not the influence will be beneficial or detrimental.

Dr. Karl Menninger, one of the great psychiatrists, made one of the wisest statements I've ever heard: "Attitude is more important than facts." Your attitude needs to remain positive and in the control position. Never let yourself be defeated by the facts.

# 11 Don't surrender leadership to frenzies.

A lot of people maintain control and they make the right decisions until they get into a frenzy, a frantic situation. This past week, as I was flying east, a gentleman on the plane waved at me as if he recognized me. I asked, "Do we know each other?"

He said, "You don't know me, but I know you. I watch 'Hour of Power' all the time."

I sat down. We chatted. He was Bob McClure, an airline captain. He said, "I fly the L1011. I've been a pilot for twenty-seven years."

I said, "If you've been a pilot for twenty-seven years, you must have a good story. What is the most unusual thing that's ever happened to you?"

He said, "During the Second World War, I was a solo fighter of an F6 Hellcat. I was on a first-bombing, strafing mission over Tokyo Bay. I took off from the aircraft carrier. I was to come in at a high elevation and make a deep, deep, strafing dive leveling out at three hundred feet above the bay."

Now three hundred feet is not very high.

He said, "I was coming down at an astronomical speed. And just as I started to level off, the left wing took a direct hit. It tipped my plane completely upside down."

I said, "Did you know that you were upside down?" (Having flown quite a bit in private planes, I know you can lose perspective quite easily.)

[101]

Take care?
People who take care
never go anywhere.

Take a chance!

Take charge!

Take control!

"Oh, yes," he said. "I knew I was upside down when I saw the ocean was my sky. Do you know what saved me?"

"What?"

"I was taught that when something terrible happens, don't *do* anything. Just think. So," he said, "that's all I can remember. I did nothing. I never touched a control. If I had not been taught that, I would have instinctively lost the horizontal position I had, and I would have tipped into the water and been killed." He added, "I still remember, when something catastrophic is threatening, *Don't do anything. Just think.*"

## 12 Don't surrender leadership to the fates.

There are all kinds of negative "fates" that social structures or the "stars" might try to impose upon you. I have been asked under what star I was born. I always reply that I don't know and I don't want to know. Too many people allow their futures to be unnecessarily predetermined by imaginary factors. Astrology is like fortunetelling and I don't like fortunetellers. They make too many negative statements.

I'll never forget this one poor anxiety-prone person who didn't have enough faith in God to go to church. Instead, he went to a fortuneteller, who said, "In your future I see poverty, bad luck, and failure until you reach the age of forty."

To which the person asked, "Then what?"

The fortuneteller looked at him and said, "Oh, after that you get used to it."

Fortunetellers, chart readers, and any others who program people subconsciously or consciously with negative self-fulfilling prophecies are dangerous people. Never allow these people to move into the control position of your life.

## 13 Don't surrender leadership to forecasts.

You know there are people who are constantly saying, "Things are bad, and they're only going to get worse." There will always be negative, cynical people who only believe that life will go downhill as time goes on.

I love the story the late Bear Bryant, head football coach at the University of Alabama for many years, told me once. Years ago, when he was coach at Texas A&M, his team was scheduled to play SMU in one of the big bowl games. He said, "All of the newspapers said that my team was going to get swamped. These were the words they used: *slaughtered, swamped, driven into the ground.* There was no way I could keep my boys from reading those negative forecasts. So I went to bed the night before the game, and I suddenly remembered all that the reporters and sportscasters were saying: 'Bear Bryant of Texas A&M is going to get beaten by three or four touchdowns.' Others were saying five touchdowns. All of these extremely negative words were in my mind as I fell asleep. I woke up early in the morning. I looked at the clock and it was one o'clock. And I was petrified. We were going to get slaughtered. That was the forecast."

Then he said, "I remembered that Bible verse: 'If you have faith as a grain of mustard seed, you will say to this mountain, "Move from here to there," and it will move; and nothing shall be impossible unto you' [Matt. 17:20]. I got up, called my coaches, and said, 'I want you to have all the players in the locker room in thirty minutes.' I pulled my pants on, put some shoes and a sweater on. I got in the car and started it. The two headlights pierced the blackness of the night. At 1:30 A.M. there wasn't a car on the road. I swung into the parking lot, went into the deserted locker room, paced, and waited. Other car lights started coming, one lonely car after another. The players came staggering in. A couple of them were still in their pajamas and bathrobes.

"I said to them, 'Did you hear the news? Have you heard what they're predicting? They say we're going to get slaughtered. Beaten by four, five, or six touchdowns. You all heard it. O.K. I want to tell you something. Jesus said, "If you have faith as a grain of mustard seed—a little mustard seed—you can say to your mountain, Move! And it will move. And nothing will be impossible to you." Now go home to bed.'"

I asked him, "How did you do?"

He said, "Dr. Schuller, we lost. But by only three points. We lost the game, but boy, we saved our pride!"

# 14 Don't surrender leadership to your foes.

I had a lot of opposition when I assumed leadership of the construction of the Crystal Cathedral. My opposition did not come from the congregation. They were very supportive in their labor, their love, and their prayers. But from outside the congregation, I had my foes. Their criticisms were hard to take. But through the whole experience I learned this: Not a single opponent, not a single foe, not a single critic offered any better solution to my problem. I soon realized that my foes really weren't interested in solving my problems.

They're not accountable. You and I will stand before God some day, and we will have to give account to Him of what and why we did or did not do certain things. Do you know what hell would be for me? It would be standing before God and having Him look at me and tell me all the things I could have done if I'd had more faith.

This leadership principle might be pretty obvious. What isn't so obvious is the next principle.

# 15 Don't surrender leadership to your friends.

Every time we have made a decision in this church, one or two of my best friends on the church board couldn't go along with it. Even in my marriage, my wife and I have not always agreed.

Somebody once asked, "How could you be married so successfully for thirty-two years when you don't always agree?" To answer that question I refer to a book my wife has written, *The Positive Family*. In that book she reveals the secret.

We have a scale of nonapproval. When we disagree, we measure the depth of the intensity of nonagreement.

We have a scale from one to ten.

1. The lowest level is, "I'm not enthusiastic. But go ahead if you want to." From there the intensity of the comments increases.
2. "I don't see it the way you do, but I may be wrong, so go ahead."
3. "I don't agree. I'm sure you're wrong. But I can live with it. Go ahead."
4. "I don't agree. But I'll be quiet and let you have your way. I can change it my way later on. Next year I can repaint, repaper, reupholster it my way."
5. "I don't agree, and I cannot remain silent. I love you, but I will not be able to keep from expressing my disapproval. So don't be offended if you hear me expressing a contrary view."
6. "I do not approve, and I make a motion we postpone and delay action until we both are able emotionally and rationally to reevaluate our positions. Give me more time."
7. "I strongly disapprove. This is a mistake—costly, not easily corrected, and I stand firm. I cannot and will not go along with it."
8. "My answer is no! I will be so seriously upset if you go ahead that I cannot predict what my reaction will be."
9. "No way! If you go ahead I have to tell you I quit; I'll walk out!"
10. "No—no—no! Over my dead body!"[3]

I must tell you that in thirty-two years my wife and I have never gone above a six in our level of disagreement.

When I feel myself getting upset, I'll say, "This is a six, Honey." Six means: "I love you very, very much. Since I can't tell what this is going to do to our relationship, which is obviously more important, let's wait and think about it. Maybe in a month or two, I'll be able to approve. However, today I can't agree with you on this. Give me time to see your viewpoint and feel what you feel."

[3]From *The Positive Family.* Copyright © 1982 by Arvella Schuller. Reprinted by permission of Doubleday and Company, Inc.

Friends can give you advice. They can share with you their opinions. But they should never have the final word. The only one who can make the decision and live with the results is you. Do what you believe you must do. Be true to yourself, to your ideals, and to your dreams.

## 16 Don't surrender leadership to the fracturing experiences of life.

A brokenness can occur that leaves people without faith for the future. A young man said to me after his wife left him for another man, "I'm never going to trust another woman."

I said to him, "Believe in dreams. Never believe in hurts. Don't let your fracturing experience shape your future."

I remember a very dear friend who had a poodle, a lovely, adorable dog. The dog died. I said to her, "Betty, when are you going to get a new puppy?"

She said, "Never again."

I said, "Why not?"

"Oh, it hurts too much to lose them. I'll never have another dog."

I said, "Betty, you can't surrender to a hurt. You can't let the grief and the hurts and the aches and the breaking experiences of life control your future decisions."

## 17 Don't surrender leadership to the flattening-out experiences of life.

I have seen families in this church that have withstood experiences that would crush others. One of these families was the Van Allen family. Both Ed and Jeanne are now gone, having passed away much too young. Ed Van Allen died when he was transporting a new airplane to a South Pacific mission station. The plane never made Honolulu. No sooner did Ed die than Jeanne got cancer. Jeanne was told that her case was terminal, that she did not have long to live. After courageously fighting a losing battle, she suddenly had a last resurgence. She came back and did some wonderful work and made some fine contributions.

At her deathbed, I asked, "Jeanne, where did you get the power to come back these last few weeks? Three months ago you were almost dead."

She said, "Oh, I began to think, 'This is it. You're terminal. Now's the time to quit, give up.' But then I prayed and this thought came to me: If I give up, two organizations will benefit—the mortuary and the cemetery. But if I hang in there for another month or so, my family will benefit. Maybe my church can benefit.

"So I said to myself, I'm going to get dressed at least once more, and I'm going to work on the telephone—the NEW HOPE Telephone Counseling—at least one day, or at least a couple of hours."

She said, "Then I began to get inspired. I thought of hundreds of things I wanted to do. I just kept saying, 'I'm gonna do this, I'm gonna to do that.' Dr. Schuller, the *'gonnas' got me going!"*

Jeanne didn't give in to the flattening-out experiences. She also practiced the final principle of leadership, the principle that encompasses all of the above.

## 18 Do surrender leadership to one thing—faith.

Let faith be in control of every decision you make and every action you take. You do that when you let the positive possibilities set your goals.

When you look at your life and where it's headed, ask yourself these questions: "Who's in charge? Who's in control? To whom have I surrendered leadership?"

Surrender leadership to faith. Surrender leadership to God. Let Him be in control of your life. Ask Him three questions: "God, who am I? Why am I here? Where am I headed?" At the very least, His answers may surprise you. They will open your eyes to the beautiful person that you are and will become, as well as to the fantastic future that awaits you.

# 6

## Ten Commandments of Possibility Thinking

Possibility thinking. What is it? In essence it is the management of ideas. Some people never have learned to manage time. Some people never have learned to manage money. Some people never have learned to manage people or themselves. Possibility thinking focuses not on the management of time, money, energy, or persons, but on the management of ideas.

What do we mean by *management*? Management is control. Management is the control of a resource in order to minimize waste and maximize the development of latent possibilities.

I am told that ten thousand ideas daily flow through the average mind. A vast majority of the ideas are negative. Possibility thinking is the disciplined separation of negative thoughts from positive thoughts by this criterion: Positive thoughts are those that hold undeveloped potential for good.

Impossibility thinkers are people who instinctively react negatively to a possibility-laden idea. They impulsively look for reasons why it can't be done. They quickly abort an idea and forget about it.

The possibility thinker looks at every idea to see if it has possibilities. If it does, he takes an option out on the idea. He does not let it slip by.

I recently received a letter from a woman in Flora, Indiana, who was presented with a positive idea, executed it, and is now managing a successful small business. She wrote:

Dear Dr. Schuller:

A few weeks ago I heard you say, "If you are laid off work, you're lucky!" I thought, *Oh, dear, really!* You said, "You probably would not have the guts enough to quit your job and start a business of your own." I thought to myself, *How did you know?*

Well, that is exactly what has happened to me. I was laid off from General Motors in Kokomo, Indiana. I kept busy with my sewing and doing for others, but that didn't pay much. I kept asking God, "If I have a talent, please help me turn it into a business."

In August, my husband and I were helping friends build a cabin in Minnesota, and in evenings we women worked on crafts. My friend said, "I am so tired of making crafts and giving them away, aren't you? Let's start a gift shop with things on consignment." She also said we had the ideal place for the shop—where I used to have my Tupperware office at one end of our garage—a room twenty-four by thirteen feet.

Now this friend had not seen this room since I got out of Tupperware seven years ago. It had become a room for "where do I put this or that? . . . Oh, just out in the Tupperware office." Now, can't you just picture our room like that? When we got back from Minnesota we had fifty names on our list of people we knew who made crafts. We got that messy room cleaned out, had a garage sale, and what didn't sell, the Goodwill got. We got six hundred dollars for stuff we thought was really junk. We thought, *If people will come out in the country for a garage sale, they should come for handmade things*.

So we got very inexpensive pumpkin-colored plaid carpet. We restained the paneling and made curtains with painted pumpkins on the tiebacks and called our place "The Pumpkin Patch Gift Shop." We opened October 1.

In the first month we have had over six hundred people here and have had gross sales of $2,533.22. Before we opened the doors on October 1, we had our long talk with God, and He is our Number One Partner. We now have ninety-four people with lovely handmade things in our place. As we look back, I can't remember any negative thoughts about this. We just feel like it had to be God's idea. We could not have done all this as fast as we have without Him. And we do thank you, Dr. Schuller, for all your help. I talk about you in the Pumpkin Patch lots of times.

This woman is a possibility thinker! She could have rejected her friend's proposal for any number of reasons. Instead, she managed the negative ideas, executed the positive ones, and now her unemployment problem is solved!

I consider myself a possibility thinker. I have pursued many ideas that initially appeared humanly impossible. The results have always amazed me. But, I must confess that there have been many other ideas that were so ludicrous that I quickly rejected them. I never gave them a chance.

Today I was given the keys to a brand-new Lincoln. The car is mine, free of charge, for twelve months. This gift was the result of an impossible dream that I was tempted to discard.

The idea first occurred to me when I was with my wife at the Honolulu airport. We were inquiring about a rental car when the clerk informed us, "We have a super bargain going right now. We have brand-new Lincolns, fully equipped and fully computerized. Normally they rent for sixty dollars a day. We can let you have one for only thirty-five dollars!"

My wife was so enthusiastic she convinced me to rent the car. It was beautiful! It handled like a dream.

That was when I got the idea: "Wouldn't it be great to get a car like this for Arvella [my wife]? After all, she has nearly eighty thousand miles on her old car."

My idea was a good idea. It was a positive idea. It could bring comfort and safety to someone I love. However, when I realized how much a car like that one might cost, I quickly dismissed the thought.

No sooner did I say to myself, *Forget it, Schuller. It's too expensive*, than this next thought came to me: *Why don't you practice what you preach? You just gave a lecture last week at a sales conference. There you told thousands of people how important it is to manage ideas. You said "Never throw away an idea just because it is impossible. Give it a chance."*

So, I decided to give it a try. I thought that I should at least find out what it cost. Maybe it would be less than I imagined. Even if it was as much as I expected, perhaps I could get one on sale. If not, I could try to increase my income somehow. I decided I would try to work it out.

As soon as I made *a sincere commitment to try*, the breakthrough came! I suddenly recalled meeting a man named Bob Eagle, who was introduced to me as "head of Eagle

Lincoln-Mercury dealership in Dallas, Texas—one of the nation's largest."

Should I call Bob and see if he would sell me one of these cars at cost? The idea seemed crazy. I was tempted once more to discard it. But then I remembered another principle I have lectured on often, "Do it now!"

I walked to the telephone, called the Dallas information operator, and asked for the telephone number of Eagle Lincoln-Mercury. I placed a person-to-person call to Bob Eagle. When the secretary heard it was a person-to-person call from Hawaii, she immediately got Bob on the line. He greeted me warmly.

I relayed to him how impressed I was with this automobile and told him that, though I couldn't afford it, it would be wonderful if I could give one to my wife for her birthday.

Bob said, "Dr. Schuller, you've really helped me through your television show. Now I'd like to help you. Let me see what I can do."

A few minutes later he called back. "There's someone I'd like you to talk to. He's Gordon MacKenzie, vice-president of Ford Motor Company."

Then, by way of a three-way conference call, I met Gordon and accepted an offer to visit the Ford assembly plant later that week when I would be in the Detroit area.

When I arrived in Detroit, I was treated graciously by Gordon and his friend, John Sagan, treasurer of the Ford Motor Company. They took me to dinner and the next morning gave me a personal tour of the assembly plant.

As we were surveying the assembly lines, Gordon MacKenzie said, "Dr. Schuller, I want you to feel free to interrupt any worker on any assembly line and ask him any question you want."

I decided to take him up on his offer and tapped a laborer on the shoulder. MacKenzie introduced me. I said to the worker, "How do you like your job?"

"I love it," he said.

"Why?" I asked.

His eyes flashed and he grinned from ear to ear. Then he

answered, pointing proudly to a beautiful new car: "That's why! I'm so proud to be a part of that car. This is absolutely the greatest automobile made in the world, today. For price and value, it cannot be beat. We have never before produced such an automobile in Detroit! And we know it!"

As I was leaving the plant I turned to MacKenzie and said, "Gordon, I am very impressed by what you're doing here. Nobody could put more quality, care, and dedication into manufacturing a car than you are."

Gordon MacKenzie realized how deeply moved I was at the dedication of the workers in that company, and he said to me, "Dr. Schuller, since you are so impressed we'd like to do something for you. Be our guest and drive one of our cars for the next twelve months—free. And see if everything we are telling you isn't really true!"

That's how I came to be the recipient of keys to a brand-new Lincoln. It never would have happened if I hadn't grabbed hold of my first idea. It makes me wonder how many potential blessings I have carelessly tossed aside because I did not dare to pursue a positive thought.

The point is this: Never underestimate the value of an idea. Every positive idea has within it the potential for success if it is managed properly. How do we manage ideas so effectively that we can be assured of success? Through the Ten Commandments of Possibility Thinking—that's how! If you will obey these commandments for possibility thinking, you will be amazed at the success that you will be able to achieve. What are they?

##  Never reject a possibility because you see something wrong with it!

There is something wrong with every good idea. Any time God gives you an idea, you can find some negative aspect to it. It's amazing how people sit in a deliberating meeting and respond to an opportunity only by finding fault with it. Don't throw away a suggestion when you see a problem. Instead, isolate the negative from the possibility. Neutralize the negative. Exploit the possibility, and sublimate the negative. Don't ever let negatives kill the positive potential that is within an opportunity.

Nothing is impossible if I will hold on to the idea that it might become possible somehow, some way, with someone's help. Only a few weeks ago I was asked to deliver a possibility-thinking seminar for the unemployed. They said, "Dr. Schuller, you believe in possibility thinking. Maybe it can help the unemployed solve their impossible problems and find a job."

Frankly, I was challenged by the idea. It forced me to review the principles of possibility thinking and apply them to an area to which I had never before attempted to apply them.

As I worked on my speech, my notes piled up higher and higher until I realized: *This could be very helpful to a lot of unemployed people. Maybe I should write a book on this subject.*

At that point I could have reacted negatively. Instead, I yielded to that positive impulse, telephoned my publisher and asked, "Could you get a book published, manufactured, and out on the streets of America in a few months? I think I have something to say that could be very helpful to the unemployed. I'd like to get it out in a hurry."

My editor, Larry Stone, said, "I'll call you back."

On Friday the phone rang. It was Larry. "Dr. Schuller, we love the slogan 'Tough times never last . . . but tough people do!' We'd love to have you write a book with that title. It could be very, very helpful to many people. And we agree that it must get out in a hurry. A lot of people are desperate and need that hope today.

"Our spring catalog goes to print in three days. If you're agreeable, we'll announce your new book in the spring catalog. It will say that your book will be coming out in six months. O.K.?"

I was excited. "You bet!" I answered.

Then he dropped the bombshell, "If we are to deliver what we are promising, we will need the first four chapters from you by November 15."

"No problem," I answered impulsively. "You'll have it!"

*Better to
do something
imperfectly
than to
do nothing
flawlessly.*

My wife had heard the conversation and said, "What have you agreed to do?" I explained. She said, "Do you know what date it is today?"

I said, "No."

"The fifteenth of November is a week from Monday."

I was horrified. "A week from Monday? There is no way I can get four chapters by that time! Tomorrow is Saturday and I'll need all day Saturday to write the two Sunday morning messages I am scheduled to deliver."

The only free day I had before November 15 was Monday, the eighth. How could I possibly get four chapters written before the fourteenth of November? I concluded inwardly that I had agreed to the impossible. Yet everything within me refused to give up on the idea. Somehow it would have to be accomplished.

On Monday morning I was not at all motivated. In fact, I was paralyzed by anxiety.

I allowed myself to be interrupted by telephone calls. I allowed myself to be distracted by other pressures.

By the time I went to bed at 10:30 on Monday night I had not lifted a pen. I had not written a thing on my book. That meant that I now had only six days left to write four chapters.

You are reading the book, so you can see that I got the chapters done in time. What saved me? Was it a positive slogan? Prodding from my wife? No. It was an obscene phone call.

On Tuesday morning, November 9, 1982, the phone awakened me at 4:30. The person on the other end never said a word. There was just some heavy breathing.

I turned over, hoping to catch another couple hours of rest, but was unable to go back to sleep. As I tossed and turned, this thought occurred to me: *Why don't you get up? Go into the library and start dictating.* But I argued with myself: *I can't dictate a book. I never dictate books! That is something in which I've never believed.* (Don't ask me why. It only illustrates my problem of locked-in thinking on a particular point.)

But then I remembered that I am supposed to be a possibility thinker. *Schuller, practice what you preach. Anything is possible. Maybe it is also possible to dictate a book. At least it will help you to get started. Remember what you wrote in* Move Ahead with Possibility Thinking: *"Beginning is half done."*

That did it. I responded to the idea. I slipped out of bed, walked to the library, and dictated in the silent darkness of the early morning. I spoke without interruption for two hours. By this time the darkness had turned to dawning. The sun was rising. My daughters were stirring in their bedrooms. The day was just beginning, but I had already written one complete chapter.

The rest of my day was full. There was no other time for writing. But I went to bed that night confident that one chapter was finished. At three o'clock on Wednesday morning I was awakened by our dogs. Our Samoyed, Doberman, and German Shepherd would not quit barking. Finally I got out of bed to quiet them down and discovered that they had cornered a raccoon under our front porch. They were barking with insane rage at this cowering, cornered creature. I tried to bribe the dogs with food to quiet them. I commanded them to be quiet. Nothing worked.

I was disgusted. I went back to bed. I couldn't get to sleep. So for the second morning in a row I went to my library and dictated another chapter for the book.

Then I called my senior editor, who edits my sermons every Sunday and consequently knows all of my material better than anybody else! That person is my daughter, Sheila Schuller Coleman. I said, "Sheila, I need to get two more chapters written in the next few days. Remember the story of Birt, Benno, and John, our NEW HOPE counselor who was paralyzed? Would you pull them together into a chapter? And would you help me polish up the other chapters that I have dictated? Could you take my lecture on the Ten Commandments for Possibility Thinkers and develop it into a fourth chapter?

"Sure, Dad!" she replied enthusiastically.

The story that I am sharing with you now, I dictated on Thursday morning at 4:30! A few hours later I left for Arizona, then Indiana. I arrived back in town late Friday night. On Saturday, I prepared two messages for Sunday. But on my desk Saturday morning were the four completed chapters of this new book, *Tough Times Never Last, But Tough People Do!*

What I would have considered to be a total impossibility became an accomplished fact!

## 2 Never reject a possibility because you won't get the credit!

God can do tremendous things through the person who doesn't care who gets the credit. Years ago, I met a man who was president and chairman of the board of a company in Minneapolis. The company had made the first huge balloon satellite, one that moved across the night sky like a star. It was a successful step in the early stages of the space program. I said to the president, "Excuse me for saying this, but I've never heard of your name or your company."

He replied, "Maybe not. We didn't get the credit, but we got the contract."

Don't worry about getting the credit. If you do, you'll become ego-involved in the decision-making moments of life. Decisions must never be based on ego needs. They must be based on human needs and market pressures that transcend your own desires. Decide today: Would you rather satisfy your ego—or enjoy the fruit of success?

## 3 Never reject an idea because it's impossible!

Almost every great idea is impossible when it is first born. The greatest ideas today are yet impossible! Possibility thinkers take great ideas and turn the impossibilities into possibilities. That's progress!

The important issue is whether the idea is a good one. Would it help people who are hurting? Would it be a great

*When faced*
*with a mountain,*
*I will not quit!*
*I will*
*keep on striving*
*until I climb over,*
*find a pass through,*
*tunnel underneath—*
*or simply stay*
*and turn the mountain*
*into a gold mine,*
*with God's help!*

thing for our country and our world? If so, then develop a way to achieve what today is impossible.

Not many days ago I was in Singapore, talking with a Nobel Prize-winning biologist who's active in genetic engineering and the forefront of gene-splicing. He predicts that if given freedom to do so, geneticists will be able to develop a plant agriculturally designed to generate an alcoholic fuel that will produce maximum mileage for sophisticated engines not yet conceived. That's possibility thinking! Just because it's impossible today doesn't mean it will be impossible tomorrow. Our goals should always be based upon whether it would be a sensational thing to accomplish.

 **Never reject a possibility because your mind is already made up!**

I'm sure you've heard the saying: "Don't confuse me with the facts, my mind is already made up!" I've had to change my mind publicly more than once. People who never change their minds are either perfect or stubborn. I'm not perfect and neither are you. I'd rather change plans while still in port, than to set sail and sink at sea.

**Never reject an idea because it's illegal!**

Listen carefully, or you'll misinterpret this commandment. Some of the greatest ideas are impossible because they are illegal today. You should never violate the law, but don't reject an idea because it's illegal. You might be able to get the law changed!

A good friend of mine, Bill Brashears, acquired fourteen property lots to develop a twelve-acre commercial center. But he ran into a major problem. There was a flood control channel through the middle of his property, and it was illegal to erect a building over a flood control channel. That could have killed the project for him, but I gave him this advice: "Never reject an idea because it's illegal. The law is inadequate—so get it changed. After all, they built the Prudential Building in Chicago over the railroad tracks. Why can't we have a little water go under a building in Orange County?" So Bill led a crusade, and the law was changed. A lot of laws on the books today need to be changed.

 ### Never reject an idea because you don't have the money, manpower, muscle, or months to achieve it!

All it takes to accomplish the impossible is mind power, manpower, money power, muscle power, and month power. If you don't have them, you can get them. Spend enough time, use enough energy, develop enough human resources, acquire enough financial capital, and you can do almost anything. Don't reject an idea just because you don't have the necessary power. Make the commitment to do what's great, then solve the problems. A supersuccessful person has very few resources, except the capacity to take an idea and marshal stronger and smarter people around him to pull it off.

Many years ago, when the beautiful Union Railroad Station was built in Cincinnati, Ohio, spectacular mosaics were created on the plastered walls. They artfully depicted the crafts and industry of the city of Cincinnati.

As years went by, the building began to sag. When it was condemned, people were horrified. What would happen to the exquisite mosaics? Destroying them along with the building was unthinkable.

Yet, when the experts were consulted, they replied, "There is no way to save the mosaics when the building is destroyed."

Alfred Moore refused to accept that answer. He could not let the mosaics be destroyed. He decided that he would find a way. That decision was the key that unlocked his mind. He thought of one possible way the twenty-by-twenty-foot panels could be moved.

He created a gigantic steel frame for the section of the wall. Then he put wire nets on the back side of the wall, and sprayed it with gunnite—the wet concrete that is used in swimming pools. Then, with a huge crane, he lifted the walls, transported them, and installed them in the new airport. They are there today!

## 7 Never reject an idea because it will create conflict!

The longer I've studied possibility thinking, the more I've come to one conclusion. You can never develop a possibility without creating problems. You can never establish a goal without generating a new set of tensions. You can never make a commitment without producing some conflict. Every idea worth anything is bound to be rejected by people who don't go along with it. To reject an idea because it may generate conflict is to "surrender leadership" to friends or foes!

## 8 Never reject an idea because it's not your way of doing things!

Learn to accommodate. Prepare to compromise. Plan to adjust. A different style, a new policy, a change in tradition—all are opportunities to grow. Get set to compromise. Learn to be equilibristic. Maintain a balance between the tension of an opportunity that demands exploitation and the limitations of the resources available at the moment. Readjust your budget. Compromise your taste. Accommodate your life-style. You may have to decide, "It's more important to succeed than it is to snobbishly adhere to my private tastes."

## 9 Never reject an idea because it might fail!

Every idea worth anything has failure potential within it. There is risk in everything. One thing the United States needs more than anything today is possibility thinking.

I've recently returned from a trip to Singapore, where they have an impressive amount of productivity. Singapore imports 100 percent of its oil, and it's not getting any discounts. If Singapore pays the same price we're paying, and it has to import everything, why is it so successful? The people there are better at possibility thinking.

Our problem in this country is with management, labor, and consumers. Consumers are told that if there is anything wrong with a product, don't buy it, and if you do buy it, sue the company. Labor has its problems. Management has its problems. I don't think there is anything worse than the no-risk mentality we have in America.

If Jesus Christ had operated that way, He would never have died on the cross. The whole principle of faith means you're prepared to make a supreme sacrifice for the greater good of other persons. There can be no assurance until that happens. Success is never certain, and failure is never final.

People look at my ministry and think it is a success. It is. But for how long? By the grace of God, *only as long as we can make it so*. Success is never carved in granite. It is always molded in clay. America thought it had it made, but now we're being surpassed. We were so successful before that, while we took long lunch breaks, others were running on ahead of us.

You never reject an idea because there's some risk involved. You isolate the risk, insulate it, and eventually eliminate it.

 ## Never reject an idea because it's sure to succeed!

There are people today who back off if they are sure they will succeed. One reason is that these persons begin to imagine the ego fulfillment this success would give, and with an excuse of being humble, they pull out.

To all of my fellow Christians, trying to follow Jesus, who say, "I should not try to be successful. I'm not trying for the top of the ladder. That's vanity. That's materialistic," I must say, that's not true! To choose poverty instead of prosperity, failure instead of success, low achievement instead of top-of-the-ladder achievement, simply for the sake of being humble, is not super-Christian. It's dumb. Only successful people can help people who are failing. Only winners will survive to give food to the hungry.

Rich DeVos, a member of our board and president of Amway Corporation, has a favorite saying: "The poor cannot help the poor." Because an idea gives you ego-fulfillment does not mean it is not coming from God. Philippians 2:13 puts it very bluntly: "It is God who works in you both to will and to do for His good pleasure." Just because an idea is going to be a success, don't be against it.

The Ten Commandments for Possibility Thinkers—where do I get them? All ten come from the Bible. All ten come from Jesus Christ—the World's Greatest Possibility Thinker. He said, "If you have faith as a mustard seed, you will say to this mountain, 'Move from here to there,' and it will move; and nothing will be impossible for you" (Matt. 17:20).

# 7

## *Count to Ten and Win!*

**M**any years ago I discovered a formula for solving insolvable problems. It's a formula that has never failed me. I call it "Playing the Possibility Thinking Game." I referred to it in *You Can Become the Person You Want to Be*, but here I will show you how it can help you manage your problems and overcome difficulties.

I discovered the exercise in creative thinking quite accidentally—or was it providentially?

The year was 1955. I had accepted an invitation to come to California to begin a new church. I was told that the sponsoring denomination would finance the purchase of two acres of land at the cost of four thousand dollars. In addition, I was given five hundred dollars. That was *it*. I was expected to come up with my own financing for the first little building. After it was built, I could start holding services and hopefully collect a nucleus of charter members. I suggested that I could start holding services in some empty hall while we were putting the financial package together and designing the first simple little chapel. "There isn't an empty hall around the town," my advisor replied. "It's impossible to find an empty hall or an empty building in Garden Grove!"

Such were the premises when I packed my family into our '53 Chevrolet to drive from Chicago to California.

I was in a café in Albuquerque, New Mexico, with my wife, my six-month-old baby boy, Robert Anthony, and my four-year-old daughter Sheila. My mind was wandering, racing ahead to my California destination, now only two days away.

"There must be an empty hall somewhere in that town!" I blurted out to my wife, sitting across the table.

Then I did something quite intuitively and impulsively. I picked up the paper napkin, and on the back side I wrote the numerals "1" to "10" vertically on the left side of the paper. I let my imagination run wild. My list looked like this:

1. Rent a school building.
2. Rent a Masonic Hall.
3. Rent an Elk's Lodge.
4. Rent a mortuary chapel.
5. Rent an empty warehouse.
6. Rent a community club building.
7. Rent a Seventh-Day Adventist Church.
8. Rent a Jewish synagogue.
9. Rent a drive-in theater.
10. Rent an empty piece of ground, a tent, and folding chairs.

Suddenly what had seemed totally impossible now seemed possible. Suddenly the word *impossible* sounded irresponsible, extreme, reactionary, and unintelligent.

This list was my first rudimentary effort in playing a game that I would play many times in the next thirty years.

I had made my list. I then proceeded to check out each of my possibilities. Possibility number one was scratched when I discovered that it was against the law to rent a school building. (That law has since been changed.)There was no Masonic Hall or Elk's Lodge in Garden Grove. The Baptists were already meeting in the only mortuary chapel in town. The Presbyterians were renting the Seventh-Day Adventist Church on Sunday. There was no Jewish synagogue. I couldn't find an empty warehouse or an empty community club building.

I was down to possibility number nine. There was a drive-in theater on the outskirts of the city. *Too far away from the center of Garden Grove*, I thought to myself. But after that negative thought, a positive thought entered my mind. And the positive thought was, *It may not be in the center of Garden Grove, but it is in the center of Orange County!* The rest is history. I went to the drive-in theater. I was told it was available at ten dollars a Sunday! And it had parking for seventeen hundred cars.

I started preaching in that drive-in theater four weeks later. I eventually spent six years preaching under the open sky without protection from the winter rains, insects, or birds.

Years later, we erected our first building. In ten years, the church grew to a membership of fifteen hundred persons. We now needed offices and counseling quarters to minister to the expanded needs of the hurting people in our community. We calculated that all of the offices needed for counselors and ministers would occupy too much ground space. Then I thought, *Why not build it in a high-rise tower?* After all, a tower could be a landmark, pointing out the location of the church to passersby on neighboring roads. The church steeple is respected and traditional on the landscapes of western Europe and the United States of America.

*Why not build a church tower, a steeple, that would not only have height—but would also be functional from the top to the bottom? Why not put a couple of elevators in the tower, divide it into floors, put a chapel at the top and fill it with offices and counseling facilities?*

It was an exciting idea. But again I had absolutely no money. But to play the possibility thinking game, you have to assume that *you won't win if you don't begin.* There's no hope of winning if you don't decide to play the game.

I decided to *win*. And to win, I needed to *begin*. I went to the bank in Garden Grove and opened a special "Tower of Hope" fund. In it I deposited twenty-five dollars. Then I went before the congregation and shared, in a message that I hoped would be inspiring, my dream of a counseling center that could minister to people in the community and across the nation. I shared with them a vision of installing telephones in the tower to receive calls from desperate people all over the United States. The phone number would be one that anybody would remember—the letters *N-E-W H-O-P-E*.

*You won't win
if you don't begin!*

In addition, I imagined that we'd have a chapel at the top of the tower, where young people could be married. They could look out to the left and see Catalina Island lying in the Pacific Ocean. They could look to the north and see the snow-capped mountains. They could look around the county and see the freeways and the highways twinkling with the lights of moving traffic and believe they could rise above human problems.

This was the picture I painted for my congregation. This was my dream of a Tower of Hope. "It will cost a million dollars," I told them. "We have twenty-five dollars from an anonymous donor. All we need is another $999,975, and up it goes!"

A couple of people came up to me afterwards and said, "It was a great sermon, Dr. Schuller. And it's a great idea. But it will take a lot of money. I don't know where you're going to get it."

That week I received a letter commending me on the idea and enclosing a check of five hundred dollars. With such an enthusiastic endorsement, I immediately went to the architect, Richard Neutra. I said, "I have an idea for a functional church tower." I sketched out my dream for him—a chapel at the top, counseling offices on the lower floors. "Now, Mr. Neutra," I asked, "I need a pretty picture of this tower."

I handed him my rough black-and-white pencil sketches and said, "Can you make it look pretty? Give it your style? And can you do it in color? And can you do it for $525?"

He smiled at me and said, "I shouldn't agree to it. But I will!" Before I knew it, the picture was delivered. It was a beautiful four-color rendering.

I posted it in the lobby of the church with the announcement: *"This* is what we are going to build!"

The poster inspired a few small gifts. In addition, I published my first book about that time and earmarked my royalties for this project. That boosted the total to six thousand dollars. That six thousand dollars began earning 6 percent interest and was compounding.

I calculated that if we never received another single contribution, that the six thousand dollars would grow into one million dollars in about one hundred years. I told the entire congregation, "If any of you think that the Tower of Hope will never be built, you're wrong! It's going to be built. We already have a million dollars. The only problem is, we can't collect it until one hundred years have passed!" They laughed. I laughed. The important thing was that the project was taken more seriously. We still needed to generate more momentum; however, I needed an idea to lift the project from its launching pad.

At that point I again picked up a piece of paper. I played the possibility thinking game. At the top of the paper I wrote "$1,000,000."

1. Get 1 person to give $1,000,000.
2. Get 2 people to give $500,000.
3. Get 4 people to give $250,000.
4. Get 10 people to give $100,000.
5. Get 20 people to give $50,000.
6. Get 40 people to give $25,000.
7. Get 50 people to give $20,000.
8. Get 100 people to give $10,000.
9. Get 200 people to give $5,000.
10. Get 1,000 people to give $1,000.

I took a look at the list of ten possible ways to get one million dollars, and unknown to me, I'd already cracked an impossibly hard nut. I had listed ten *possible* ways to do what was *impossible* at that moment.

I never did believe I could get a one-million-dollar gift from a single individual. Consequently, I never tried possibility number one.

I did hire a professional fund-raiser to help me organize a campaign. "We'll ask one person to give a hundred thousand dollars, and we'll have other contributions in varying brackets, fifty thousand, twenty-five thousand, and ten thousand dollars," I told my organizer.

"Do you know of anybody who could give one hundred thousand dollars?" he asked.

I said, "I really don't." But then I thought, *Well, there is probably one family that could give ten thousand dollars a year. In ten years that would add up to one hundred thousand dollars.* I was willing to wait ten years for the building. As soon as I thought in those longer terms of years, my problem became manageable and solvable!

We launched the campaign. We called on all of the members of the church. One family, the Vernon Dragts, pledged the hundred thousand dollars over a ten-year period. Actually, they paid it long before that time was up!

When we announced we had a pledge of one hundred thousand dollars, we stimulated enough momentum that the congregation began to believe that this idea was not only possible, it was highly *probable*! That's when I learned that people want to join an exciting, adventuresome, and challenging idea that looks like it will succeed.

The Tower of Hope was built! We borrowed more than eight hundred thousand dollars, aiming to repay it through pledges over the next ten years. In 1968 the tower was opened and stands today as a magnificent landmark in California.

An impossibility became a possibility as soon as I began to play the possibility thinking game. More than any other exercise that I have used, it has stimulated the creative solution to an impossible problem.

I have used it often because each time I solved one problem I found I was faced with another. Twenty years after I had started the church that God called me to build, I had successfully solved countless problems. The tower was built, and the television ministry was launched and financially self-supporting.

But now we faced a new problem. We had outgrown our sanctuary. We needed a larger building. Because of the six years of worshiping in a drive-in theater, I found myself now driven by a deep compulsion to order a structure that would give me an uncluttered view of the sky.

Six years in the drive-in theater revived my country childhood love of the sky and its impact on the worshiping soul.

Without those years I *never* would have been deeply shaped to desire an all-glass building. The comments I made to the architect, Philip Johnson, were, "I really don't want a building. I want to worship in a garden. God's idea of a church was the Garden of Eden."

When Philip Johnson delivered a six-inch plastic model of what would eventually be called the Crystal Cathedral, I fell in love with the concept. But I shuddered at the thought of what it might cost.

After all, I had not given him any limitations when it came to the budget. (I had decided to live by the principle that I had taught: "Nobody has a money problem—only an idea problem.") When he had asked me what kind of budget restrictions he would have to keep in mind, I replied, "Mr. Johnson, we can't afford a million-dollar building, we can't afford a two- or three-million-dollar building, we can't afford a four-million-dollar building. We can't afford anything! Therefore, it doesn't make any difference what it costs!

"The important thing is that the building should generate enough excitement that it will in itself attract the money."

Unhampered by budget restrictions, Philip Johnson unveiled this absolutely spectacular design. On my desk rested the model of what I believed would be one of the great architectural structures of the centuries. "What will it cost?" I asked the architect.

"I think you can build it for seven million dollars," he replied. I gulped. I didn't reveal what I was thinking: *Seven million! So much money!* It was far more than I could handle. It emotionally defeated me for a moment. Our cash flow could not handle such an increase. We would have to raise the money in cold, hard, unborrowed cash. Seven million dollars was a bigger figure than I could comprehend.

When an all-consuming dream fills the human mind with an all-consuming desire, only to be followed by the harsh reality that the entire concept is impossible—then the emotional spectrum moves from an all-time high to an all-time low. Excitement and peak enthusiasm give way to severe discouragement and depression. That was my experience.

## BUT TOUGH PEOPLE DO

I turned to my book *You Can Become the Person You Want to Be* and read the chapter that outlined the possibility thinking game. Once again I took a piece of paper and wrote "$7,000,000" at the top. I wrote "1" to "10" vertically. I prayed intensively. I totally committed the impossible dream to the God whom I believed inspired the dream. I opened my mind to ideas and soon found myself facing ten possible ways to do what I knew was impossible.

1. Get 1 gift of $7,000,000.
2. Get 7 gifts of $1,000,000.
3. Get 14 gifts of $500,000.
4. Get 28 gifts of $250,000.
5. Get 70 gifts of $100,000.
6. Get 100 gifts of $70,000.
7. Get 140 gifts of $50,000.
8. Get 280 gifts of $25,000.
9. Sell each window—10,866 windows—at $500 per window—$5,000,000 plus.

That was as far as I got. I was already enthusiastic. I believed that the project was possible where only minutes before it was a total impossibility. I'd cracked the hardest nut I was ever asked to crack in my life!

I never did ask any person to give seven million dollars. Why not? Because I doubted I could have maintained my own freedom. I was afraid I could have been intimidated by any person that would donate such a large sum of money to the Cathedral! I would be tempted to become a slave as some politicians have to some single, powerful, financial source.

I did move to the second possibility, although I could not comprehend anyone making a gift of one million dollars. I belong to a denomination that is the oldest Protestant denomination with an unbroken ministry in the United States of America—The Reformed Church in America. Fifty-four Dutch colonists, all members of the Reformed Church in the Netherlands, bought Manhattan Island in 1628, built a Dutch windmill, and held worship services in the loft. That church continues today. It is the well-known Marble Collegiate

Church in New York City. In more than three hundred years our denomination has never received a single gift of one million dollars from a living donor.

Again I prayed and recalled reading how one person had contributed a million dollars to a southern California YMCA building many years before. I made contact with the donor. He agreed to see me. I shared with him the blueprints and the model of the Crystal Cathedral. He was fascinated by it. I said to him, "It'll never get built until people take it seriously and believe in it. They won't believe in it unless we get a major gift. Would you, could you, make a lead-off gift of one million dollars?" I will never forget the immediate look in his eyes. It was one of sadness.

"I'd like to, but I can't."

I wasn't surprised. It was a long shot on my part. After all, we didn't know each other.

"May I pray before I leave?" I asked.

"Of course," he said.

I found myself praying, "Dear God, was it Your idea or was it my idea to build this Crystal Cathedral?" and I waited. I wanted to hear His answer deep down in my heart. I asked a second question, "Dear God, was it Your idea that I ask this man to give one million dollars? Or was it my idea?" And I waited long for the reply. Then I continued, "Dear God, I'm so thankful that he said he wants to do it and would like to give it. But he has also said he cannot. Is it possible for You, Father, to figure out a way for him to do what he would like to do?" I waited. Long. Silently. Then I closed the prayer with "Thank You, Father, for listening. Amen."

The next morning at 11:07, the telephone rang in my study. It was the donor. "Dr. Schuller, that building has got to be built. You're right. It'll never be built until people believe it. People won't believe it until there is a major gift. I don't know how, and I don't know when, but I'll give the first gift of one million dollars." I screamed with delight.

It was possibly the single most ecstatic moment in my life. Within sixty days he delivered fifty-five thousand shares of his company's stock at a value of over $18 a share. When sold, it netted $987,000 cash in our special savings account! We were on our way!

I quickly moved on to another possibility in the list of ten possibilities. We announced the sale of windows at $500 per window. Within six months, we successfully sold ten thousand windows. Most of them were being purchased at $25 a month for a twenty-month payment plan.

The project moved from an impossibility to a possibility simply through the possibility thinking game!

I wouldn't want to leave you with the impression that it was all that easy. When it looked as though the cash would be readily available through the above strategies, we made a calculated decision to increase the cost of the building from seven million to ten million dollars by building an entire structure underneath the floor of the Cathedral. This additional structure would provide offices for the entire music department and television production department.

I looked once more over the list of ten ways to raise money. I decided to give possibility number two another try. I approached a donor in Chicago, Illinois, who promised, "I'll give you the tenth million when you have nine million dollars raised in cash." Success looked easy and certain. But then we were hit with inflation, which boosted the price beyond the expected price of ten million to more than fourteen million dollars! That did not include the architectural or engineering fees which would be 8 percent of the construction cost— an additional one million dollars. That was not all. This did not include furnishings and special electronic equipment, which would boost the price by yet another two million!

What was anticipated as a ten-million-dollar project now looked closer to seventeen million! If I were to be totally honest with you, I'd have to say that those were the darkest days of my life. Four months had passed since we had collected our first million dollars. By this time we had spent almost two million in architectural fees, engineering costs, and other beginning expenses.

I called my key persons and offered to abort the project. "You can't do that," I was told. "Your integrity is at stake.

*Don't kill
the dream—
execute it!*

People want their names on windows. We promised it to them. You have to follow through. Think bigger! And don't contemplate anything less than the fulfillment of the God-given dream."

I followed that advice. We prayed. We dug the hole. We started construction. The bank offered a loan of three and a half million dollars. That was surely not enough. But added to the money we were raising, it was a boost.

We launched another major fund-raising drive to try to collect another million dollars on a single Sunday. I had used an inheritance check of ten thousand dollars some years before to purchase an ocean-front condominium for thirty-eight thousand dollars. I found that it had escalated in value to one hundred seventy-five thousand dollars. I contributed it to the million-dollar Sunday. The momentum was established and the million-dollar Sunday offering was a success!

Two months later an unsolicited offer from a total stranger in Chicago, Illinois, came to me in the form of a letter that said in essence, "I've seen pictures of your proposed Crystal Cathedral. I think it is very exciting. What's the financial status to date? Would an extra million dollars from an old gentleman in Chicago be helpful?" I flew to Chicago and met with him and his wife.

"When do you need the money?" he said. "Actually," I reported, "we are building the building on a pay-as-we-go basis. We will have exhausted our cash and are being told by our contractor Clair Peck that he will stop construction if we have not put another million dollars into the escrow account within thirty days."

The gentleman looked across the room at his wife and said, "Well, Mary, I think we can give Dr. Schuller a million dollars within the next thirty days, don't you?"

Within thirty days, a cashier's check in that amount was delivered!

Two months later he invited me back to Chicago to celebrate his birthday at a very small and intimate gathering in the country club on the North Shore. As I left the dinner party, he handed me an envelope and said, "Dr. Schuller, I

[137]

want to be selfish on my birthday and give myself a lot of fun. Here is a letter that I've written very selfishly to give myself a great deal of joy. Read it in the car, and you'll understand."

I got in the car and opened the envelope. There was a simple little note that said in effect, "I find my greatest joy in giving gifts to people and projects I love." And with the note was another million-dollar cashier's check for the Crystal Cathedral—our fourth million-dollar commitment!

Construction continued without abatement. And in September 1980, the building was completed. The final cost was nearly twenty million dollars. The only mortgage was a three-and-a-half-million-dollar, ten-year, 9½ percent bank loan against pledges outstanding that would all be collected in another twenty-four months. We could say the building was dedicated "debt-free."

The entire project was successful, all because I was able to count to ten!

Anyone can count to ten—and anyone can be a success! It's true. Count to ten and win. This simple possibility thinking game can help anyone with any problem. I even shared it with the city leaders of Flint, Michigan.

When I was leading the unemployment seminar there, included on my schedule was a noontime luncheon with five hundred city leaders. I knew there were twenty-five thousand people unemployed. So I suggested that the city really needed to create twenty-five thousand new jobs. "And if you think that's impossible," I challenged them, "let's count to ten and believe that we can win." At the top of the blackboard I wrote "25,000 Jobs." Below I listed vertically ten possible ways to create twenty-five thousand new jobs.

1. Get 1 company to move into Flint and produce 25,000 new jobs.
2. Get 2 companies to move in, each providing 12,500 jobs.
3. Get 5 companies to hire 5,000 people each.

4. Get 10 companies to hire 2,500 people each.
5. Get 50 companies to provide 500 new jobs each.
6. Get 100 companies to provide 250 new jobs each.
7. Get 200 companies to provide 125 new jobs each.
8. Get 250 companies to provide 100 new jobs each.
9. Get 500 companies to provide 50 new jobs each.
10. Get 1,000 companies to provide 25 new jobs each.

We were thinking constructively. We had many possibilities that, moments before, hadn't been there.

I challenged the civic leaders. "How can you possibly find these companies?" Answering my own question, I suggested, "Try using the '1 to 10' technique with each of the above possibilities. First, make a list of ten companies *in the world* that could possibly be persuaded to move to Flint, Michigan, and produce twenty-five thousand new jobs." Seeing the look of hope in their eyes, I continued, "But I hope you don't succeed! Why? Because any city that is dependent on one single industry for twenty-five thousand new jobs is too vulnerable! A much better solution would be to find several companies that will create new jobs.

"Go to the existing companies and challenge them to expand their markets and increase their sales productivity to the point that they'll need to hire more people. Look at all of the possible job-producing forces in this world. Consider the federal government. Perhaps it could be motivated to create new jobs in this town. Consider the state and county governments. Consider overseas operations. Look at the companies in Germany, Japan, and Korea that might be persuaded with incentives to come to Flint, Michigan!"

I wish I could report, as of this writing, that the above "count to ten and win" technique had produced twenty-five thousand new jobs in Flint. I cannot report that. But I can report that hundreds of new jobs have been created. And beginning is half the battle!

I have no doubt that if a power committee were established to pursue all of the possibilities that the city could actually create twenty-five thousand new jobs! It might take five years to do it. It might take ten years to do it. It might be accomplished in two or three years. But it's possible!

But you say, your problem is not financial? Maybe it isn't. And maybe it is!

Let me ask this question: "If I were to give you a million dollars in cash, do you think you could solve the problems you are facing today?"

Think about it for a day or two. Think about it for a week. And if the answer could conceivably be yes, then go after a million dollars!

Count to ten and win. Why does it work? What are the dynamics that cause it to be so effective? I said it in *You Can Become the Person You Want to Be*, "Consider the mind set that results from 'game attitude.'" When you adopt the attitude that it's only a game, emotionally you are free. What are the attitudes characteristic of someone who is playing a game? They are:

1. Risk-running: The fear of failure is absent. "If I lose, it's only a game." You dare to think in almost reckless dimensions. This is the arena in which progress is always made.
2. Record-breaking: This mental attitude causes you to think bigger, reach farther, try harder, than you ever have before. You are putting yourself in a frame of mind where you can think bigger than you have ever thought before. Almost always the inventive solution to every problem is that simple. Spend more money. Hire more people. Form a new organization. Travel farther. Telephone an expert in Europe, etc.
3. Commitment-freeing: Since it's only a game, you can quit any time you want without ruining your reputation. You are free from the subconscious tension generated by the fear of involvement and ongoing responsibilities. Because it's only a game, you can relax in total freedom from responsibility.

When you adopt such game-playing attitudes you generate a mental climate conducive to creativity. This is the secret behind the possibility-thinking game, "Count to Ten and Win."

The word *possibility* is another key to the success of this formula. The very word *possibility* creates a mental climate conducive to creativity. Simply suggesting that something might be possible releases creative brain cells from their invisible prison of subconscious defense mechanisms.

To understand the cybernetic power of this word, consider its antonym, that dirty thirteen-letter word *impossibility*. When uttered aloud, this word is devastating in its effect. Thinking stops. Progress is halted. Doors slam shut. Research comes to a screeching halt. Further experimentation is torpedoed. Projects are abandoned. Dreams are discarded. The brightest and the best of the creative brain cells nosedive, clam up, hide out, cool down, and turn off in some dark, subterranean corner of the mind. In this defensive maneuver, the brain shelters itself against the painful sting of insulting disappointments, brutal rejections, and dashed hopes.

But, let someone utter the magic words *It's possible*. Those stirring words, with the siren appeal of a marshaling trumpet, penetrate into the subconscious tributaries of the mind, challenging and calling those proud powers to turn on and turn out new ideas! Buried dreams are resurrected. Sparks of fresh enthusiasm flicker, then burst into new flame. Tabled motions are brought back to the floor. Dusty files are reopened. Lights go on again in the darkened laboratories. Telephones start ringing. Typewriters make clattering music. Budgets are revised and adopted. "Help wanted" signs are hung out. Factories are retooled and reopened. New products appear. New markets open. The recession has ended. A great new era of adventure, experimentation, expansion, and prosperity is born.

Now you too can play the possibility thinking game. Here's how:

Rule number one: Begin by believing that you possess latent gifts of creativity. You will respect, trust, and admire your own thoughts. *Every* person can be creative.

Rule number two: Don't play it alone. Play it with problem-solving people. Play it with possibility-thinking people. Play it with people who have a record of achievement and success. You *can* play it alone. But a lot of ideas might come from others.

All it takes is one idea to solve an impossible problem! It might be one of those ideas that you will write down on the piece of paper. Or it could be a combination of several of the ideas that are put down on the paper.

Remember this. You won't start winning without a beginning.

# 8

## *The Faith That Can Move Your Mountain*

So you've tried to believe, and still you're unemployed? You think you've applied faith to your problem, and it still won't go away? You've exercised all the faith you can muster, and difficulties still abound?

Someone once said to me: "Was Jesus wrong? Did He make a mistake when He said, 'If you have faith as a mustard seed, you will say to this mountain, "Move from here to there," and it will move; and nothing shall be impossible for you' [Matt. 17:20]?" My answer is one that can give you the inner toughness to see your tough time through until light breaks around you.

Faith is indeed the greatest miracle-working power imaginable. Faith never fails a person; we fail when we give up on our faith. However, if we cut out any one of the five phases of faith, we will be disappointed with the ultimate results.

Faith is like a seed. If a seed is not planted, it can't bear fruit. But planting is just the first phase. Unless the seed is watered, it won't sprout. Sprouting is the second phase. Once the seed is planted and watered, growth will begin. But unless the plant is nourished, it will not reach full maturity. It will not blossom, which is the third phase.

Then when the buds are beginning to form, if the proper climatic conditions do not exist, the stalk will produce no fruit. There will be no ear on the corn. Bearing fruit is the fourth phase of the cycle. Only if each phase is properly nurtured can a seed reach full maturity. Finally, when the fruit is ripe, it must be harvested at the precisely correct time, or winds, rain, or overripeness can cause it to drop to the ground, where it will rot. Even as there are five phases to fruit-bearing, from the planting of the seed to harvest there are five phases to the full cycle of mountain-moving faith.

## The Nesting Phase

The first phase of faith is the nesting phase. That's when an idea drops into the mind as an egg is deposited in the bird's nest. Some people experience only this first phase of faith. For too many people, faith never gets beyond the nesting phase. The unhatched egg rots in the nest. The idea passes through the mind without being taken seriously.

I don't think anything kills the potential miracle-working power of faith more than a lack of self-confidence. Faith is indeed most fragile at birth.

The thought of picking up a new career in mid-life is probably an impossibility in your own imagination. Part of this insecurity or lack of self-confidence is because we tend to develop a negative self-image, based on our low position on the ladder of life. People think that if they were really brilliant, they would be president of some corporation. If you were appointed president of a major corporation today, what would that do to your self-confidence?

When President Woodrow Wilson's secretary of labor died, one of the White House maids caught the president off-guard with a request: "Mr. President, my husband runs a little store on Pennsylvania Avenue and really works hard. I wonder if you would consider making him secretary of labor."

Startled by her unexpected and rather unreasonable request, the president replied, "Well, Mary, that's a very critical position. It requires a big man."

She replied, "Well, if you put my husband in that position, he'd be a big man."

[144]

Faith begins when you begin to believe in the ideas that God sends to you. Greatness does not depend upon your position in life, but upon your respect of the positive ideas that flow into your imagination! The head of a well-known company decided to test the creativity of average people and selected at random, ten uneducated persons from the bottom of the corporate ladder of one of his factories. The company president led them into the executive headquarters, had them sit in big leather chairs around a huge table, and stood before them to explain why they had been chosen: "It has come to my attention that all of you have remarkable gifts of creativity. This is the reason I called you together today. Our company is facing a problem, and I believe that you people can come up with a solution." He explained the nature of the problem and left the room for a few hours.

When he returned, he discovered that they had had a very effective brainstorming session and had, in fact, come up with a breakthrough idea! They had found an answer to the problem that had been overlooked by the top corporate research and development personnel. Obviously the executives in charge of the research and development were suffering from locked-in thinking.

The truth is that the average "bottom-of-the-ladder" person is potentially as creative as the top executive who sits in the big office. The problem is that the person on the bottom of the ladder doesn't trust his own brilliance and doesn't, therefore, believe in his own ideas.

This top executive appealed to the employees' pride and stimulated their self-respect. This is how he explains it: "Every person is creative, but a lot of people don't believe in their own creativity. When I told them they were smart, they believed it. *They came up with a solution because they were not well enough informed to know that their suggestion couldn't be done.* The rest of us never seriously considered their approach because, in our minds, it was technologically impossible. But we established their idea as a goal and were able to solve what we had assumed to be an impossible problem!"

Every human being has virtually equal creative potential.

Why isn't the average person more creative? No matter how complex the answer, one simple reason dominates. Basically, people do not believe that they are creative. Because nobody has ever told them they are creative, they have never tried to be.

Our tendency is not to do anything about the incredible ideas that come to our minds. Years later, when we read that somebody else has turned an idea into a great success, we may lament to ourselves, *I thought about that once. Why didn't I do something about it?*

As a pastor, author, and television spokesman, I find that I must constantly communicate to the masses this confidence: "All of you are brilliant!" And of course, this is true. All of us have incredible creative potential because all creative ideas come from God and all of us can tap into this wisdom.

Common people are brilliant if only they believe in their own ideas. Most human beings have the same basic brain capacity. The major difference is the attitude that a person has toward his own ideas!

At an international psychological congress in Paris, France, Dr. H. E. Gruber of Rutgers University reported that research has led to the confident belief that "child prodigies are not born, they are developed." If a child prodigy is not a genetic freak, but a product of environmental stimulation, then every human being is a potential genius. It means that somehow we have to begin to trust our better and brighter ideas. *Believe in your own brilliance!*

Faith will die in the nesting phase unless you believe in the positive ideas that drop into your mind.

A man from the Orient once traveled around the world in search of the wisest guru. He was told that this man lived in a cave high up in the Himalayas. So he loaded his horse with supplies, set off across mountains and deserts, and after months of traveling, came to the foot of a high mountain. He led his horse up the narrow path through the crevices until he came to a cave.

"Are you the guru who is known around the world for his wisdom?" he asked the old man sitting in the cave.

The old man rose to his feet, walked out into the full light of day, looked into the face of the traveler, and said, "Yes, I am known for my wisdom. What is your question?"

"Wise old man, how can I become brilliant? Where can I find wisdom?"

The wise old guru stared for a moment into the weary traveler's anxious eyes and asked in reply, "Where can you find your horse?" And with that he turned and walked back into the cave.

The answer was obvious. The traveler's horse had been with him all the time; brilliance and the capacity for wisdom had been within him all the time.

Jesus said it: "The kingdom of God is within you" (Luke 17:21). God drops ideas into your mind every day like eggs in a nest. The first stage of faith is believing in yourself.

The positive ideas that flow into your brain come from God. Don't reject the ideas simply because of your awareness of your own imperfections. Perfectionism keeps many people from ever embracing the kind of faith that could mature into a mountain-moving force.

An often-told folk tale illustrates the futility of perfectionism: A man found a beautiful pearl with one tiny flaw. He thought if he could remove that tiny imperfection, the pearl would be the world's most priceless. So he peeled off the first layer. But the flaw was still there. He took off the next layer, thinking the flaw would surely be removed, but it remained. He continued to take off layer after layer, until, finally, the flaw was gone—but so was the pearl!

Of course, no idea is perfect. No idea is without its built-in problems. But trust that the positive potential in an idea is powerful enough to merit your continued support.

*The me I see is the me I'll be.* To make sure you develop mountain-moving faith, build a positive self-image. If you see yourself as a person who is going to become more educated and knowledgeable, then that's precisely what you will become.

Your mind's image of yourself will release powers of self-actualization. Hold a mental picture, and it will unquestionably, invariably turn into a physical reality. Hold a negative picture, and negative results will happen. Positive results follow a positive mental picture. This is the irrevocable law of faith built by God into the universe. Draw now a positive picture of yourself, believe in your ideas, and faith will survive phase one.

# 2 The Testing Phase

Faith's second phase is the testing phase. No person plunges recklessly and irresponsibly ahead with every idea that moves through his brain. Ideas must be tested by asking the questions that rise out of your own value system. *Decision-making is easy if there are no contradictions in your value system.*

It's easy to make major decisions at the snap of a finger if we know the questions we have to ask to get reliable raw data as answers. A positive idea implies questions like: "Is this really necessary?" "Is it really a human need-filling idea?" "Can it be inspiring to others?"

The Crystal Cathedral, which stands on our campus, has been called a monument to possibility thinking. That could well be true. I recall very vividly the day when the bids came in while we were preparing to build the ten-million-dollar building. Suddenly we were faced with construction bids that topped fifteen million dollars! I wanted to quit.

In fact, I wrote out a news release announcing that we were aborting the project. But before I could release the story, I received two letters—one from Australia and one from Michigan.

The letter from Michigan was from a Roman Catholic nun:

Dr. Schuller, thank you for your plan to build the Crystal Cathedral. I'm on the board of directors for a hospital. We were talking about adding a wing to the hospital but the idea was voted down because the cost would run six million. I asked the members of the board, "Did you hear what Dr. Schuller is planning to build in California?" They were silent. I told them, "He is planning to raise several million dollars to build a Crystal Cathedral. If he can find several million to build a cathedral can't we find six million for a wing in a hospital?"

Dr. Schuller, that inspired all of them to reverse their decision. They went ahead and decided to build the wing and somehow solve the problem and somehow raise the money. The statement that went around the room and swayed the decision was: "If Schuller can do it, so can we."

At the same time I received a letter from an Australian minister:

Dr. Schuller, thank you for your plans to build the Crystal Cathedral. I was in a committee meeting in which the churches of Australia were contemplating building a youth ranch as a recreational and inspirational facility for young people. But the cost was going to run nearly two million dollars. Nobody believed it was possible. I asked them, "Have any of you been watching Schuller on television?" Nobody raised a hand. I told them that I'd been listening to you and that you were planning to build a Crystal Cathedral. "If he can find millions of dollars to build a cathedral, don't you think that all of us, working together, planning together, praying together, believing together, can somehow raise two million for a youth conference center?" And, Dr. Schuller, that sold the day! I'm writing to tell you the decision has not only been made, but over one million dollars has been collected! We are going to succeed. We owe it to you.

How do you test the ideas that come into your mind? I test mine by this universal principle: *Will my faith, acted upon and firmly embraced, cause my life and my activity to be an inspiration to somebody else to become a better person or to achieve more in his life?* The truth is, everybody is an inspiration to somebody else. Anybody who has ever attended the Special Olympics and watched handicapped children jump over hurdles and race down the track understands what I am talking about. Suddenly tough times become good times when our positive reaction becomes an inspiration to others.

Everybody can be an inspiration to somebody else. Patty Wilson, a member of our church, was thirteen years of age when it was discovered she was epileptic. Her dad did everything he could to convince her that she shouldn't have a negative self-image because of this illness. He knew that she would encounter discrimination, that there would be those who would not hire her because she was epileptic. He knew that, without a positive self-image, she would never amount to anything. Somehow he had to communicate to her that she too could react positively to her problem and that her life would be an inspiration to others.

One day, Patty's father was driving to work when he saw a man running along the sidewalk. He wore runner's clothes, but there was something strange about his shoes. They were shaped like horses' hooves. Mr. Wilson did a double-take and threw his car into reverse. He found out that Peter Strudwick had been born with no feet. His custom-made running shoes, resembling hooves, enabled him to run. That one incident inspired Patty's dad to start running: "If he can run, so can I."

It was at this point that he vowed to teach Patty that she could be supersuccessful too. Just because she was epileptic didn't mean that she had to be handicapped. He was going to make her believe in herself. As Patty watched her dad run each morning, she became interested and was soon running alongside him. Day after day, week after week, month after month, the father-daughter team ran through the neighborhood.

Then an idea entered Patty's mind, in the nesting phase: "How can I encourage people to treat epileptics like normal people?" That question gave rise to a second idea. She found out the women's record for long-distance running and set a goal to break it. She decided to run from Orange County to San Francisco, a distance of four hundred miles, at the end of her freshman year of high school. That became her major goal, testing it on this simple principle: "Can it inspire a lot of other people, who consider themselves handicapped, to set exciting goals for themselves?" She concluded that, with enough faith, she could attain her goal and in the process inspire a lot of other people. When her faith passed from the nesting to the testing phase, she decided that she would pay the price and succeed. At that point her faith entered into the third phase.

# 3 The Investing Phase

The third phase of faith is the investing phase, the point at which you make a public commitment. You commit time, money, energy, and—possibly the most valuable products of all—pride and prestige to the publicly announced project. At this point many people find their faith faltering. If, by an act of will and prayer, you determine that you will make the public commitment, the odds are overwhelming that you can succeed.

Unfortunately many people let their faith die when they fail to put up the risk capital.

Patty made an investment of one year in tough training. She said, "At the end of my sophomore year I'll run from Orange County to Portland, Oregon [a distance of one thousand miles]." But she didn't stop there. "At the end of my junior year," she said, "I'll run from Orange County to St. Louis, Missouri [two thousand miles]. And at the end of my senior year, when I graduate from high school, I'll celebrate by running from Orange County, across the United States of America, to Washington, D.C. I want to shake the hand of the president of the United States."

Patty set the impossible goal of running four hundred miles from Orange County to San Francisco, California. And she made it. Of course, by that time, she had spent nearly an hour every day in training—running every morning, getting herself in top physical condition. And at the end of her second year she expanded her goal.

By this time, thousands of people were inspired by her. A book entitled *Run, Patty, Run* was published. At the end of her sophomore year, she was ready to try for Portland, Oregon.

On the day the event was to occur, Patty's high-school

There will never be
another now—
I'll make the most
of today.

There will never be
another me—
I'll make the most
of myself.

classmates stretched a big paper banner across the street. On it, they had written in red ink, "Run, Patty, run!" There were some simple ceremonies: the high-school band played, the crowd grew silent as I offered a prayer for her success, and I took a medallion from around my neck to place around hers. On the back of the medallion were the words of the Possibility Thinkers' creed: "When faced with a mountain, I will not quit. I will keep on striving until I climb over, find a pass through, tunnel underneath, or simply stay and turn the mountain into a gold mine, with God's help."

Then Patty started running, ripping through the paper banner and leaving it shredded behind her. She trotted down the road—taking the first few steps, then the first block, then the first mile. Driving behind her at a safe distance, was her mother, a registered nurse, with medication on hand, in case Patty should have a seizure. Written on the back of the van were the words, "Patty Wilson. World's Women's Long-Distance Running Record Holder. Running from California to Oregon." We followed her every day with our prayers. She did great for twenty-eight miles, when she cracked a bone in her foot. She was ready now for the fourth phase of mountain-moving faith—the arresting phase.

Before we look at the arresting phase, let me ask you; "If your problem isn't going away, have you really given it all you've got?"

If you're still unemployed, have you invested everything you possibly can in getting a job that would at least bring a dollar or two or three an hour? Remember that mountain-moving faith will never fail you, but you can fail it if you aren't willing to pay the price. You might have to pay the price of greater humility—starting back once more at the bottom of the ladder. You may have to invest more months or years in mid-life study and retraining.

When we have to back up our ideas with hard work or cold cash, it's easy to get cold feet. The going gets tough when we are forced to either put up or back out. Many people fail their faith at this third phase. They are just not faithful enough to invest everything they've got into their dream.

Try it. But get ready for the fourth phase.

# 4 The Arresting Phase

The nesting, the testing, the investing phases almost invariably lead to the fourth phase: the arresting phase. You've started. You've made the commitment. You've put your name on the line. You've started your run.

Now problems attack you. Troubles block you. Defeat seems certain. You begin to think you've bitten off more than you can chew. You wonder if you've made a terrible mistake with your investment. The arresting phase of faith is God's way of testing us before the final victory.

He wants to make sure: Are we really depending on Him? Will we really be grateful if we make it? Can He trust us with success? Are we going to prove humble enough to handle the big prize?

For Patty Wilson, the arresting phase came when she hurt her foot. Her parents took her to the emergency room of the hospital, praying that her injury wouldn't be serious. Doctors X-rayed her and concluded that she had, in fact, fractured her foot. One doctor told her, "Patty, you better not run. If you do, you risk permanent damage."

Patty knew there were thousands of people who were expecting her to run and complete the trip. "Doctor," she said, "if you wrapped it very tightly, don't you think I could keep running?"

"Yes, you might be able to run with the fracture if it were tightly bound," he explained. But he added, "You'll get blisters, and you can't run with blisters."

"But a blister is nothing more than water under the skin," Patty answered. "My mother's a nurse. Couldn't she just take a syringe and slip the needle into the blister and draw the water out?"

The doctor looked surprised, but said, "Yes, I suppose that might be possible." And with that, Patty had the doctor show her mother how it was to be wrapped every morning.

The arresting phase was only that. It was not terminal. It was an arresting condition. She went on and kept running— five hundred, six hundred, seven hundred, eight hundred, nine hundred, and one thousand miles. She decided to take the coastal route, not realizing that it was three hundred miles farther. She only thought that it would be far more scenic—and it was—but one thousand miles went into eleven hundred and eleven hundred to twelve hundred, and finally thirteen hundred miles brought her to the outskirts of Portland, Oregon. The governor of the state got his running suit on, joined her, and ran the last mile with her! The entire town was out to greet her. What a welcome she got! She had endured the pain. She had paid the price. She had survived the arresting period and had succeeded. She had learned that faith has incredible mountain-moving power if you will hang on and not give up when you seem to be surrounded by impossibilities.

I remember the day when I received the telephone call that an elder of my church, Stanley Reimer, had had a twenty-two minute cardiac arrest. *Twenty-two minutes?* I knew what that meant. Obviously that was a considerable amount of time during which oxygen was not reaching his brain.

They had managed to get him breathing again, but he was in what was called a "death coma." He was placed in the intensive care unit immediately, and although his body was breathing on its own, there was no other sign of life. The neurosurgeon told Stan's wife that there was no hope: "If he keeps breathing, he'll be a vegetable all of his life. He'll never close his eyes. They'll be open in a death stare exactly as you see him now."

As soon as I heard the news, I rushed to the hospital, praying all the way. "God, what will I say to him? What will I say to his wife? Will I even be able to talk to him if he is in a coma?"

I remembered that, in theological seminary, the professors had taught us: "Some day, as a pastor, you may talk to some-one in a death coma. When that happens, only think *life*, only talk *life*, only believe *life*. If you are ever at the bedside of a patient who is presumed to be dying—in a 'death coma' so deep that they cannot respond in any way—keep thinking *life;* keep talking *life;* keep praying *life!* The patient may lack the power to move his lips or manifest a physical indication that he is hearing you, but his conscious and subconscious mind may in fact be getting your messages. So you must not place a negative thought in his mind."

With that recollection I went into the intensive care unit where Stan was lying. There was Billie, his wife, standing at the bedside, tears streaming down her face. Stanley, my once-outgoing friend, looked like a statue. He could not move. From all practical appearances, he was dead. His eyes were wide open but indicated no life or responsiveness whatever. I put my arm around Billie and prayed with her. Then I took hold of Stanley's hand and I said softly, my lips close to his ear, "Stanley, I know you cannot talk. I know you cannot respond to me. But I know that, deep down within you, you can hear me. I am your pastor. This is Reverend Robert Schuller. I've just come from the church, where everyone is praying for you. And Stanley, I've got good news for you. Even though you've had a bad heart attack and are in a coma, you are going to recover. You are going to live. It's going to be a long battle. It's going to be hard and tough. But you are going to make it, Stanley!"

At that point, I had one of the most moving experiences of my life. Suddenly a tear rolled out of his staring eye! He understood! No smile; no quiver of a lip; but a tear rolled out of his eye. The doctor was shocked. Billie was shocked. One year later Stanley was able to speak full sentences. He was able to hear. His faculties were becoming normal. Today he walks and talks and laughs and is alive! A miracle, you say? Of course.

"If you have faith as a mustard seed, you will say to this mountain, 'Move . . .' and nothing will be impossible for you" (Matt. 17:20). In the darkest times, simply remind yourself that faith can move any mountain.

It was my pleasure and pride to be a close friend of the late

## BUT TOUGH PEOPLE DO

Senator Hubert Humphrey. When I heard that he was in New York City to have major surgery for a malignancy, I sent him a telegram. The telephone rang, and the famed senator said to me, "Hello, Bob. I'm so glad I got hold of you." His voice sounded strong. He continued, "I'm going into major surgery in just a few hours. I just wanted to thank you for your inspiring telegram. My staff just brought in a large stack of telegrams and letters, neatly pressed and sorted. I was browsing through a few of them and guess which telegram was on the top of the pile?"

I replied, "Well, obviously, the telegram from the president of the United States."

Laughing, he said, "No, Bob, yours was. I have it before me right now. I'm drawing power and strength from it this very moment. Let me read to you what you sent to me.

And he read, "God wanted me to send this Scripture verse to you: 'For I know the plans I have for you, . . . plans for good and not for evil, to give you a future and a hope" (Jer. 29:11, TLB). Later the senator would tell me that this Scripture passage gave him holding-on power in a dark time. Holding-on power is that which gives faith the strength to move mountains. For even mountains erode in time, if exposed to wind and rain.

Every project I've ever tackled has gone through its severe arresting phase. And at that point in time, you have the choice to hang on or to give up. You and you alone reserve the ultimate choice: Quit or keep believing. Which response will inspire the most people?

Tommy Lasorda, the world-famed manager of the Los Angeles Dodgers baseball team, has been a close friend of mine for many, many years. He keeps on the wall of the locker room a poem that is very familiar to many people. But it's good to reread it. After all, it's never the same poem the second or the third or the fourth time you read it. We change. Our life's situation changes and, therefore, our perception of the message changes. Here are the powerful words of Edgar A. Guest:

### Don't Quit

When things go wrong, as they sometimes will,
When the road you are trudging seems all uphill,
When the funds are low and the debts are high,
And you want to smile but you have to sigh,
When care is pressing you down a bit,
Rest, if you must—but don't you quit!

Life is queer with its twists and turns,
As every one of us sometime learns,
And many a failure turns about
When he might have won had he stuck it out;
Don't give up, though the pace seems slow—
You might succeed with another blow. . . .

Success is failure turned inside out—
the silver tint of the clouds of doubt—
And you can never tell how close you are,
It may be near when it seems afar;
So stick to the fight when you are hardest hit—
It's when things get worse that you mustn't quit!

Don't trust the clouds—trust the sunshine. Don't set your compass by the flash of lightning—set it by the stars. Trust the sun—don't trust the shadows. Believe in your dreams—don't believe in your despairing thoughts. Have faith in your faith—and doubt your doubts. Trust in your hopes—never trust in your hurts. And you will move on eventually, effectively, inspiringly to faith's final phase: the cresting phase.

## 5 The Cresting Phase

Yes, the crowning phase of faith is the cresting phase. The mountaintop is scaled! Success finally is achieved! A habit is broken. The money starts flowing your way. The chains are loosed. The bones are healed. The doctor tells you you can go home now. You walk back into the sunshine. A broken relationship is healed. The emptiness and loneliness of life is filled with a new friend and loved one. The court case is

*Decision-making*
*is easy*
*if there are*
*no contradictions*
*in your*
*value system.*

settled. The economy turns around. A job opportunity comes your way. The winter passes; the spring returns. God never fails to let the sun outlive the storm. And those who keep on keeping on ultimately survive successfully and, in the process, are an incredible inspiration to others to keep bravely fighting their battles, too.

Jesus Christ's life reflects all five phases of faith. By the time He was twelve years old, He knew what God wanted Him to do in His life. He had His calling. The *nesting time* of His faith was when He realized that He had to be about His Father's business.

The *testing* phase of His faith came when He spent forty days in the wilderness being tempted by Satan.

The *investing* phase of His faith came when He spent His years walking in the plains and deserts of God's land, preaching, teaching, and investing his life's energies, thoughts, and ideas and committing His prestige to the public eye. He experienced His time of popularity. The crowds followed Him everywhere. He looked supersuccessful!

But then the *arresting* phase came for Him in the Garden of Gethsemane. Hours before He walked to His death, He prayed, "Abba, Father, all things are possible for You. Take this cup away from Me; nevertheless, not what I will but what You will" (Mark 14:36). And He was crucified. It looked like the dream was dead. Everything was coming apart. His disciples had betrayed Him, deceived Him, and deserted Him.

But then came the *cresting* phase. Easter morning came, and with it the big breakthrough. We who are Christians know that He is alive today. He rules over a kingdom of believers in this world who have been saved from their self-doubt, from their self-condemnation, from their sin and shame, into the job of serving God and our fellow human beings through creative possibility thinking.

The cresting time will come for you too if you will hold on and never believe in *never*. The storms will pass. And the birds will come out to sing again!

## BUT TOUGH PEOPLE DO

When
the night is past
and
the dawning of the new day
is
about to break
with
fresh hopes and dreams,
then
you will hear . . .
the singing of the birds.

When
storm clouds break
to drift away
leaving bright patches of blue
with
golden shafts of sunlight
on
flower and leaf
sparkling with fresh drops of diamond rain,
then
you will hear . . .
the singing of the birds.

Yes
there are those times and places
when
the cold winter ends.
Springtime returns.
The dark night of the soul
is dissolved in a happy daybreak.
The storm is over.
Then
you will hear . . .
the singing of the birds.

—R.H.S.

## Now—Believe and You Will Achieve

Mary Crowley, president of Home Interiors, a very prosperous business, was with her husband in Nassau, the

Bahamas, some years ago. On Sunday morning, they found a local church filled with the local citizens—all black, except Mary and her husband. She tells the story of how the huge silver-haired preacher with the thundering, rusty, gravelly voice kept pounding home one theme to his people all morning: "Be somebody! God never takes time to build a nobody. Everybody God creates is created to be somebody."

The God who created you gave you a brain that's brilliant. You were able to learn to read, and you have been able to read this chapter. You have a great deal of determination. You've followed the book up to this point. The fact that you are reading these words is proof of the fact that you are cut from great cloth. You are as deserving and as capable of achieving success as any other person alive in the world today! God created you to be somebody who could be an inspiration to many people. Open your mind to receive possibility thoughts. They will come like eggs dropped in a nest. Tenderly receive them and be prepared to trust in them through the testing phase, the investing phase, the arresting phase. Never abandon the dream until you've reached the cresting phase!

# 9

## *Prayer: The Power That Pulls Everything Together Successfully*

Every principle we have shared with you in these pages is a key ingredient in the recipe for success. We come now to the final and most important technique necessary for effective life management. If you've followed all the steps outlined earlier, then by now you have (1) put your problems in proper perspective, (2) applied the twelve principles of managing problems positively, (3) taken charge and control of your situation, (4) tackled impossibilities with the Ten Commandments for Possibility Thinking, (5) counted to ten and won, and (6) applied the faith that will move your mountain. But through each of these stages, undergirding and overriding all the principles we have developed in the preceding pages, there must be a steady and unfailing practice of positive prayer if you are to succeed.

God guides praying people through tough times until the beautiful breakthrough finally comes. I have recently experienced a remarkable evidence of this guidance, and I can tell the story now for the first time.

One of my toughest times came two years after the completion of the Crystal Cathedral and involved my only son. Ever since he was a young teen-ager, he felt called to commit his life to Jesus Christ and to full-time ministry.

He graduated from Hope College in Holland, Michigan, and completed his theological work in California at Fuller Seminary. He began work as a part-time assistant in our ministry and had as his great goal to "spend my life working with my dad as his associate and partner in the Crystal Cathedral."

Such was the path he chose to walk. But the relationship between my son and me was about to take an unexpected turn.

## Holy Week 1981

As the meeting of the church board of the Crystal Cathedral drew to a close on Tuesday night, I turned to my son and, on impulse, said to him, "Do you have anything to report to the board?"

Caught off-guard, he heard himself say something he never had planned to verbalize. "Yes, as a matter of fact, I do." After a pause, he shocked himself and everybody else by saying, "I feel I have to resign from the church." There was a ghastly silence.

"I want to be a great preacher like my father." I thought I saw tears in his eyes. I saw him swallow a lump in his throat. "I don't believe I'll ever be able to be the man my father is unless I walk the kind of path he walked," he continued. "I've been praying a long time, and I really believe God wants me to get out and start my own church from scratch the way Dad did."

At that point his lips trembled and his eyes brimmed with tears. In all the twenty-six years of his life, I could not remember seeing him shed tears. When he was disciplined or scolded as a child, he took the deserved punishment with a stiff upper lip.

"Please excuse me." Choking back the tears, he pushed back his chair and slipped into the adjoining restroom. All of us at the table—elders, deacons, fellow ministers—sat silently looking at each other. Finally, Bob returned. He walked out tall, ramrod straight, smiling from ear to ear, but showing a redness around his eyes.

"Excuse me for that," he continued. "All my life I envisioned being only at this church. I was only six months old when my father started it. But I feel God now wants me to leave."

At that point, twelve elders and deacons stood up and formed a living chain, arms linked, and embraced my son. We prayed that God would bless him and guide him in every decision and at every step of his way. After the time of deep prayer, I looked at him and asked, "What are you thinking of doing?"

"I think there is room for another wonderful positive Protestant church in the southern part of this county," he said, "and I'm praying that God will lead me there if that is what He wants."

The meeting swiftly adjourned; it was nearly ten o'clock at night. Before my son left the room, I asked, "Bob, can we get together tomorrow?"

"Yes," he answered, "I'd like that. I have to go down to San Diego. Maybe you could ride with me."

I left a note on my secretary's desk, instructing her to cancel all of my appointments for the next day, explaining that an emergency was taking me out of town. Being with Bob was the most important thing I had to do.

The next morning we left the church together, to begin the ninety-mile trip south. We'd been traveling for about eighteen miles when I said, "Bob, starting a new church from scratch, as you hope to do, is a lot tougher today than when I was a young minister a quarter of a century ago."

Bob looked at me and stopped me properly with this statement: "Then maybe you'd better stop preaching your possibility thinking, Dad!"

He had me, and I had no retort. "But where do you expect to buy land today, Bob?" I asked, adding, "You know when I started this church, we were able to buy land for six thousand dollars an acre. Today there isn't much vacant land to be bought. And if you can find an empty parcel, it would cost you over one hundred thousand dollars an acre!"

He raised his right arm and with one long finger pointed through the window to the huge expanse of undeveloped ranch land directly in line with our car. An American flag flew from a flagpole on a sloping green hillside surrounded by palm trees. It was the famous ninety-two-acre Rancho Capistrano.

"I have thought and prayed, and I believe that God is going to give me a piece of that land," Bob said confidently. I was floored by his powerful, affirmative faith.

"Why, Bob, that might just be possible," I answered, for the first time getting a little excited about his dream. "After all, that's where John Crean lives, and he's the man who gave the first million dollars to launch the Crystal Cathedral fund drive. In fact, it was in that house, in that grove under the American flag, that I had asked John for a lead-off gift that would be big enough to guarantee the successful launching of the Crystal Cathedral campaign.

"You know, Bob," I continued, getting more and more enthusiastic, "I remember now that John said to me once, 'I don't know what I'm going to do with this big ninety-two-acre ranch. But I guess God has a plan for it. I know I don't intend to keep living here all my life.' You know, Bob, he just might give you a few acres."

"I'm sure he will," Bob said. "I've prayed about it, and I feel strongly, without an ounce of doubt, that that is exactly what God has in mind."

"Then make a date with John and approach him," I said. "It's your job, you know, not mine."

By the end of the day on Wednesday, we had made our trip to San Diego and returned home. Shortly after the sunset of this day in Holy Week, my son called John Crean for an appointment "to get together and talk."

"How about tomorrow?" Mr. Crean offered.

"Sounds great," said Bob.

The next day—Maundy Thursday—they met for lunch. Bob called me at breakfast and said, "I'm having lunch with John Crean. Pray for me."

"Bob," I said, "do you realize that it was on Maundy Thursday five years ago that I sat down with him and asked him to give the first million-dollar gift? Now on Maundy Thursday

*Brownouts
do not
have to be
burnouts.*

five years later, you'll ask him to make possible the birth of a new church. But don't be surprised if he says no, Bob, and don't be discouraged. After all, he said no the first time I asked him to give a million dollars. It was only after he prayed it through that he came back and made the gift."

I couldn't wait for Thursday afternoon to get the word from my son. The phone rang late in the afternoon.

Bob's voice had a quality about it that I had never heard before: "Dad, you'll never guess what John Crean has done."

"Tell me quickly," I demanded.

"Well, I asked him if I could have a small chunk of the ranch to start a church. He said to me, 'Bob, you're too late. Last night Donna and I gave away the entire ranch to somebody else.'"

It was the biggest shock of my son's life and a bigger shock to me.

John Crean went on to explain to my son that for more than ten years he had found health, healing, and spiritual strength by attending retreats sponsored by the Jesuits. Few, if any, organizations in the world are more experienced in running retreats effectively than the Jesuits.

"Donna and I prayed and came to the conclusion that God wanted the ranch to be a retreat center. Since the Jesuits really know how to run retreats, we have offered it to them. In fact, we signed the papers last night, deeding the entire ninety-two-acre ranch to them."

It was good news and bad news. The good news was that John Crean was giving the land to a wonderful organization of godly men for a fantastic cause. The bad news was my fear of what it might do to my son's faith in God's guidance through answered prayer. Meanwhile, I had a dream I had never shared with anyone. I had long dreamed of having a retreat center. Now, I was also spiritually distraught at having lost the opportunity to acquire a piece of property on which I would have been able to have fulfilled my unspoken dream of launching retreats for married couples, burned-out ministers, or persons with problems with alcoholism.

Mr. Crean was a voting and an active member of the "Hour

of Power" program's board of directors, but I had never shared my secret dream with him. He never had known of my heart's desire. Naturally, there was no reason why he should consider offering the property to us. Had he known how deeply I had wanted to get into this healing ministry myself, maybe he would have offered part of it to the Crystal Cathedral and part to the Jesuits. We could have made a little chunk available for a church site for my son. Was it too late? Perhaps we could purchase a part of it from the Jesuits. I picked up the telephone on Saturday and called Mr. Crean. "Is your gift of the ranch carved in granite, or poured in concrete? And, if so, is the cement dry?"

"Oh, yes, I'm afraid it is, Bob," he answered. "You know, the ranch is worth nearly ten million dollars and I'm giving it to them without any strings attached, so I'm sure they will accept it. They are very enthusiastic about it, or I wouldn't have signed the gift conveyance.

"Of course, they have to sign the papers to legally accept the gift. All I've asked is that they get the signed papers notarized and sent to me within the next six months. After all, I do want to have it all taken care of before we get into the last quarter of the year when I will have to calculate my own tax situation."

I was quiet for a moment before I said, "I wish I had known that you wanted to turn it into a retreat center, John. I had secret dreams myself. But I am sure you did the right thing, for you are a man of prayer. I know that. I've never met a man that prays more sincerely than you do, John."

With that I hung up, but my heart was enormously heavy. We would not be able to use Rancho Capistrano for the renewal conference grounds of which I had secretly dreamed. I had hoped to get to that project after the Crystal Cathedral was finished. It had taken nearly ten years to conceive, promote, develop, and construct the Crystal Cathedral! Now in my mid-fifties, that project was completed and I wanted to get into the development of the conference facilities. But the only potential piece of property that might have been available to me had been given to someone else.

## July 1981

Three months passed after the Creans had signed the papers giving the property to the Jesuits. John Crean invited friends, relatives, and leaders of the Jesuit community to his ranch for a special birthday party where he announced to everyone that the gift was being given and was being accepted. The Jesuits moved in a brass cross, candles, and a communion set, using the pool table in the game room as a place for their private morning Mass.

## August 1981

"I am going to need the gift accepted, signed, and notarized," John Crean told a prominent Jesuit official. But for some reason the signed papers didn't come back. There were, after all, internal considerations that needed clarification by several important persons at different levels in the hierarchy.

Crean unburdened his heart to me: "I have never worked so hard to try to give a gift away. I don't know why they haven't signed the papers and accepted it. I wish I had given it to you, Bob, but it's too late."

## September 1981

"The six months will be up on Monday," Mr. Crean instructed his attorney. "Please write to the Jesuits and tell them that I will need to have the papers accepting my gift signed and notarized by 4:00 P.M. on Monday, September 4. If I do not receive an acceptance at the end of this six-month period of time, I will feel directed by God to dispose of it another way."

On Monday, September 4, I was in my library when the telephone rang at 4:04 P.M. It was Donna Crean, John's wife:

"Bob, I wondered if you could drop around tonight. John would like to talk to you."

"Donna, you know this is Monday. Monday night is my date night. You know my wife and I never go anywhere on Monday nights except on our date."

"I know that, Bob," she answered. "Maybe you could just drop around the ranch on the way out to dinner. It won't take long. Let me give you a hint of what John wants to talk about. The gift of the ranch fell through, and he'd like to give it to you."

I cried; I squealed; I almost fainted!

Two hours later, Arvella and I were sitting in the same room of the same house where five years before I had asked a total stranger to give a one-million-dollar gift to launch an incredible project to be called the Crystal Cathedral. Now I was in the same room to receive the gift of a ninety-two-acre ranch.

"John," I said, with quivering voice, "you know this is an answer to prayer. It all started when my son, in prayer, asked for a place to start his church."

At that point, John Crean interrupted, strongly and intensely. "Bob, I am giving this to you for a retreat center and for your church purposes. It is not for young Bob. He has to earn his own way. He has to experience his own struggles. It is my dream that this will be a retreat center, not just another church."

I had to respect his strong feelings, but, at the same time, I was crushed inside. What would I tell my son? I would not have been sitting in that room receiving that gift on that night, if my son had not first pointed the way out of his own prayer experiences.

## November 1981

My son accepted the fact that his father was the beneficiary of the ranch and that he would never be able to have even one acre of it for a church. He searched unsuccessfully for an empty hall. He tried to use a drive-in theater, but the city council rejected his application, contending that it would create too big a traffic problem. He looked for a warehouse to rent. None was available. He finally found a college gymnasium, and in November 1981, he started a church service, hoping some people would come. The crowd grew slowly but strongly, through December, January, February. Meanwhile, the ranch stood idle. I had lost my enthusiasm for its development.

## March 1982

John Crean and I met and agreed that we needed to have a long talk about developing the ranch. "Let's spend two or three days together on the boat," he offered. I agreed. "You know, I am very impressed with the job young Bob has done," he said, as we sailed the Pacific, looking for marlin. "My brother has been going to young Bob's church. He has joined it, did you know that?" Crean asked. He turned and looked at me, continuing, "A lot has happened during the last year. Young Bob has proven himself. If he'd like to use the old barn at the other end of the property, make it into a little chapel, and have his church meet there, I think that might work out O.K."

He went on: "Donna and I have been praying, and we believe in the principles practiced by the members of Alcoholics Anonymous: 'Let go and let God.' Totally relinquish and release your entire position to God Almighty. Let Him do exactly what He wants to do the way He wants to do it, in your life. We feel we have to do that as far as the ranch is concerned. Do what you want, in the way you want, Bob. I believe you will pray for guidance; I believe God will guide you; and I believe you will do the right thing as you follow Him."

No sooner had John Crean made that profound spiritual profession than a surge of release and inner strength came to me. I can only describe it as the reality of God flowing through my mind and my mood.

Today, as this book is published, my son is holding church services in what was the barn on the ninety-two-acre ranch. Two services with growing audiences are worshiping God in this newborn church! The first of three carefully designed retreat centers is under construction. The beautiful rolling ranch land with a private lake, lovely woods, trees, and waterfalls will be preserved as a Garden of Eden—a place where tired and burned-out souls and marriages can find renewal and new life!

Two years have passed since my son first prayed and was pointed to the ranch. Two years after his prayer, he is holding services on the property that he was led by faith through prayer to claim in the name of God.

His faith went through every phase—the nesting phase when God dropped the idea; the testing phase when he asked whether this was indeed the best and only place; the investing phase; the arresting phase when he was told he could not use it, and, today, he is enjoying the cresting phase of faith.

The times of hope, despair, enthusiasm, and depression have all passed. Today the sun is shining. The sky is blue. The dream has come true!

And I have just finished writing a letter to the Jesuits:

My dear brothers in Christ,
    You have been relieved of the responsibility of maintaining and managing the ranch. We have accepted that awesome responsibility. And in a few months we'll have luxurious bedroom facilities, chapel facilities, and dining facilities available for you, my good brothers, to come for a retreat if you find the rooms suitable.
    After all, we do not own the land. God owns it. We have only been made stewards and caretakers of it. And all human beings are God's children. All of us are brothers. If we can be of service to you, please let me know.

As this book goes to press, I am just beginning what I expect to be a five-year project of developing the gardens and the structural facilities of the Rancho Capistrano Renewal Center. It will be a project that I expect will keep me creatively occupied with peak enthusiasm. After that, I expect to spend the rest of my life using the place to erase tensions, fears, sins, and stress from the hearts of those who come to the place where the swallows come back every spring.

There will be one Bible verse etched in stained glass dominating this entire garden renewal center. It is the promise of God found in the Song of Solomon: "And the time of the singing of the birds has come" (2:12; paraphrased).

The storm has passed. The birds are singing. The night is over. Tough times never last. Tough people do! That's really true if we live moment by moment, day by day, in complete surrender to God in prayer. Through prayer, God gives the power to hold on to tough times until the breakthrough comes.


But those who wait on the LORD
Shall renew their strength;
They shall mount up with wings like eagles,
They shall run and not be weary,
They shall walk and not faint
(Is. 40:31).

I have found immense strength through this promise of God. As I wait upon Him in prayer I find the strength to go on. The terrible danger in tough times is that we lose our emotional power to remain enthusiastic and creative. But the solution God offers is prayer, the power that pulls everything together successfully.

## Prayer—The Power That Pulls Everything Together Successfully

We all know what it means to be burned out. There are people who get burned out professionally, creatively. There are institutions that get burned out productively. There are families and marriages that get burned out. There are individual personalities that lose their enthusiasm for life.

The problem with burnouts is that they inevitably lead to crash landings.

I don't want to see your life crash about you. Neither does God. That's why He's given us a solution to the burnout problem. His solution is prayer.

When times are the toughest and it seems as if you are as low as you can go and when possibility thinking hasn't had the results you expected, you are in danger of burnout. It's precisely at these times you need God because when you remain in touch with God, you are immune to burnout. You say, "But don't you get terribly down at times?" Yes, but remember I said you can be immune to *burnouts* not *brownouts*. A brownout is a temporary power failure. It is not a permanent resignation, divorce, or bill of sale. You may feel down in a brownout, but you don't abandon the ship as you would in a burnout. It's important to know the difference. In a brownout the power will come back on. A burnout? That's a toughie. To keep a brownout from becoming a burnout you must remain in touch with God—and that's what prayer is. But remember, keeping in touch with God won't eliminate your problems . . . it will only help you manage them. The late comedian Grady Nutt said it: "God should be a resource in the struggle, not a way around it."

How do you renew your strength and spirit during a brownout time? How do you pick yourself up in time to prevent a burnout and prove the truth of this book: *tough times never last, but tough people do!*? Let's look at the word *renew*. I'm going to deal with each of the five letters that make up the word *renew* in the hopes that you will know and will remember how to renew yourself whenever you feel you're about to burn out.

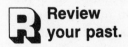

## R Review your past.

Where have I come from? What was keeping me going? Review the persons that have been in your life, close to you, as well as the projects and problems you faced. Review your private practices, your philosophy of life, your value system, and your religion.

Review what was the source of your emotional energy. What turned you on in the past? Why aren't you excited now? Was it a special person or a project that inspired you before? Has the person left or is the project now complete?

Or were you being challenged by a problem, and the problem is now solved? Perhaps you were challenged by an adversary. The spirit of competition motivated you.

Was it a private or public life-style that kept you going? Have you forsaken your ideals? Have you accommodated yourself to questionable ethics or a dubious moral standard? And is this like a silent termite eating away the youthful enthusiasm?

Was it a false expectation that enticed you and led you onward and upward? Shakespeare said that many of our goals in life are really like needles in haystacks: "You shall seek all day until you find them, and when you find them they are not worth the search."

Too often our goals rise from a defective value system. And the energy to remain enthusiastic in life, marriage, and career is often drawn from the search and the hunt rather than from the final harvest and the ultimate ingathering.

What was the taproot of your positive emotion that kept your light burning through the years? Review your life carefully.

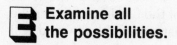

### Examine all the possibilities.

What would you set as your goals if . . . ? What would you do if you had the money, if you had the education, if you had the training, if you had the contacts, if you had the support base? What would you do if you had the marketing system, if you had the right people on your team? What would you do if you had the time, if you had the plant, if you had the equipment? What would you do if you knew it could not fail?

There are far more possibilities than you think. Examine them.

## Name the price you're willing to pay.

Are you willing to go to school for two or three years? Are you willing to move? Are you willing to go through six to eight months of physical therapy to walk again? Name the price you're willing to pay.

When Henry Ford transported Thomas Edison's entire laboratory to Dearborn Village, he also brought the trash pile. Why? Because he wanted everybody to see how much Edison had to throw away in order to finally have some success. Every sales person knows this. There's always a pile of rejections in order to get the "yes." What price are you willing to pay?

When I first saw the model of the Crystal Cathedral, I said to my wife, "That is fantastic! If giving leadership to the development of that cathedral would cost the price of high blood pressure and even a fatal heart attack, I'd gladly pay it for that building." I meant it. When you feel that deeply about something you are going to make it.

## Elect the best possibility, no matter what the price.

Choose the best; shun mediocrity. Mediocrity has a way of shriveling up enthusiasm. But commitment to excellence taps an incredible source of energy. Elect the best, no matter what the price tag.

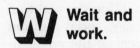

## Wait and work.

Probably nothing is more difficult than to keep waiting, working, plodding, and maintaining patience through dark times. But we must. And in God's good time, hope and help will come our way. Oftentimes someone's unexpected, off-the-cuff comment or curt answer to an important question can be the breakthrough to a new emotional sunrise.

Henry Ford was born on a farm, left the farm at the age of sixteen, and got a job as a mechanic in Detroit. Then he became a fireman in the Detroit Edison Company and worked his way up until he became the chief engineer. Of course, Edison was just a big name to him. When Thomas Edison was visiting the company, Henry Ford told himself that if he ever got close enough to this famous inventor, he would ask him one question. Ford got the chance in 1898. He stopped Edison and said, "Mr. Edison, may I ask you a question? Do you think gasoline is a good fuel source for motor cars?" Edison had no time for Ford; he simply said yes and walked away. And that was it. But that answer turned Ford on. Henry Ford made a commitment. It was in 1909, eleven years later, that he turned out the Tin Lizzy. He took criticism, but during those eleven years he worked and he waited, and he waited and he worked. He experienced brownouts, but never burnouts.

"Those who wait on the Lord shall renew their strength." The Lord might strengthen you through some person, or a chance meeting. It may come through someone God uses to encourage you. I know this is true because there have been times when I needed to be encouraged. And there have been other times when God used me to give encouragement to someone else. "Wait on the Lord." Remain in touch with God through prayer.

You've heard of Florence Nightingale. But did you know that she was born to wealth and social prominence in London, England? This brilliant young girl from a socially prominent, wealthy family wrote in her diary in 1851 at the age of thirty-one, "I see nothing that I desire today, other than death." She came close to burning out. But she renewed herself. How? She *reviewed* her life. Money, social position didn't do anything for her. Then she *examined* the possibilities. If only she could help people. She wanted to be a nurse. Her mother and father said that such a status was beneath their dignity. But she *named* the price. She was willing to be ostracized by her parents and society. She *elected* to be a nurse. Her mother wrote, "We are two ducks, my husband

and I, and we've given birth to a wild swan." But Florence Nightingale's biographer said, "The mother was so wrong, for Florence was not a wild swan but an eagle." The Crimean War broke out. Florence chose to go. "Possessed by demons," her family said. "Victim of a nervous breakdown." She was ostracized, criticized, considered insane. But for three years she waited and worked among the dying men, their blood, their amputated legs. She came home three years later in 1859, and she wrote and published notes on how hospitals should be operated. And she changed hospitals. You and I have the benefits of it a century or more later.

"Wait on the Lord" in prayer and He will renew a dream. And a brownout will give way to a light-up.

Brownouts are not necessarily burnouts. Tough times pass. Tough people survive. If there is only one principle you remember after you put this book down, let it be this: Brownouts do not have to be burnouts.

It's terribly important that we hang on in the face of hope and never call a brownout a burnout. If we do quit, we will later on look back and say, "I realize now it was just a phase—just a period of time—just a natural transition I was going through. I shouldn't have packed up; I should have seen myself through it. When the kids were all little with all the diapers, that was an age. When the company was young and struggling and I had to do my own secretarial and janitorial work, that was an era. Those times would not have lasted forever.

Every institution, every individual, every job has its ages, passages, periods, eras; we have to be careful to hold on. When the brownout is only a brownout and not a burnout, the power will come back on. When there is a temporary overload on the emotional system, we must rest, wait upon the Lord, and the new dawning will come.

The most dangerous thing in the world is to make an irreversible negative decision during a brownout time. Don't sell your real estate because there is no electricity in the building. It's just a brownout, not a burnout. Never cut a dead tree down in the wintertime. I remember one winter my dad needed firewood, and he found a dead tree and sawed it down. In the spring to his dismay new shoots sprouted around the trunk. He said, "I thought sure it was dead. The leaves had all dropped in the wintertime. It was so cold that twigs snapped as surely as if there were no life left in the old tree. But now I see that there was still life at the taproot." He looked at me and said, "Bob, don't forget this important lesson. Never cut a tree down in the wintertime." Never make a negative decision in the low time. Never make your most important decisions when you are in your worst mood.

Wait. Be patient. The storm will pass. The spring will come. New feelings will come over you, and they will be positive. Keep waiting affirmatively and positively in prayer for God's strength to return.

In the early days of our church history, I went through a prolonged period of two years when an associate minister was conspiring to replace me as the senior minister of the young church. He managed to attract several of his supporters from the church board. They had secret meetings during the week. I knew this was going on and didn't know how to handle it. I abhor confrontations. My natural inclination was to pack up and split.

Yet, I was the senior minister assigned by the denomination with the responsibility of getting the church organized. I was reared to be responsible and accountable. "You never go fishing until you've done the chores," my father used to say to me.

I couldn't possibly leave the church with the job undone. I had to hold on. It was not a burnout time, but it was surely a brownout time. I slipped cards with inspirational thoughts written on them under the glass top of my desk. One was a statement Jesus made: "No one, having his hand to the plow, and looking back, is fit for the kingdom of God" (Luke 9:62).

Another sentence was written by a Dr. Butler of Baylor University: "When things get rough don't move. People and pressures shift, but the soil remains the same no matter where you go."

## BUT TOUGH PEOPLE DO

Wait on the Lord, and He will strengthen your heart!

I have had my brownout times. I still get them from time to time. Today I find my life is highly visible. I have made the discovery from personal experience that when someone's work achieves high visibility through the publication of books or through television appearances, he will be vulnerable to a wide interpretation by people and institutions who may or may not understand and interpret him correctly. It has never been easy, and it remains difficult for me today to keep going with enthusiasm when erroneous and negative interpretations are made of my work.

I have learned that if you are a leader, you will be called upon to be the front person. "The point man" is what they call it in the military service. And the point man is always at the top of the needle. It is impossible to be at the top of the needle without getting pricked.

I find that encouragement and sincere compliments are a major source of encouragement to me. They keep my light bright. When they are replaced by cynical criticisms from people who are probably ill-informed, ill-motivated, or un-educated, I must return to my Ultimate Source. In prayer I must return to God who gives me my direction and orders and keep going, for prayer is the power that pulls everything together successfully.

In the *Reader's Digest*, December 1982, a marvelous little piece of philosophy appeared that may be helpful at this point. It is entitled "Anyway."

People are unreasonable, illogical and self-centered.
*Love them anyway.*

If you do good, people will accuse you of selfish
ulterior motives.
*Do good anyway.*

If you are successful, you will win false friends
and true enemies.
*Succeed anyway.*

Honesty and frankness make you vulnerable.
*Be honest and frank anyway.*

## TOUGH TIMES NEVER LAST

The good you do today will be forgotten tomorrow.
*Do good anyway.*

The biggest people with the biggest ideas can be shot down by
the smallest people with the smallest minds.
*Think big anyway.*

People favor underdogs but follow only top dogs.
*Fight for some underdogs anyway.*

What you spent years building may be destroyed overnight.
*Build anyway.*

Give the world the best you have and you'll get kicked in the
teeth.
*Give the world the best you've got anyway.*[1]

The point of this piece of philosophy is that you should
find joy and light in doing God's will regardless of how people will interpret it or accept it. Above all, "to thine ownself
be true." Wait on the Lord, and *He will renew Your strength!*

Prayer is the umbilical cord that allows you—with your
embryonic ideas—to draw nourishment from a source that
you, like an unborn infant, can neither see nor fully know or
comprehend—God our heavenly Father! Prayer is the power
that pulls everything together successfully.

With this prayerful attitude, tackle your problem today.
Turn it over to God. Take out a sheet of paper. Pick up a
pencil. And get ready for the ideas that He will drop into
your mind. Together let's get ready for action!

[1]Reprinted with permission from the December 1982 *Reader's Digest* and RESPONSE, a
newsletter of Presbyterian Church of White Plains, White Plains, NY, Marjorie
W. Timmons, editor.

# PART
## III

*Beginning
Is Half Done!*

# 10

## *Alphabet For Action*

In difficult times, people too often lose the ability to face the future optimistically. They begin to think about their tomorrows negatively.

They forget that the tough times will pass. They concentrate on the problems of today rather than on the opportunities of tomorrow. In so doing, they not only lose the potential of today, they also throw away the beauty of tomorrow. That's the real tragedy of tough times.

Frank Sinatra said it: "Dr. Schuller, your messages are medicine to my mind. Somehow, every time I listen, I have the courage to step into tomorrow."

I have to give credit where credit is due. I wish *I* had thought of those words: ". . . the courage to step into tomorrow." If there were one thing I could give to every person, it would be the courage to step into tomorrow. Probably you are not in need of opportunities; they are already there. You just have to have the courage to step into tomorrow and grasp them.

It doesn't matter how young or how old you are—if you want your life to thrive you must have the courage to step into tomorrow.

Last week, a six-year-old boy came to me and said, "Dr. Schuller, may I have your autograph? And will you write something special? I'm going to be a preacher too when I grow up." Isn't that sensational? Six years old, and he has a plan.

I'll never forget Grandma Finley. I met her one summer while I was working on the Campus Afloat Ship, connected with Chapman College in Orange, California. I was acting as professor of philosophy and history. In our student body was Mrs. Finley.

We all called her "Grandma Finley" because she was eighty-four years old. She had been traveling worldwide since the end of the Second World War. As I recall, her trips had included six visits to the Soviet Union.

Word of her reached the people in New Zealand, and so when our ship docked in Auckland, the press was waiting to meet Grandma Finley.

I happened to overhear the interview. A reporter said, "Grandma Finley, is it true you've had six trips through Russia?"

"Yes."

"Is it true that you've been traveling to a different country every year, for thirty-four years?"

She said, "Yes."

"And is it true you're eighty-four years old?"

"Yes."

And then the reporter said, "Well, I suppose this is your last cruise."

She was offended, shocked, and upset. She said, "The last cruise? Of course not! I belong to the CMT Club."

"What's the CMT Club?"

"That's the 'Can't Miss a Thing Club.' I'm not going to miss a thing. My bus is leaving. Good-bye." She took off, trotting halfway to the bus.

Whether you are six or eighty-four years old, you have a tomorrow. You can choose to face it positively—and make the most of it—or you can throw it away.

Recently, while I was in New York, I rode in a cab from downtown Manhattan to Long Island. During the hour-long ride, I worked on the message I was to give. I took out my daily itinerary for my three-day visit to the city and began to make notes on the back.

I looked over the notes I'd just made. In frustration and dissatisfaction I tore off the page with what I'd written, put it on the seat, and started over. I wrote down my thoughts on the next page of my itinerary. I was pleased with my new efforts.

When I reached my destination and got out of the car, I suddenly remembered that the piece of paper I'd left on the seat of the cab was my itinerary for the next day. I said, "Hey, I've got to keep that." As I retrieved it, I added, "I almost threw away part of tomorrow!"

Maybe that's your problem. Maybe you've thrown away part of your tomorrow. Perhaps you've had a dynamic idea on which you've neglected to capitalize. You've carelessly tossed it aside.

Every idea is worth considering. Most ideas are worthy of action. The most tragic waste is the waste of a good idea. I ask you now: Is there some great idea in your life that you have still not dealt with affirmatively?

Everyone has within him some idea of something that he should have started but hasn't. Maybe it's to quit smoking. Maybe it's to lose weight. Maybe it's to get started on a physical fitness program. Maybe it's to join a church. Maybe it's to accept Jesus Christ as your Savior and Lord. Maybe it's to read the Bible, which you may never have done. Maybe it's to start a new business. Maybe it's to go back to school. Maybe it's to take a positive attitude toward your marriage, discarding the negative attitude you've had far too long. Maybe it's to quit drinking. I don't know what it is, but everyone, I have no doubt, has an idea of some area in which he should be taking some action for self-improvement. It's a great idea.

*Now*—what will you do with that idea? America is known for its waste. We waste money, energy, gasoline, fuel, time, clothing, and paper. But nothing is as tragic as the waste of a good idea! So, if there's a good idea in your mind right now, don't waste it!

How do you keep from wasting it? Very simply, begin to do something about it!

When I took a course in English composition, I confess that I received a very low grade. My teacher said, "Bob Schuller, I think you can make a living by talking; you're a good talker. But don't ever try to write." God bless her.

I remembered her negative thought when something stirred inside me some years ago, suggesting I put my thoughts into writing. I felt sure I should write a book. But I thought, *I can't write a book. Smarter people than I have told me I'd never be able to.* And then I remembered: Beginning is half done. So I took out a piece of paper and typed, *"Move Ahead With Possibility Thinking* by Robert Schuller." I bought a loose-leaf binder and stuck the title sheet in it. Beginning is half done! Before I knew it, I had written a book!

Just because you're flunking something doesn't mean you *can't* pull good marks in it.

Since then, the level of my accomplishment is due, in large measure, to that one sentence. Beginning is half done! Get started! Winning starts with beginning!

What kind of a person are you? Often we hear the question: How do you treat people? A far more important question is this: How do you treat ideas?

Treat ideas like newborn babies.

Treat them tenderly . . .
    They can get killed pretty quickly.
Treat them gently . . .
    They can be bruised in infancy.
Treat them respectfully . . .
    They could be the most valuable things
    that ever came into your life.
Treat them protectively . . .
    Don't let them get away.
Treat them nutritionally . . .
    Feed them, and feed them well.
Treat them antiseptically . . .
    Don't let them get infected with the germs
    of negative thoughts.

## BUT TOUGH PEOPLE DO

Treat them responsibly!
Respond! Act! Do something with them!
—R.H.S.

How do you treat good ideas? By *acting* on them, that's how!

## Decide to Decide

You handle ideas by making some kind of a decision. Winning starts with beginning! And to begin, you must do something *now*.

What do you do when you have a good idea? Just observe how differently people respond to ideas:

1. Insecure people hibernate. They run away from good ideas. They're afraid they might fail or that they might have to spend too much effort. And, like a bear which feels the first whisper of a winter wind and rushes off, tail between his legs, to hide out until the sun comes back months later, some people hibernate.

2. Lazy people luxuriate. They don't pay much attention to ideas. They want to enjoy the pleasures of this life. They'll get serious later on, probably when they're old. Maybe they'll even get religion.

3. Wounded people commiserate. They say, "Oh, it's a good idea, but I couldn't do it. I've tried it so often. I've tried to lose weight. I've tried all kinds of diets, but I keep getting fatter." Or, "I've tried to quit smoking twenty times in my life, and I've even torn up the package of cigarettes and thrown it in the wastebasket." Or, "I've tried to quit drinking, but I can't." Or, "I've tried to get along with my wife, but we still argue." Don't commiserate.

4. Foolish people procrastinate. They put off acting on their ideas. "Later on, when I'm ready, I'll do something about it," they say. "I'm not ready yet." Let me give you a sentence that could change your life: Don't wait until you're ready to make big decisions, or you'll never accomplish half

[189]

of what you could. The difference between the high achiever and the low achiever is this: The high achiever almost always makes decisions before he's ready to move.

Who would honestly say he was ready for marriage when he got married? When I look back, I realize I was not. And the day I joined the church, as a young boy of sixteen, in a balcony in a northwest Iowa country church, I heard the minister say, "Today is the day of salvation." And I thought, *That's right, Reverend. You really are right.* I don't know what came over me, but I got out of that pew and gave my life to Jesus Christ. But you know, I wasn't ready for the challenges, the temptations, the problems that I was to run into. Don't wait until you're ready, or you'll never make the move!

5. Wise people dedicate. They're do-it-now people. No grass grows under their feet. That's why they don't waste the most precious thing in the world—a good idea. They don't waste a good moment or a good opportunity.

How do you handle your good ideas? Don't hibernate. Don't luxuriate. Don't commiserate. Don't procrastinate. Dedicate yourself to that idea that has come from God. And then you can become the person you want to be!

How do you dedicate? How do you get started? Let me give you this clue: Don't wait for an inspiration. Use your head, and your heart will follow. Don't wait until you feel like it to make the move. If you wait until you feel like it, emotion will run you instead of reason. Many times two people who rationally know they belong together marry and develop love, where love did not exist.

Frequently I tackled an idea and said, "I'm going to do something about it," although I didn't feel like it. When I started writing this book, I did not feel like it! If I had waited until I got inspired, nothing would have happened. A published author will tell you how to write. Simply set a specific time to go to the typewriter and type. And you may not feel like it when you start, but pretty soon the inspiration comes.

You may need to go on a diet, but you don't feel like dieting. You're waiting until you feel like it. Don't! Discipline

*Beginning
is
half done!*

yourself for one full day, and then for two days, and do you know what? After two days you'll feel like it! Use your head, and your heart will follow!

I've learned another thing: I can do anything I think I can . . . but I can't do anything alone. I've taught this, preached it, written it, and tried it, and it's true. I always need someone to support me! Don't try to handle your dreams alone. It won't work.

Winning starts with beginning, and beginning starts with a single action.

Do something great with a great idea. Whatever it is that you should be doing—a concept for self-improvement, a dream, a goal, or a commitment to Jesus Christ—I want you to do it. Decide that this is going to be the day you're going to do something about it!

Life today is nothing more than a collection of results of the choices you have made. And I would now add this sentence: Today's decisions are tomorrow's realities.

Plan your future because you have to live in it. That means that you must be mature enough to change your mind. Show me a person who never changes his mind, and I'll show you a very immature, childish, stubborn person.

To really succeed in life, all you have to do is (1) get started! and (2) never quit. Those are the only two hurdles you need to clear to become the person God wants you to be!

Let me call your attention to a powerful Bible verse: "For [God] says: 'In an acceptable time I have heard you,/ And in the day of salvation I have helped you.'/Behold, now is the accepted time; behold, now is the day of salvation" (2 Cor. 6:2).

You didn't think when you got up this morning that this would be the day your life would change, did you? But it's going to happen because the only thing that stands between you and grand success in living are these two things: Getting started and never quitting! You can solve your biggest problem by getting started, right here and now.

Together you and I are going to create an *alphabet for action*.

## BUT TOUGH PEOPLE DO

For each letter of the alphabet we will assign a possibility-thinking verb—not a noun, not an adjective, but a verb. Verbs are action words, and this is an alphabet for action. For example, here are some verbs that start with *A*.

**Attack** your problem with courage and your possibility with enthusiasm.

**Ask** the *market* what needs are undeveloped; the *masters* how to develop a new product; your *mind and heart* what your real motives are and what price you're willing to pay.

**Add** up your strength. You can see. You can hear. You can read. You can telephone. You are stronger than you think you are.

**Adjust** your mind to the changing times. You'll never begin until you get with it.

**Accept** the irrevocable negative realities. And accept the fact that you can be successful—somewhere, somehow, someway—anyway. I have a friend, David Wong in Hong Kong, who keeps this slogan on his desk: "Hallelujah anyway!"

As you move through this alphabet, I want you to think of your own verbs. I will give you one in each case and leave blanks where you can add your own. Earnestly pray that God will give you the right verb (it may or may not be the same verb I suggest). Then take the action that will lead you down the path that He wants you to walk. With God's Holy Spirit leading your life and your mind, you will help write this closing chapter. You and God will join in the final authorship. Then truly this book will be an answer to the prayer: "Lord, give me the guidance to know when to hold on and when to let go and the grace to make the right decision with dignity. Amen."

Whatever words you choose, remember this: *Pick positive, not negative, words.* Positive words provoke positive results. Negative words promote negative results. The difference? How can you tell positive words? You can feel them.

Yes, you can feel the mood they generate. Positive words inspire positive emotions: *humor, courage, optimism, faith, con-*

[193]

*fidence*. Whereas negative words stimulate negative emotions: *suspicion, fear, distress, anger, doubt, depression, sadness, worry, jealousy.*

Remember this: *The words you choose will change your mood for better or worse.* Architects say, "The client shapes the structure—from then on the structure shapes the client [the occupant]." Carefully censor the words, and you'll be molding and manipulating creatively and constructively your mental attitude and your personality. You and only you will design and shape your personality. Make it great and joyous. For you'll have to live in it. From then on, your personality will shape your destiny. The right words will manage or mangle you. Choose them carefully and positively.

# A Affirm

*Affirm* that you can do it. You can find a job. You can change careers. You can learn to walk again. You can recover and not spend the rest of your life in the hospital. You can make it. You can succeed. But you must first affirm: *I deserve to succeed as much as anyone else.*

Every human being is born with one gift from God: The *privilege* of deserving to succeed. People aren't higher up the ladder than you are because they are more favored by God than you. You are as good as they are. And if you don't think so, then that's your problem. If so, I hope I can help you with it. You must affirm: *I deserve to succeed;* and *I have the ability to succeed.* Everyone has within himself latent, innate ability. It probably needs to be honed, educated, trained, and refined, but it can be done.

If you doubt your abilities, I can show you people who have learned to believe in their limited abilities enough to succeed far more than experts say they should. In a school for the severely mentally retarded in Mitchell, South Dakota, I've seen Down's Syndrome children with an average IQ of 36, writing sentences complete with verbs, nouns, and prepositions. There are vast, undeveloped areas in the most retarded mind. The reason more "handicapped" persons fail to develop their latent abilities is that other people don't believe they can. I've heard people say, "Don't waste your time on them." It's a tragic attitude.

I'll never forget Gail Bartosh. Her memory will always be an inspiration to me. She died just a few months ago and many of us miss her. Gail had Down's Syndrome. She spent the past twenty-six years in our church where her father had served as an elder. She believed in her possibilities and, the last ten years of her life, was a salaried, self-employed, self-sustaining person. She worked in the nursery and in our custodial department. People loved her!

*Affirm.* Anybody can amount to something if he will affirm himself and his abilities. Below, begin your own alphabet for winning.

A_____

_____

_____

 **Believe**

*Believe* that somehow, some time, somewhere, through someone's help, you can achieve your heart's highest goal. All these words are important. The *A* stands for affirmation, belief in yourself, *B* is a belief that you can make it happen, but not by yourself. You can make it happen somewhere— but not necessarily where you are today. You can make it happen some way, even if you have to do things differently. You can make it happen some time—maybe not today, maybe not even this year. Perhaps this is the year of transition, during which you'll need to retool yourself intellectually and professionally with a new skill or a new trade.

No matter what your problem is, somehow, somewhere,

some way, some time, there is someone who has the key of wisdom to set you free.

**B**_____

_____

_____

 **Commit**

*Commit* yourself to a dream. You *affirm* you're created in the image of God, that you have latent abilities, that you deserve to succeed as much as anybody else, and after you begin to *believe* that somehow, some way, somewhere, some time, through someone, you can make it. When you are inspired with a dream, God has hit the ball into your court. Now you have to hit it back with a commitment. Most people fail right here on letter *C*, because, with every commitment, comes the risk of failure. Nothing devastates or holds people back more than the fear of failure.

A man who lost an election said to me, "Dr. Schuller, I feel like a total failure."

But I replied, "Anyone who announces his candidacy and campaigns for public office, only to lose, is not a total failure. In fact, nobody who tries to do something great but fails is a total failure. Why? Because he can always rest assured that he succeeded in life's most important battle—he defeated the fear of trying."

People who never declare their candidacy because they're afraid they'll lose, or people who never make an application because they're afraid they'll be turned down, or people who never try because they're sure they'll fail have lost the first battle. They have lost to fear. They have been knocked out before they even got in the ring.

Try. Go back to school, take a course. If you fail, at least you can have the pride of knowing you have conquered the fear of failure. You have won the one battle that knocks people out before they get started. *Make a commitment.*

C_____

_____

_____

 **Dare**

*Dare* to try. *Dare* to love. *Dare* to make a commitment. *Dare* to take a risk.

If you don't dare to take a risk, you'll never get ahead. You'll never solve your problems.

To laugh is to risk appearing the fool.
To weep is to risk appearing sentimental.
To reach for another is to risk involvement.
To expose your feelings is to risk exposing your true self.
To place your ideas, your dreams, before a crowd is to risk
    their loss.
To love is to risk not being loved in return.
To live is to risk dying.
To believe is to risk despair.
To try is to risk failure.
But risks must be taken, because the greatest hazard in life
    is to risk nothing.
The people who risk nothing, do nothing, have nothing,
    are nothing.
They may avoid suffering and sorrow, but they cannot learn,
    feel, change, grow, love, live.
Chained by their attitudes they are slaves; they have forfeited
    their freedom.
Only a person who risks is free.[1]

_____
[1] *President's Newsletter,* Nov. 1982, Phi Delta Kappa, Bloomington, Indiana.

D_____

_____

_____

 **Educate**

*Educate* yourself. Don't be tempted, as many are, to take shortcuts, to avoid the hard years of serious study. The training may be a grind. But those who are too lazy to learn, who never gain the knowledge they could have, weaken their chances for success because knowledge is power. Ultimately, the knowledgeable person who has the right answers is the one who will impress the powerful people. So, get smart!

E_____

_____

_____

 **Find**

*Find* the talent, the possibilities, the time, the money, and the way. There's a great Bible verse: "It is the glory of God to conceal a matter" (Prov. 25:2). God does not lay it all out in the open. No. The diamonds are deep in the earth. Pearls are concealed in oysters. The gold has to be carefully mined. Your real talent dwells deep down within you, and you may not have discovered it yet.

"It is the glory of God to conceal a matter." Why? Because the "matter" is much more exciting and meaningful when you have hunted for it and discovered it.

You have great possibilities hidden deep within yourself.

## BUT TOUGH PEOPLE DO

They wait to be discovered. They may be hidden at the core of a problem, or buried deep under a personal tragedy. Perhaps your greatest opportunity is wrapped up today in a blanket called "tough times." But find the positive power in the problem that you are facing. Find the help that is waiting for you, waiting to help you succeed.

An old Roman proverb says, "When there is no way, we will find one or build one." And a study of the building of the Roman roads confirms that they carried out that attitude.

F_____

_____

_____

## G Give

A *giving* attitude is the secret to successful living. When you have an attitude of "I want what I want, when I want it," people can tell, and they are repelled. A lawyer friend says he has learned to smell a person's motives.

The secret of success is simple. Adele Scheele, the noted career guidance expert, said it, "If you're in a company, your aim should be to make that company more successful, more productive, more effective than it's ever been before." When you want to give something back over and beyond what you've earned in your paycheck, then you are going to be noticed.

There is a legend of a man who was lost in the desert, dying of thirst. He stumbled on until he came to an abandoned house. Outside the dilapidated, windowless, weather-beaten, deserted shack was a pump. He stumbled forward and began pumping furiously, but no water came from the well. Then he noticed a small jug with a cork at the top and a note written on the side: "You have to prime the pump with water, my friend. P.S. And fill the jug again before you leave." He pulled out the cork and saw that the jug was full of water.

Should he pour it down the pump? What if it didn't work? All of the water would be gone. If he drank the water from the jug, he could be sure he would not die of thirst. But to pour it down the rusty pump on the flimsy instruction written on the outside of the jug?

Something told him to follow the advice and choose the risky decision. He proceeded to pour the whole jug of water down the rusty old pump and furiously pumped up and down. Sure enough, the water gushed out! He had all he needed to drink. He filled the jug again, corked it, and added his own words beneath the instructions on the jug: "Believe me, it really works. You have to give it all away before you can get anything back."

The principle was well stated by the apostle Paul: "He who sows sparingly will also reap sparingly, and he who sows bountifully will also reap bountifully" (2 Cor. 9:6).

If you want to succeed, you have to "go for it" and give it all you've got.

The people who really succeed are the people who give extra effort and push themselves beyond their normal limits. There is a principle: "New powers are discovered every time you push yourself farther than you've ever gone before." There are deeper layers of energy, talent, and creativity within you, waiting to be tapped. No person ever fully discovers and develops all the potential within himself. Nobody ever drills the deepest well. Everybody—in his limited lifetime—falls short of uncovering the deeper talent and hidden possibility that lies far beneath the surface of his own consciousness.

**G**_____

_____

_____

*Every beginner is a winner!**

*At least he won over inertia and procrastination and a fear of starting.

# H Hope

*Hope* is holding on, praying expectantly. It's never giving up. It's never quitting.

A father once said to his boy, "Son, you gotta set a goal and never quit. Remember George Washington?"

The son said, "Yes."

"Jefferson?"

"Yes."

"Abraham Lincoln?"

"Yes."

"You know what they all had in common?"

"What?"

The father said, "They didn't quit. Remember Azador McIngle?"

The kid said, "No. Who was he?"

"See, you don't remember him! He quit!"

*Hope.* It is one of the most beautiful words in the New Testament. "And now abide faith, hope, love . . ." (1 Cor. 13:13).

At the International Psychiatric Congress in Madrid, Spain, which I attended, one of the main lectures was on the healing power of hope. Doctors, renowned psychiatrists from all over the world, gathered to discuss and agree that the single most important healing force is hope: hope of recovery, hope of loving and being loved, hope of making it, succeeding.

Carol Lovell is alive today because she had hope. Doctors attribute her survival after five bullet wounds in the head to hope, as much as anything else.

On September 4, 1981, Carol went to work early at the restaurant where she was employed as a bookkeeper. The building was empty, and she let herself in with her key. Soon Carol heard a knock at the door and recognized the man who stood there as a new custodian.

After she opened the door to him, he began slapping her around and demanded that she open the safe: "You're gonna be dead if you don't open the safe."

So, Carol opened the safe and gave him the money. *Now, she thought, he has what he's come for. He'll leave.*

But, the man was not done with Carol. He pulled her into the employee restroom, raped her, and shot her twice in the head.

Somehow, Carol maintained consciousness. Sure that her wounds would kill her, she prayed, "Lord, help me. I don't know how to die. I'm afraid. Give me the strength to die. Show me how." And then suddenly, she was able to pull herself to her feet. She thought, *I want to live; I don't want to die.* She ran to the front of the restaurant, and picked up the wrong phone, only to realize that she could not call out. She panicked when she realized her mistake, ran back to the office, and called a friend. She was asking her to call an ambulance when the man returned.

Seeing Carol, he shot her three more times. She fell to the floor, where she lay until the police and ambulance arrived.

She remained alert and amazingly calm as she described her attacker and informed the emergency attendants that she was wearing contact lenses. She was so calm, in fact, that the doctors felt freer to take time to determine the best way to remove the bullets from her head.

Her sister, Linda, arrived and began to fill her mind with hope and positive instructions. She told Carol, "You're going to be O.K. You're going to make it. Don't let your brain swell. Don't let your body bleed."

Amazingly, her brain never did swell, a common reaction to such a brain injury.

For weeks as Carol lay in intensive care, her sisters continued to feed her with positive thoughts and Scripture verses.

After six months of surgery, recovery, and therapy, Carol was walking and talking as she had before the accident. Her only residual difficulty after her attack has been an arm that tends to be uncooperative.

Carol's survival is incredible. She attributes her healing to hope. As she said to me, "Only prayer and positive thinking kept me going!"

Tough times never last, but tough people do. If you want to succeed, if you want to conquer, then *hope*—hold *o*n, praying *e*xpectantly!

H_____

_____

_____

## ▯ Imagine

Possibility thinking is in actuality the exercise of dynamic, creative, sanctified *imagination*.

Sir Edmund Hillary, who attempted to scale Mount Everest, lost one of the members of his team in the failed effort. He returned to a hero's welcome in London, England, where a banquet held in his honor was attended by the lords and ladies and powerful people of the British Empire. Behind the speakers' platform were huge blown-up photographs of Mount Everest. When Hillary arose to receive the acclaim of the distinguished audience, he turned around and faced the mountain and said, "Mount Everest, you have defeated me. But I will return. And I will defeat you. *Because you can't get any bigger and I can.*"

I recently went through a rigorous training program for a long-distance run. In the five-mile stretch I covered every morning for two weeks was one hill that was really a toughie. The first morning, it almost forced me to walk. The second morning wasn't much easier. The third morning, I believed it was better. On the fifth morning as I approached it, I began to repeat a Bible verse: "every mountain and hill shall be made low" (Is. 40:4).

Then I recalled Hillary's comment, and I said to myself,

"God is going to strengthen me. God will make me bigger and tougher. That hill is a toughie. But *it can't get any tougher, but I can.*" It's amazing how easily I ran that hill, once I allowed my mind to become controlled by these positive thoughts.

Imagine solutions to your problem. Imagine yourself scaling your mountain. Imagine yourself crossing the finishing line.

I_____

_____

_____

## J Junk

*Junk* the junk food of your mind. To keep hope alive, to be a creative imaginer, you have to throw out the tremendous load of junk food that we feed into our minds and emotions. What is emotional junk food? It's self-pity: "Why is this happening to me?" It's jealousy: "I don't think he's that good. He should have been laid off, instead of me." It's worry and anxiety. It's fear. Negative thoughts that stem from racial prejudices are also junk foods of the mind. People may have tried to put you down because of your color or national heritage, but you don't have to let them defeat you.

My friend Jester Hairston is an American treasure, an international institution. There isn't a high-school choir in the United States of America that hasn't sung one of the compositions or the arrangements of Jester Hairston. He is unquestionably the world's leading composer and arranger of Negro or Black spiritual music. I asked him, "What do you call it?"

He answered with a smile, "Negro, colored, Black, Afro-American folk songs."

"Jester, have you ever been the victim of racial prejudice?"

"I have been all my life. But I don't see any reason why I

should feature it. I have tried to outlive it. I can't just ignore it, but I have tried to outlive it. And I don't harbor the hatred of some people."

Jester has learned to junk the junk food of his mind. He has learned to outlive prejudice. Consequently, he has been a bridge-builder. His music, based in the roots of early Black American folk songs, has been sung by people the world over.

J_____

_____

_____

 **Knock**

*Knock* out depression, knock out discouragement, knock out all kinds of forecasts of gloom and doom. You may not be able to control everything that happens to you, but you can control how you will react. Even if the doctor has given you shattering news, you don't have to be knocked down. You can get up and fight. You can win—perhaps over the disease, but most certainly over the depression.

No one has fought more gallantly and won more graciously over the battle of cancer than beautiful Marguerite Piazza. This extraordinary woman sent me a cassette tape in which she told her story. I played her cassette one day while riding in my car. I was so moved that I had to pull over to the side of the road until she was finished.

It was in the peak of my career, performing in New York City, when I noticed a pink spot on my right cheek. I thought it was one of those 'zits,' as the kids say. I assumed it would go away. So I just put a little extra make-up on. But it didn't go away. Every time I was at the doctor for laryngitis or some other minor ailment I'd refer to my spot. They'd examine it, but always responded, "It's nothing. Don't worry about it." So I didn't. But it did not go away.

At this time, I was at a point in my life where I was known as the lady who had everything. I was one of the ten best-dressed women in the world. I was reported to be very beautiful. I was a star at the Metropolitan Opera. I had created a thing called "the act" for supper clubs. I was the first one to have dancers and all that kind of thing. *Variety* claimed it was the birth of a new form of show business. (Of course, today everybody does it.) I was married to a wonderful man who was a great, Southern gentleman and fun to live with. He had everything going for him.

Suddenly my world fell apart. Billy died of heart failure. Two weeks later, that spot on my cheek was diagnosed as melanoma, the worst form of skin cancer. It usually kills within seventeen months if it is not totally removed. They tried in three different operations to remove that melanoma from my cheek. They wanted to save my face because I was in show business. I was supposed to be beautiful, and you know show business is a business of beautiful people. If they did the radical surgery, I might end up like Scarface Lil.

The three operations weren't enough. The doctor said, "Marguerite, you must have radical surgery if you're going to live. You do have a choice. You can take a chance and decide not to have the radical. In so doing, you will keep your beauty, but you'll probably end up in a coffin. Or, you can let us do what we have to do—the radical. Then you'll have a possibility of living."

I was scheduled to sing that night. The house was sold out. The theater was packed with people who had come to hear me sing and see me dance.

What do you do at a time like that? Well, you do what you're paid to do. I was paid to lift people. So I prayed for strength. I went on. And each time there was a costume change between scenes or acts, and I took the costume off, hung it on the hanger, and got the new dress on, I hung my troubles on a hanger, left them in the closet, and went on stage. I sang my heart out and danced for all I was worth. The people loved it.

I did what I had to do on stage, and I did what I had to do for my children—I had the complete, radical surgery. Yes, I had six young children. I had no sisters or brothers. Now that their father was gone, I was all that they had. So, I promised the Lord if He would just let me live so I could take care of my children, that I'd never complain.

I went through the radical. They removed my entire right cheek, all the glands in my neck, the carotid artery, and the muscle in my right shoulder. I was the worst-looking sight you'd ever see in your whole life.

I came home. I showed the children what had happened, and I explained to them that I was going to be O.K. They were still very shaken from the recent death of their father. Yes, sir, I was going to be O.K.! I didn't know if I could go back into show business or go back into supper clubs. It takes a lot of fortitude, and I didn't know if everybody would accept me with this scarred face.

I had ten or eleven plastic surgeries to remove the scars. I'm singing again. I'm performing for my Lord, and He has pleased me. He has brought a wonderful man into my life who has become my husband and has been a great father to my children.

I liken my experience to that of a child who is totally absorbed in something. My son Gregory would be reading a book or watching the tube and I'd say, "Gregory, come here." He wouldn't seem to hear me. I once asked the doctor, "Do you think that child is deaf?"

He said, "No, of course not. He has a great sense of concentration. But, Marguerite, if you want his attention, go up to him and shake him a little bit. He'll look at you. Then tell him what you want."

That's the way it was with me and the Lord. He needed my attention. I wasn't doing exactly what He wanted me to do yet. So He shook me—with a second cancer. I couldn't believe it. But there it was. I went through seventy-two hours of radiation and another operation. That is when I learned that stress can kill you. It almost killed me because I was filled with stress. Stress was controlling me.

*If there's anything I've learned through all of this, it's that the mind is extremely important. What you focus your thoughts on will be manifested in your outer life. If you think stress and fear, they will manifest in your life. And if you think love and understanding, they will also manifest and bring to you all of the things that God wants you to have.*

[208]

## BUT TOUGH PEOPLE DO

Do as Marguerite did—knock out depression, discouragement, forecasts of gloom and doom. Take control of your life and your future by knocking out all negativity.

K_____

_____

_____

 **Laugh**

You must keep a sense of humor and be able to *laugh* at yourself. Have you heard the story of Oral Roberts, Billy Graham, and Robert Schuller? The story goes that they all died earlier than planned. Peter met them at the gate: "I'm sorry, guys. Your rooms aren't ready yet. You'll have to wait downstairs in hell until your room is ready."

Before long, Satan called and said, "Peter, hurry up and get these guys out of here. Oral Roberts is healing the sick. Billy Graham's saving all the souls, and Robert Schuller's raising money to air-condition the place!"

Believe me, you can't be a successful possibility thinker unless you can laugh at yourself and laugh at life's difficulties. If you keep your sense of humor and laugh, then you'll be able to love. I really don't think it's possible to love until you laugh first. People who try to love before they laugh take themselves too seriously.

There are too many counterfeit forms of love and too many people who say, "I love you because I need you," or "I love you because I want you." Such possessive forms of love are not real. They seek to *get* something from the other person instead of *giving* something. When you laugh, you can love, because then you're loving people because they need you and the joy you can bring to their life.

L_____

_____

_____

 **Make it happen**

You can make it happen when you *manage*, because possibility thinking is really another label for dynamic mental management. You make it happen.

Colonel Norman Vaughan is a man who has led one of the most exciting lives imaginable. He made it happen. He wanted adventure so he went after it.

The son of a financially capable father, Vaughan was a sophomore at Harvard when he picked up a paper and read: "Byrd to the South Pole." He felt destined to go. Something said to him, "Get going. Close your books." So he did. The next day he was at Admiral Byrd's house.

Norman rang the doorbell. The maid came, but wouldn't let him past the door. She said that only those who had an appointment could see Commander Byrd.

He was nothing but a college kid. After a moment of disappointment he turned and walked down the steps to the sidewalk. When he hit the sidewalk, he quickened his pace and almost ran to the newspaper office to see the man who had written the piece on Admiral Byrd. He asked the reporter to intercede for him and relay his hopes to Admiral Byrd.

It worked. Commander Byrd accepted his proposal.

So Norman left Harvard immediately. He went to where Admiral Byrd was assembling his dogs, and he devoted a year to the commander's work, sleeping on the ground in a tent, winter and summer. In order to eat, he volunteered to be a waiter at the nearest inn, in exchange for leftover food.

Admiral Byrd reviewed Norman's efforts and decided to take him on the expedition.

Since he had had experience driving dogsleds, Norman

was classified as one of the five professional dogsled drivers. They took ninety-seven dogs, ten teams, to unload the two ships. The entire expedition was one of the most exciting events in which anyone could ever participate. Norman was there because he made it happen. Admiral Byrd did not come to him. Norman's father did not approve of his quick departure from Harvard, so he did not finance Norman's venture. Norman wanted to make it—and he did. He made it happen!

He told me, "The most challenging moment of the whole expedition was when Admiral Byrd asked me if I could pull a Ford Tri-Motor from the ship out to Little America, a distance of nine miles. I said that I didn't know but that I'd try. So we put a long hawser from the ship out across the snow toward Little America. I brought all ninety-seven dogs with the various teams together in front of that airplane. We harnessed the dogs to that hawser and tried to get them started.

"In order to start a heavy load, you lift the gang line, and drop it. Well, lifting the gang line for ninety-seven dogs took two or three other men with me. We lifted it and let it go. And supposedly, when there was a slack in the line, all the dogs would pull. We worked an hour and a half, until suddenly, through no particular reason any of us could ever detect, the ship moved. When it moved, all ninety-seven dogs began to pull. We didn't stop until we hit Little America. We jogged along in front of that airplane with our dogs. And that's the largest sled dog team that was ever harnessed up until that time."

Do you want excitement? Do you want your dream to come true? Then make it happen!

**M**_____

_____

_____

**Negotiate**

If you want to get from *A* to *Z* in the Alphabet for Action for Possibility Thinkers you have to be able to *negotiate*, to compromise. You can't have your way all the time.

When we started in the drive-in theater twenty-five years ago, I began to dream of a church of my own. My first dream was for a forty-acre plot. However, when a forty-acre parcel became available, we couldn't afford it. So, I negotiated, I compromised, and I decided that we *actually* needed only ten acres. That's all we bought. Later on, we added another ten acres. Better half a loaf than none!

Scale down, if necessary. Don't be embarrassed. It's better to change plans while the ship is in port than to save face, only to sink in the middle of the ocean. Be willing to start smaller and add to your plans as you grow.

N_____

_____

_____

 **Overlook and overcome**

If you've made it to *O* you'll have been successful enough to know that you can't succeed without a team. You can't get very far without some kind of organization. That means that you will have to work with people. They're not going to be perfect; there will be times when they will let you down. They're going to make mistakes, and if you demand perfection from them, you're going to be hard to work for. The good people will leave. Therefore you have to overlook your own and other people's imperfections. When you overlook, you'll be able to overcome.

Do you have a problem that is so big that you don't know

how to handle it? Then maybe you need to overlook and look over.

What do I mean by "look over"? Let me explain it with a story.

One day a pastor went walking in the country and saw a cow looking over the wall. As he stood looking at the cow, he was approached by a member of his church who asked him, "Is something wrong, pastor?"

He replied, "Well, I'm having troubles."

The farmer said, "Pastor, look at the cow. What's that cow doing?"

"She's looking over the wall."

The farmer said, "Why do you think she's looking over the wall?"

"Oh, I don't know."

"She's looking over the wall because she can't see *through* it."

I must tell you that during my twenty-seven years in this church, I have come up against some walls I couldn't see through.

I've come to the conclusion that there are lots of problems that can't be solved. In my first book, *Move Ahead With Possibility Thinking*, there was a chapter entitled, "There's a Solution to Every Problem." I don't believe that any more. I think there are some problems that can't be solved. However, every problem can be overcome, manipulated, molded.

O_____

_____

_____

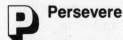 **Persevere**

*Persevere;* don't give up. Tough times never last, but tough people do.

You may have heard of Kathy Miller. Millions saw her story

when it was made into a movie for television. But, I want to share it with you because if anyone has persevered over tough times, it has been Kathy Miller.

When Kathy was thirteen, going on fourteen, she was struck by a car. This beautiful, bubbly, popular young woman, who had once been a runner, was suddenly motionless and silent. She lay in a coma, week after week without any sign of life.

Eleven weeks after the accident, Kathy regained consciousness, only to face her toughest battle. The accident had left her brain-damaged. She was like a baby who had to learn to eat, drink, walk, and talk. And when she finally got to the point where she was able to try to resume her life, she was bitterly disappointed.

By then her friends were in high school. They had continued to grow and mature, while Kathy had suffered a major setback. She had reverted to childhood, and had lost weight to the point where she weighed only about fifty pounds. She was skin and bones, and her speech and body motions were far from normal. When she compared herself to others, she fell short. Nobody could relate to her. It was a tough time for her.

But Kathy had a dream that kept her going. Her dream was to run in the North Banks 10,000 meter run.

Barely able to walk, running such an arduous race seemed absurd. But Kathy was determined. She trained vigorously, building her body for the race.

She wanted to run the course. Finishing would be like winning for Kathy.

On the day of the race, all of the other runners sprinted far ahead of her. Before long, she couldn't see them. All alone she ran, step after step, her body aching, her heart pounding, her lungs burning. Often she fell, sprawling face down onto the pavement. But she picked herself up, put one crippled foot a few inches ahead of the other, and dragged her other leg up to meet the foot. She repeated this process countless times. As she persevered, the blocks stretched into miles. The sun had risen high in the sky and was beginning to descend as Kathy neared the last stretch of her run. Just as she began to fear she couldn't continue, that she would have to quit, she saw some friends from high school who had felt uneasy around Kathy's disabilities. Now they were cheering her on: "Go, Kathy! Keep going! You're doing great!"

Kathy made it. She finished the race. She's a winner. In fact, she received the Philadelphia Sportswriters' Award as the most courageous athlete in America and the International Award for Valor.

She graduated from high school with honors—straight A's.

I said recently to Kathy, "You're a winner. You have persevered. But tell me, what do you say to people who lose, even after they've given it all they have?"

She replied, "To me, winning is not necessarily being first or best at something. When you give it all you've got, then you win. Winning to me is just that: Giving what you've got for the Lord, just coming through whatever trial you face."

I asked her another question: "What do you say to someone who has problems, who's really hurting?"

"My word to them would be to just hang in there and keep plugging at it. Know that you're winning through Christ and that He's there and He'll help in His perfect timing!"

*Persevere.* It's a very important word in our alphabet for action.

**P**_____

_____

_____

 **Quit**

*Quit* complaining because life isn't as nice as you want it. Look at what you have left, never at what you've lost. Quit remembering all of those negative, haunting memories.

## TOUGH TIMES NEVER LAST

This past week, I called on a dear friend of mine, Mrs. Putnam. She lives in Cleveland on the shores of Lake Erie. Not too long ago, at eighty-three, she fell and broke her hip. She said to me from her chair, "I was unconscious for three days; they thought I wouldn't live, but I did." Then she looked at me and said, "Dr. Schuller, how do you stay happy all the time?"

I said, "Well, for one thing I decided long ago to throw out all of the excess baggage of my mind. By that I mean the baggage of bad memories. Throw it out."

"How do you do that?"

Before I answered her, I looked at a picture of her deceased husband, hanging on the wall. He was a fantastic man, one of the great American lords of industry. I also noticed the picture of her son in uniform, killed in World War II. Now here she was, unable to walk. She repeated her question, "How do you unload the bad memories? How do you rid them from your life?"

I said, "Mrs. Putnam, can you stand?"

She said, "Oh, I think so."

I stretched out my hands. She took the blanket off her knees, and took hold of my hands. I held her tightly above the elbows and slowly led her until she was four feet from the window. And I asked, "What do you see?"

She said, "I see Lake Erie."

"I'll bet when you were younger you used to stand here on the lawn and throw a stone and you'd watch it fly into the lake."

She said, "Oh, yes, but I haven't done that for many years."

"Did you know that your mind can throw a bad thought a lot farther than your arm has ever thrown a stone? Mrs. Putnam, any time an unpleasant memory or any unpleasant feeling or a negative thought comes into your brain, I want you to stand, if not physically, at least mentally, right here and look through the window. With your mind, throw that thought through the glass until it sinks deep into the lake. Then I want you to sit down and read these lines." And I handed her a piece of paper on which I had just scrawled four lines from an anonymous author:

> I shut the door on yesterday
> and threw the key away.
> Tomorrow has no fears for me
> Since I have found today.

She said, "I can do it!"
So can you if you'll quit complaining!

Q_____

_____

_____

 **Reorganize**

If you haven't yet succeeded, then you have to say, "I need to *reorganize*." When you fail, you will need to reorganize. And when you succeed you will need to reorganize.

Whether you've failed or succeeded, chances are, there are parts of your life that need reorganization. The only person who doesn't have to reorganize constantly is the person for whom life and business has become static. Anybody whose life is static is dead.

I've been reorganizing the past month. I took a few days off with my wife and we prayed. I asked these questions, to myself, to God, to my wife:

1. Who am I?
2. Where have I come from?
3. How did I get here?
4. Where do I want to go?
5. How can I get there?

I knew who I was last month, and last year, but I'm constantly changing. I need to frequently reevaluate who I am and where I am going. And right now I'm reorganizing my life around the answers to those questions.

A few years ago the doctor told my wife that she had a cancerous tumor in her breast. Just before the surgery, she called her doctor and me to her bedside and said, "After the surgery I want to know what the score is. If cancer has spread through my body, and I have only twelve months to live, I want to know right away, because there are two things I want to do before I die." We agreed. However, thank God, her surgery was successful. We believe she's permanently cured. But about a year or two ago, I remembered what she had told me just before her surgery. I asked her, "Honey, do you remember what you said to me just before surgery? What are the two things you wanted to do?"

She said, "Number one, I wanted to organize all my closets and drawers. I didn't want to be dead and have other people go through the drawers and closets and say, 'Boy, what a mess!' The second thing I wanted to do was write a personal letter to each of my children."

Reorganize. Times change. You may have to change your whole corporate structure. You may have to abolish some departments. Sometimes you have to go back to get on the right track. Maybe you need to advance. Perhaps you need to retreat or regroup. Maybe you need to scale your operation up or down, maybe even close down. Whatever your situation is, chances are that you need to reorganize.

R_____

_____

_____

**S** **Share**

God can do tremendous things through the person who doesn't care who gets the credit and is willing to *share* the credit, *share* the power, and *share* the glory.

More than one company has been successful, only to reach a certain leveling-off period where it began to die. The reason? The guy who started and developed the business reached a point where he couldn't handle all the administration, but he couldn't bring himself to delegate it to others. Some people are afraid to delegate because they think no one else can do as good a job as they.

I've gone through that. But I came to this conclusion. It's better to let somebody else do a worse job than I would do, than not have it get done at all. The surprising thing is that, more often than not, they do a better job of it than I would have done!

Share your feelings and share your gratitude. Say "Thank you" to the people who helped make it happen. At the point of success, don't forget to share appreciation. I don't forget the fact that I'm totally dependent upon friends and members of the church who keep the ministry going. Share your appreciation by using that powerful word, "Thanks."

In a cynical moment of interviewing, a newspaper reporter said to Rudyard Kipling, "Mr. Kipling, I just read that somebody calculated that the money you make from your writings amounts to over one hundred dollars a word." Mr. Kipling raised his eyebrows and said, "Really? I wasn't aware of that." Then the reporter said, "Here's a hundred-dollar bill, Kipling. Give me one of your hundred-dollar words."

Kipling looked at the hundred-dollar bill, finally took it, quietly folded it up, and said, "Thanks." Then he turned and walked away.

S_____

_____

_____

 **Trade-off**

When you have begun to reorganize and share, then you will have to get ready to *trade-off.* That means that you will have to decide what you will give up in order to keep what you've got.

A minister friend of mine who played golf told his wife how important it was. He said, "It's good for my work. I meet important men and women on the golf course." But one day as he was heading for the car with his clubs, his little four-year-old boy, watching at the screen door, said, "Daddy, can I go with you?"

The minister said, "Sorry, son, you can't go golfing with me." The little boy's eyes filled with tears. The father waved, started the car, and drove off. He had only gone about two blocks when he turned around, drove back, rushed into the house, swept his son in his arms, and said, "Hey, buddy, would you rather go fishing?" At that point, he made a great trade-off, exchanging one human priority for a better one.

The other day I was in Paul Harvey's studio in Chicago as he was making his broadcast. Paul said, "It's time for me to go on the air; but why don't you join me in the studio? It's live, you know." I went in the studio. He closed the door. The red light was blinking. He cleared his throat. "Good morning, Americans, this is Paul Harvey speaking." And away he went. He said, "I happen to know somebody, a minister, who, I'm told, chose to fail in order that he could choose to succeed. Is that right, Robert Schuller?"

I said, "Right, Paul Harvey. I chose to fail at golf, because I wanted to succeed as a father. Yes, I traded-off my hobby of playing golf in favor of my desire to be a successful dad." At this time, maybe you have to trade-off power for peace, dollars for joy, and glory for the greater joy of seeing other people grow.

T_____

_____

_____

*The me
I see…
is the
me I'll be!*

## Unlock

*Unlock* some human values you never experienced before—faith, hope, and love. Let these values be the driving force propelling you toward true success. What is success? It is being in a position to help others who are hurting.

I know of no man who is more successful than Dr. Howard House.

If you were to ask medical doctors around the world to name those doctors that rank in the highest category of specialists concerning surgery and diseases of the ear, the first to be named would be Dr. Howard P. House of Los Angeles. He is president of a world-renowned, unexcelled research center for the development of solutions to hearing problems.

I recently had the honor of meeting this remarkable man. I was immediately impressed by the love and concern he had for the people he helps. He told me he first decided to become a doctor when he announced to his father, a renowned dentist, that he would follow in his footsteps.

His father surprised him, however, by responding, "If I had it to do over again, I would go to medical school and then into dentistry, because you can't divorce the teeth from the rest of the body."

Years later, when Howard finished medical training, he apologized to his father for going into medicine instead of dentistry. His father replied, "Do you remember that evening when I suggested you go into medicine instead of dentistry? Why do you think I did that? Because medicine is a much broader field. It offers many more opportunities for research and development and care of people."

*Concern for people.* This is what motivated Dr. House. This is what spurred him to learn all he could. At the close of his medical education, as Howard was being drawn towards a specialty in eyes, ears, nose, and throat, his father asked him, "Howard, is there anyone in this country that knows more about eyes, ears, noses, and throats than you do?"

Howard had to say, "Of course."

His father said, "There will never be a better time than now to visit each one of those doctors and see what motivated him, what made him the man he is today." So in 1937 he set out for Stockholm, Sweden, to see for the very first time a new operation to restore hearing performed by a Professor Homgren. When Howard House saw this remarkable surgery, he decided at that moment that it's much more important to create a sense of hearing for a person who is hard-of-hearing than to give him a better-looking nose.

Since then he has performed more than thirty-two thousand ear surgeries. And along with his brother Bill, he has developed an implant of minute wires that restores hearing after otoschlerosis, a progressive hearing-loss disease.

They have also developed the cochlear implant, little electrodes in the inner ear that bring hearing to deaf children.

He has placed implants in more than two hundred such patients, the first in 1968. He recalled to me the joy he felt recently when, for the first time, he did an implant on a three-year-old child: "Just to watch this child delight with hearing for the first time, sounds lost because of meningitis when she was a year and a half old! She loves the sounds! She loves to hear the sound of her feet as she walks on the floor. It brings tears to all of our eyes when we see this little girl's response."

Literally thousands of doctors come from around the world to the House Institute to learn the techniques of the House brothers.

"A brilliant man," you say. Yes, you are right. Smarter than you? I doubt it. I've seen his college transcripts. Are you ready for this? At the end of his first year in college he had a 2.0 grade-point average. He had mostly *D*'s, including a *D* in chemistry. He even had one *F*. The following year, he didn't do any better. In fact, he did worse. He ended up with a 1.35 grade-point average. The third year, he perked up and got all the way up to a 2.2. At that point, Howard went to see Dean McKibben at the University of Southern California and told him he was interested in going into medicine. The dean said, "You're not serious."

But he did tell Howard that if he worked hard and came back the next year with a better grade, he'd have a place for him. So Howard dropped a number of extracurricular activities. His grades improved. Thanks to Dean McKibben, he entered medical school.

Today, more than thirty-two thousand people have discovered the glory of sound thanks to a caring, dedicated man—Dr. Howard House—but only because he unlocked the love and faith in his heart and let them be the driving force of his life.

U_____

_____

_____

 **Visualize**

*Visualize* the dream before you. Don't ever lose the vision. When you lose the vision, you're dead. Where there are no dreams, people perish.

A young lad came to college as a freshman and checked into his room. The first thing he did was hammer a big brass letter *V* on his door. Everybody asked him what it was for, but he wouldn't tell them. He kept it polished, and it was always the first thing put up in his room as he moved from dorm to dorm. Finally he graduated and at the commencement exercise, his name was announced as valedictorian. When he walked across the stage, there in his left hand was his polished brass letter *V*.

Set new goals. Believe you can reach them. Visualize defeat and you will be defeated. Visualize ultimate success, and you will achieve it! *What you see is what you'll be.*

I recently spoke at a convention of two thousand salespersons employed by an obviously very successful direct sales business woman. The leader's father, who was a university graduate, was understandably disappointed when she dropped out of high school. As a result of his disappointment, this woman developed a terribly negative self-image. After years of feeling like a flop and a failure, she was introduced to possibility thinking. As a result she made a trip to California and worshiped in the Crystal Cathedral.

Soon after, she learned of a good, useful product that people needed. She believed in it. Friends encouraged her to market this product and become a salesperson. "But," she said, "I can't be a salesperson. I don't know anything about it. And besides I'm not very smart. I never finished school." But before she threw the idea away for good, she remembered these words: "With God all things are possible." She gave it a try. She succeeded, and a few days ago I spoke to two thousand of her employees.

Success all starts in your head, and every person has the freedom to choose to be a success or not. It's that simple: Choose to succeed. See yourself as a successful person, and you will be a successful person.

Visualize. *The me I see is the me I'll be.* You can be anything or anyone you want to be if you can learn to believe in yourself.

It is true that God gives different abilities and different gifts to different people, but, ultimately, success doesn't come through special abilities. You can look at people in your profession who are higher up the ladder than you are. You know that you are as talented as they. Conversely, you can look down the ladder only to see a crowd of equally talented people nipping at your heels.

Neither success nor self-esteem necessarily comes through *talent*. Nor do they necessarily come through *territory*. Some people surmise that they would find success if they lived in a particular town or state. Although it is easier to succeed in America than in any other country, merely living in America does not guarantee success.

I was in Hong Kong not long after the Communist takeover, when the Chinese poured onto that island. I was in Berlin shortly after the Wall went up to keep people rushing from the East to the West. Today, people are fleeing to America. Why? Because life is easier in America than in any other country. But, ultimately, success doesn't come from where you are but from the way you think! It comes from visualizing your dream. That's why possibility thinkers who may not have the talent, the territory, or the training achieve the impossible. They go through tough times and they survive. Why? Because they believe in themselves. They feel that they have as much right as anyone else to be happy and to be successful.

You won't find real success or self-worth through the right *ties*, nor will you find it in mere undeveloped *talent*, nor in living in the right town, community, country, or *territory*. You won't necessarily find success or self-esteem through *training* either.

Success comes from visualizing yourself the way you want to be. Do you think you are terrific? You are! You just have to believe in yourself. I probably won't be able to convince you of it, for persons can't be convinced they are beautiful if they don't think they're beautiful.

I recall every one of my four daughters, at least once in their lives, when they got a new haircut or permanent, asking me, "How does it look?" I would say, "It looks great." But in their uncertainty they replied, "Oh, I don't think it does. I bet it doesn't look good at all!"

Even though I thought it looked great and I told them so, they remained unconvinced. The same is true for you. I can convince you of your talents, but I can't convince you of what you can accomplish in life. Only one person can convince you . . . God. The way you think about yourself depends on the way you think about God. I call it possibility thinking. It's the secret of success! Why is it so powerful? It's powerful because of what it does for you. It tells you that you are potentially as smart and inherently successful as any other person.

How do you visualize yourself? *The me I see is the me I'll be.* I want you to ask yourself this question: "What new goals would I set for myself, if I could be sure that I would succeed?" Think about it. Pray about it. And get ready to act on it.

Paul said it: "I can do all things through Christ who strengthens me" (Phil. 4:13). Where do I get my dreams? Why, from Jesus Christ. God put you in this world. He has a dream for you. Open up to His dream and see yourself as He sees you. "As he [man, woman, or child] thinks in his heart, so is he" (Prov. 23:7).

I shall never forget him. I met him this past year at a conference. He was only twenty-two years of age, but one of the top salespersons. The young man had been diagnosed a few years earlier with cystic fibrosis. After his fatal disease was discovered, nobody would hire him. He was told, "You won't live long enough to make it worthwhile."

His father and mother were poor. They could hardly pay the medical bills.

He thought, *I may be sick; I may be dying; but I can still do something. It would be much better to accomplish something great than to just sit here and wait to die.* So he accepted an invitation to join a direct sales business. He was a terrific salesman, because, as he said, "I don't have long to live, so if I want to break any records, I'd better do it in a hurry."

When I saw him, he was wearing a Hawaiian shirt. He said, "Do you know why I'm wearing this shirt? After I made enough money to put a savings account aside to take care of my funeral expenses, I gave some of the rest to the Lord, and I decided to take my mother and father to Hawaii. We just got back. We had a wonderful time!" He was only skin and bones under the Hawaiian T-shirt. He's no longer with us. But, boy, he's really alive now, for he knew the Lord.

*The me I see is the me I'll be.*

How do you see yourself?

There are too many people today who are suffering from an inferiority complex. There are several factors in our society that could contribute to it. Too many rely on these factors as excuses for not being all that they could be. Others are hurt and they say, "What's the point of trying, just to get knocked down again?"

But some people have learned to rise above the blows that life has dealt them. They discover that they are somebody special, regardless of what others say or how they are treated. They keep proving the truth of this book. *Tough times never last, but tough people do!*

I think of the woman who emigrated from Mexico to the United States with her husband and children. On their way to "paradise," at the border in El Paso, Texas, her husband deserted her, leaving her stranded with the children. A divorcee, twenty-two years of age with two kids, she was poverty-stricken. With the few dollars in her pocket, she bought bus tickets to California. There she was sure she could find work. She did find a job—an awful job, working from midnight until six o'clock in the morning, making tacos. She earned only a few dollars, but she ate meagerly and saved a dime from every dollar she earned.

Why did she save? She saved because she was visualizing a dream—she wanted to own a taco shop. One day she took the few dollars she'd managed to save, went to a banker, and said, "There's a little place I'd like to buy. If you'd loan me a few thousand dollars, I can have my own taco shop."

The banker, impressed by her, decided to take a chance and loaned her the money. She was twenty-five years old and the owner of a little taco shop. She worked hard at it, and eventually, she expanded and expanded until today, fifteen years later, she has the largest wholesale business of Mexican products in America. She went on to become the treasurer of the United States. Her name is Ramona Banuelos.

She was asked, "What's the biggest problem facing your people in America today?"

She replied, "Children are growing up in America thinking they are inferior. I'll never forget the day my little daughter came home from school and said, 'Mama, am I Spanish or Mexican?' When I said, 'You're Mexican,' her face dropped. She was so depressed. She said, 'I wish I were Spanish.' When I wanted to know why it mattered, she answered, 'Because the Spanish people are very smart and Mexicans aren't.'"

Ramona Banuelos said, "That's not true! Mexicans are not inferior!" To prove her point, she took her children to Mexico, and she showed them the ruins of the Aztec temples, telling them, "These were built by Mexicans not Spaniards." She showed them the wide boulevards and the great architecture. "These were built by the Aztecs; that's the blood you have in you. Be proud you are a Mexican—you have good blood in you!"

You are somebody. You bet you are. No matter what your race, no matter what your color, no matter what your ethnic background, you are the child of a survivor! That's right! If you trace your roots to Africa, Europe, Mexico, or Malaysia, or wherever, you will find times of great suffering in the history of your people.

Success doesn't come through the ways you may think it comes, it comes through the way you think! Think positively. Visualize success!

V_____

_____

_____

 **Work**

There is no substitute for *work*.

The other night, my wife and I took the world famous pianist, Roger Williams, to dinner in appreciation for the times he has donated his talents to our ministry. At ten o'clock, he said, "Well, I really have to go. I must get to work."

"Work? At this time?"

"Yes, it's a rehearsal," he said. "I will go home and rehearse from ten o'clock till about two o'clock. I'll sleep for about three or four hours, and then I'll get up and rehearse for another two hours."

I asked, "Do you do that every day?"

He said, "Oh, yes, every day."

The people at the top of the ladder work harder than anyone else. Why? Because they have gotten into the habit of working hard. There is no substitute for it. Success is spelled w-o-r-k.

If you ever flunked a college course, it wasn't because you weren't smart enough. You just didn't apply yourself. The difference in IQ isn't that significant on a college level; the difference is in application.

A little boy in patched overalls asked a rich general contractor in fancy clothes, observing the skyscraper rising under his supervision, "How can I be rich like you when I grow up?"

The tough old construction man looked at the little fellow and, using the crusty language of one who had come up from the soil of labor, said, "Buy a red shirt, son, and work like hell."

The startled little boy obviously didn't understand what the older man was telling him. The man pointed to the workmen crawling around several stories of the open steel framework of the rising skyscraper and said to the boy, "Look at those men working there. They all work for me. I don't know them by name. I've never met some of them. But look at that fellow in the red shirt. Everybody else is wearing blue. I've noticed that the man in red works harder than anyone else. He comes in every morning, just a bit earlier than anybody else. He seems to work faster than anybody else. He is the last one to clock off the job. He stands out from the crowd because he wears that red shirt every day. I'm about to go over there and ask him to be my supervisor. From there, I suspect he is going to rise to the top and maybe become one of my vice presidents.

"That's how I made it, son. I decided to work a little harder and a little better than anybody else on the job. And if I wore blue overalls, nobody would ever notice me. So I always wore a striped shirt. I worked harder. I stood out from the crowd. I was noticed. I got the promotions. I saved my money. And that's how I got where I am today."

W_____

_____

_____

 **X-ray**

If you're pursuing a job, if you're on your way toward a goal, if you've got a dream, and you've gotten this far, then it's high time you stopped once more and *x-rayed* your deepest motives.

There are people who have high moral and ethical integrity in their businesses. If you took a moral, spiritual, and an ethical x-ray of one of these people, put it up on the board, and flipped the light on, you'd say, "Wow, he's in great shape!" However, if you saw your own x-ray, you might not like what you see. You've been making a lot of money; that's great. I tell people, "Make all the money you can legally. Save all you can. Then give all you can. But if dollars become an end in themselves, then you're in trouble."

You need to ask yourself, first, "What do I really want to accomplish?" Then ask yourself, "If I continue the way I am, will I get to where I really want to go?" Then you ask a third question: "If I get there, will I be happy? And will that really fulfill me at my deepest level?" That's what you call x-ray.

X_____

_____

_____

# Y Yield

In a great verse from the Book of Romans, Paul said, "Yield yourselves unto God" (Rom. 6:13 KJV). When it's all said and done, you must have done this long before you come to the Z of the alphabet for action.

By the time you've asked, "Where have I come from; what do I want; where am I going; will I be happy if I get there?," then you must be ready to yield it all to God. By the time you get through the x-ray, you may find out that you've been running after the world, but neglecting your own soul. Jesus said it: "For what will it profit a man if he gains the whole world, and loses his own soul?" (Mark 8:36).

Yield yourself to God, because you're very close to the Z, and the Z is the end.

The late Senator Hubert Humphrey said to me, shortly before he died, that he wanted to come to the end of his life with pride behind him, love around him, and hope ahead of him. How will you come to your end? What will it be like? After life, what do you take with you? If you leave it behind, who gets it?

I met a man on a plane. I did not recognize his face, though his name is a household word. He said, "Dr. Schuller, I want to tell you—I like you on television."

I said, "Thank you."

"My wife and my mother never miss you either."

"Thank you."

He said, "My name is Bear Bryant."

I said, "It's always super to meet a great Christian."

He protested, "I'm not sure I am a Christian!"

I asked, "Well, don't you believe in Jesus?"

"Yeah, I believe in Jesus, sure."

"Why do you think you're not a Christian?"

"Well," he said, "first of all, I don't have the feeling. These born-again Christians have a feeling that I don't think I have.

I've talked to Billy Graham, I've talked to Oral Roberts, and I'm talking to you. I still don't have that feeling.

"And a second thing bothers me," he said. "There are some things in the Bible I just cannot understand. It says in the Bible that this prophet sent some bears to eat up some little kids. I don't think God would want a bear to eat up little kids."

I said, "What else?"

He said, "The third thing is, I do some things I shouldn't do. Like smoking; I shouldn't smoke if I am a Christian."

I said, "Coach, I want to be your coach on the spiritual plane. A Christian is not somebody who understands and believes in every word in the Bible. That's not the definition of a Christian. When you get to heaven, God isn't going to ask, 'Do you believe in every word in the Bible?' That's not the judgment. I think Christians all believe the Bible is the Word of God, but there may be some things they have difficulty understanding. You're not saved by the Book, you're saved by the blood.

"Also, Christianity isn't a feeling, it is a faith. I'd have to agree with you—I've never had a moment when I would say I was 'born again' in the sense that one day was black and the next day, white. I never had that. Christianity is faith, not feeling.

"Finally, being a Christian is surely not a matter of being a perfect person. I have my sins, too. I'm not perfect."

He said, "I wish I knew that, if the end were to come, I would go to heaven."

I said, "Well, I can help you there."

I took a piece of paper, and I wrote Jesus' promise: "The one who comes to me I will by no means cast out" (John 6:37).

I said, "Look at that, coach. That's a promise Jesus made. I know that when my end comes, I will step into the sunshine and not into the darkness. There will be eternal daylight, not eternal darkness, for me. I believe in heaven. If I believe in a yes, there's got to be a no. If I believe in light, there's got to be darkness. If I believe in heaven, there has to be a hell.

[233]

"Not everybody's going to heaven, coach. When I go there, I'm going to be carrying in my hand and my heart this promise of Jesus: 'The one who comes to me I will by no means cast out.'

"Jesus is my Friend. He would never turn a friend away. Do you believe that?"

He said, "Yes, sir."

I drew a straight line and dated it. I said, "O.K., coach, sign it."

He looked at the paper and said, "Well, I don't know if I can be sure if I should sign that or not today."

I said, "*I* can't be sure that this plane will land, either."

He said, "I'll sign it!"

Yield your life and your problems to God. Once you've given God control of your life, it won't be free from difficulty. God has not promised that our skies will always be blue, but He has promised to see us through.

My daughter Sheila gave her life to God years ago. Her life has been full—a fulfilling career, a loving husband, and two delightful boys, Jason, two, and Christopher, three months.

Yet her life had not been free from tough times. Last Saturday, the phone rang as we were busy preparing for my daughter Carol's birthday party. I answered the phone. It was Sheila.

"Dad, I'm here at Children's Hospital. It's Christopher. They say he has asthma, a double ear infection, and spinal meningitis. They did a spinal tap. It's positive. There are some cells in the spinal fluid." Then she broke down: "Pray for my baby."

Sheila and her husband, Jim, followed the nurse down the hospital corridor. She held her hot little baby close to her. When she glanced up, she saw to her surprise, written on the doors, "Intensive Care Unit." They stepped into a world of machines and individual rooms with windows. Through them, they could see other babies, some in oxygen tents, all hooked up to monitors.

The nurse took Sheila's baby from her, undressed him, hooked him up to monitors, and placed him in a steel crib.

Then the doctors came in, hovered over him, and examined him thoroughly.

The primary doctor said, "Mr. and Mrs. Coleman, we will be starting an IV with medication for the asthma and antibiotics for the infection and meningitis. My suggestion to you is to go home and get some rest. Your baby will need you more tomorrow than today."

So Jim and Sheila went home, leaving Christopher in the care of his nurses. They went home to their toddler Jason who needed them too. But when they stepped into their home, it felt strangely empty. When Jim went down the hall to tuck Jason in for the night, he glanced in the empty nursery. He went in and placed Christopher's little blue Bible in the empty crib.

As Sheila picked up the toys Jason had left around, she felt a pang of emptiness. When she looked at Christopher's empty infant chair, oh, how she missed the big, beautiful smile of her little butterball.

As she went to turn out the lights, she decided to leave on the light that shines over the picture of Jesus in their family room. The next morning Sheila awoke suddenly and remembered the empty crib down the hall. She thought of her baby in the hospital and ached to hold him.

The clock said, "4:30," but Sheila was unable to sleep. She went downstairs. Looking at her picture of Jesus, she prayed, "Lord, I need to feel You. I need to *feel* that You are real." In her mind He spoke to her. She saw Jesus in His soft, flowing robe, holding Christopher just as she wanted to hold him. Christopher seemed at home in His arms, just as he did in hers. Then she felt her Lord say, "Sheila, he's my baby too."

Sheila said to me later, "Dad, when Jesus said that, I didn't know if He meant that I was going to get to keep Christopher for a while longer, or if He was going to take Christopher to be with Him. But, it didn't matter. Either way, it didn't matter. For I had such peace. I felt my whole being bathed in peace because I had yielded my baby and my problems to Jesus. I knew that Jesus loved Christopher as much as I did, and that He was holding him for me even when I couldn't."

[235]

Yield your life and your problems to God. Let go and let God. A friend sent me this poem. I think it's terrific.

**Let Go and Let God**

As children bring their broken toys
  with tears for us to mend,

I brought my broken dreams to God,
  because He was my Friend.

But then, instead of leaving Him
  in peace to work alone,

I hung around and tried to help
  with ways that were my own.

At last I snatched them back and cried,
  "How can You be so slow?"

"My child," He said, "what could I do?
  You never did let go."
  —UNKNOWN

## Z Zip it up

Jesus said, "I am the Alpha and the Omega, the Beginning and the End, the First and the Last" (Rev. 22:13). If you live by this creed, x-ray your motives, and yield it all to God, then you come to the end and you can *zip it up.*

You can face whatever is ahead of you, and with Christ as your Friend, you can succeed.

Z_____

_____

_____

When the Queen of England visited Southern California, Mayor Tom Bradley invited a small group of celebrities to a private luncheon for Her Majesty and Prince Philip. I was honored to be included in that small group.

At the event a lady approached me whom I did not recognize. "You don't know me, Dr. Schuller," she said, continuing, "but I'm John Wayne's daughter. I know that you and Dad were good friends. I know that you prayed for him before his surgery in Newport Beach. But I don't know if anybody told you about what happened in his life before he died." She smiled, her eyes glazed in a mist of love.

"He never missed your telecast. One Sunday morning you did something you very seldom have done. You said, 'There must come the time in our life when we really surrender our life entirely to the Lord. Today may be the day when you should slip out of the chair, get down on your knees, and yield your life completely to God. Ask Him to forgive you of your sins. Ask Him to save your immortal soul.'"

Now as she looked at me, John Wayne's daughter said, "Dr. Schuller, my father was so sick in his bed—but he got out of his bed, got down on his knees, and prayed your closing prayer with you and turned his life completely over to the Lord!"

Probably no person has an image for being a tougher tough guy than John Wayne. Yet, even he found that to face the ultimate battle he needed superstrength. And that's what God provides when we turn our lives over completely to Him.

"If God is for us, who can be against us?" (Rom. 8:31) That is the ultimate secret of becoming tough enough to face the toughest battle and win! Only then can you be sure that your life will prove the truth of the title of this book: "Tough times never last, but tough people do!"—eternally!

It is my prayer that this book has been an answer to the most important prayer that you could be praying today:

*Lord,*
*give me*
*the guidance*
*to know*
*when to hold on*
*and*
*when to let go*
*and the grace*
*to make*
*the right decision*
*with dignity.*

# TOUGH MINDED FAITH FOR TENDER HEARTED PEOPLE

# To

*the thousands of good people*
*who believe in me enough*
*to encourage me with*
*their prayers and support*
*—even though we may never*
*have a chance to meet*
*face to face.*

# Contents

# Introduction

"Of course you can! It's possible! All you do is start and take one step at a time," the guide in the Cologne Cathedral said, encouraging Mrs. Schuller and me to take the challenging climb inside the tower. "It'll be worthwhile—I guarantee you," he promised, continuing, "the thrill of making it to the top is fantastic!" He kept nudging us on: "Come on, it's just one step, then the second, then the third, and before you know it, if you don't quit, you'll have a few hundred behind you, and you will make it! And you will never forget it!"

How right he was. "One step at a time." And we did it! The view was sensational. The ecstasy of achievement still stirs my blood as I recall it. Now, my friend, let me be your guide to super-successful living. My promise? You can climb to the top! My secret? All you have to do is get motivated today—and stay motivated every day until you achieve your God-inspired goal!

How do you do it? Get started! And keep at it one step at a time.

Simply start each day with a positive step up the tower of faith!

Yes, here are 366 steps on a walk of faith designed to build within your personality and soul a mountain-moving, motivational *faith*.

Yes, faith is a noun—but it must become a verb! Action! So I have selected 366 verbs, each designed to reveal a facet of that sparkling diamond we call faith. The self-motivation to get up and get going—that's what faith is all about! Then I have selected 366 faith-generating, human-motivating Bible verses to start off each day. By exercising these verbs and the

[249]

powerful Bible verses in your daily life, you will release inner emotional powers from their imprisonment. Yes, subconscious emotional restrictions can bind and repress the incredible potential emotional strength that lies dormant within you *right now!* For decades, I have carefully studied the emotional blockages that constrict the forceful flow of emotional strength. I have outlined here 366 days of motivational treatment that will surely, steadily, slowly, but successfully give you emotional freedom! Find yourself free at last! You will reach a point somewhere along this walk of faith where you will feel as if you are power-driven! You will sense that you are upward bound! You will feel tremendous emotional health, energy, and power being released within you! You will finally experience the incredible, powerful truth in this promise of Jesus Christ: "If you have faith as a mustard seed, you will say to this mountain, 'Move . . .'; and nothing will be impossible for you" (Matt. 17:20).

You will have developed in a one-year spiritual fitness program a tough-minded faith that will make it possible for you to go through tough times with surviving power!

What greater gift could I give you? What greater blessing could God bestow upon your life than the gift of a tough-minded faith for a tenderhearted person?

O.K.? Let's take that first step and never stop for the next year.

You'll never be the same again.

ROBERT HAROLD SCHULLER

## Trusting the unprovable

"You will seek Me and find Me, when you
search for Me with all your heart."—JEREMIAH
29:13

"I would love to be a believer, if I knew it was the truth," an **1**
intelligent young Japanese man said to me. "Prove it to me.
That's what the unbelieving world is waiting for. We're scientific. We want *proof* before we believe."

"But that's a contradiction," I answered. "If there is proof,
there no longer is room for belief. For faith believes in that
which cannot be proven. Let me sum it up in this sentence:

**When proof is possible, faith becomes impossible."**

The young man asked, "But if God wants us to be believers,
why didn't He prove Himself to us?"

I quoted Hebrews 11:6. "Without faith it is impossible to
please [God]."

The same is true in human relationships. When somebody
believes in you before you've earned their trust, you have been
honored! When they trust you even though you didn't display
your credentials, faith is born.

I remember the people who believed in me when I started
our ministry. I was unknown. I had no reputation. Yet they
believed in me before I could prove myself to them. To this
day I have deep affection for and gratitude to those special
persons.

God knew what He was doing when He established the belief system. When you strip away all mystery and leave the
truth naked and mathematically scientific, something sweet
and attractive is lost.

There will always be the unknown. There will always be
the unprovable. But faith confronts those frontiers with a
thrilling leap. Then life becomes vibrant with adventure!

## Dreaming God's dream

"Be renewed in the spirit of your mind."—
EPHESIANS 4:23

**2**  What's the purpose of life anyway?
Only to eat, drink, work, play, make love?
Or do you have a brain designed to dream dreams?
Is your mind created to be an architect, drawing plans?
Can you imagine beautiful accomplishments?

Think of this:
The human being
is the only creature in the universe
that has the capacity for exercising creative imagination!

This divine quality of *dreaming*
what you want to be,
where you want to go,
what you'd love to do,
projects you hope to achieve,
goals you'd like to reach—
all of this makes you human
and the most unique creature in all of creation!

You really are "made in the image" of the Creator–God!
So you are fulfilling your destiny
as a child of God in human flesh
when you start dreaming the beautiful
dreams God Himself is inspiring in your mind.

A radio is designed to pick up the sounds that are here in this room now!
A television is engineered to pick up the moving pictures that are in the air waves around you now.
Your mind was invented and created by God to pick up the messages and mental pictures He is sending your way.

That's exciting!
Faith is dreaming God's dreams!

## *Breathing your native air*

"I have come that they may have life, and that they may have it more abundantly."—JOHN 10:10

It's terribly important to understand that a believer is a normal person. Faith is the mark of normality. A persistently negative and cynical attitude is a mark of emotional illness.

Birds were designed to fly. The air under the wings of a bird is the natural habitat of the flying fowl.

Water is the natural habitat of the fish.

**Faith is the native air to be breathed in and out by human beings.**

It is normal to have faith. It is abnormal to be cynical. Therefore you welcome all stimuli that would encourage you to have faith. Reject all negative forces that would destroy faith and replace it with unbelief.

When you practice positive belief, you are more controlled by positive emotions—love, joy, courage, faith, enthusiasm.

These are the qualities of an emotionally healthy person. Persons who are not breathing the natural air of faith, but are breathing the polluted air of doubt and unbelief, are quickly susceptible to a lower morality. They are quickly consumed by negative emotions—all of which are measured and marked as symptoms of something less than true wholeness and health as a human being.

You were created to be a believer!

Faith is finding your native air.

That's why you feel so great when you're optimistic!

Thank You, Father, for causing me to be a normal, healthy human being by motivating me to walk the walk of faith. Amen.

## Wanting more out of life

"Delight yourself also in the Lord,/And He shall give you the desires of your heart."—PSALM 37:4

**4** Faith is a choice, not an argument.
It is a decision, not a debate.
It is a commitment, not a controversy.
Faith fulfills some need in your heart.
It can be defined as wanting more out of life.

Even the superaffluent are attracted to faith; they soon realize that all of their wealth, social standing, and personal power leave a void in their lives. When you have more money than you can enjoy what is left?

Saint Augustine said: "Our souls are restless till they rest in Thee." We suspect that out there, somewhere, there is always something more. From where does this intuition for "something more" come? It is built into our nature.

The human being has been called an incurably religious animal by instinct and nature.

**Be careful what you want—you'll get it! Wanting is believing, and believing produces results.**

Strong faith is often the expression of deep desire.

Likewise doubt is the lack of desire. A host of conscious or subconscious forces can keep you from wanting to believe. Fears of what God might do *to* your life or *in* your life can keep you from wanting to believe. Internalized guilt can make the possibility of God a threatening concept. Deep-seated negative emotions can kill the desire to believe leaving you with a negative inclination to doubt. Having trouble believing? Why don't you want to believe?

Our Bible verse today contains God's promise of blessings upon faith. God promises to bless the person who has strong desires. This is because in God's eyes desire and faith are one and the same: "He shall give you the desires of your heart."

*FAITH IS . . .*
## *Doubting your doubts*

"God is not the God of the dead, but of the
living."—MATTHEW 22:32

"There lives more faith in honest doubt, than in half the    **5**
creeds," Alfred Lord Tennyson wrote in *In Memoriam*.

I find that some people who have serious questions about
the existence of God want desperately to believe. Their probing inquiry reflects thoughtful doubt.

Actually, they are far more responsible and serious in their
pursuit of a commitment to God than those who blindly re-
cite cold creeds without really daring to explore the tough
questions.

**Doubt can be a positive force when we learn to doubt
our doubts and have faith in our faith!**

It is quite apparent that the believer in God and the Bible
has as strong a foundation for a rational system of belief as any
doubter has for the philosophy of irreligion he has fabricated.

Faith in God will
    increase your moral strength,
        increase your days of joy,
            reduce your days of despair.

I've never seen a person who has been more respected as a
leader in the philosophy and faith of religion than Jesus
Christ.

Jesus believed in God. He believed in prayer.

He believed in heaven and hell and eternal life.

He believed in salvation.

He believed in every single human being!

He believed in possibility thinking and He believed in faith.

If your doubts collide and clash with the viewpoint of Jesus
Christ, it is the better part of wisdom to believe the believer
and doubt the doubter. Then you are on your way to a great
life.

## Surfing on the waves

"The LORD on high is mightier/Than the noise
of many waters,/Than the mighty waves of the
sea."—PSALM 93:4

**6** I am one who enjoys the seashore, where the water laps
lazily over the sandy edge. It is there I find tranquility and
creativity. But on occasion, I have watched surfers ride the
wonderful, wild, and wicked waves. They inspire and motivate me!

Quietly, patiently, the surfers lie waiting on their slender,
slippery surfboards, poised and ready to leap to action at any
moment!

Suddenly, there it is! The beginning of a swell in the ocean
foretells the birth of a wave.

The surfer suddenly leaps barefoot on his surfboard, catching the rising crest of the fresh breaking wave. He is lifted high
and carried far by the curling, sweeping, arching, flight of
foam. The ride is on. Bending knees absorb the shocks, swells
and swirls. Arms outstretched slice the wind like eagles
wings. The trusting torso struggles to maintain balance. From
time to time the waves win out as the sportsman is wiped
out—sent off his board and into the sea. But riding or falling
he wins! His challenge to the surf has won him victory over
fear. And so he ends in safe shallows where he turns and pad-
dles out again to catch the next wave.

These same waves that carry the surfer into the shallows
send the timid bather running and squealing, hoping to escape
what threatens to overwhelm him. As the bather turns his
back to escape what he views as a threat, he increases his
chances of being knocked down and sent sputtering into the
foamy surf.

Faith is surfing on the waves of life.

**Faith faces the fears and turns the negative into a posi-
tive. Doubt runs from fear and is overwhelmed by it!**

Dear God, thank You for inspiring me today. I know that
together, You and I can ride out the waves of negativity. Amen.

## Batting all alone

."Choose for yourselves this day whom you will
serve, . . . But as for me and my house, we will
serve the Lord."—JOSHUA 24:15

Faith—we shall see—is sometimes a collective and some- **7**
times a very private matter. When a nation unites to defend
its peace and freedom against an invading enemy, we see an
illustration of collective faith.

But when an institution delegates enormous decision-making powers to the chief executive officer, the decisions will
become painfully private. The presidency of the United States
has been described as the loneliest office for that very reason.
The buck stops at his desk. He is up to bat. Alone! One man
against the world.

Faith, we soon discover, is a very private matter. Our most
important decisions cannot be passed off to anyone else. Consider the basic decisions. (1) What am I going to do? What
career will I pursue? In a free society, *you,* and you alone, must
decide! Out in front of you are nine members of another team
plus a stand full of spectators watching to see how you will
perform! No state bureaucracy will select a profession for you!
That's being in the batter's box alone! (2) Who will be my one
essential friend? Whom shall I marry? Or shall I remain single? No government agency, no academic advisory council can
make that decision for you. You are in the batter's box—
alone! That calls for strong, private faith! (3) What religious
choice will I make? I can choose to believe in nothing or I can
choose to believe in something. Atheism or theism.

It's your decision. You're up to bat. You can't avoid the moment. Sure, you can run scared, throw the bat to someone else
in the dugout—avoid the choice—call yourself an agnostic.
But then—face the consequences—you're out of the game!

Choose faith: take a swing at it! Become a believer.

**After all—faith is *the only positive option open to
you.* The other alternatives are negative! And nothing
positive ever follows negative decisions!**

## *Sitting in the front row*

"O God of our salvation,/You who are the confidence of all the ends of the earth."—PSALM 65:5

**8** Why do people rush to get the front seats in a football field, at a baseball game, or in the live theater, while the front seats in the average church are the last to be occupied? The answer seems obvious.

We want to maintain space between ourselves and others who might conceivably intimidate or threaten us. We want to be "in" but remain at a safe distance. Sit in the front row? Never! We might be noticed.

Perhaps you are still struggling with an inferiority complex, so you stand outside the circle or attend only large gatherings where you can hide in the crowd. Why don't you have enough faith to be aggressive? Will you ever have the faith to sell yourself? If not, what doors will remain locked to you forever? What human experiences will never be enjoyed?

Can this fear be overcome? Can such behavioral patterns, probably rooted deep in childhood, be corrected and changed?

Yes! Of course! You and I simply need more faith in ourselves and in God. Decide today to tackle this lifelong pattern of negativity with self-confident aggression.

**The best seats in the house are waiting for the people of faith!**

Don't miss out on the action! Grab a seat for yourself in the front row now. The same people who dare to sit in the front row are the "go-get-'em" type who are almost always one step ahead of the competition. They're going places!

You'll meet new friends. One of the new friends you'll meet who will change your life will be the new you!

## *Angling for the catch*

"You shall increase my greatness."—PSALM 71:21

My boyhood days of the wide-open spaces of an Iowa farm **9** were happy times. I had freedom to roam the fields and fish the streams. I enjoy no memory more than that of the corncob "dobber," floating on the placid Floyd River. As long as I had a cane pole, a can of worms, and a pocket full of faith, I was in heaven.

The largest fish I ever caught were catfish. Imagine how my eyes grew large when I saw pictures of marlin leaping out of the water in sports magazines in the barber shop. But that kind of fishing was reserved for the professional sports fisherman. There was no chance for an Iowa farm boy to go fishing like that. Right?

Years later, however, I found myself living in California, only a few hundred miles from where they fish for marlin. Could I get there? How much would it cost? My next thought was a negative one, "No, I'm only a cane pole fisherman from Iowa."

But possibility thinking had already changed my life. I told myself:

**"Go for it. Give it a try. You might surprise yourself and succeed."**

And I did!

That's the kind of faith you call "angling for the catch." It's the kind of faith that produces results. Unemployed people find work. Lonely people find friends.

Today, Lord, You are telling me that I can achieve that long-held dream if I'll only go for it. I'm going to be superpositive; I'm going to go fishing for what I really want in life! Thank You, Lord. Amen.

## Knocking down the high bar

"For the LORD will be your confidence,/And
will keep your foot from being caught."—
PROVERBS 3:26

**10** Oftentimes faith meets success at the point of failure. For
example, the pole vaulter who runs and then vaults over the
bar a little higher each time never really knows how high he
can jump until he fails to scale the bar.

He succeeds when he fails!

For failure isn't a matter of not reaching your goal!

Failure is failing to give your project all that you've got!

**Success is achieving the maximum of your potential
in the situation you are in.**

When you honestly have attempted your ultimate best,
then you have been successful, in spite of failure. The people
who are really failures are the people who set their standards
so low, keep the bar at such a safe level, that they never run
the risk of failure.

Faith is daring to face an embarrassing failure. It's only after
the pole vaulter knocks down the bar raised to its highest level
that he knows he's jumped as high as he can—today!

Success comes at the point where we can't do any better
than we are doing at this moment. The applause doesn't come
until you've given all you have to give. Spectators love the
winners and they love the losers, as long as both give it their
best!

Dear God, thank You for this boost You have given me today. I understand now that I really am not a failure. I am succeeding because I am doing my very best. Thank You for Your
confidence in me. I will keep on keeping on! To God be the
glory. Amen.

## *Whistling in the dark*

> "If I say 'Surely the darkness shall fall on me,'/
> Even the night shall be light about me;/Indeed,
> the darkness shall not hide from You,/But the
> night shines as the day;/The darkness and the
> light are both alike to You."—PSALM 139:11–12

**11**

As a young boy on an Iowa farm, before the days of electricity, I was often exposed to the threatening mysteries of the dark. When I was afraid to go out at night to check on my horse, my father reassured me, "There is nothing to be afraid of, Bob. And if you are afraid, just whistle!"

Believe it or not, it really worked.

Dad must have sensed that I needed to learn to venture out in new and potentially threatening situations without the usual support system.

So one night he refused to go with me to bring the horse in from the pasture. On my own I ventured forth, whistling in the dark.

As I entered the darkened stable with my horse, I was scared nearly out of my wits by the voice of a man! It was my father, coming to meet me half-way.

Often, I am still called to go out into the darkness, alone. And I always find that whistling gives me courage.

> **Positive affirmation is like whistling in the dark. It gets me there and keeps me going, even at the darkest point of the journey.**

We are all called to walk in the unknown darkness.

We are not moving in the area of faith when we walk only in broad daylight and can see where we are going.

Head out into the unknown today. Whistle in the dark. For "the darkness and the light are both alike to [God]."

Thank You, Father, that You know where the path is leading. I am trusting You. I am not afraid of the dark anymore. Thank You, God. Amen.

## Stepping on the scale

> "'I have walked before You in truth and with a
> loyal heart, and have done what is good in Your
> sight.' And the Lord said to Hezekiah, 'I have
> heard your prayer . . . and I will add to your
> days fifteen years.'"—ISAIAH 38:3–5

**12**  The inch-by-inch principle is building your faith. The little things you do today for someone else will add up to a lifetime of joy!

You can be genuinely optimistic about the prospect of enjoying life.

You have faith today to be able to accomplish the incredible by using the inch-by-inch principle.

Faith is answering the telephone, it is balancing the checkbook, and it is stepping on the scale!

Faith is confronting reality, not running away from it. If a telephone call brings bad news, have the faith to deal with it inch by inch. If finances are depleted—inch by inch, turn the problem around. If the scale says you're overweight, have the faith to tackle your problem slowly and surely—inch by inch!

**Faith is not a contradiction of reality, but the courage to face reality with hope.**

Recently I prayed for guidance. Gradually—over the past two years—extra pounds crept up on me. "Step on the scale every day." The message was loud and clear! I have been doing that! And writing it down! And I'm succeeding!

Affirmation: Today I shall begin to praise myself by being honest. I am going to stop kidding myself. I'm the last person I want to cheat. And I am cheating myself if I'm not being honest.

Today I shall step on the scale. I shall begin to turn my life around. I am facing up to my reality.

I am not afraid to face any negative situation, for I know that with God all things are possible!

## Expanding the base

"You enlarged my path under me;/So that my
feet did not slip."—PSALM 18:36

When is faith fulfilled? With a wedding? Graduation? Grand
opening day? Victorious election day? When is the dream
fulfilled?

**13**

"Faith is never fulfilled. It always gives birth to a new
dream," my son, the Reverend Robert Anthony Schuller, observed as he preached his first sermon in his new sanctuary.
And he's right!

The truth is, faith is never fulfilled—it is always upstaged!
At the very moment faith appears to be fulfilled, it is transcended by a new dream. "Now that I'm married we can. . ."
"Now that we are in business, let's. . ." "Now that we have our
new property, we will. . ."

Yes, just when faith seems to be fulfilled, it is upstaged by a
new dream. And it is this new dream, "see what we can do
now," that keeps faith alive. The new dream calls out to faith,
"Come along with me; I need you. After all you got me started
and brought me here. Don't let me down now. I can't get along
without you."

Faith, after all, isn't needed unless there's a gap between the
"is" and the "ought." Faith cannot exist unless there is a
chasm between the "I have it" and the "I want it."

So, when we succeed in our walk of faith, we learn an important life principle.

**Unless I am expandable, I am expendable.**

Growth is synonymous with life. Keep dreaming, and you
keep growing.

# Shooting for the moon

"Oh, give thanks to the LORD, for He is good!/
For His mercy endures forever./To Him who
made great lights . . ./The sun to rule by day
. . ./the moon and stars to rule by night."—
PSALM 136:1, 7–9

**14** When God created the universe, He did so with an unlimited expenditure of divine creative energy! There are heavens and galaxies that will never be fully explored.

M-31 in the constellation of Andromeda is a galaxy millions of light years away from planet Earth. If NASA can develop a spacecraft that travels at the speed of light (186,000 miles per second) it still would take a few million years just to reach the edge of that galaxy. It is safe to say we'll never reach it! In fact, it may be the geographic location of heaven!

Faith is shooting for the moon! Yes, it's planning to reach heaven someday. To the believer, heaven is the ultimate destination of the road of faith.

But until then, we need to shoot for the moon right here and now. What do I mean? I mean that a possibility thinker uses every possible opportunity to be outstanding! Throw yourself into your work with everything you've got.

**Again and again the person who fails, fails because he is not willing to shoot for the moon, to give his dream *all that he's got.***

It is that 100 percent effort—some athletes refer to 110 percent effort—that gives a champion the winner's edge. The difference between the number one and the number two spot is sometimes a matter of fractions of seconds.

Faith is shooting for the moon! It's putting all your eggs in one basket.

If you really believe in what you're doing, then don't hold anything back.

Give it your all—go for it!

## Splicing the gene

"I have made you hear new things from this
time./Even hidden things,/and you did not
know them."—ISAIAH 48:6

Could this incredible Bible verse possibly refer to genetic **15**
engineering that is happening today? Did it refer to the splitting of the atom earlier in our century?

**I often marvel at how God keeps so many secrets to
Himself. Slowly, patiently, He releases new insights
and allows each new generation the joy of making its
own contributions!**

When science is on the verge of a new frontier, there are
always negative, fearful eyes that see only the potential dangers. It strikes me as a contradiction when some people who
are known as "people of faith" suddenly lose their faith when
it comes to moving into uncharted scientific realms. God created the genes, and the potential for life forms to be successfully created through gene splicing. God ultimately holds
the final judgment and course of life in His hands.

Christians who walk the walk of faith look positively at the
constructive possibilities in scientific discoveries, such as
gene splicing. Possibility thinking sees dangers and potential
difficulties in every forward move that we might make. But
we do not reject an idea of vast positive potential because
some incredible dangers might be unleashed. Rather, we take
the discovery and try to identify the potential negatives.

**We eliminate, isolate, insulate, or sublimate the nega-
tive!**

That's walking the walk of faith. Faith is splicing the gene!
It's welcoming the adventure God reserved for a time like
ours!

## Probing for answers

> "Ah, Lord GOD! Behold, you have made the
> heavens and the earth by Your great power and
> outstretched arm. There is nothing too hard for
> You."—JEREMIAH 32:17

**16**    I know a chief executive who often calls in his top research
people to ask: "What questions do I need to ask you to get the
answers that will give me the knowledge I need to make the
right decision?"

Faith is probing for answers. Some people are so paralyzed
by their problem that they do not know how to begin to find
the answer.

*The search for faith begins with questions.*

When you know what questions to ask, you *believe* that
someone, somewhere, sometime, somehow can come up
with the right answer! So, believing is probing!

Faith is a needle:
- It has a sharp point.
- It provokes progress.
- It disturbs the status quo.
- It points to the need for answers.
- It probes until no corner is left unexplored and no possibility is left unexamined.

"That was tried, and it failed," the negative thinker may say.
But faith probes deeper into the situation. Perhaps someone
went about it in the wrong way—perhaps it was not possible
yesterday—perhaps with today's new technology and chemistry it might be possible!

Like an unsettled sea with a depth that defies measurement, restless faith churns until it finds hidden springs in the
bottom of the ocean floor! There are vast resources that God
wants to give the person who will never give up believing.

**Believing is spelled p-r-o-b-i-n-g!**

## *Becoming normal*

"And when Jesus went out He saw a great
multitude; and He was moved with compassion
for them, and healed their sick."—MATTHEW
14:14

In the Broadway play *The Man of La Mancha* Don Quixote **17**
is near death. He has been mocked and scorned because he is
such a positive thinker! Finally, in a splendid self-defense, he
asks the ultimate question. "Who is crazy? Am I crazy because I see the world as it could become? Or is the world crazy
because it only sees itself as it is?"

Who is normal, the cynic or the believer? The positive
thinker or the negative thinker? The believer in God—or the
atheist? The despairing pessimist or the hopeful optimist?

By now we all know the answer! We must affirm that health
is normal, and sickness is abnormal. That basic value judgment is beyond controversy.

Unbelief is a sickness, and skepticism is damnably dangerous. It gives birth to a multitude of spiritual demons that
can malignantly destroy your mental health and spread an
epidemic of despair wherever you go. As soon as you surrender yourself to negative thoughts, you become host to an
infectious spiritual disease and become the carrier of another
epidemic of gloom and doom.

It is normal for a child to dance and laugh and play. It is not
normal for a child to be downcast, morbid, withdrawn, and
sulking in isolation. It is normal to be a happy believer.

Who is crazy? The realist or the idealist?

The answer is obvious. The Beautiful Dreamer, with His
exalted visions of glorious possibilities, is the Uplifting Force
in society! He comes bringing solutions. He then becomes the
Great Physician, the Healing Source, the Hopeful Friend. We
can follow Him.

His name? Jesus, the Lord. My Savior. My friend.

## Integrating yourself

"Let the peace of God rule in your hearts, to
which also you were called in one body; and be
thankful."—COLOSSIANS 3:15

**18** In his book *Games People Play*, the psychiatrist Eric Berne
defines three ego states in the human being. There is the *parent* ego state, the *child* ego state, and the *adult* ego state.

By that, he means there is in every human being the *child*
that remains within us. This explains why, as mature persons,
we sometimes act very childishly when we are frustrated. The
child-quality within us never leaves us, nor should it completely. For then we cease to enjoy the childlike quality of
wonder.

There also lives in us, through our memories, the *parent* to
scold or mold us. In unexpected times we recall the stern or
sweet voice of the father or mother, and we find ourselves responding or resisting.

Finally, there is the *adult* ego state. By this Eric Berne
means the real and rugged individual who is today a free individual.

Are you a single person? Or are there several different persons within you? Are they kind? Cruel? Patient? Impatient?
To what extent is your personality fragmented?

The secret of mental health is to achieve a maximum degree of integration until there is an overwhelming magnetic
force at the core of your personality that brings isolated and
fractured elements of your being into a oneness.

The atheist tries to integrate his life around a vacuum—a
belief in nothing.

**The believer becomes integrated around one dominant
overwhelming Magnetic Force that pulls life together.
That Force is Jesus Christ. That power is the power of
belief.**

Thank You, God, that You are the Magnetic Force integrat-
ing my life.

# Discovering your natural habitat

"We are His workmanship, created in Christ
Jesus for good works."—EPHESIANS 2:10

You are discovering who you are, where you belong, and **19**
what a marvelous creature you really are. Once you learn to
breathe your native air, you discover that the path of faith is
the central corridor, the mainstream, the number one boule-
vard that runs from one end of the Garden of Eden to the
other!

**The exciting process of discovery is always a mark of
authentic living.**

You have already discovered that to live is to grow. And you
have made a marvelous growth-producing discovery when
you came to know that living by faith is living the healthy and
natural way.

You were designed as a human being to be the brains and
the body that could execute God's good work on planet Earth.
Once your faith has motivated you to a genuine commitment
to faith in God, you find your values changing, your priorities
reshuffling, and your goals being reviewed. Christ Jesus literally changes your life and retools you to do good work!

In the process of this good work you find joy, self-esteem,
and dignity. You have discovered your natural habitat.

- Now you know why you were born.
- Now you understand the divine purpose behind human
  life.

No other animal has the capacity to be a believer in God.
That's your unique heritage.

Thank You, God, for enabling me to make this discovery.
Amen.

# *Thinking God's thoughts*

"For I know the thoughts that I think toward
you, says the LORD, thoughts of peace and not
of evil, to give you a future and a hope."—
JEREMIAH 29:11

**20** Each new year is an appointment to become an authentic
optimist.

Each new day is justification for being enthusiastic about
life again.

Each dawning is God's invitation to start over and build a
new life, beginning with the present moment.

Every new week is an opportunity to make new and noble
resolutions! Every Monday morning you have a standing appointment to meet new opportunities!

What does it mean to have faith?

Faith is opening your mind for God's thoughts to flow in.
And when His thoughts flow in, life will change, for you will
have a dream. You will see possibilities in the day—the
week—the month—the year that is waiting to unfold.

Faith moves mountains.

### The greatest power in the world is a positive idea.

And the most powerful positive idea is one that comes directly from the God who created the world and broke sunshine through the black of night.

Today I will think God's thoughts. This very moment, I will
open my mind to let God's thoughts enter my brain. I will
listen to the idea that comes from God, and it will turn me
into a new and different person. I feel a freshness and a newness coming over me now as God's thoughts begin to take
control over my consciousness.

I am set free, liberated, by new thoughts that come from
God. Now I know what possibility thinking is—it is the mental activity that happens when I let faith take over.

Thank You, God, that I am being born again. Your Holy
Spirit is filling my mind with your thoughts. I am excited
about today, and I'm excited about my future. Amen.

## *Praying for guidance*

"Show me Your ways, O Lord,/Teach me your paths./Lead me in your truth and teach me,/For You are the God of my salvation . . ."—PSALM 25:4

The walk of faith is an adventure in a holy partnership. You **21** are a human being with a mortal starting point at birth and a mortal terminal point at death. The span between your birth and death is your earthly life. Your purpose is to fit into a holy scheme, and become a participant with God. He created the world and all of us human beings for the purpose of creatively achieving His holy and happy purposes.

**You are walking the walk of faith when you dream God's dreams and seek God's guidance.**

Therefore, faith is not merely a super-aggressive activity into which you plunge with a gung-ho attitude, to achieve the first impulse that explodes in your mind. Rather, faith is a steady, stable, and steadfast process of opening your conscious and subconscious mind through prayer to the Holy Spirit. The eternal God will shape your will and direct your way!

**God promised He will give you guidance.**

In the depth of your heart, you know with an unflinching certainty, and with an invincible awareness, the course of action your life must take. This is God Himself, answering your prayers for guidance. He gives you a strong and powerful will to proceed along the determined pathway. Consider these prayers of affirmation:

I am driven by a divine destiny.

I am praying for guidance now.

I am opening my mind consistently and constantly to God, the way the tip of a branch is unceasingly alert and responsive to the wind!

## *Setting a goal*

> "One thing I do, forgetting those things which
> are behind and reaching forward to those things
> which are ahead, I press toward the goal for . . .
> the upward call of God . . ."—PHILIPPIANS 3:13

**22**    Faith is not merely thinking holy and happy thoughts.

**God's thoughts must take the form of good and
godly goals.**

No act of faith is more dynamic, more constructive, than
setting incredible goals!

Have you noticed how negative thinkers avoid setting
goals?

"Goals—who needs them? I'll just wing it, thank you. I pre-
fer to roll with the punches."

"I don't want to get trapped by a commitment. Isn't that
what happens when you set a goal?"

"I've had enough disappointments. I don't want to be set up
only to be let down. Goals? No more failures, thank you."

Failure is not a matter of failing to meet your goal. Failure is
not making the most of the possibilities seen and unseen,
known and unknown, in your present and in your future!

Use faith to set positive goals, and you'll be sure to rise to
the higher plateau. I guarantee that . . .

• when you set a challenging goal, you'll be farther ahead
tomorrow than you are today. Even a little can turn out to be a
lot!

• you'll be a happier person. Someone stopped me recently
and asked, "Why do you always seem to be in such a happy
mood?" My answer: "Because I've always got unfulfilled goals,
and my goals distract me from my worries!"

• you will feel that your life has value!

If you have goals, you are bound to inspire somebody who is
hurting. You will discover your own worth.

Goals—what are they anyway? They are impossible problems awaiting to be solved by someone with this incredible
power called faith! So get set to set goals, and move upward!

*FAITH IS . . .*
## *Charting the course*

"Let us run with endurance the race that is set
before us."—HEBREWS 12:1

You are walking the walk of faith, thinking God's thoughts, **23**
seeking God's guidance, and setting good and godly goals.

Now, how can you possibly succeed when your goals are
beyond your grasp? Did you go overboard? Are you thinking
too big? Should you scale down your dreams? How can you
possibly pull off what seems to be an impossibility?

What you must do is think, plan, and chart your course
through the uncharted waters before you.

You cannot expect God's ideas to automatically evolve as
actualized achievements. You must assume responsibility to
make success happen. You must develop a strategy and a
scheme that will allow you to succeed.

**If you fail to plan, you plan to fail.**

Now exercise your faith by affirming . . .

I am trusting God to give me wisdom to chart my course as
carefully as a captain who looks at a map, chooses his route,
and calculates the time and resources needed to finish the
journey.

I want to reach the destination and see God's dream for my
life accomplished. I am planning to make it possible.

I am excited. I am ready to begin! I am going to fulfill my
divine destiny.

I am confident that
• if there's a will, there's a way.
• if it's God's will, He will show the way.
• if I keep the faith, He will show me how!

Thank You, God, for giving me the motivation to run the
race. Thank You for the wisdom to chart the course that
fulfills Your successful plan for my life!

## *Believing I will make it*

"He [God] who has begun a good work in you
will complete it . . ."—PHILIPPIANS 1:6

**24**   Deliberately exercise your faith by repeating these positive
affirmatives:

I am thanking God—today—that He has a plan for my life.

I am motivated to seek and serve God's will.

I am trusting that God has inspired me to begin—surely He
will guide me to succeed.

I am walking the walk of faith.

I am thinking God's thoughts.

I am setting goals.

I am charting a course.

I am believing that I will succeed.

I am disciplining my mind to weed out negative thoughts.

I am rejecting all thoughts of discouragement.

I am visualizing myself making steady progress.

I am basing my ultimate success on the character of God.

God never starts a project and abandons it!

God is no quitter. He is a finisher!

**God gave me a dream; motivated me to set a goal; and
He will keep stimulating me to succeed.**

I will keep on believing in success, for I know that success
is inevitable as long as I focus my belief on eventual success.
*I will make my life an exclamation mark!* Surely God
wants me to be successful. He certainly does not dream up
plans for people to fail at! Because I am responsible for my life,
I will decide to succeed. I am believing I will make it.

God, who has begun a good work in me, will complete it!

*FAITH IS . . .*
## *Scanning the horizon*

"Set your mind on things above, not on things
on the earth."—COLOSSIANS 3:3

We define *horizon* as the place where heaven meets earth. **25**
But it is also where today's state-of-the-art ends and tomorrow's new developments move in.

Faith refuses to surrender control to negative doubts of yesterday. Doubt adds up all of the bungled debts, fruitless research, foiled efforts, and shattered dreams.

**Doubt finds its life by digging in the cemeteries of bur-
ied hopes.**

**Faith finds its life by scanning the horizon, knowing
there will be a sunrise tomorrow.**

Today is the beginning of a new age. What medical breakthroughs will be made before the sun sets today? What new
technological achievements will be possible by the end of this
year, or this decade?

Faith is belief in the future. It is scanning the horizon for
new ships that will sail into view, carrying treasured cargo of
new discoveries. Faith expects and predicts headlines of new
cures and breakthroughs that will be announced in the next
365 days.

Affirmation: Today I will cultivate a mental attitude that
expects progress. I will steadfastly scan the heavens!

Through positive prayer, I look forward, expectantly and excitedly! Thank You, Father, for what You are planning to do in
my future. Amen.

## *Possibilitizing*

"For a dream comes through much activity."—
ECCLESIASTES 5:3

**26**    Today, I want to introduce you to a new word—*possibilitizing*. It means coming up with solutions where none were apparent; creating a way when there has been no path. This involves the process of research and development, which leads to new inventions.

Are you faced with a seemingly unsolvable problem? Then possibilitize! Play "the possibility thinking game." It's an incredibly practical and extremely valuable technique for solving rugged problems.

Make a list of one to ten on a sheet of clean white paper. Now open your mind to God in prayer. Then *list every possible way* of accomplishing the impossible problem, no matter how wild, how far out, or how preposterous it seems—until all ten lines are filled.

Begin right now by listing here the first thoughts that come to your mind:

 

_____

_____

 

_____

A few decades ago, the idea of taking a healthy heart out of a dead body and transplanting it into the chest of a living person with a decaying heart would have been unthinkable.

As long as they are not immoral or unethical, list your ideas. You'll be surprised at how God operates! As you write your ideas down on paper, if one has come from Him, it will grab you. You'll not be able to shake it. It will become a part of the answer!

**Possibilitizing—it moves mountains!**

# Assuming "it is possible"

*". . . but with God all things are possible."*—
MATTHEW 19:26

Faith is the process of *acting upon glorious assumptions.* **27**

If you attempt to achieve an objective that is easily reached, then you are not moving within the circle of faith.

Faith is not necessary unless your projects are humanly impossible.

Unless there is strong reason to doubt, you are not living in the higher altitude of real faith.

You must commit yourself to projects where there is a possibility of failure before you can claim to be walking the walk of faith.

How does faith move us forward when success is uncertain? Faith moves us onward by giving us the courage to act upon positive assumptions. We assume that:

**With the help of God, the impossible can be possible.**

There will never be progress until someone acts upon a grand assumption. Surely, you have the right to assume that God, who made your dream, will also make it possible for you to succeed.

Keep moving forward, steadily, assuming that when you reach the door it will swing open! Even Moses moved toward the Red Sea, assuming that a way would clear for him to cross it!

O God, with Your help today, I believe the impossible can be possible. I assume that my problems are solvable; that help will be forthcoming; that new breakthroughs will come my way; and that positive and exciting new healings will flow into me. I believe that today's assumptions will become tomorrow's grand accomplishments! Thank You, God. Amen.

# Viewing success positively

"You shall also be a crown of glory/In the hand
of the LORD,/And a royal diadem/In the hand of
your God."—ISAIAH 62:3

**28**    Is it possible that some people are more afraid of success
than failure? Can it be that they are unsure what success will
do to their lifestyle? Will they lose some of their old friends?
What new pressures and temptations will come into their
lives?

I am constantly surprised to find Christians who are afraid
of success. Many suffer from the hang-up that success contra-
dicts the Christian virtue of humility. They associate success
with pride; therefore, they refuse to consider it. Faith views
success positively. Don't be afraid of success!

**God can do great things through successful people
who are dedicated to Him!**

The cynic cannot save the world. The doubter cannot share
faith, hope, and love. God's work needs all the success it can
get!

Faith welcomes success and then uses it positively.

How does faith deal with success positively?

• Faith does not *fear* success.
• Faith does not *fight* success.
• Faith *accepts* success as *noble.*
• Faith *pursues* success with enthusiasm.
• Faith *welcomes* success with gratitude.
• Faith *shares* success.
• Faith *uses* success to solve the problems of the world.

I'm so grateful, Lord, I know that it's no sin to succeed? I'll
not be afraid of winning. Amen.

## Fearing failure courageously

*"Come, . . . I will teach you the fear of the*
*LORD. . . . who desires life? . . . do good;/Seek*
*peace and pursue it."—PSALM 34:11–14*

A successful black multimillionaire and entrepreneur told **29** on a national television interview how, fifteen years earlier, he had plunged into a business opportunity that came his way.

When no bank would take a chance on him, he sold his idea to friends and relatives, convincing them that they should loan him one hundred dollars here and five hundred dollars there.

He was asked by the interviewer: "How do you explain such an unusually high record of sales that first year?"

He spoke up swiftly and sincerely: "The fear of failure! I couldn't possibly contemplate failure. I was so afraid I might fail that I just worked and worked and worked!"

**The possibility thinker is turned on by the fear of failure; an impossibility thinker is turned away from ever trying!**

Fear of failure *can* be a positive force! It not only keeps us going but *pushes* us to produce more than we ever thought we could!

What that black entrepreneur didn't know is this: with his drive, determination, and positive mental attitude, he was already a success. He succeeded before he even knew it! Even if his business had ultimately failed, he would have learned enough to tackle any opportunity that came his way.

It is true—*the fear of failure can be the insurance policy of success.*

Lord, give me the drive, the determination, and the positive mental attitude today to succeed. With Your leading, I can't possibly contemplate failure. Amen.

*FAITH IS . . .*
## *Risking failure bravely*

"The Lord is my light and my salvation,/Whom shall I fear?/The Lord is the strength of my life,/Of whom shall I be afraid?"—PSALM 27:1

**30** You are really making progress in your walk of faith. When you made the decision that you dare to fail, you conquered an enormous obstacle that stops 90 percent of the people from experiencing mountain-moving faith.

Now you can move ahead to pray specifically, engage contracts, make forward-moving commitments, reaffirm original goals, and set forth immediate goals that shall mark progress in your walk.

### Faith is impossible without risk.

Unless you're running the risk of failure, you're not totally living within the parameters of faith.

Unless there is the possibility that you can experience a rejection, or a defeat in your project; then you're obviously playing it so safe you can't lose. This means you are not even on the playing field of faith.

God does not promise to bless the coward. However, His promises are packed full of reassurance for those who are brave in heart. Are you in the playing field of faith? Ask yourself these questions:

What goals would I set for myself today if I knew I could not fail? _____

What announcements would I make to the world if I knew I could succeed? _____

Affirmation: Today I'll make my decision based on the good that can be accomplished if I succeed, not on the pain I would experience if I suffered failure! Then truly I can know that I'm being controlled by possibilities instead of problems!

Glorious achievements happen when you and I decide to dare to run the risk of failure!

# Defusing the fear of failure

"He shall set me high upon a rock./And now
my head shall be lifted up above my
enemies."—PSALM 27:5–6

You have taken a giant step forward on the walk of faith. **31**
You dare to fail! You *will* risk failure bravely.

Today you will defuse the fear of failure once and for all.
The fear of failure is the explosive bomb that can blow you
out of the water and devastate your destiny. How can you defuse this fear, once and for all? By analyzing intelligently what
the fear of failure really is.

Ask yourself this key question: Why does the fear of failure
frighten me? _____

_____

The fear of failure is really a fear of rejection, of embarrassment. (What will my friends say? What will my loved ones
think of me?) The fear of embarrassment is the fear of the loss
of respect of people who support me emotionally.

And the fear of rejection is really a fear of a loss of self-
worth, self-esteem, and self-respect. I can live without much
money, and I can live with just a few friends, but I can never
live with myself if I hate myself! And I'm really afraid I'll hate
myself if I try—and don't succeed.

How do you defuse this fear? It's simple! Tell yourself that
there is no shame in trying to do something great and failing.
It is much more an embarrassment if I am a coward, lacking
the courage to *try* to do something wonderful and worthwhile.

**There is more self-esteem generated in honest and no-
ble failure than there is in cowardly retreat from great
opportunity!**

"So I'd rather attempt to do something great and fail, than
attempt to do nothing and succeed!"

## *Scoring in the first round!*

"Wait on the Lord,/Be of good courage,/And He shall strengthen your heart,/Wait, I say, on the Lord!"—PSALM 27:14

**32**  Once you dare to risk failure and defuse the fear of failure, you have scored in round one.

From now on you will dare to try.

Once you have attempted to do something great, it is impossible to be a total failure.

At least you have succeeded in conquering cowardice.

You have dared to step into the ring.

Round one in the fight of life is daring to try even though you know you might fail.

To make a commitment to attempt something great, despite the very real possibility of failure, marks you not as a reckless fool, but as a daring person of great faith.

Most people lose the battle of life by never conquering the fear of failure *enough* to attempt to climb the biggest challenges God puts before them. They've never even stepped into the ring! They were knocked out before the first round!

Until you have enough nerve to set some "gutsy" goals, you run the far greater risk of becoming a total failure!

Affirmation for today: I'll never be a total failure, for at least I can conquer the problem that stops most people. I have looked the fear of failure in the face and I've stared the enemy down!

### I'm trying—therefore, I am a success!

Every competitor is a winner! The losers never tried. Every contestant is a winner! The losers never made it to the contest.

Here I go!

No matter how it turns out, I'm getting one award—the badge of courage! Thank You, Lord!

FAITH IS . . .
## Expecting to succeed

"In all your ways acknowledge Him [God]/And
He shall direct your paths."—PROVERBS 3:6

Can faith really move mountains? Can faith really release **33**
hidden healing powers in dying people? Can faith attract divine and human powers to transform your life? Can you expect your prayers to be answered if you believe?

Of course! For by believing, we exercise the mental practice
of dreaming God's dreams and seeking God's goals.

**And God deeply desires that His plan for your life will
be fulfilled.**

The question is, how can you move your faith from low
gear to high gear? By practicing the mental habit of *expecting
positive results*. In this practice of mental expectation you
strengthen your faith!

You wish you had a tougher faith? Then put your faith on a
vigorous fitness program.

To begin with, give your faith a good diet of spiritual miner-
als and vitamins. Withhold all negative consumptions that
would make your faith "sick."

To maintain the health and the vigor of your faith, it must
be exercised regularly! How?

Ask yourself these questions: Am I really expecting to succeed? Am I mentally keen on achieving my desired goal? Am I
genuinely enthusiastic about the prospects of success?

Faith that passes the fitness test must register high in expecting to succeed. Stretch your faith today by increasing your
expectations!

Affirmation for today: I affirm that my goals are definitely
going to be realized. I am a lot farther today than I was when I
was merely daydreaming. I am committing myself 100 percent to making my dreams come true.

I am expecting to succeed!

I can feel my faith getting stronger already!

## Drawing mental pictures

"Where there is no vision, the people perish."—
PROVERBS 29:18 KJV

**34**   If I asked you to draw a picture, how would you go about it?
You'd probably reach for a blank piece of paper and some
pencils or crayons. Or you'd reach for a canvas, with oil paints
and brushes.

I am no artist, but I can teach you how to draw pictures in
the mind. Your mind is the canvas. Your willpower is the
brush. Your thoughts are the oils and colors. Within your
mind is an incredible assortment of colors; every idea is a potential color! Begin to "see" ideas in "color." Ideas that are
happy can be colored red, yellow. Depressing thoughts? Color
them gray. Angry thoughts? Color them black. Loving
thoughts? Color them blue. Forward moving, growth ideas?
Color them green!

Today choose to become an artist with ideas. No training is
necessary. God gives gifts of imagination—your thoughts.
Now use your creative power to draw the mental image of the
dream *accomplished.* See the finished project in the mind.

**The me I see is the me I'll be. If I cannot see it, I will
never be it. Until I believe it, I will never achieve it!**

It may be helpful to you to actually take out a blank piece of
paper and draw a picture of what you want to accomplish.
Sketches on paper plant an image on the brain. The subconscious, like a roll of undeveloped film, picks up the image
and the picture is drawn. And at this very moment faith
moves into a motivational phase. Energy and enthusiasm begin to be released.

Have fun! Become an artist with ideas.

O God, give me a vision, a mental picture of the person you
want me to be, the project you want me to pursue, the objectives you want me to manage toward actualization. I open my
mind like a screen to the Holy Spirit. I will paint the pictures
within my imagination now. Thank You, God. Amen.

## *Announcing your intentions*

"O Lord, open my lips,/And my mouth will
show forth Your praise."—PSALM 51:15

Look at the upward steps that the walk of faith is taking. **35**
Faith takes the first step in dreaming. It climbs higher
through drawing mental pictures, and it takes a giant step upward through the public announcement of your goals!

I suppose this is one of the most frightening steps that you
can take in the walk of faith. As long as you keep your mental
picture to yourself and secretly harbor your unspoken desires,
then the dreaming is relatively safe. But once you open your
mouth and tell the world what you intend to do, then you
place your integrity on the line. You place your reputation as a
believable person on the line once you announce your intentions. Now you must either produce or be proven unreliable at
best and a phony at worst.

The public declaration of commitment intensifies the risk.
You can immediately expect opposition and criticism to come
out of the woodwork. Negative thinkers will leap forward—
"It can't be done," "It won't work," "Somebody else tried it
and failed." Or they'll attack your motives. "What kind of an
ego trip are you on?"

**Take the leap of faith upward today. Tell the world
what you're going to accomplish.**

Don't be afraid of criticism. Just as criticism and opposition
will come, so support will come from unknown and unexpected sources. The power of a positive idea is greater than the
power of a negative idea.

O Lord, open my lips, and my mouth shall show forth Your
praises. I shall tell the world of the dream You have given me
and what You and I will attempt to accomplish for Your glory.
Amen.

[285]

## Getting excited about succeeding

> "For who is God, except the LORD?/And who is
> a rock, except our God? It is God who arms me
> with strength,/And makes my way perfect."—
> PSALM 18:31–32

**36**   Now that you've drawn the mental picture and announced your intention, you are getting excited about the idea of success.

You can pass the course.

You will succeed in the examination.

You are going to get married and make it work.

You are going to set physical-fitness goals, and will succeed.

You are going to establish a new career, open a new business, take a challenging trip.

It's all going to happen! How can you get so excited about succeeding? Because God is your Rock, your Refuge, your Fortress. He called you! He installed you! His power and His vision enthrall you!

Read Psalm 18:31–33. Here the psalmist tells us what we can expect from God . . .

**It is God who arms me with strength.**

**It is God who makes my way perfect before me.**

**He makes my feet like the feet of a deer . . .**

swift and skillful in maneuvering, sometimes slow down rocky pathways and sometimes swift in the race on the meadow, sometimes powerful for the plunge across the canyon or the leap across the stream or the bounding lunge to the upper rock!

There God sets your feet on the high places! And you, from your vaulted vantage point of spiritual height catch a vision of success so bright!

Thank You, Father, that You have given me the dream—and now the gleam—of success. I need that today! Amen.

*FAITH IS . . .*
# *Allowing for the impossibles*

"As you do not know what is the way of the
wind,/Or how the bones grow in the womb of
her who is with child,/So you do not know the
works of God who makes all things."—
ECCLESIASTES 11:5

Is it possible for the sun to rise in the west? At first thought, **37**
the answer is, "No, it is impossible." But—

**Faith allows impossibilities to become possibilities.**

There are several ways impossibilities can become possibilities.

There may be supernatural laws that override natural laws.
Or there are probably natural laws known only to God.

Recently, when I was in Europe for a religious conference, I
was asked to make a fast trip to Washington, D.C., for an important appointment. The only way I could reach my destination in time was to fly via the Concorde—the supersonic
transport plane that hits speeds of over fifteen hundred miles
an hour. Our plane was to leave the Paris airport in time to
watch the sunset. Unfortunately, a problem arose and the
plane was delayed. Consequently it was nine o'clock and dark
before we took off.

"We missed the sunset," I lamented. And then it happened. I
watched a replay of the sunset! I saw the sun rise in the west!
Because our plane was traveling faster than the speed of the
rotation of the earth, we literally caught up with the sunset. I
watched the sun rise from the western horizon to a position of
four o'clock in the afternoon as we landed in the sunshine in
Washington!

Faith is allowing for the apparent impossibilities to be realities.

O God, give me the humility to make allowance for the
possibilities that I am tempted to reject as totally unrealistic!
Help me to see that I cannot grow as a person until I am willing to be a believer. Amen.

## *Aiming to achieve the best*

"[God] is able to do exceedingly abundantly
above all that we ask or think, according to the
power that works within us."—EPHESIANS 3:20

**38**     Have you noticed that people who do not walk the walk of
faith are also the people who have no clear-cut aim in life?
These people "wing it" without any plan. They fail to set
achievable goals. They often take refuge behind the pious
phrase: "God knows what's best for me and He will provide
it."

### If you aim at nothing—you're sure to hit it!

The truth is, the person who sets low goals achieves little.
*The size of the dream will determine the size of the person
you will become.*

There are no great people in this world; there are only ordinary people. The only difference is that some people set
higher goals, dream bigger dreams, and settle for nothing less
than the best!

Excellence is the motto of great people. All-out effort is the
hallmark of their character. They focus on goals and aim carefully at a measurable, manageable target the way a crack rifle-
man sights the target, takes aim, and fires! All the while they
confidently trust God to give them a victory.

Today, are there problems that transcend your ability to
solve them? Are your dreams beyond your reach? Then stop
leaning on your abilities and start trusting God's abilities. He
is able!—"to do exceedingly abundantly above all that we ask
or think . . ." (Eph. 3:20). You just aren't able to think big
enough to match God's abilities!

Affirmation: I know that I can never dream big enough to
match God's dreams! He's always ahead of me and beyond
me!

# Verbalizing victory

"For whatever is born of God overcomes the
world. And this is the victory that has
overcome the world—our faith."—1 JOHN 5:4

Do you remember the marvelous and true story of Babe **39**
Ruth? The bases were loaded, and there were two strikes
against him. It was a crucial inning. Suddenly, Babe Ruth
stepped out of the batter's box, lifted his bat, and pointed it at
the stands off in center field, indicating to the crowd that he
was going to hit the ball out of the park. The pitch came
across the plate. He swung. And the ball sailed exactly to
where he had pointed!

> **When you dare to predict your own success, you at-
> tract support and you produce the pressures that will
> ensure your success.**

I've never been good at the game of pool so I marvel at the
pool player who can point to his goal and say, "Number six in
the corner pocket," then shoot, and make it! He verbalizes
victory—beforehand!

It takes a lot of faith to announce your grandiose intentions!
"What if I fail after I made the announcement?" Be proud that
you had the courage to try!

Today, ask yourself this question: Do you believe in God
enough to announce what the two of you are going to do together? It's your responsibility to demonstrate that much
faith. It's God's responsibility to make it happen.

When you verbalize victory you give yourself a new injec-
tion of enthusiasm. People will say that you talked your way
into success. That's only partially true. You acted out your
faith. In the process you put the ball back in God's court. Isn't
it marvelous how God planned for life to be such a challenging game of faith?

FAITH IS . . .
## Unlocking your positive emotional powers

"You are my hope, O Lord GOD;/You are my
trust from my youth./By You I have been
upheld from my birth;/You are He who took
me out of my mother's womb./My praise shall
be continually of You."—PSALM 71:5,6

**40**  Tremendous power is released when you begin to thank
God for making you the way you are.

I know of no one who doesn't wish to change something
about his or her appearance.

Even winners of beauty contests see some imperfection in
their physical makeup. Some say, "I wish my nose were
shaped a bit differently." Others say: "Don't you think my
chin protrudes a little?"

And what about you? How satisfied are you with your physical appearance? Have you accepted yourself as you are? Tremendous power will flow into your life once you do.

I did not choose my race, my skin color, my ethnic origin, or
the time of history in which I was born.

There was a destiny that predetermined the basics of my
life. I call that Destiny *God.*

**I will unlock the emotional powers within myself by
believing that God knew what He was doing when He
created me the way I am.**

Affirmation: Today I shall praise God for the positive people
He used to mold my life—a teacher, a parent, a relative, a
minister, a friend.

Thank You, God, for those moments when You give me
opportunity to lift my sights and improve myself! Thank You,
Father, that You created me with wisdom and beauty in mind.
I thank You that I have been led to take this walk of faith. My
faith is unlocking positive emotional power within me now!
Thank You, God. Amen.

FAITH IS . . .
## *Plunging before you are positive*

"Do you not know that those who run in a race
all run, but one receives the prize? Run in such
a way that you may obtain it."
—1 CORINTHIANS 9:24

An exciting illustration of faith is portrayed in the running **41**
of a race. The runner jumps at the starting gun, even though
he cannot be sure he will win. But one thing is certain.

**The person who does not start can never win!**

This means that another truth becomes markedly evident:
Every starter is a winner. The losers are those who never tried.
If you need to be sure that you will win, if you need to be
confident of success *before* you make a commitment, *then
you are not even walking the walk of faith!*

It is the element of uncertainty that adds excitement to life.
The predictable always produces boredom. The element of the
unpredictable always generates the interest and involvement
of spectator and participant alike.

So the person who walks the walk of faith is alive and is
keeping others alive, speculating on his success. He is news,
because he has entered the race before he is positive that he
can win.

God's promises are not offered to the "play-it-safe" spectator
in the stands, but to the "let's-take-a-chance" player in the
middle of the game!

Take this positive plunge: Today I'm going to double-check
my life. Have I plunged ahead with the new opportunities that
came to my mind only a day or two ago? If not, then today I
will step on the starting line, I'll put both hands to the ground.
I'll step up on tiptoe. I'll look ahead at the course. Here I go!
I'm running the race. This time, I'm not a spectator in the
stands, but a *contestant* and *participant!*

## *Deciding to begin*

"In the beginning God created the heavens and
the earth."—GENESIS 1:1

**42**  God has given you a dream. Now you must prepare to make
brave decisions.

Faith is not daydreaming, it is decision making!

*Even God's ideas aren't worth anything—until a believer
acts upon them!* We exercise our faith when we make the
toughest decision—the decision to get started.

### Procrastination is an exercise of doubt.

Postponing tough decisions is, more often than not, the result of a lack of faith.

God does not promise to bless us, until we make a commitment to live and walk by faith.

We cannot expect God to bless our profession of faith until
we stop doing nothing and start doing something.

Faith is deciding to begin. Affirm with me:

### Today I shall tackle my biggest enemy—inertia.

I will walk.
I will run.
I will talk.
I will write.
I will launch the project.
I will tell people what I am starting.

And I will trust God to enable me to keep moving once I
demonstrate enough faith to get going! I really am walking the
walk of faith. I am going to start today.

**In deciding to begin, I have solved my biggest problem.
I'm going to succeed, for beginning is half done!**

## Entering the contest

"Commit your way to the LORD./Trust also in Him,/And He shall bring it to pass."—PSALM 37:5

As a young child I never entered contests because I never wanted to lose. I did not want to compete because I always wanted to win. Looking back, I realize how preposterous the whole negative-thinking process was. Obviously, if I never entered the contest, I never would win!

There is more to winning than never losing! In the walk of faith

**43**

> **The person who enters the contest has already won a battle. He has overcome the fear of failure!**

What contest are you preparing to enter?

What competitions should you engage in?

You can at least compete with your own best record!

Why don't you enter the contest of "generosity champion"? Wouldn't it be wonderful to be known as one of the most generous persons who ever lived?

Why don't you enter the "encouragement contest," and win the gold medal for doing more than anybody else to encourage the discouraged?

Why don't you enter the "honesty contest"? In the final judgment honesty pays off. What company would knowingly hire a dishonest person?

Why don't you, in the name of Christ, compete against negativity, sin, evil, and greed?

Almighty God, there is a race I should run,
    a contest I should enter,
        a competition I have to get involved in.
Show me the way, and I will follow. Win or lose—I'll know I've kept the faith! Thank You, Father. Amen.

## *Leaving your ruts*

"Your word is a lamp to my feet/And a light to my path."—PSALM 119:105

**44**    It takes the power of God to release us from negative, locked-in thinking. It takes guts to leave the ruts.

Is it possible you are in a negative-thinking rut?

If aeronautical engineers in the 1920s said it was impossible to fly faster than the speed of sound, is it possible you might be placing your faith on some negative precept? What ideas are limiting your growth? What opinions are restricting you?

Ruts have a way of becoming security blankets in your second childhood. Most little children have their favorite blanket. Many of your negative, deeply ingrained opinions and well-entrenched conclusions become emotional security blankets, holding you back

—from daring to go out in business for yourself,

—or daring to go back to college,

—or daring to tackle a physical fitness program,

—or daring to learn another language.

It takes a lot of courage to make a major career change in midlife!

It takes a lot of faith to pack up and move to a new city, state, or country.

What ruts are you in? You're free to leave that rut. A rut, you know, is a grave—with the ends knocked out.

Come alive. Climb out of it. Tackle some exciting new possibilities today! Just make sure you are guided by God Almighty and His holy Word. Be certain you are not jumping out of the frying pan into the fire. God's "word is a lamp to my feet/And a light to my path"! Follow it. Get started today by accepting His challenge.

## Committing to action

"Go your way; and as you have believed, so let
it be done for you."—MATTHEW 8:13

Miracles never happen just through meditation—but with **45**
mighty action! Read carefully in the Gospels the words of
Jesus and notice the verbs. *Follow, go, seek, ask, knock.* The
walk of faith is not merely the serene, silent, spiritual, un-
speaking stroll of a holy man in the stillness of the sunrise or
the secret silence of the sunset.

> **Faith is the mental activity that draws God into our
> mind and imagination until a passion begins to in-
> flame our wills, motivating us to action!**

It is then that the commitment is made. And what is a
commitment? It is entering into an honorable contract, pledg-
ing oneself before the problems are solved. Every commitment generates a new set of problems. And if we waited until
we saw solutions to problems before we made the commitment, we would obviously not be walking the walk of faith! It
is for that reason that commitment—
  in marriage,
    in religion,
      in interpersonal relationships,
        in devotion and dedication to your career goal
        or the fulfillment of a project
becomes self-inspiring.

Walk the walk of faith today. Make a fresh commitment to
God, saying prayerfully and sincerely:

"God, I'm ready to take the plunge. Give me the push that I
need, and I'm trusting that with Your help we'll tackle every
problem at every turn of the road with a positive mental attitude! And together we'll succeed joyously!"

## Inking the agreement

"For behold, I have made you this day/A
fortified city and an iron pillar,/And bronze
walls against the whole land."—JEREMIAH 1:18

**46**     Until I'm solidly committed to an appointment, I write it in pencil. But then comes the time when it needs either to be erased or written in ink! That's the point of commitment.

Faith is inking the agreement. It's pouring the concrete! It's breaking the mold and throwing the pieces away.

On the grounds of our Crystal Cathedral is a beautiful bronze statue of Christ surrounded by sheep, sculpted by Henry Van Wolf. When we purchased the Good Shepherd statue and were completely satisfied with the finished bronze piece, the sculptor asked that the mold be destroyed, thereby protecting the uniqueness of the work that would stand on our property. I had no choice in the matter. It was a directive of the sculptor. He didn't want copies made.

> **Irrevocable commitments that offer no loopholes, no bail-out provisions, and no parachute clauses will extract incredible productivity and performance.**

One of the reasons my marriage has been so successful is because there isn't a single ounce of doubt in our minds that it has to be, it must be, and, therefore, it will be, a happy relationship until the end! We really meant it when we promised to love each other "for better, for worse; for richer, for poorer; in sickness and in health, till death us do part."

Inking an agreement is making a commitment to continuity. Try it. Believe me, that kind of faith moves mountains!

# Imagining the positive possibilities

"But those who seek the LORD shall not lack
any good thing."—PSALM 34:10

List on a piece of paper all the resources you need to achieve **47**
your desired goal. Overlook nothing. Do you need more time
or money,
    education or tools,
    books or credit,
    property,
    consultants or friends,
    specialized technicians,
    or marketing plans?
Make sure you've included everything. Have you included
on the list your own positive imagination, your faith?

Now, look down the entire list and number the items according to their importance. What, in your list, will prove to
be the single most important factor to your success?

That's right—your own faith, your own power of imagination!

**What you imagine is what will transpire. What you
believe is what you will achieve.**

When you imagine positive possibilities, you release enthusiasm. You are driven with a strong desire to succeed. Nothing
is more important on that entire list than your own faith and
imagination!

You have the power to control pictures that are put into
your mind. Do not allow yourself the destructive luxury of
imagining all the negative possibilities.

Imagine the positive possibilities actually happening. You
will get so excited that the best people in the world will be
attracted to your side.

Everybody wants to associate with a winner!

Think success, and you'll achieve it.

## FAITH IS . . .
## *Initiating positive action*

"I will go in the strength of the Lord GOD."—
PSALM 71:16

**48**  By now you have observed that faith is not a plateau, it's a pyramid. It's not a sidewalk, it's a ladder. Faith is wading in the shallow water and moving on to the depths.

Wanting more out of life is the incentive to get going. Mountain-moving faith requires that you and I be initiators!

Be prime movers, leaders! A leader is the first person who stands up out of his chair and says, "O.K., gang, let's go!"

Our world today needs positive leaders of faith. Good things don't just happen. You have to make them happen!

People frequently comment on the success of our church. "Things seem to be going great for the ministry of the Crystal Cathedral."

My answer almost always is, "Yes, because people pray, prepare, plan, and promote these achievements. We initiate our own success. It doesn't just fall into our lap."

Where do you get the courage to be an initiator; a self-starter; a motivated individual? Draw motivation from faith.

I have been motivated for years by a phrase that is printed on the masthead of my little hometown paper in Alton, Iowa. I read it all of my childhood days: "The saddest words of tongue or pen are these: it might have been."

Become a "do it now" person. The world is out there waiting to follow those who have the faith to move ahead. Be the *initiator* of good and the *imitator* of God Himself!

**I believe it will work, if I work it!**

[298]

# *Assuring yourself of success*

"There is not a word on my tongue,/But behold,
O LORD,/You know it altogether./You have
hedged me behind it and before,/And laid Your
hand upon me."—PSALM 139:4–5

Faith is not folly. It's a responsible confidence rooted in the **49**
assurance that a wiser providence maneuvers your life. Confidence is not human arrogance. Rather, possibility thinking
and self-assurance are the reflection of an abiding trust in the
Lord who knows us perfectly. He has only our best interest in
mind.

Our relationship with God allows us to be affirmative. Exercise your growing faith now with these declarations:

> **"I'm on the right road. I am walking the walk of faith.
> I have made the decision to follow the Lord."**

> **"I have given my life to God and He is in control of it."**

> **"The God who has command over my life is protecting
> me from hidden shoals that could sink the ship of my
> soul and spirit."**

> **"God is opening doors that will surprise me with new
> opportunities."**

> **"God is closing doors that I want to go through be-
> cause He knows they will lead to my failure and de-
> struction."**

Thank You, Father, for assuring me of success on my walk
of faith. I know I'm on the right road. I thank You, Lord, for
opening and closing doors, thereby guiding me on my daily
walk. I sense my faith growing stronger as I declare my faith
and affirm You as Lord of my life. Thank You, O God.

## Arranging to arrive

"Your eyes saw my substance,/being yet unformed./And in Your book they all were written,/The days fashioned for me,/When as yet there were none of them."—PSALM 139:16

**50**     **It's terribly important that in the walk of faith you maintain your sense of responsibility.**

Faith seeks positive action through
• careful calculation
• wise planning, and
• clever arranging.

The greatest example of this is God Himself, the Divine Arranger, the Master Organizer!

Any scientist, chemist, or physicist will tell you how neatly and brilliantly every cell, genetic chain, and piece of matter is wondrously made and organized.

The way in which two microscopic elements meet in the womb to create a human being is wondrous. How beautifully today's Bible verse records it: God's eyes saw your substance before you were formed; He arranged your days before you were born. There is a divine plan for your life on earth.

God challenges you to so arrange the elements of your life that you might fulfill His plan. He assigns you the responsibility to consider all of the resources, time, energy, money, and relationships, and then arrange them to keep on target.

It is essential to put your life in good order. This is especially true of the health of your eternal soul and its relationship with the heavenly Father. Make sure that your life is so carefully arranged that when your calling comes to make the transition into eternity, you will arrive at heaven's gate without fear. You can do that now by committing your life to the God who made you.

Be sure of this—God will never turn one of His friends away!

## Desiring to arrive

*". . . when the desire comes, it is a tree of life."*—PROVERBS 13:12

More than anything else, faith is an all-consuming desire to succeed!    **51**

**Faith without passion is soda water without the sparkle.**

"You don't lack faith," I said to a young man who had just complained of that problem. "Your faith lacks drive." Somehow a strong desire must be injected into the project of living, or faith will fizzle out and failure will overtake you.

Open a can of cola or soda water and let it stand for a few hours—and the fizz will all be gone. What the sparkle is to soda water, is what an inner passion to succeed is to mountain-moving faith. If you've lost your desire, if the fizz is gone, and the beverage is flat, then you need a new birth of divine desire!

How do you get it?
1. Perhaps you need to take a complete break, a holiday, a vacation.
2. Double-check your motives. Are you too self-serving?
3. Draw close to a hurting person. Feel his anxiety, loneliness, and emptiness. Know that, through your success, you can put a smile on his face and a sparkle in his eye; the passion will return.
4. Invite God to totally control your moods and your mind! For God Himself is the holy passion of helpful, appealing love which will override all other inclinations!
5. Calculate—who will be helped if I hang in—and succeed? And who will hurt—if I quit and fail?

*FAITH IS . . .*
## Complimenting yourself every day

"Do not cast away your confidence, which has a
great reward. For you have need of
endurance. . . ."—HEBREWS 10:35

**52**   Practice all the faith you can by complimenting yourself,
honestly, genuinely, and fluently! Be effervescent in complimenting yourself today.

As Christians we sometimes become so programmed to humility, coupled with the awareness that we can accomplish
nothing without the grace of God and the goodness of our
Lord, that we fail to give ourselves adequate credit.

God knows you and I need a pat on the back. There are
nobler dreams that God wants us to pursue; there are bigger
battles to be fought. The need to endure to the end compels us
to give ourselves all the motivation possible.

Self-congratulatory remarks—in the privacy of your prayer
time with God—are in order!

> **In the presence of God, in the privacy of prayer, take
> time to applaud the great human being that you really
> are!**

You are a redeemed child of God! Let your light shine!

Try complimenting yourself every morning when you begin
the day by praying.

Thank You, Father, for giving me enough faith in myself,
and in Your goodness to me, to give myself these compliments! I thank You that I have been created with a mind capable of dreaming dreams! I thank You that I have a heart
through which the love of Jesus Christ can flow to human
beings around me. I thank You that I do have talents, abilities,
and gifts that You can use. I thank You, God, that my life is
definitely on the right road. Stay with me, Father, all the way.
Amen.

## FAITH IS . . .
# *Educating your mind*

"When wisdom enters your heart,/And
knowledge is pleasant to your soul,/Discretion
will preserve you;/Understanding will keep
you."—PROVERBS 2:10–11

There is only one *now*—I'm going to make the most of today. There is only one *me*—I'll make the most of myself. **53**

People who have a lot of faith believe in themselves and
their potential enough to invest everything to make the most
of the one life they have.

How?

If you believe in yourself, you'll educate yourself.

You'll pay the price to become informed. Perhaps you need
to go back to school, or aim for another degree.

Do you need to be brought up to date on new technology?
Today more than ever before, a neglected intelligence is folly.
"A mind is a terrible thing to waste" is the slogan of the United
Negro College Fund.

Faith means being good stewards of the treasures God has
put at our disposal, the opportunities He puts before us, the
gifts He has given us, and the resources He has entrusted to
our care.

Is any treasure more valuable than your ability to think?
Remember, faith and intellect are not opponents. The smarter
you become, the stronger your faith can grow. Be wise. Seek
the counsel of the smartest people. Go to the person you
would like to work for and ask what you need to do to qualify
for the job you would like.

Keep this formula in mind today.

**Inspiration + preparation + self-motivation = suc-
cessful faith**

Prepare yourself to become a leader. You can do it—you are
a possibility thinker.

FAITH IS . . .
## Auditioning your ambitions

"For out of the abundance of the heart his
mouth speaks."—LUKE 6:45

**54** Now that you have educated your mind don't assume that a degree will automatically unlock any door. Education merely entitles you to go out and sell yourself with integrity! Your credentials only give you the right to audition your ambitions in the market place.

There was an advertisement: "Help wanted: office boy." One positive-thinking youngster rushed to answer the ad, only to find a long line of boys ahead of him waiting to be interviewed. He was afraid that by the time he got to the door, a selection would have been made.

So he wrote this note: "To the boss: My name is Johnnie. I'm number thirteen in the line. Don't hire anybody until you've interviewed me!"

He handed the note to the secretary, who brought it into the office. A moment later she came out, approached young Johnnie, and said, "The boss would like to see you." It was no surprise that he got the job!

**If you don't believe in yourself, who will? You owe yourself every possible chance!**

Faith is auditioning your ambitions. Jesus said, "Let your light so shine before men, that they may see your good works" (Matt. 5:16). And He cautioned us not to "light a lamp and put it under a basket, but on a lampstand" (Matt. 5:15).

Don't be afraid of boasting. You are only witnessing honestly to the talents God has given you! Remaining a silent, shrinking violet can be a sin of ingratitude to God for the position and privilege He has bestowed upon you.

Are you arrogant? Lacking in humility when you step forward? I think not. Rather I suspect you are a dynamic possibility thinker! You're good—by the goodness of God and both of you know it! Go for it!

# Underscoring your positive thoughts

*"You have put gladness in my heart."*—PSALM
4:7

Today let's underline the positive thoughts. Let's honor cre- **55**
ative ideas. Let's take the constructive ideas and crown them
with a leadership role in our life.

Look at a person who's moving forward, making commitments in faith, and you'll see somebody whose actions underscore his positive thoughts. Observe the person who is setting
goals and going for them with all his might and you'll see
somebody who has turned the leadership of his life over to a
dynamic faith.

Stop and think of the most creative thoughts you've had in
the past twenty-four hours. What have you done with those
ideas?

Now go back and underline the most exciting ideas you've
had in the last year. What have you done with them?

Life becomes what you make of it, and what you make of
life depends entirely on how you manage the ideas that come
to your brain.

> **Wisdom is the gift of spotting a positive idea and un-
> derscoring it by letting it become incarnated into ac-
> tion.**

Here's a positive thought that you can underscore right
now:

God is alive.

He is there even if you do not feel His presence.

He is guiding your life by directing positive thoughts into
your mind to keep you on the pathway of faith.

This is proof of God's existence and His goodness.

What a tremendous thought!

## Adopting an orphan

"God has dealt to each one a measure of
faith."—ROMANS 12:3

**56** Many positive ideas come into your mind like orphans.
They don't seem to be your own. But be prepared to adopt
them, especially when they are loaded with possibilities.

**Faith is adopting an orphan; it's buying without a war-
ranty; it's paying in advance; it's ordering from a foreign menu; it's traveling away from home without
reservations.**

Our wedding took place in a little country church in Iowa.
After the reception, we rushed to the car under a shower of
rice and headed off for a weekend honeymoon. As we drove
toward the direction of the state border, my wife asked,
"Where are we spending the night?" I looked at her dumb-
founded. In all of the excitement of the wedding, I completely
forgot to make reservations!

"I thought we'd probably stay in a hotel somewhere in Minnesota," I said.

"You mean you didn't make reservations?" she asked.

We still laugh about that today, over thirty years later! As it
turned out we had a wonderful room, and a wonderful night.

In the first years of our marriage we supplied our house
with used utensils and appliances that were auctioned off by
moving companies. It was fun to watch unopened barrels
wheeled onto the platform and auctioned off. Nobody had any
idea what they were buying. They could be filled with old
clothes or, possibly, fine crystal and silver.

A positive idea sometimes comes across your mind like a
sealed box at an auction. Who knows what great possibilities
are waiting in that orphan idea? Adopt it!

This is your chance! Grab it.

# Tuning into positive thoughts

"Make a joyful shout to the LORD . . ./Serve the
LORD with gladness;/Come before His presence
with singing."—PSALM 100:1–2

Faith is tuning into positive thoughts. When an uninvited **57**
and unwelcomed negative thought comes into your mind,
tune it out by tuning in a good idea.

When my children were growing up, they often had childish
sibling quarrels. They usually ended up pouting and sulking.
Then I would take my finger and brush it lightly across the
forehead from one side to the other saying, "Your mind is like
a radio. And right here is the dial." Then I playfully switched
the ear on the right and then the one on the left and said,
"These are the little turning knobs. Why don't you turn the
dial and pick up a happier channel?"

On more than one occasion when this little exercise didn't
seem to achieve the immediate desired objectives, we joined
as a family at the table and sang a happy song. Even though
none of us were celebrating a birthday, we sang the happiest
song we could think of. We knew "dear someone" would be
glad we remembered his or her birthday!"

You and I have the power to choose the wave lengths we
will tune into—wave lengths that will generate harmony or
disharmony within your mind.

Imagine that the positive emotions are radio stations waiting for you to tune in and get turned on. Here are some positive wave lengths for you to select:

L–O–V–E
H–O–P–E
J–O–Y
P–E–A–C–E
C–O–U–R–A–G–E
C–H–E–E–R

If you really want to—you can find sources—like radio stations—sending out these signals. Tune them in, and you'll
*come alive!*

[307]

## FAITH IS . . .
### *Filtering the thoughts*

> "Whatever things are true, whatever things are noble, whatever things are just, whatever things are pure, whatever things are lovely, whatever things are of good report . . . meditate on these things."—PHILIPPIANS 4:8

**58** A faith that is committed to success in the pursuit of an excellent and noble idea will require fine tuning. Fine tuning happens as you develop the practice of filtering the thoughts that come through your mind. Gradually your conscious level will rise as it relates in sensitivity to
what is positive and what is negative,
what is good and what is evil,
what is productive and what is counter-productive,
what is constructive and what is destructive,
what is healthy and what is unhealthy.

**Your faith will be strengthened or insulted on a daily basis by the thoughts that enter your mind.**

You can choose many of your thoughts by selecting the reading material, the television programs, and the deliberate exposures that you choose to encounter.

Still, there are the thousands of unsolicited stimuli that hit the average brain from a variety of unpredictable sources in the course of a single day. Consequently, a filtering system must be built into your mind that screens out the negative while allowing the positive to pass through. The Bible verse of today gives you the blueprint for establishing a six-layer mental filtering system.
1. Is it true?
2. Is it noble?
3. Is it just?
4. Is it pure?
5. Is it lovely?
6. Is it positive?
Now meditate on these things!

# Minding the storehouse of the mind

> "'Therefore give to Your servant an
> understanding heart to judge Your people, that I
> may discern between good and evil.'" (The
> prayer of Solomon)—1 KINGS 3:9

No wise builder builds a house until he knows the mate- **59**
rials available to him. Likewise, anyone who walks the walk
of faith requires constant spiritual nourishment. You must
have an adequate supply of positive beliefs for emergency use
in the battle against negative and destructive forces that can
conquer you.

I remember a young man, a member of my church, who
suddenly became uninterested in his faith and went into a
period of depression. He finally asked me for help. I asked him
the basic questions. "What have you been reading lately?"
"Have you been reading your Bible?" "Inspirational literature?" "Have you been listening to positive-thinking people?"
He admitted he had allowed himself to be exposed to much
negative thinking.

I shared with him the old computer programmer slogan,
GIGO—Garbage-in-garbage-out. If you program garbage into
the computer, garbage will come out of the computer.

A psychologist friend of mine, who was counseling a client
suffering from depression, put on a dramatic demonstration.
He filled a glass with water, then added some dust to it. He
reached in the ash tray for a cigarette butt and dropped it in.
He reached underneath a chair and, finding a dried piece of
gum, added it to the glass of water. Now he mixed the polluted mixture thoroughly and proceeded to pour it into a nice
clean cup. As he did, he said, "You will only pour out what
you have put in."

**At least once a week hear a positive-thinking message
from some positive-thinking church. Add to that positive Bible readings and positive prayer, and then your
faith will remain vital and alive.**

## *Imprinting the self-conscious mind*

> "For You are great, and do wondrous things;/
> You alone are God./Teach me Your way, O
> LORD;/I will walk in Your truth."—PSALM
> 86:10,11

**60**     It's important to understand how faith works, from the scientific and psychological perspective as well as from the theological and scriptural perspective.

We have already studied previously that the subconscious mind is like
- a film in a movie camera
- the tape in a tape recorder
- a chip in a computer

Knowledge is stored permanently.

We now know that the human being never forgets anything. Every experience we ever have had is indelibly recorded within us.

We may lose the powers of conscious recall. But under deep psychoanalysis we can usually recollect experiences that have long been forgotten in the depths of our memories.

When you exercise positive faith by imagining, visualizing, or picturing in your brain the expectant achievement, you are in effect making a cybernetic imprint. Your strongly held beliefs leave an indelible stamp on your subconscious, almost like a tattoo on the skin. As you evaluate the thoughts that you allow into your conscious mind, remember this:

**Each thought becomes a tattoo on the skin of your memory either for good or ill.**

Therefore, it is vitally important to your mental muscles that you control what you will allow to be imprinted on your eternal memory.

Thank You, Father, for teaching me the power of faith.

## Censoring the negatives

"Behold, I stand at the door and knock. If
anyone hears My voice and opens the door, I
will come in."—REVELATION 3:20

Possibility thinking includes the process of positive censor- **61**
ing. It involves sifting out the good from the bad.

Faith asks the question: Does this idea deserve my attention or the trademark of my name? Maintaining a constructive critical overview is a constant process.

Faith is not afraid to censor. It stands guard at the portals of
your mind, checking the ethical and moral credentials of the
ideas that could disrupt, disturb, and possibly destroy your
attitude of faith.

So firm up your willpower.

Assign responsibility to the spiritual laws that manage your
thoughts. Without guidelines, controls, and censorship, life is
like an airplane with a drunken pilot. A crash landing is always looming.

I have made several trips into Egypt to study ancient Egyp-
tology. Pharaohs often are portrayed with a cobra poised over
their heads. King Tut not only is pictured with a head gear
featuring a cobra—but also a vulture. The cobra was to attack
the poisonous ideas before they entered his head. The vulture
was to consume the rotten ideas.

> **You need Jesus Christ to help control your thinking.
> He stands at the door of your mind and heart waiting
> to come in.**

Lord Jesus Christ, my mind was designed to be a mansion
with many rooms. Will You come and be the Doorkeeper at
the main entrance? Admit only those guests who would bring
honor to the household. Dismiss the unworthy from my doorstep. Welcome those honorable visitors that would flood my
mind with hope and health and happiness.

Lord, will You come to be the Guest of Honor? Amen.

## Starving your enemies

"Do not be overcome by evil, but overcome evil with good."—ROMANS 12:21

**62**  Do positive-thinking people deny the reality of evil? Not at all. We recognize that there is an opposite to everything; when we declare our faith in positive thinking we automatically acknowledge the alternative—negative thinking.

So we can expect to encounter enemies as we walk the path of faith. Possibility thinking is a threat to impossibility thinkers. Positive thinking is a judgment on negative thinking.

**Faith is a positive attack on doubt.**

What enemies have you encountered, so far, on the walk of faith?

In the walk of faith we describe an enemy as anybody who diminishes your faith in yourself, in your neighbors, and in almighty God!

Therefore, our strongest enemies are the negative thoughts that come into our minds.

Who then is your greatest enemy? You may lament the fact that those closest to you do not give the encouragement you think they should. But nobody puts you down more than you do yourself. Nobody has rejected more of your best ideas than you have!

How many good ideas have come into your mind only to be discarded by you?

So how will you handle an enemy? If you can't convert him, starve him. Whatever you do, don't feed your negative thoughts! Starve your negative thoughts by ignoring them.

Feed your positive thoughts with faith. Fill your mind with beautiful affirmations and powerful promises that are abundant throughout the Bible.

My promise to you is this: Your walk of faith will be productive, prosperous, and worthwhile!

## *Washing the windows of the mind*

"The path of the just is like the shining sun,/
That shines ever brighter unto the perfect
day."—PROVERBS 4:18

If you tune in positive thoughts and censor out negative **63**
ones, will these dynamic exercises of a daily, disciplined faith
keep the windows of your soul sparkling continually? No, not
completely.
- Accidents can dent a new car.
- Spills can stain clean clothes.
- Upsets can frustrate a good person.
- Storms can litter the clean year.

Recently I attended a religious conference in Amsterdam.
Each morning we saw Dutch people washing their windows,
even if there was no dirt on them, no rainfall to stain the glass,
no heavy dew that would dry and leave a misty film.

That's a good practice for us also.

Faith is washing the windows of the mind, every morning
beginning the new day, bright with God's love, and each night
washing away the film of negativity.

Have you noticed how quickly windows that were clean
can lose their sparkle? From somewhere a film comes, cloud-
ing the reflection of the sun.

Are the twinkle and the sparkle of faith gone from the win-
dowpanes of your soul? Is the reflection of God's love no
longer mirrored brightly in your life as it used to be?

> **Ask the Holy Spirit to come in each morning and
> again in the evening to wash the skylights of your soul.
> Visualize the Lord, living within your mind like a
> bright light of love and faith!**

Lord, make my life a window for your light to shine
through, and a mirror to reflect your love to all I meet. Amen.

## Mining the deeper thoughts

"O LORD, You have searched and known me./
You know my sitting down and rising up;/You
understand my thought afar off."—PSALM
139:1–2

**64**  I have long marveled at the courage of the miners who dare
to dig deep shafts in the heart of the trembling earth, in search
of diamonds, gold, or precious ore.

**A vibrant and shining faith comes from mining deeper
thoughts, exploring deeper and darker regions of your
soul.**

Joshua Lightman tells of a colleague, a professed atheist.
The young Jewish man, undergoing depth analysis to understand his subconscious feelings, recalled a long-forgotten experience. His mother had enrolled him, at the age of five, in a
synagogue school to "learn about his heavenly Father." This
little boy's earthly father was cruel; therefore, he believed all
fathers were cruel. In a negative emotional reaction he made a
decision *not* to meet "another father"—God. When he discovered that his atheism was rooted in negative emotional-
ism, not healthy intellectualism, he was liberated and became
a believer!

Are there blockades that need to be blasted out of the way
before you can discover the wealth within your grasp? Delve
into your conscious and subconsciousness—mine the depths
of your faith. God has searched you and knows you. He *understands* your thoughts afar off.

O Lord, my Father, You know every experience I have ever
encountered. Heal me of deep obsessions, of negative experiences that would prevent me from believing with joy. Then
may my faith sparkle like a diamond! Thank You, Lord.
Amen.

## *Tolerating your imperfections*

"Do you not know that you are the temple of
God and that the Spirit of God dwells in
you?"—1 CORINTHIANS 3:16

How's your self-image today? Having trouble accepting **65**
yourself after goofing, bungling, or sinning?

Are you pulled down by a painful awareness of your shortcomings and your frailties?

Then today is the time to reprogram your mental attitude,
remodel your self-image, and give your self-esteem a "faith-
lift."

• Remember that even though you are imperfect, you still
are a child of God.

• Decide to join the human race. Nobody's perfect; no one
is sinless! Who do you think you are? Why are you so rough
on yourself?

• The power of God within you can compensate for your
imperfections and inability.

• Tolerate your imperfections, and keep striving for excellence!

• But never tolerate your own negative thinking!

• Do separate yourself from negative thinkers who put you
down! You need to be built up.

• Gravitate to positive people who give you a lift!

• Choose—willfully and deliberately—to be a "bigger" believer! Yes, you are designed to be a positive thinker.

God is within you now, living in the best thoughts you are
thinking.

Affirmation: I shall tolerate my weakness and shortcomings by shifting my focus to the mighty power of God.

**God is able to do great things through imperfect
people!**

Thank You, God, for living in me. Knowing this, I claim
Your power, Your holiness, Your ability, and Your wisdom,
that my weakness may be made perfect in Your sight. Amen.

## Deprogramming your computer

"Let us know, let us pursue the knowledge of
the LORD. His going forth is established as the
morning; He will come to us like the rain, like
the latter and former rain to the earth."—
HOSEA 6:3

**66** The mind is like a computer. Think of yourself as a multi-
track, supersophisticated recording device. From the moment
you are born, this complex, four-track tape recorder starts running and never stops!

On one track you record in the memory and subconscious
every sound you ever hear.

On another track a video camera starts filming everything
your eyes see from the moment they open and begin to focus.

On still another track your subconscious begins to record
sensual experiences—pain and pleasure. The entire psychological system of Pavlovian behavioral modification takes off
on this track.

On still another track, another subconscious recording
starts the moment you are born. This channel will record
every emotional experience you ever encounter.

God created your memory to record the audio, video, sensual, and emotional trips you'll take in life.

We have all experienced *deja-vu,* that experience whereby
something we see, hear, or smell touches the replay button of
our subconscious recorder and we immediately experience a
visual or emotional flashback. We are suddenly caught up in a
mood—pleasant or unpleasant. We cannot explain why. A
long forgotten experience from the distant past is trying to
surface in the memory. The vague recollection hazily lingering in the subconscious memory only succeeds in "filtering
through" as an unclear mystifying mood.

So you realize how important it is to limit the negative input in your life. Every time you repeat a negative word or
phrase, you contribute to the collective underground pollution of your mind.

Deprogram, then *reprogram yourself with positive words,
positive affirmations, and positive prayers.*

This is mountain-moving faith at work!

*FAITH IS . . .*
## *Programming your computer for success*

"The fruit of the Spirit is love, joy, peace, longsuffering, kindness, goodness, faithfulness, gentleness, self-control."—GALATIANS 5:22

Knowing that the mind is a complex recording system, you **67** choose to either program it for failure, or for success. Today, program these positive thoughts:

> **Faith puts positive thoughts into my mind, knowing they will flash back on the digital screen of my conscious mind at the press of a button.**

- I am programming my mind to see the good in bad situations.
- I am programming my computer to react positively to negative situations.
- I am programming my computer to create a subconscious mental picture of my success already achieved.
- I am affirming only positive expectations.

I marvel that God gives me the freedom to program my computer any way I choose. If I fill it with inaccurate data, that's exactly what will come out; so I am treating my subconscious mind seriously. I cannot be frivolous in playing mental games. I cannot take a lighthearted attitude toward negative fantasies that flash through my mind.

God gives me the freedom to choose what my life and destiny will be. I shall prove responsible to this awesome responsibility. I know that success is certain if I program positive thoughts for great possibilities.

Thank You, God, for all the positive encouragement You send my way. Your blessings are so many I cannot count them all—love, joy, peace, kindness, goodness. . . . What a rich reservoir I can tap when I program Your power into my life. Thank You, Lord. Amen.

## Supposing —positively

"Surely His salvation is near to those who fear Him."—PSALM 85:9

**68**    Life proceeds on the basis of many unproven assumptions. Faith moves ahead, acting on suppositions that may or may not be verifiable. A negative-thinking person assumes the worst will happen, and then wonders why his negative expectations are always fulfilled. But a positive-thinking person assumes that the best will happen and sees positive results!

Faith is *supposing—positively.* A negative thinker says, "But suppose it won't work." A positive thinker says, "Suppose it *will* work!" The negative thinker says, "But suppose it can't be done." A positive thinker says, "Suppose it *can* be done! I don't want to pass up this opportunity!"

*Faith practices the art of creating positive alternatives to negative assumptions!* Here's how supposing positively works: An idea comes to mind, an opportunity presents itself, a problem confronts us. Now watch the "supposing positive" mind at work: "*Suppose* this idea came from God?" "It sounds impossible, but *suppose* I give it a try?" "*Suppose* I announce my plans?" "Then *suppose* some people believe that it's a great idea and come to my support!" "*Suppose* I pray about this and believe it is the right thing to do." "Is there reason for me to *suppose* that God will bless me?"

There is no *supposing* when it comes to the faithfulness of God! The word in the Scriptures is *surely!* "*Surely* His salvation is near to those who fear Him." "*Surely* goodness and mercy shall follow me/All the days of my life;/And I will dwell in the house of the LORD/Forever" (Ps. 85:9; 23:6 italics added).

**God's promise is that He will replace our positive *supposing* with His *absolute surety*.**

## *Experiencing impossibilities*

"Your sun shall no longer go down,/Nor shall
your moon withdraw itself;/for the LORD will
be your everlasting light."—ISAIAH 60:20

Is it possible to live where the sun never sets? Yes, northern **69**
Sweden is the land of the "midnight sun." Some years ago
when I was on a preaching mission in Sweden, we traveled to
the northernmost point of the earth, which is reachable by
commercial floating vessels. On the third day of the cruise, at
11:00 P.M., there was only blue sky around us.

We watched the sun drop until it was low in the sky and
looked as though it would disappear. But then it began to
move to the right, parallel with the horizon. At midnight, still
as bright as day, the sun moved across the horizon without
setting. It was a great experience to witness one of those days
when the sun never sets.

When you experience something that you always assumed
was an impossibility you can be sure you've been believing!

**Faith is the practice which allows for the possibility of
apparent impossibilities to become actual scientific
realities.**

Walking the walk of faith is the attitude of keeping your
mind open to new possibilities that only God knows about!

"God is the sum total of the vast unknown," said my friend
Dr. Arnold Beckman, founder of Beckman Instruments. This
explains why some of the greatest scientists alive in the world
today are believers in God.

The next time you face a problem or a challenge that appears to defy solutions, keep an open mind to the impossibility. . . . It might be possible after all!

Today, O God, I am going to keep an open mind to experience some new surprises of spiritual growth. Today, I am going
to believe that the impossible really is possible! Amen.

# Rising above depressing situations

"To whom then will you liken Me . . . ?/Lift up your eyes on high,/And see who has created these things. . . ."—ISAIAH 40:25–26

**70** What do you do when the analysis of your condition leads to a depressing diagnosis?

What do you do when your doctor tells you that you have an incurable fatal disease?

How do you keep an open mind to the possibility of a cure when there is no known cure?

You practice faith! You rise above the depressing attitudes and situations.

Think of the locks that enable a boat to rise and proceed up a stream that otherwise would be impossible to navigate. When ships travel upstream they are "locked" into an enclosed area which is then filled with water. Ships weighing tens of thousands of tons, are lifted easily through the floatation power of water. The lock system enables ships to sail on and on through higher bodies of water.

What do you do when you are trapped with a negative analysis that appears to block your way through life?

> **Lock in your mental attitude with positive thinking and allow your mind to float upward by the invisible, silent, escalating flow of the spirit of faith which only the eternal God can give.**

Suddenly you are moving forward again!

You are rising above the shoals that would have grounded you.

O God, today I feel Your enormous power streaming into my life, flooding my soul. I am rising like a giant ship, lifted by water. I am floating above the negative predictions because I know my condition is never hopeless! My faith is escalating! Thank You, God. Amen.

*FAITH IS . . .*
## Scaling the wall

"For by You I can run against a troop;/By my
God I can leap over a wall."—2 SAMUEL 22:30

You have heard about those incredible incidents where an **71**
average human being exhibits almost superhuman strength in
an emergency situation. It's a frequently recurring phenomenon.

Two people are working on an automobile. One is underneath the car. The jack collapses. The car falls. The companion
finds himself picking up the car and rescuing his companion
from certain, crushing death. Where did the strength of a giant
come from?

Do you know how strong you are? Do you know how high
you can jump? We really don't know! For every single human
being, without exception, has the potential to tap into physical power that far transcends normality. We just don't know
the how, the why, and the wherefore.

What that means to you today is that you can scale that
wall! The "impossible" obstruction! You can leap over that
fence of frustration! Suddenly you can surmount that obstacle
as your spirit soars!

Any person becomes a bigger person when he becomes ob-
sessed by a "giant complex"! You can be a giant, too. You are
as big as you think you are!

Think "leaping over" thoughts and you will scale that wall!

> **The "will" is more important than the "skill" when it
> comes to scaling a wall.**

You will not fail to scale the wall. "By my God I can leap
over a wall." Break wide open with big-thinking belief and—
away you go!

## Dividing to conquer

"Look, the LORD your God has set the land
before you; go up and possess it, as the LORD
God . . . has spoken to you; do not fear or be
discouraged."—DEUTERONOMY 1:21

**72**    One day president of McDonnell Douglas Corporation, Walter Burke, received a telephone call from President John F. Kennedy. "Mr. Burke, we need a rocket with enough booster power to put a man on the moon. I have already been told all the reasons why it can't be done. Now you go ahead and solve the problems to get the job accomplished!"

"How did you ever begin to tackle such an impossible assignment?" I asked Walter Burke.

"I learned many years ago that one large problem is really a collection of many little problems," Mr. Burke said. He explained:

**"The way to tackle an impossible problem is to break it down and solve the several little problems one at a time."**

You tackle each one until only one stubborn problem remains. Now all attention is focused on this remaining obstacle and the breakthrough happens! You have divided and conquered the total problem one chunk at a time.

It worked for Walter Burke and it will work for you. When you face a seemingly insurmountable problem—divide it.

Part of the problem is a decision you need to make.

Part of the problem is your lack of patience.

Part of the problem is your negative attitude.

Part of the problem is your preoccupation with yourself. You can handle all of these parts of the problems. Right?

You will succeed in conquering the insolvable problems! What a great feeling of success you'll experience!

# Challenging the negative judgment

"There are many who say,/'Who will show us
any good? Lord, lift up the light of Your
countenance upon us.'"—PSALM 4:6

Many problems continue to remain unsolved because **73** negative-thinking experts say, "It can't be done." Remember Walter Burke? One day I asked him, "How did you ever manage to believe that it was possible to develop a rocket big enough to put a man on the moon?"

He answered, "I was a student in aeronautical engineering in St. Louis, Missouri, in the 1920s. At that time, we were taught as a matter of scientific truth that the speed of sound was the absolute, ultimate limit we would ever be able to travel. The reasons made sense: (1) the weight of such a machine, because of the amount of fuel needed, would render it unflyable; (2) we believed an object crossing the sound barrier would disintegrate."

"And how did we ever break through such locked-in thinking?" I asked Dr. Burke.

"Well, the Second World War came along," Dr. Burke explained. "And in the emergency, farmers from Iowa and Nebraska were drafted. We put them in a cockpit and in a matter of days taught them to fly an airplane. We never bothered to teach them aeronautical engineering. With a few victories, they were promoted to officers. Well, these uneducated officers got together and decided we ought to focus our energies on developing a jet engine that could fly faster than sound. They did it. *Because they didn't know it couldn't be done!*"

The next time somebody tells you, "It is impossible!" "It can't be done!" "It's hopeless!" "It's terminal!" challenge the negative assumption.

**God doesn't know the meaning of *impossible*.**

That's what faith is all about.

[323]

## *Analyzing inquisitively*

> "Understanding is a wellspring of life to him who has it."—PROVERBS 16:22

**74**　Stop and analyze the creative people who have been responsible for big breakthroughs and have made distinctive contributions in the world of science, art, humanity, and religion. You will find that each has an inquisitive nature.

After all, thousands, even millions of people must have sat under a tree and had an apple hit them on the head, but all they did was complain! According to legend, Newton looked up and ask, "Why did the apple fall *down?*"

If you are having problems with your faith, perhaps you need to be more inquisitive. Do not fear that your faith in God can ever be shaken by an increased intelligence. Make sure the sources of your newly acquired knowledge are persons who are not prejudiced and who are not proclaiming as fact assumptions that are rooted in negativity.

Can you see how widely the poison of negative thinking has penetrated our culture? How often have you and I been heard saying, "Curiosity killed the cat"? In fact, curiosity has been responsible for many scientific achievements and medical breakthroughs!

**The inquisitive nature of the human being is a God-implanted impulse, designed to entice us down the road of faith toward exciting progress!**

Analyze God Himself. You'll be surprised how this can be the beginning of new growth into a maturing religious consciousness. The possibility thinker who pursues his inquisitive nature is the one who will find the buried treasure!

Thank You, God, for the faith to analyze Your Word today. I will no longer be afraid in Your presence. My finite mind cannot begin to understand the vastness of Your infinite knowledge. Walk with me today and teach me a new truth about Yourself. Amen.

*FAITH IS . . .*
## *Actualizing your positive fantasies*

"Your old men shall dream dreams, your young men shall see visions."—JOEL 2:28

I once did a study of those great people we call "geniuses." I observed a recurring quality in them—the amazing quality of positive, childlike fantasizing. Great people are intuitive and imaginative. They have the capacity to let their minds fly into wild and wonderful flights of fantasy. It was said of Walt Disney that he never stopped being a little boy.

Faith is actualizing *positive* fantasies. Obviously, negative fantasizing that leads to antisocial behavior must be restrained. Faith tests your fantasies. Are they positive? Will they help society? Will they bring happiness? Dare to dream the most wonderful dreams in the world!

Now make your fantasies come true by believing they *can* come true, even though they appear to be totally and completely impossible! Your fantasies will attract attention if you dare to talk about them! At first you may not be taken seriously, but your fantasies will soon become realities as you take the first strong steps forward.

**Positive people will intuitively respond to your positive dreams. Encouragement will come from places and people you least expect. Believe in your positive fantasies and you will begin to actualize them.**

I speak from experience. An all-glass church? A Crystal Cathedral? A fantasy? Yes—and today, it is a fantastic reality!

Positive fantasies become positive realities when by faith you start to do something about them. Make them happen. They will become tomorrow's talked-about achievement.

# Stretching your imagination

"Enlarge the place of your tent,/ . . . Lengthen
your cords,/And strengthen your stakes./For you
shall expand to the right and to the left."—
ISAIAH 54:2–3

**76**   The word *imagination* comes from the root word meaning
"to image." Every person has the ability to imagine. It is the
mark of the image of God within us. The trick is to stretch
that imagination! Expand it higher, wider, longer, and deeper.
Think bigger thoughts, and bigger results will come your way.

**Measure a person by the stretch of his imagination.**

You can tell where he is going by how expansive his powers
of imagination are.

It was said of Joseph Stalin that he kept a world globe on his
desk. He used it as a device to help him think bigger! The
conquest of the world was his goal.

Today the tentacles of Communism have effectively
reached around the world! It has become, along with Christianity and Islam, one of the three leading ideologies, in terms
of worldwide power and following.

Now consider Jesus Christ. He, too, had a vision of world
conquest. A simple, untutored, uneducated Carpenter left this
challenge with twelve of His followers: "You shall be wit-
nesses to Me in Jerusalem, and in Judea and Samaria, and *to
the end of the earth*" (Acts 1:8). The results?

Today, more people claim to follow Christianity than any of
the other major world philosophies.

Christ needs you to expand His ministry around the world.
Can you stretch your imagination that far? Nobody—except
yourself—can tell you how big you can think!

You have the freedom to dream as big, beautifully, and
bountifully as you want!

*Since it doesn't cost a dime to dream you'll never short-
change yourself when you stretch your imagination!*

*FAITH IS . . .*
## *Managing to achieve the impossible*

"Through wisdom a house is built,/And by understanding it is established. By knowledge the rooms are filled/With all precious and pleasant riches."—PROVERBS 24:3–4

Can you say—
- I've taken the plunge?
- I'm pushing myself to the limit?
- I believe in success and I will manage until I succeed?

**77**

**The impossible can become possible through wise management.**

Management is taking control of a situation in which you will be held accountable for the results.

Think of this: Responsibility means that you will be held accountable for your successes or failures. If you have to answer for your performance then you are ipso facto in a management role. Then you must have freedom to control.

The word *control* implies the exercise of leadership. Leadership is the force that sets the goals. It is the force that analyzes problems that make certain situations *appear impossible*. Leadership is the managerial power that sets goals to solve problems, clear the way, remove obstacles, invent solutions, hire experts, until what once seemed impossible now becomes possible.

Leadership takes control of a situation to reshape, rearrange, reorganize, and retool the operation until the project turns around! Be patient. It takes time to stop a freight train. It will take time to turn impossibilities into possibilities, but you will make it!

Perhaps you have to learn to manage by setting definite goals. *Your situation isn't impossible—you simply have to exercise leadership!* Don't confuse indecision for problems!

What is one of the first arts of a good manager? It's making hard decisions!

*FAITH IS . . .*
## *Planning to solve unsolvable problems*

"Ask, and it shall be given to you; seek, and you will find; knock, and it will be opened to you."—MATTHEW 7:7

**78**   The walk of faith inevitably leads you into a position where you face problems. On first sight, these problems may appear unsolvable! The fact is

**We are not operating in the arena of faith unless we are dealing with problems that at the present moment appear unsolvable.**

Is your walk taking you to the brink of a possible failure? If not, you may be living so safely that your faith can be called into question.

Your faith moves from the infantile stage to the adult stage when you face seemingly impossible situations. At that point, your faith is no longer mental fantasizing, but active planning.

How do you put your faith in action? Simply count to ten, pause, and pray. Then listen to every wonderful, wild, and wacky idea that enters your mind and which might conceivably whittle away or chip off a corner of your enormous problem. Write the ideas down. Before you know it, you will have listed ten ways to solve your unsolvable problem. This is the process of planning solutions to your problems through possibility thinking! This is faith on the adult level.

So set goals. Today! Make them impossible enough to get God involved! You—and God—will come up with a plan to make them happen!

Let my prayer and yours today be these words of an old hymn:

O for a faith that will not shrink
Though pressed by every foe
That will not tremble at the brink
Of any earthly woe!

## *Pursuing your objective relentlessly*

". . . be strong in the Lord and in the power of
His might."—EPHESIANS 6:10

Human behavior can be dissected and divided into three **79**
sections:

(1) Intellectual—when you walk the walk of faith you use
your head. Be smart about it.

(2) Emotional—be inwardly secure enough that you do not
fear the mysterious and marvelous geysering of positive emotions. Enthusiasm is a mark of health—not illness. However,
it's not enough to merely "experience a religious feeling." In
fact, many people with a strong faith never do have an emotional conversion experience. It's possible to be "born again"
and not know the exact hour or time.

(3) Volitional—faith must be applied to daily life. The word
*volitional* comes from the root, *velle* which means expressing
tremendous proven internalized energy that becomes exter-
nalized energy in the pursuit of an all-consuming objective!

Faith moves from emotional and intellectual stages to a volitional stage when you are determined and disciplined. All
great athletes who have won medals or earned crowns have
done so because of tremendous faith. They believed they
could win! And *then* they exploded with an inner volition.

Have you discovered this capacity in yourself? It's there. If
you have experienced it, you know what I mean. But if you
haven't, you've got to believe that there is a lot more within
you than you ever experienced.

**It begins when faith becomes an act of the will; when
belief is translated into dynamic willpower.**

O God, help me to discover the power that comes from
within me when I make up my mind wholeheartedly to pursue my objective relentlessly. Amen.

## Splurging in possibilities

"Then Mary took a pound of very costly oil . . .
and anointed the feet of Jesus."—JOHN 12:2

**80** "It may help you," I explained to a new Christian who asked
about his new-found faith, "to think of the walk of faith which
you have just started as a symphony in four movements."

The first movement of faith is the *urge*—deep within yourself there was a voice that said, "There is something more."
Intuitively you suspected that you were missing out on something. An inner urge nudged you to open up your mind to the
possibility of a religious reality that until now you had
avoided. There was a hunger deep within yourself that
nothing seemed to really satisfy in spite of your successes and
achievements.

The second movement of faith is known as the *surge*. What
started as a gentle thought—*It would be wonderful if . . .*—
grew into a passion: *I want it! I need it!*

The third movement of faith is known as the *purge*. Negative thoughts rushed in to destroy your desire and torpedo
your dream with negative forces. This movement was filled
with discordant notes and contradictions.

All of the destructive thoughts *must* be purged. Abort all
negative thoughts before they can take an embryonic fix in
your mind.

The fourth and final movement is the *splurge*—you made
the leap. You went all out for it. You put everything on the
line. You held nothing back. It is the splurging of your dream
that will make it come true!

**Like that beautiful woman who opened the flask and
poured all of the costly perfume over the feet of Jesus
in a display of extravagance, I'm going to give my
dream my all-out effort; for I am a believer!**

# Making daring decisions

"I have set before you life and death, blessing
and cursing; therefore choose life, that . . . you
. . . may live."—DEUTERONOMY 30:19

Success never happens until you make it happen. And you **81**
make good things happen when you make decisions that
cause a movement to begin. You can be sure that you are
walking the walk of faith so long as you make those decisions.

How can you make a decision when there is risk involved?
How can you make a decision when dangers may follow?
The answer, of course, is this:

**Life, by its very nature, rejects protectionism.**

Do you refuse to make decisions because problems and perils might result? Do you want to play it safe? That's one of
life's rare impossibilities! When you play it safe, you can be
sure you will face the dangers that inevitably come: boredom;
lack of growth; stagnation; emotional death! The zest that
comes from decisions will be gone. What is left is a shriveling
and shrinking spirit with false promises of security.

Of all the cruel illusions there is none more insidious or
disastrous than the alluring call of safety and shelter when
you retreat from taking a risk!

*The truth is, if you continue to make daring decisions, you
will succeed—at least you will succeed in filling each day
with excitement!*

The promise from the God of life, abundant and eternal, is
only offered to those who dare to walk the walk of faith.

Keep walking that path by daring to make the decision you
have already postponed too long!

*Success is no accident. Success is a commitment—not a
coincidence!* Decide today where you want to be five, ten,
twenty years from today.

*FAITH IS . . .*
## Snapping the trap

". . . that we may know the things that have
been freely given to us by God."—1
CORINTHIANS 2:12

**82**  I grew up out in the country, on a farm at the end of a road. I discovered early in life that I did not appreciate living at the dead end of a road.

There wasn't much excitement there! The only cars that ever came down that road were those of relatives, friends, or someone who was lost. Whenever a lost traveler realized that he was on a dead-end road, he would turn around in a cloud of agitated dust and retreat over his fresh path clearly marked in the dirt, racing faster to make up for lost time.

I learned this lesson early in life: *Dead-end roads never go anywhere.*

Dead-end roads are traps. As a young man I never allowed myself to be trapped by conditions that weren't leading me upward, outward, and onward.

I quickly made this youthful observation: I could walk away from dead-end roads! Yes, I could get out and walk when I couldn't drive any farther. But I would never stop and sit in a parked car spending my life on a dead-end road.

Are you trapped today in a job that has no future? Is your life bogged down at a dead end with nothing exciting in your future path? Even God cannot steer a stalled car. Get out and move. It takes guts to leave the ruts.

Analyze your obstruction. Who, or what, is blocking you? Chances are, you are your own greatest obstacle.

Faith is snapping the trap!

So set new goals.

Chart a new course.

Consider a midflight correction and a midlife change.

**You are free to go anywhere from where you are!**

## Peeling the orange

"Behold, now is the accepted time; Behold, now is the day of salvation."—2 CORINTHIANS 6:2

At the core of faith, there is that innermost, indivisible cell called commitment. Faith always commands some decisive action. More often than not, it represents an irreversible decision. **83**

Faith is peeling the orange. It's cracking the egg. It's opening the can of Coke! Faith is delivering the ice. Now you either consume it, or throw it away.

Faith is serving the soufflé hot from the oven! You must eat it, or watch it deflate. What's left cannot be saved or stored.

Our family always remembers one night when we had a family party. Our favorite dessert, a baked soufflé, was just taken out of the oven and put on the table when there was a knock at the door. It was a police officer, commanding, "Come out quickly! There are armed robbers who have escaped from the police. They are believed to be in the grove behind your house. There will be shooting so we need to evacuate you now!"

Two hours later we returned. The robbers were captured, and the soufflé was a deflated, miserable sight. But we were alive and safe. There are those tides and times in the affairs of human life when we must take action—now! There can be no procrastination! To delay is fatal!

Dear God, what decisions are before me now that require firm action on my part?

**Give me the faith to make the move at the right time in the right way. Protect me from the false security that indecision foolishly promises me. Today I shall move from faith. I shall not be mesmerized by fear.**

Thank You, God, for giving me the faith to make decisions courageously. Amen.

## Stepping out of line

"And do not be conformed to this world, but be transformed by the renewing of your mind. . . ."—ROMANS 12:2

**84** Do you dare to be a maverick? A maverick is a spunky, spirited calf that doesn't run with the herd but ventures out into the beckoning canyons.

Mavericks are essential to the survival of the herd. A herd with no mavericks huddles together with backs to the wind, heads down, shoulders together, seeking to survive the storm. More than one herd of cattle has frozen to death that way. Where is the one who can break out of the group, put his head to the wind, and venture out to find shelter from the storm or discover new grazing ground?

Early in my ministry I was labeled a maverick by a rigid institutionalist in my denomination. My first reaction, I confess, was negative. I was offended. But when I checked on the definition, I admitted that I was indeed a maverick and proud of it. For being a maverick is a characteristic of people who walk by faith. When you start looking at what everybody else is doing before you make a move, you surrender leadership to your social group.

**Dare to be a wise but wonderful nonconformist.**

Look at the leaders of the world! They all step forward and upward and onward. And that's beyond the line of conformity—always.

Let God have command over your life. When the Holy Spirit of the living God guides and leads in your life, you will be "transformed by the renewing of your mind." You will break out of the mold and be unique!

O Lord, give me enough faith to step out of line and move ahead with courage toward the dream You have given me. I shall dare to be a maverick today. Thank You, God.

## Flying with an unknown pilot

"Examine yourselves as to whether you are in
the faith. Prove yourselves."—2 CORINTHIANS
13:5

Today I'm going to give you a checkup on your walk of faith. **85**
How shall I grade you? Are you passing the course? The good
news I have is that you, indeed, are passing with higher marks
than you expected. The fact that you have continued this far
on the walk of faith shows that you really are a believer.

Even on the days when you wonder about the very existence of God and were tempted to doubt His presence and
power—even on those days your faith gets a passing grade!

Why? You are a believer even when you do not feel it.

The walk of faith is like traveling on an airplane. You never
see the pilot at the controls. You've probably never met him
face to face. His credentials are not hanging on the wall of the
plane. Yet you step into the plane, believing he is there and
that he can handle the flight.

There isn't a day that you can't assume there is a God in
charge of this incredible flying vehicle called planet Earth.
That's *faith!*

> **We ride this spacecraft called Earth, traveling at an in-
> credible speed, and we assume there is a pilot at the
> controls! That's *faith!***

The world would soon turn to madness if there was no
heavenly Pilot in control, no God at all! Our hearts tell us
there is a Pilot even when we have never met Him face to face.
We may not know Him, but we trust Him! That's *faith!*

Yet, by faith we know Him!

By faith we believe in Him!

When we become acquainted with Jesus Christ, the unseen
Pilot comes out of the cabin and we meet Him, in person.

When we do know Him, that's *faith!*

Thank You, Lord, that I really do believe in You. I assume
You are there all the time—and You are! I have a stronger faith
than I realize.

# *Adventuring into new territories*

> "Where can I go from Your Spirit?/Or where
> can I flee from Your presence? . . . If I take the
> wings of the morning,/And dwell in the
> uttermost parts of the sea,/Even there Your
> hand shall lead me."—PSALM 139:7–10

**86**   When we trust the Pilot at the controls of our lives, then we are ready to venture into new territories.

Is anything quite as exciting as an adventure? Can you imagine how dull life would be if all risk were removed; if you knew exactly how everything would turn out before you plunged; if the outcome were certain when you made the commitment?

I recall a positive-thinking friend who received the news she had cancer. She needed surgery and then chemotherapy. The prognosis was grim, and the outlook was grave.

Yet when I came to call at her bedside, I saw an excited sparkle in her eye. "I've never taken this kind of trip before!" she said. "I think it's going to be quite an adventure—enlightening, and potentially life-enriching, if not lifesaving." And she really meant it. That's faith!

When a member of my church knew that she was at death's door and was soon to make the transition from earth to heaven, she was genuinely excited. As she patted her Bible affectionately, she said, "My suitcase is packed. My bills are all paid. My passport is in order. I've been looking forward to this trip all of my life."

## Faith—it's seeking adventure into new territories!

Are you starting a new business? Are you unemployed? Did you get laid off? Maybe you need to move to a new locality, learn a new trade, or be reeducated. Maybe you need to take a trip you've never taken before!

Look upon each new day as a new adventure into new territories! With God as your guide you need not be afraid. We cannot travel beyond His care and keeping.

*FAITH IS . . .*
## Liberating your creative powers

"For you shall go out with joy, and . . . peace;
the mountains and the hills shall break forth
into singing . . . and all the trees of the field
shall clap their hands."—ISAIAH 55:12

When we begin to breathe the breath of faith we discover we **87** are becoming creative persons. How exciting!

When we become believers and walk the walk of faith, we find salvation from life's tensions—sin, fear, anxiety. When we walk the walk of faith, we become whole and healthy normal persons. In the process our stress level is drastically reduced. Tensions that attack us are noticeably eliminated, and the peace of mind that naturally results sets the stage for creativity.

Have you noticed? In the quiet hours of the early morning you get your brightest ideas. That's because those are the times when you are protected from the possibility of unwelcome, pressure-producing interruptions that stimulate tension. Deep relaxation allows creativity to happen.

In a garden we are creative, for

**The sounds and sights of nature relax the soul.**

We find it natural to believe in God when we behold the starry heavens from the mountaintop.

There is a reasonable explanation for the greater prevalence of religious belief in the rural countryside. The farmer is closer to nature. He is in his natural habitat. The person who is surrounded by the tension-producing sounds of engines and sirens finds that his eyes and ears, designed to be channels of tranquility, have become blocked from the flow of creativity.

Faith in God liberates the creative powers, for faith gives me peace of mind! Tranquility is conditioning for creativity.

Thank You, Father, for creating me to be a partner in the creative work in this world. I open my mind to Your ideas. I believe that Your ideas can be translated into constructive creative activity. Thank You, Lord. Amen.

# Advancing with boldness

"The kingdom of heaven is like treasure hidden in a field, which a man found and hid; and for the joy over it, he goes and sells all that he has and buys that field."—MATTHEW 13:44

**88**     It's easy to see why some people fail. They are under the lordship of an unholy trinity—acidity, frigidity, timidity.

Some fail because of *acidity.* Their personalities are bitter. They are poisoned with negative thinking. There is acid in their souls.

Others fail because of *frigidity.* They're cold. They lack the warmth of affection to attract good people. Love is missing in their lives.

Still others fail because of *timidity.* They demand guarantees of safety before they move. They need all the problems solved before they make a commitment.

Successful people are controlled by a faith that dissolves acidity with sweet thoughts, thaws out frigidity with an enthusiastic attitude of kindness, and replaces timidity with boldness.

Today, move forward with faith. Take at least one step forward in some area of your life.

Where should you advance? To what degree? Pause now to pray that God will show you where you are holding back and where you ought to be moving forward. God knows you better than you know yourself. One thing is certain:

**You'll never get ahead until you start advancing.**

In our Bible verse a person is walking across property with a "for sale" sign on it, stumbles on hidden treasure, hides it, then what? He moves fast! Sells everything—and buys it!

You are walking across opportunities today! Spot them, grab them—fast.

FAITH IS . . .
## *Stimulating positive emotions*

"We also should walk in newness of life."—
ROMANS 6:4

Living the faith stimulates positive emotions. In the same **89**
way, doubt constantly feeds negative emotions. Doubt is an
anesthetic. Skepticism drains the spirit. Unbelief makes us
drowsy. Negative thinking turns us into dreary people, fearful
of our fears and worried about our worry. What a despairing
cycle!

But you are out of the rut! You walk the path of faith. Stimulate positive emotions today: Jesus Christ has freely saved
me from all doubt! *My faith stimulates my hope.* Like a bird
awakening the others with a song, until all are singing a happy
chorus, so one positive thought alerts and awakens others until I am moving on a higher energy plane.

My faith stimulates positive thinking, and positive thinking stimulates me to see all of the possibilities.

> **I have made commitments.**
> **I am involved.**
> **I'm pursuing a project.**
> **I am out of the ruts.**
> **I'm on the way.**
> **The adventure's begun.**
> **The countdown has started.**
> **Blast-off is inevitable.**
> **I'm now swept up into dynamic action**

God is encouraging me. The Lord is nudging me forward.

Thank You, Father, for drawing me into this circle of excitement. Thank You, for saving me from the sad cycle of deadly
skepticism and fatiguing boredom. Humor has returned to my
life. Joy has stepped into my morning. I hear the birds sing
again. I'm overwhelmed by an abundance of blessings. Thank
You, Lord. Amen.

## *Agreeing to advance*

"For you shall go out with joy,/And be led forth
with peace;/The mountains and the hills/Shall
break forth into singing before you,/And all the
trees of the field shall clap their hands."—
ISAIAH 55:12

**90** You are moving upward, forward, and onward!
  • You are deprogramming yourself of negative input.
  • You are reprogramming yourself positively.
  • You are transcending human distractions and inade-
    quacies.
  • And you agree today to advance in your walk of faith until
    you give God complete lordship over your life.
Faith is the process of agreeing to allow positive forces to
control you. Your inadequacies help you recognize that you
need to be led by somone smarter than yourself.
Agree to advance and turn the leadership of your life over to
God!

> **When you turn leadership of your life over to God,
> then you agree to advance, even though you do not
> know where God will lead. Remember, faith is moving
> beyond the realm of the sure into the realm of the un-
> certain.**

Faith means you enter an agreement before all the questions can be answered!
Affirmation: Of one thing I am sure: As long as Christ is the
leader of my life, I'm in the best of company! I shall be advancing. And that's all-important!
O Lord, I'm putting everything I am into my belief in You.
Deep within in my heart I feel right about this move, even
though I don't know where You will lead me. Thank You,
Lord. Amen.

## Escalating your expectations

"For as the heavens are higher than the earth,/
So are My ways higher than your ways,/And
My thoughts than your thoughts."—ISAIAH 55:9

Now that you're on the move, stretch your faith until it is **91**
big enough to unfold the plan God has for you!

**Make your thinking big enough for God to fit in!**
**Let the size of your faith set the size of your goals!**
**Match your expectations to God's abilities!**

Visualize a scale in your mind—one of those old-fashioned
scales with two trays balanced against each other. In one tray
place your beliefs about God—His goodness; His might; His
wisdom; His connections with sources and resources, financial, intellectual, emotional, and organizational. The God that
you believe in is on one scale.

Now on the other side, place your expectations—how far
you want to go, how high you wish to climb, how rich you'd
like to become. (Remember, it's not a sin to be wealthy; it is a
sin not to be generous!)

By now you are in the process of escalating your expectations. You think bigger than when you first started. You increase the size of the goal you eventually expect to reach.
That's great! That means your faith is growing. That means
you are under the influence of God and not evil.

You are an optimist, not a pessimist.

You are a possibility thinker, not an impossibility thinker.
Browning said, "A man's reach must exceed his grasp, or
what's a heaven for?"

Reach for heaven today.

Reach for God's way.

Reach for His thoughts.

Faith is escalating your expectations!

*FAITH IS . . .*
## *Declaring your positive intentions*

"Let the words of my mouth . . ./Be acceptable
in Your sight,/O LORD!"—PSALM 19:14

**92** God will lead you out of the wilderness of complacency and
despondency once you have enough faith to declare your
positive intentions. Enormous power is released once you
make a public announcement of what you are going to accomplish. You put your integrity on the line. When you declare
your intentions publicly and positively, the pressure is on to
produce! Publicly announcing a project is one of the most successful, yet most painful, ways I have utilized to accomplish
my goals.

Be careful to declare your intentions only to positive people! You will need all the help you can get.

Even so, be prepared for negative reactions from those who
will resist or resent your goals. To some people, you will appear to be a threat, to others, a wild-eyed idealist. Still others
will simply laugh at your plans. After all, they're impossible,
aren't they?

But,

**Once the idea becomes a word, it will come to life.**

There is incredible creative power in the spoken word. It
was with a spoken word that God created the world. Christ,
who is called the Incarnation of God, is referred to as the Word
"made flesh" (John 1:14 KJV).

Do you really want to succeed? Then practice faith. Declare
your intentions positively and publicly with enthusiasm and
integrity! And you cannot fail, unless you give up on your
dream.

## Talking positive talk

"Anxiety in the heart . . . causes depression,/But a good word makes it glad."—PROVERBS 12:25

Faith is more than positive thinking. It's positive talking. **93**
- Fantasizing becomes incarnate in verbalizing.
- Ideas take the form of the spoken word.
- Believing becomes speaking.
- There is incredible emotional power released through the spoken word.

**By the word of God the heavens and the earth were created. God spoke—and it happened!**

Read the Bible and underline the words *say, speaks, spoke, word.*

Until persons speak, they remain a mystery. Christ was God exposing Himself in a language people could understand. He is God speaking to us by lip and by life. Once a dream is articulated in a public announcement, you are committed. Once you program your mind with positive language and positive words you are programmed for action.

Faith must rise to the level of affirmation.
- Declare you are the person you want to be.
- Tell yourself you have already accomplished what you hope to accomplish.

When you are in a downward mood, never verbalize a negative emotion. Rather, declare positively, "I feel great!" You are expressing incredible faith and belief that God will hear and answer your prayer in an instant.

The kind of faith you need now is to affirm that you are succeeding. You are making progress even if you can't see it, or feel it! You know you are because God is on your side. Trust Him and talk positive talk.

# Patting yourself on the back

"For You have made him [us] a little lower than
the angels,/And You have crowned him [us]
with glory and honor."—PSALM 8:5

**94**     Take time today to applaud yourself. For in congratulating
yourself you are glorifying God by recognizing the goodness of
His grace.

- I am a truly remarkable creation!
- There isn't another human being just like me.
- I believe in myself.
- I congratulate myself for the person I am and the person I
  am in the process of becoming!
- I have survived a great deal.
- I have been given incredible endurance.
- There is nothing I cannot accomplish once I set my mind
  to it. I have proven that more than once.

**By the grace of God, I am somebody marvelous!**

- I am praising and applauding God for the good work He
  has done within me.
- God loves me so much that He would stop at nothing to
  save my soul! The cross of Jesus Christ is proof of that!
- I am proud to be known as a believer.
- God's love is flowing through my life.
- I am a channel of His joy.
- I am doing a lot of good through my positive attitudes.
- I am building up others around me through my faith.
- I am really a wonderful person.
- God is crowning me with glory and honor.
- I am still a Christian in the process of maturing. I am
  improving.
- I am growing spiritually.
- I'm pressing on the upward way; new heights I'm gaining
  every day.

## FAITH IS . . .
### *Exercising enthusiasm always*

"Rejoice in the Lord always. Again I will say, rejoice!"—PHILIPPIANS 4:4

One thing will become apparent as you walk this walk of 95 faith. Faith is a walk. That means exercise!

People who never walk, jog, or move around soon become flabby and weak. It doesn't take long for human muscles to lose their resiliency.

**Faith is exercised when we exercise enthusiasm. Enthusiasm is the emotion that feeds faith and keeps it alive.**

Faith drinks of the cup of enthusiasm and takes off with youthful energy.

To walk the walk of faith can be perceived as the constant revitalization of our innate inclination to be enthusiastic, for enthusiasm is the mark of an emotionally healthy person.

By contrast, lack of enthusiasm is evidence of something less than peak mental and spiritual health. Tragically some educators see youthful enthusiasm as something to eliminate. Enthusiasm is often viewed as an emotional weakness; whereas cold, calculating rationality is viewed as the epitome of mental alertness.

Not so! You are a healthy person when you are enthusiastic. Enthusiasm is a mark of youth. It is the fountain of energy.

Exercise enthusiasm today. Begin by counting your blessings. Begin with God! He is alive! You can be enthusiastic about His love for you!

Now express enthusiasm about faith—itself! The late Dr. Daniel Poling had a positive addiction. Each morning he would turn his face toward the new light and repeat aloud— *very loud*—several times, two words: "I believe!" "I believe!" "I believe!" "I believe!"

Try it! It will really give you faith! Energy! Life!

# Exaggerating enthusiastically

"My soul shall make its boast in the LORD."—
PSALM 34:2

**96**   What is exaggeration? (a) A sad symptom of an inferiority complex? Sometimes. (b) A deliberate deception to con someone? Sometimes. (c) A positive attempt to convey a true impression? Yes! Sometimes exaggeration is just that.

Consider the artist who exaggerates the size of a human hand. He is giving the honest impression of strength.

Consider the musician or the actor who exaggerates the soft and loud tones, thereby giving an honest expression of the dynamic range.

Consider the reporter who exaggerates the attendance. He is giving an honest impression of a big crowd.

Consider the pastor of a fast-growing church who reports membership as "nearly one thousand" after the roll call has passed six hundred. He is conveying an honest impression of great growth.

"My soul shall make its boast in the LORD." There is such a thing as honest exaggeration.

Exaggeration is honest when it is really an "advance announcement"—when your overstated numbers will be "right on" by the time people hear the news.

Exaggeration is honest when it is the expression of an "inner vision seen" in the mind of a positive believer!

It is an audacious and daring act of faith to declare that you have already achieved what you prayed and believed you would achieve.

Yes, it's dangerous! For now, you either have to produce the predicted results or be labeled a braggart and a liar and lose credibility. But this risk can be used as a powerful, positive pressure to produce.

Yes, the powerful practice of making "advance" announcements will release incredible, positive forces.

**Positive exaggerations generate great expectations that stimulate enormous enthusiasm.**

[346]

## Fortifying yourself

"The LORD is my rock and my fortress and my deliverer."—PSALM 18:2

The walk of faith does not guarantee that we are completely **97** protected against the disintegrating forces that are always around us. Like termites in a wooden beam or dry rot in the timbers, moral decay can set in subtly and insidiously.

Where did your enthusiasm go? What happened to your drive? You thought that you had your act together, and now you seem to be coming apart.

Enthusiasm and confidence are not welded to your spirit— they're glued. The bonding can lose its adhesive quality quickly if you allow disintegrating forces to come into your thinking or action.

Faith is fortifying yourself; building an invisible shield of faith around you.

Walk out into the new day imagining that there is an invisible barrier of impenetrable and indestructible material that surrounds you like a fracture-proof bubble.

> **Deflect the poisonous darts of negative thoughts with holy stubbornness.**
> **Your mind is fortified by faith!**
> **Through persistent positive thinking develop an immunity that instinctively, intuitively, fights off the would-be invaders of negativity.**
> **Positive projects provide built-in prevention.**

Because you are walking in faith, negativity, pessimism, cynicism, unbelief, like invading germs, drop dead before they ever reach you.

Thank You, Father, that I have a faith that fortifies me against the destructive spiritual forces loose in our world. I have the ultimate security, for You are beside me. Thank You, Lord. Amen.

## FAITH IS . . .
# *Upgrading my standards*

> "For You have formed my inward parts;/You have covered me in my mother's womb./I will praise You, for I am fearfully and wonderfully made;/Marvelous are Your works,/And that my soul knows very well."—PSALM 139:13–14

**98**　　It's amazing how an actor will perform at his peak when he knows an important person is in his audience.

More than one athlete has knocked himself out because he knows that his dad is in the grandstand! The story is told of a boy who always had to settle for second-string position. Yet his father never missed a game. After his father's death, the son, with tears in his eyes, said, "Coach, please let me start tonight. I want to play for Dad."

The coach, knowing that the boy's dad had never missed a game, agreed. The young man's performance on the field astounded the coach. When asked to explain his phenomenal level of achievement, he said, "Coach, I played that one for Dad. My father never missed a game, but he never saw me play—until tonight! You see, Coach, my father was blind."

How much better could you be doing in the game of life?

> **God is in a front-row seat watching your performance on the stage of life today. He is applauding the moment you move into the scene. What previously untapped levels of energy and creativity and accomplishment will you reveal?**

You can do more than you have done.
You can go further than you have.
The Lord deserves the best of whatever you can be.
Today, upgrade your standards!
Raise that goal!
Set your sights on higher targets.
Our Lord is watching you—now!
He'll applaud you.
So will I.

## *Improving yourself constantly*

"Add to your faith virtue, to virtue knowledge,
to knowledge self-control, to self-control
perseverance, to perseverance Godliness, to
Godliness brotherly kindness, and to brotherly
kindness love."—2 PETER 1:5–8

Does this verse show where the path of faith leads? Will we **99**
never reach a point where we've got it made? Does this mean
we will constantly have to improve ourselves?

Absolutely! That's what spares us from death. For plateaus
are boring. Nothing is as dull as yesterday's race when it is
over! Who cares to look at the bumper stickers of last year's
political campaign?

**We must always be living in today—and tomorrow!**

What is exciting to know is that the real stimulation of life
never needs to diminish with age. Real excitement comes as
you make constant commitments to new projects that hold
creative challenge.

You can continue to feel young as long as you live, because a
youthful attitude is basically a commitment to progress. You
can have that no matter how old you are! You never need to
grow too old to escape the opportunity for self-improvement.
The walk of faith calls you to improve yourself constantly,
consistently, and continually!

Affirmation: I shall choose one of these elements within
today's Bible verse and focus on improving myself. It may be
faith,
virtue,
knowledge,
self-control,
godliness,
kindness, or
love.
Then my life will remain fruitful no matter how old I am!
Thank You, God, for this glorious promise.

*FAITH IS . . .*
## Welcoming a new day

"This is the day which the Lord has made;/We will rejoice and be glad in it."—PSALM 118:24

**100**  How do you welcome a new day? I invite you to join me in this positive meditation:

What surprises do You have planned for me today, Lord?

I am excited about the abilities that I have at my disposal.

I am able to see, and think, and hear!

I am able to read.

I have the ability to plan.

I am excited about the hours and minutes that this day holds.

I am suddenly conscious, heavenly Father, that You give to all human beings the same number of minutes and hours in every day.

And I am well aware of the fact that the most important resource I possess is not money but time!

**For time is life.**

With the gift of time I have the opportunity to laugh! to love! to talk! to think! to pray! to give of myself to people whose paths will cross mine. Surely, my dreams will come true because I am blessed! I am alive! I am being given the priceless gift of another day to live! I take the time to carry my dreams out. Today I can move them forward!

My problems can be solved for I am walking the walk of faith! For I am filled with genuine thanksgiving. I will use the gift of this day wisely. I will do something about my life's opportunities and obstacles, its dreams and disappointments.

O God, thank You for treating me fairly!

You have given me a fresh day with freedom to do something constructive!

This faith gives me hope.

Thank You, Father. Amen.

# Grabbing the magic moment

"Then you shall see and become radiant,/And
your heart shall swell with joy."—ISAIAH 60:5

There are magical moments of life that come unexpectedly, **101**
and then, suddenly, they are gone!

There is that magical moment when the darkness of the
night disappears and the sky becomes light. The first bird
awakens and throws its head back to announce the new day.
His early song awakens the others, who join in a heavenly
chorus.

To capture that magical moment, you must learn that the
birds do not wait for you. The beautiful but very brief symphony will not be delayed until you finish your domestic
chores. So bow to the birds! Have faith that other activities
can wait.

It is the same with the sunrise. There is that magical moment just before the sun rises above the horizon when the
orange sky becomes brilliant with color. And just as quickly
as it appears, the resplendent glory of the sunrise fades. The
high point has passed. The exquisite elegance is no longer
there.

> **The brilliant moments of magic never last long. Plan,
> accommodate, and adjust your schedule so you will
> not miss the magic when it comes. Faith is carefully
> planning to capture the highest, happiest, and holiest
> moments in life.**

Moments of inspiration do come. The soul seems to soar for
a brief moment when we sense God's presence.

Drop everything when this moment surprises you, for the
beauty of the fast fleeting moment will not wait for you. Grab
it! It is God's special gift to you.

## *Delighting in discovery*

"Behold what manner of love the Father has bestowed on us, that we should be called children of God!"—1 JOHN 3:1

**102** People with faith to explore make grand discoveries. Like a father who leaves wrapped gifts hidden where his children will find them, so God waits behind doors left ajar, where He watches His children venture in.

What delight He takes in watching us discover and then open the carefully planned surprises.

**God delights in our delights.**

He may or may not open the door far enough to expose His generous Self. We may not even know where the gifts have come from. To Him it does not really matter. But how His heart leaps when He hears us say, "Father did it. Isn't He wonderful!"

As God's children we may never see His face or hear His voice, but we sense a goodness and love that planned something good and beautiful for us!

One morning, as I opened God's gift to me of a new day, I hummed the familiar tune, "Morning Has Broken." Then these words came to me:

Dawn is awakening, bright with a new light,
calling our hearts to love while we pray.
Thank God for living.
Thank God for breathing.
God's recreating new life today.

Father, the doorway of a new day is opening. Who is turning the knob? Who is opening the door? Who will show His smiling face? It is joy opening the door to release the new day to my life. God is alive. He is blessing me. Alleluia.

*FAITH IS . . .*
## *Alerting myself to the good in the "now"*

"Every day I will bless You."—PSALM 145:2

Faith gives one of the most beautiful invitations that any **103**
person can covet! Have you ever envied someone for being
invited to an affair where your name was not on the list?

Well, every person is invited by faith to come into "today"!
Step into the joy of the present moment.

- **Today there are flowers blooming. You are invited to
  notice them.**
- **Today there are birds singing. You are invited to listen to them.**
- **Today there are people who are crying for help. You
  are honored with the invitation to comfort them.**

Imagine being invited by God to a special showing in a
beautiful theater to witness a premiere event never seen by
any human being before! You step into the theater. You have a
prize seat. The stage is before you. You sense that something
is happening on stage. You are unable to experience it because
the curtains of yesterday and tomorrow remain closed—your
preoccupation with the past and your anxiety about tomorrow can cause you to miss today's premiere showing.

Now the curtains begin to separate. The stage is wide open.
You experience the music, the dance, the drama—the living
and the loving, the laughing and the crying, the dreaming and
the despairing, the struggling and the succeeding—all happening this very moment! It's exciting. It's life! You must not
miss it.

Today is the tomorrow you dreamed about yesterday! It has
arrived. You are in the center of God's love. Praise your God!

## Taking a chance on tomorrow

"Tomorrow the LORD will do wonders among you."—JOSHUA 3:5

**104**  The true stories of amazing accomplishments experienced by possibility thinkers who act on faith make unbelievable reading.

For instance, a friend of mine, Christy Wilson, was a missionary in Afghanistan. He missed the comforts of life in America, not the least of which was his favorite food—Long Island duckling. He proceeded to order fertilized duck eggs! He assumed that they could be transported by air and arrive in Kabul, the capital of Afghanistan, before they were spoiled. That's faith!

When the shipment finally arrived, after long delays, there were fewer than two dozen eggs left. Only two hatched out! Would you believe that one was a male and the other a female?

Of course, that was all he needed. They reproduced and soon Christy had a very successful enterprise.

Meanwhile, an epidemic was becoming a near national disaster: the sheep in the country were being killed by a tiny parasite.

Then it was discovered that the parasite was spread by snails. Ducks love to eat snails. So Christy Wilson's ducks spared the country from an agricultural and, consequently, human tragedy.

One day a member of the royal family heard the story.

Christy Wilson was summoned to the king's residence. The whole story came to light and the missionary was finally recognized and given credit for importing the ducks and saving the sheep. He received royal honors! That is a historical recorded fact!

Believe in tomorrow! Who can count the apples in one seed?

## FAITH IS . . .
### *Trusting in tomorrow*

"Surely goodness and mercy shall follow me/All
the days of my life."—PSALM 23:6

You sense a new enthusiasm flowing through your life at **105**
this moment, for you are walking the walk of faith. Today
your faith will become stronger as you learn to trust in tomorrow.

Your course, however well it is charted, may require adjust-
ments. But, if you keep your eyes fixed firmly on the goal,
then your future is your friend. You need never be discouraged, because God is walking beside you in this walk of
faith.

God plans your today and all of your tomorrows. Trust
Him! The storms may rage. The plan may fail to unfold as
rapidly or efficiently as you had hoped. But every tomorrow is
a new opportunity to take a fresh grip on your goal and catch a
strong hold on your commitment!

**Tomorrow will not fail you unless you choose to
throw it away.**

Yes, you may make mistakes but you are not stupid. For
God gave you intelligence and common sense. Use it now!
God is reminding you through His Holy Spirit that something
good will happen tomorrow.

So, trust in tomorrow! For trust releases incredible power,
which sustains energy and releases enthusiasm within you!

Believe that tomorrow will give you time to move your projects forward.

Believe that tomorrow will give you the opportunity to take
positive action that will prove beneficial.

Thank You, God, for this power that is coming from You
now! Thank You that there will always be a tomorrow. And
You are creating it. I know that there is bound to be a lot of
good, waiting behind the next sunrise. Amen.

## *Celebrating the unknown*

"Oh, satisfy us early with Your mercy,/That we may rejoice and be glad all our days."—PSALM 90:14

**106** Enjoy the present moment. You know your past mistakes are forgiven, your pathway for tomorrow is planned. You do not know what the future holds, but you know who holds the future.

• So celebrate the blessings that are waiting for you!
• Praise God for the blessings He is planning for your life.
• Celebrate the unknown!

That's living in faith.

It is the unknown that provides the magnets to draw you into tomorrow.

If the future could be predicted, the excitement of uncertainty would be replaced by the boredom of the predictable.

Today I welcomed my fifth grandchild. My heart took a happy leap as the news reached me by long-distance telephone. I offered thanks to God for new life.

Then, in prayer, I talked to that invisible little grandchild only a few hours old: "Scott Anthony Coleman, welcome aboard! Today is the first day of the rest of your life. You have stepped into a fantastic world, filled with opportunities to love!

"What does your future hold, young man?

"Where are you going in life?

"I am so happy I don't know.

"It gives me the freedom to imagine the most wonderful life possible for you! Your father and your mother share with you their most precious gift, God's gift of faith."

**The unknown is our great cause for celebration, for God is there!**

# Facing the future unafraid

"And the LORD, He is the one who goes before
you. He will be with you, He will not leave you
nor forsake you; do not fear nor be
dismayed."—DEUTERONOMY 31:8

I have given two daughters away in marriage. Both times **107**
they were beautiful brides in long white gowns with their
arms circled through mine, walking with nervous excitement
down the aisle to meet their grooms and make their lifetime
commitments in faith! Believe me, they really held onto my
arm!

In the same way, God leads you down the aisle to be married
to a great cause and a great project that awaits you today!

Loop your arm through God's and you will face your future
unafraid! "The LORD, He is the one who goes before you. He
will be with you, He will not leave you nor forsake you; do
not fear nor be dismayed."

Affirmation: I have no fear of the future because I am completely convinced that the situations I have been thrust in are
providential!

- I am doing God's work.
- I am walking in the center of His will.
- He is leading me.
- I am following Him.
- He is guiding me.
- I am making His chosen decisions.

**He only asks me to believe—that He may relieve!**

He relieves me of responsibility when it's beyond me, and
He knows when and where that is. So I sing with hope in my
heart:

> Be not dismayed, whatever betide
> God will take care of you.
> Beneath His wings of love abide
> God will take care of you.

*FAITH IS . . .*
## Timing your move

". . . come before winter."—2 TIMOTHY 4:21

**108**   Is it possible that some people have an intuitive gift of timing? Is it a special gift of God? Surely it must be His Holy Spirit at work in the lives of His people, for timing is everything.

"He who hestitates is lost" . . . "Time waits for no one" . . . "Haste makes waste" . . . "Make hay while the sun shines" . . . "Come before winter." The age-old proverbs and classic clichés sometimes seem confusing and contradicting. You need the wisdom of God to know how to schedule the calendar of life and when to make the moves.

One thing is certain. It is most important to announce the schedule when you make a commitment. Put a time frame around your plans. Once your goals are established, then fit them into a calendar.

Motivation loses steam quickly if you cannot see progress. Consequently, you must schedule some goals to be accomplished today.

In your timing, plan for emergencies. When I was growing up we were never late for church or community events because my mother always insisted that we "leave enough time for a flat tire." We never had a flat tire, so we were always the first ones at church.

Set your goals. Then plan to achieve them by timing your moves.

Finally, be prepared to adjust your calendar to God's calendar. "Come before winter."

**Time waits for no one. Give your goal and dream all you've got! Let go—and let God make it happen in His way.**

# *Rescheduling your timetable*

"The LORD knows the days of the upright,/And their inheritance shall be forever."—PSALM 37:18

It's often possible to take a positive mental attitude toward what appears to be an impossible situation—*if you have enough time.* **109**

In all the promises God has made, never does He surrender control over the schedule. He promises that we can move mountains and achieve the impossible if we will keep on believing. But He doesn't say *when* or *how long* it will take.

**Give God time, and He will perform the miracle.**

When a human condition appears to be totally impossible, don't check out; ask for an extension of time. The hotel sign reads, "Check-out time is 12:00 noon." Don't believe it if you run into a predicament! Ask and believe. They will extend the check-out time.

Just don't be locked into an ironclad schedule. Don't surrender leadership to a clock or a calendar. Of course you set time-dated goals. Of course you generate energy by creating urgency. But be prepared to *revise your timetable before you bury your dream!*

Every passing hour of every passing day and every new month increase the possibility that things will turn around.

What you may need is not more faith, but more patience. The impossible may become possible when you take the long look.

As we walk the walk of faith, we must become more God-like. And one quality about God is His immeasurable long-suffering and patient attitude.

What great impossible deeds could you accomplish if you had a forty-year goal?

If you are tempted to abandon your dream—don't!

Help me, my God and Father, I pray. Amen.

*FAITH IS . . .*
## *Revising your schedule*

"My times are in Your hand."—PSALM 31:15

**110** Faith is a constant process of reviewing the calendar against your accomplishments. Just because it's impossible today doesn't mean it will be impossible tomorrow.

When you set goals, put a time limit on them. Without it you are normally and naturally lazy and lethargic more often than you want to admit. It's amazing how much you can accomplish in a short period of time if the pressure is on.

What do you do when you have not succeeded in meeting your time limit, and it becomes apparent that the project will take longer than you expected?

You keep walking the walk of faith. You revise your timetable:

"It's not impossible; it just takes a little longer." Suddenly seemingly unachievable projects become very realistic!

What can you accomplish if you take ten years? You might be able to get a new degree. Perhaps you can acquire a much larger financial base. You might even be able to overcome that handicap.

Keep walking the walk of faith. Don't give up believing: just revise the timetable!

**God has never promised to deliver an answer to prayer according to our timetables.**

Dear Lord, if I fail to meet some of the goals that I have set, don't let me quit. Give me the ability to stretch the project out over a longer period of time. I'll wait for the rain to fall. I'll expect it, and I'll hang in there, knowing my times are in Your hand. Thank You, Father. Amen.

*FAITH IS . . .*
## *Recognizing the reality of miracles*

"Everyone who is called by My name,/Whom I
have created for My glory;/I have formed him,/
yes, I have made him."—ISAIAH 43:7

How would you respond if someone challenged your faith **111**
with: "Show me a miracle—and I'll believe in it!" You could
answer: "Take a look at me—I'm one! Then take a look in the
mirror. You'll see another one!"

The fact that you are alive today is nothing short of a miracle! Your life is the continuation of an unbroken genetic string
reaching back all the way to the first parents. Look back at
your family tree and see how many times the cord came close
to being severed. Was it in the Civil War? Was it in a plague
epidemic? Was it on a slave ship crossing the waters from Africa to America?

You are a survivor of survivors of survivors! How often you
yourself have survived near-death experiences, you will never
know!

Your life has a special purpose. There is a reason why you
are alive today. You are a walking miracle! Whatever your racial origin, ethnic identification, educational level, or economic bracket, *you are special! You are a winner! You are
alive!*

So give your life totally today to the God who brought you
here. Let Jesus Christ—the Ultimate Survivor, who rose from
the dead on Easter morning—be your best Friend, and share
His wonderful love with the people you come into contact
with today. That, at least, is your reason for being here.

**God must have believed that you'd be a good person to
spread His love around in the world today! God has
not let you down. You won't let Him down either. You
have every reason to be supergrateful. Think of it:
Saved for such a high and holy purpose.**

# Designing for survival

"You are my hiding place and my shield;/I hope in Your word."—PSALM 119:114

**112** The walk of faith is a day-by-day, week-by-week, month-by-month, year-by-year process of building a solid fortress reinforcing the human spirit against assaults of the enemy of doubt. This daily motivational guide is building such a wall of faith.

Each day we add one brick upon another, until we have developed a philosophy of possibility thinking that is designed to save the human spirit from being broken and crushed in the worst of times.

Richard Neutra, the famed architect with whom I worked in designing our Tower of Hope, wrote a book entitled *Survival Through Design*. Neutra believes that architecture should be designed to envelop the human emotions in healthy, positive surroundings. "Some structures and houses really are haunted," he once told me. "By that I mean that some structures are designed in such a way that the sun never shines in. You never feel the play of light. The ceilings are so low, they come down on you. You feel oppressed, instead of liberated and surrounded by light. The corners are gloomy. Hence the structures produce the moods that will haunt the human spirit with depression and gloom."

Even as great architecture attempts to design for emotional survival, you are designing a faith that will allow you to survive the emotional storms of life.

**Dear God, help me to keep praying and believing day by day, week by week, to develop such an impenetrable shield of faith that the fiery darts of doubt will be deflected in the worst times of life. Amen.**

## Feasting on the beautiful

"Man shall not live by bread alone, but by every word that proceeds from the mouth of God."—MATTHEW 4:4

**113**

I'm driven by the awareness that through Jesus Christ any person can be transformed into a beautiful person. I have watched a cold eye become misty with the warmth nourished and fed by a spiritual love of God. That is a fantastic experience! I feast on beauty! "We shall not live by bread alone."

Allow me to quote Richard Neutra again. Often he reminds me, "Beauty is practical, too!" Then he tells how his clients would object to his designs and wanted to replace the reflection pools, lawns, and fountains with practical asphalt and cement. He would wisely reply, "But the human being was designed to live in a garden. He needs beauty to sustain his soul and his spirit. Put him in a concrete jungle, and he'll become a concrete beast. He'll lose his sensitivity to beauty. And when that happens he'll cease to see the potential of beauty in human beings around him. Then he will begin to treat them abusively and violence will be the result."

**Beauty is not an option—it's a nonnegotiable necessity!**

Beauty is what keeps the human family human. And that's the first step toward becoming Godlike, which is our heavenly Father's plan. The next time you hear somebody criticizing a work of art or architecture as "a waste of money in a hungry world," remember this: What good is it to sustain human life if the human beings are not really human? This is why I am so incurably attracted to Jesus Christ. Everything I know about Him leads me to see Him as the most beautiful human being who ever walked on planet Earth.

Jesus, come into my life and fill me with Your beauty. May my life be beautiful, too. I can be a beautiful creature if Your love will shine through my eyes. Thank You. Amen.

# Acquiring an appetite for beauty

"Consider the lilies, how they grow . . . even Solomon in all his glory was not arrayed like one of these."—LUKE 12:27

**114**     When a person acquires a sense of beauty, you can be sure he or she is walking the walk of faith. For beauty is spiritual value that is the result of a belief system.

**If you want to succeed in the walk of faith, you must acquire a sense of beauty.**

Once addicted with an insatiable appetite for beauty, you'll never be able to surrender your dreams to the tempting offers of lesser values.

People often ask me: "Where did you get the strength to take the idea of the Crystal Cathedral and see it through to its debt-free completion at such an enormous cost?"

My answer is simple. "Somewhere along the line I acquired an uncompromising and insatiable appetite for beauty." I saw the Crystal Cathedral as a work of art that would inspire persons for centuries to come. And that hunger for beauty kept my commitment to the pursuit of the project fueled and sustained!

A commitment to excellence demands an enormous amount of effort. One can quickly become fatigued at fighting the majority of persons and forces that gladly want to compromise quality on the altar of mediocrity.

What keeps you from burning out before you have finished the project? How can you conquer that tough, unyielding, recurring weakness in your personal behavior?

The answer is obvious: Get the kind of faith that will not surrender to anything less than the best. It's a tough faith that will not compromise in its loyalty to beauty.

Beauty is bread, too! It feeds the soul!

## *Adorning your mind with beauty*

"And the desert shall rejoice and blossom as the rose; it shall blossom abundantly and rejoice."—ISAIAH 35:1–2

It is not accidental that the Christian religion has produced **115** the richest outpouring of great art in paintings, sculpture, and architecture. That's because God is the Source and Creator of beauty. He makes the desert "blossom as the rose."

If God can make a dry, barren desert come alive with a garden of flowers, then He can certainly turn us into beautiful personalities. He can redesign, restyle, remodel, and redecorate our minds with beautiful thoughts. When that happens, our eyes reflect the difference. The lines around our mouth change the shape of our lips, and smiles come naturally. When God becomes the source of our thinking, the mind that was dull with boredom begins to blossom with beautiful ideas and dreams.

God adorns your mind with beautiful ideas, and suddenly your life becomes amazingly fruitful!

**God's promise is that even the most barren life can be turned into a garden.**

A friend recently told this story: "I have a little house on the beach. I love watering the sand!" Laughingly, she continued, "I know it sounds funny, but it relaxes me." Suddenly her eyes flashed. "And you'll never believe what has happened! Grass has started to grow!" she said, excitedly. "Honestly! The beach turned into a front lawn where I watered it. Everyone was astonished. So was I. Apparently there are all kinds of miniature seeds mixed up in all of that sand."

Thank You, God, for being the Source and Creator of beauty! I know now that I can be beautiful, too—through Your thoughts. Redesign and redecorate my mind today so that I may bloom where I am planted.

# Detailing for excellence

"And let the beauty of the LORD our God be upon us,/And establish the work of our hands for us."—PSALM 90:17

**116** "God is in the details" is a favorite quotation of the late famed architect, Mies van der Rohe. When Mies van der Rohe taught architecture at the University of Illinois, he required his students to draw in every single brick in an entire wall! "It will force the stone masons to put in the precise number of bricks," he said. "Only then can you be sure that the fine detailing at the edges will come out the way you want them to come out."

Many students complained. They simply wanted to draw a few bricks in a small section with the instructions: "Follow this form for the entire wall." But of course, when that pattern was followed, some bricklayers became a bit generous with the cement and the mortar. The building didn't end up with exactly the number of bricks that would have given the most beautiful impression.

### God is in the details.

Beauty comes through the final refinement. The exquisite and elegant emerge when the white dot glistens in the eye of the subject on the canvas. A room can be well appointed, but put a garbage pail in the middle, and the charm and beauty are spoiled. It takes a lot of faith to resist the temptation to overlook or overdo.

Affirmation: Today I shall examine the details of my life. Do I yield carelessly to shortcuts and forget the details?

Faith focuses on the final product, the ultimate accomplishment, the completed act.

Faith knows success is in the details, for God is in the details.

## Specifying the details

"But the very hairs of your head are all numbered."—MATTHEW 10:30

The walk of faith, then, focuses on the finishing touch, the **117** final dab of the artist's brush, the fine tuning of the tightened string.

The compulsion to excellence assures excitement! And that's where the road of faith really leads the committed person. If one instrument is slightly off tune, the orchestra is noticeably less than its best.

Through nearly twenty-five years of collaborating with two of the world's most esteemed architects of the century, Richard Neutra and Philip Johnson, I have learned this principle of success:

> **Greatness comes through the toughness of being very specific even in the details!**

So, how do we achieve success in life? We cannot assume that others will adequately carry out the details unless we specify them carefully.

Apply this principle now to your private life, your prayer life, to your Christian walk with God.

Apply this principle to your own professional pursuit.

Building a reputation, a character, or a life achievement in personality development demands a devotion to the details.

What causes you to behave your worst? Be specific!

What are your shortcomings and sins? Be specific!

Specify in detail what you need to accomplish before you achieve your desired objectives.

Dear God, thank you for specifying the details of my life when even the hairs of my head are numbered. How great You are! Teach me today to be concerned about the fine details that make me a more effective believer. Thank You, God.

*FAITH IS . . .*
# *Weaving a beautiful pattern*

"In all things showing yourself to be a pattern
of good works."—TITUS 2:7

**118** Faith looks upon life's projects as commitments to

- start
- develop
- *complete!*

A beautiful piece of embroidery doesn't happen except for
the patient, persistent commitment to a completed work of
art. That *first stitch* is an act of faith.

I've watched my wife and daughters do beautiful embroidery, and I've seen remarkable weavers at work, particularly in
mainland China. There I saw weavers working on a carpet
that had been in progress for over twenty-two years. It was
estimated that it would take another fifteen or twenty years
before it would be completed.

Your attitude toward this walk of faith is one of lifetime
commitment. You are *developing* a pattern of living! A new
life pattern will steadily, slowly, and beautifully emerge as you
keep making decisions, spotting opportunities, solving problems, and shuttling the colorful threads through the loom of
your life. With the passing of years, your personality unfolds,
and your reputation is established as a beautiful creation by
faith under the influence of an inspiring Creator—God!

**Sow a thought, and you reap an act.**
**Sow an act, and you reap a habit.**
**Sow a habit, and you reap character.**
**Sow character, and you reap destiny!**

Even the dark experiences of life can add character to the
pattern if you weave them in with a positive attitude.

## FAITH IS . . .
### *Cutting the cloth*

"She makes linen garments/and sells them/. . .
Strength and honor are her clothing;/She shall
rejoice in time to come."—PROVERBS 31:24–25

You bought just the right amount of yardage. After all, the **119**
material was very expensive.

But this is a very special project.

You laid the pattern on the cloth, and it's going to work out
perfectly.

There will be no leftover scraps.

There will be no waste.

There is no room for error on this job.

An old Russian tailor's proverb is "Measure three times but
cut only once!"

Now the scissors are in your hand.

You put the sharp edges to the cloth and apply the pressure.
You have cut the cloth.

You have made an irreversible commitment! You have exercised faith!

> **Making an irreversible move which runs the risk of
> permanently wasting a resource, gambling that the
> outcome will work, is cutting the cloth!**

I remember seeing a beautiful piece of pure silk yardage on
the shelf of my mother's closet. This gift of exclusive Chinese
cloth had been brought to her by her brother, a missionary to
China. Often she would talk about what she might do with it.
She wanted to make sure she used it for the right thing, but
she was always afraid to ruin the special material. The sad
thing was that, when she died at the age of nearly eighty, it
was still there on the shelf.

She never did make anything out of it. We unfolded it to
find that it had faded on the edges.

It was good for nothing!

What patterns must I lay out today, O God? Give me the
courage to make the right choices and to cut the cloth! Amen.

[369]

## Mixing the recipe

"Oh, taste and see that the LORD is good."—
PSALM 34:8

**120**   A childhood memory will always live within me. It is a picture of my mother baking apple pies, kneading the dough for homemade bread, or mixing up one of her fabulous desserts. The remarkable thing about Mom was that she never used a recipe. She had it all in her head. She would catch a little flour in her hand and sprinkle it in. She would take the salt shaker and give a few shakes. She'd take a cap off a bottle of vanilla and pour some into the mixture. I always became a little uneasy. "Mom, are you sure you are putting in the right amount of ingredients?"

She would always smile confidently and say, "Oh, don't you worry. It will come out right!"

Faith is mixing the ingredients before you can be positive that the outcome will be satisfying. That's the dynamic success principle that is before us today.

As you expose your mind to new truths from other disciplines, can you be sure that your philosophy of life can accommodate and absorb new truths?

Essentially, when we live by faith, we are declaring that we have enough confidence in God and in ourselves that we can mix ingredients together into á harmonious and productive service. It may be a faculty in school; the work force in the company; the membership of the local church. It may be something as commonplace and beautiful as a family.

**Life ceases to be stale when we dare to come up with a new recipe.**

Dare to invest time, energy, food, thought, or other treasured resources in a new experiment. In the process you'll grow spiritually, intellectually, or emotionally.

*FAITH IS . . .*
## *Smelling the flowers*

"For lo, the winter is past,/The rain is over and gone./The flowers appear on the earth;/The time of singing has come."—SONG OF SOLOMON 2:11–12

I see a flower blooming today! As I reach for it, I breathe deeply of its fragrance. A natural high lifts me as I breathe the breath of God coming from it. **121**

Faith is smelling the flowers; it's enjoying the sweet fragrances of faith, hope, and love that blossom in the Garden of Belief.

A friend of mine, Bill Camp, is nearing one hundred years of age. Historians credit him for importing the first cotton to California from the Deep South.

Shortly after his move west, Bill's wife died. He set about hiring a housekeeper, who came and stayed for over forty years until she died. Bill said, "I asked three things of her: (1) Cook a delicious meal, (2) keep a clean kitchen, and (3) *keep a fresh flower on my table every day.*"

Try to find the means to place a blooming flower on your table. A beautiful blossom resembles a circle of positive-thinking people who bring color to brighten the day. When they leave, it is as if the perfume of joy lingers behind.

Can I be a blossom like that, spreading joy to brighten someone's day?

### I will bloom where I am planted today!

I must develop the habit of nurturing each positive thought, for that's like smelling the flowers along the way.

Thank You, Father, for the gift of flowers, for the fragrance and beauty You've created in each blossom. Thank You that the most beautiful flowers are the positive thoughts that come from You. They're free! As I smell the flowers now, I feel nearer to You, O God. Thank You. Amen.

## *Plowing the ground*

"No one, having put his hand to the plow, and looking back, is fit for the kingdom of God."—
LUKE 9:62

**122**     Who are the great possibility thinkers of all time?

Would you name the space scientists who put a man on the moon? Certainly they qualify.

But throughout the ages, I contend that the greatest possibility thinkers are the farmers.

I recall my father's plowing the ground in Iowa. Plowing was a great commitment. Once the ground was broken and prepared, the precious seed was planted.

I remember my grandfather's telling me how virgin prairies were originally broken into cultivated farmland in the midwestern states of America. The pioneer tied a red handkerchief to a long stake and hammered it in the ground. Then he retraced his steps, put his hands to the plow, and with his eyes firmly fixed on the red flag, he commanded his oxen or his horses to pull! Never once did he look back; otherwise he would plow a crooked row.

Can you imagine the faith it took for that farmer to keep looking ahead without turning for a moment to see how well he was doing?

People who reach their goal are the ones who keep pressing forward until they reach a point when God allows them to pause long enough to see how the Lord has blessed them! It all begins to add up, doesn't it? Faith works because it keeps your eye firmly fixed on your goal.

**Keep the faith . . . keep looking ahead!**

How would you like to make the Possibility Thinkers Hall of Fame? You can! Start plowing and never look back!

FAITH IS . . .
## Planting the seed

"In the morning sow your seed, and in the
evening do not withhold your hand; for you do
not know which will prosper . . . or whether
both alike will be good."—ECCLESIASTES 11:6

Every spring we planted seeds on my father's farm.    **123**

Ask any farmer what faith is and he will tell you it is planting seeds. In an act of faith a farmer throws seed away in the
hope that they will come back multiplied!

Most of us today are not farmers of the field; but we can
become farmers of ideas when, as possibility thinkers, we
treat ideas as seeds.

**Any fool can count the seeds in an apple, but only God
can count the apples in one seed.**

Take an idea and treat it like a newborn child. Feed it, nourish it, protect it, and clothe it, for that seed might sprout and
become a full-fledged project for the good of our human family and for the glory of God.

The farmer runs the risk that the seed may rot in the soil.
We run the risk that our ideas may never materialize as we
hoped.

But the person who is unconditionally committed to a lifetime pilgrimage on the path of faith will inevitably come out
far ahead of the person who chooses to surrender to doubt and
despair.

Got an idea?

Plant it!

Nothing happens until you do something to start to make
something happen!

Plant the seed of faith today in your home, your place of
work, your community. Speak a positive word—only a sentence—about your faith in God to someone.

# *Watering the tender shoots*

"See how the farmer waits for the precious fruit
of the earth, waiting patiently for it until it
receives the early and the latter rain. You also
be patient."—JAMES 5:7–8

**124**   At no point is the farmer's faith tested more than when he
searches the sky in the dry season looking for a cloud that
might hold the promise of moisture. Once the young seeds are
sprouted, the short, tender roots can quickly dry out and die
for want of drink. The Iowa farmer depends entirely upon natural rainfall. Without it his crop could be a disaster.

The California farmer, quite by contrast to the Iowa farmer,
cannot expect enough natural rainfall. Consequently, he in-
vests enormous sums of money in irrigation systems. He buys
the water long before there is any guarantee that a harvest will
be gained. That's faith.

Parents exhibit a similar faith when they invest everything
they can in their child without any assurance that this investment will really bear fruit.

Watering the tender shoots? That's faith!

It is payment in advance.

It is knocking yourself out for a good grade long before the
final exam.

It's putting out your best effort on the job before the
paycheck is extended.

When my son graduated from high school, he wanted to
take his prom date to a fancy restaurant. To make sure he
could afford it, he visited the place a week ahead of time, pre-
ordered the entire menu, and paid everything up front. "Gosh,
I just hope the place doesn't burn down before prom night," he
said. We laughed. He believed!

**The walk of faith demands effort before the outcome
can be assured.**

It's an exciting way to live, isn't it!?

## *Fertilizing the plants*

"He who tills his land will be satisfied with bread."—PROVERBS 12:11

It would be so much simpler if life were all a matter of cash **125** on delivery.

Or would it?

The farmer puts investment on top of investment, effort on top of effort, output on top of output, before he is assured that it will pay off as he waters and fertilizes the plants. He does it simply because he has faith in the tender growing shoots.

Some people fail because they don't have enough faith to plow the ground.

Others fail because they don't have enough faith to plant the seed.

Still others find that their supply of faith runs out at the stage when they have to start fertilizing the plants. They ask, "How much must I invest before I can expect a return? How do I know that I'm not putting too much into this project?"

These are fundamental questions that everybody is going to ask somewhere along the walk of faith, so it is time to remember that everything nice has its price.

Prosperity demands payment in advance—and as you go along—as well as a final payment on delivery!

It is part of God's design to keep us depending upon Him at every step in life's walk.

**There is no phase in faith when we can "go it on our own."**

God, help me to believe in my dream enough to keep giving it my best effort today! Forgive me if I have been neglecting it! I'm going to give it a shot of nourishment now with new effort. Amen.

## *Pruning the trees*

> "I am the true vine. . . . Every branch in Me
> that . . . bears fruit [the Father] prunes, that it
> may bear more fruit."—JOHN 15:1–2

**126** It has always shocked me to watch an expert pruning trees or shrubs. It appears to be such a violent act.

When I watched my father trim fruit trees, I was shocked that he would cut off the very branches from which I had just picked fruit the previous season.

I pleaded with him, "Dad, not those branches—they're the ones that bore the most fruit!"

But my father would patiently reply, "The new growth will come out in the spring—*that's* what bears the best fruit."

My father was correct in his prediction, but it took tremendous faith to cut off the branches that bore the best fruit, trusting in new branches yet unborn.

In the Bible passage beginning with John 15, verse 1, we see how important success is in the mind and teaching of our Lord. Success can be defined as bearing fruit (being productive) and fulfilling God's plan for our lives.

We also see that the pruning of dead branches is essential to success.

Do you need to prune an obsolete product from your inventory?

Do you need to retool, restyle, or update your efforts?

Do you need to reeducate yourself in future technology?

Keep growing—or start dying. Faith requires tough pruning. Believe in the knife like the surgeon believes in the scalpel.

> **O God, give me the courage to say good-by to the old that needs to be buried with dignity before I can say hello to the new that waits with youthful vigor to step in as my new friend.**

## Harvesting the crop

". . . whose hope is the LORD. . . . shall be like a
tree planted by the waters, which spreads out
its roots by the river . . . nor will cease from
yielding fruit."—JEREMIAH 17:7–8

We can all understand that it takes a lot of faith to plow the **127**
ground, to plant the seed, to water, fertilize, and even prune
the growth. But to harvest the crop? How is that an act of
faith? Isn't harvest time a time for thanksgiving? Now is the
time for relaxation. Right? Wrong!

Harvesting requires its own walk of faith, for the farmer
who harvests believes that his crop will find a buyer in the
marketplace.

Likewise, when I finally have a sermon prepared, I deliver it
in the faith and belief that it will be helpful to others.

When you complete your college education with the degree
tucked away in your pocket, you'll need a new level of faith.
To make the most of your education, you have to tackle the
job market.

And once you've achieved a financial base and have acquired some savings, can you relax? Hardly. As a crop rots in
the field if it isn't harvested, so a financial fortune quickly
dwindles away unless it is invested wisely. Inflation alone will
reduce it rapidly.

Success can tempt you to take it easy. If the joy of the harvest, plus the high price paid to achieve it, tempts you to retire
and retreat from future expansion and growth, then you're in
real trouble! Even while my father harvested the crop he was
planning a new crop for the following year.

How wise are the words of Viktor Frankl:

**"The *is* must never catch up with the *ought*."**

Not having a new goal is to be feared more than not reaching a goal.

O God, give me faith strong enough to harvest the crop!

[377]

## *Developing progressively*

"When you walk, your steps will not be hindered,/And when you run, you will not stumble."—PROVERBS 4:12

**128** The high-flying trip of success doesn't usually happen swiftly and spontaneously. American success stories are of people who developed their businesses progressively. Faith progresses step by step. Each step is an exercise in possibility thinking.

Step 1 is *setting*. This is the stage similar to the chicken's waiting for the egg to hatch. You think things through. You do some raw market research. You do not leap forward impulsively. There is a lot of faith and possibility thinking in this first step.

Step 2 is *fretting*. Once you have an idea, begin to imagine the real obstacles you have to overcome. It's unrealistic not to prepare for this overcoming step in developing your project. Hopefully, you have been well prepared in this walk of faith to survive this stage—and the next one, too.

Step 3 is *getting*. Now it's time to get out and crack each problem one at a time. Refuse to surrender leadership to frustrations or forces that surround you.

Step 4 is *sweating*. You may have second thoughts. You may even ask yourself, "Is this what I really want?" Remember that it's usually darkest just before the dawn. God is setting things up for a miracle.

Step 5 is *netting!* You netted your catch! You reached your goal. Now what? Now you can find time to be alone and creative. You are not the same person you were when you took that first step. In this walk of faith, step by step, you have developed and progressed along with your dream.

**A dream developed never leaves you where it found you. It makes you the person God wants you to be.**

## Mapping out the trip

"He who walks with integrity walks
securely."—PROVERBS 10:9

A great deal of faith is required when mapping out a trip **129**
before you hit the road. The same is true of the walk of faith.
For faith is a commitment to your highest values and noblest
calling. Begin by asking the questions:
Where will this road lead?
What if this becomes a habit?
What if others imitate me?
What if my children follow in my footsteps?
What if the whole world lived this way?
Occasionally our family vacations in Hawaii. We enjoy eating breakfast at the beautiful Kahala Hilton hotel dining room
overlooking the beach. Nearby is a private walkway leading
through a tunnel of trees. There is a sign posted which reads
"private."
One day our family visited a condominium near the hotel.
From the condominium we walked back through a wooded
area and came out to the same spot where the sign was. There
we found ourselves in front of the hotel's breakfast room. My
little daughter said, "Oh, that's where the road leads!"

**Map out your trip. Make sure you know where the
road leads. Know where you want to go.**

Today, check out your private life. Are your personal relationships healthy? Are your associates positive—or negative?
Take a long look at your goals. If you keep following the
path you're on, where will you end up?
Will you be pleased and proud once you get there? Will your
children be proud of you once you're gone?
Today, Lord, I'm going to walk the walk of faith. I'm going to
map out the path of my life carefully to make sure that I'm
walking in faith. Thank You, God. Amen.

## Disciplining yourself to succeed

"I discipline my body and bring it into
subjection, lest I myself become disqualified."—
1 CORINTHIANS 9:27

**130** Faith is focusing all of your conscious and subconscious
thought and your natural and supernatural powers to create a
spiritual cable more powerful than any steel cable.

**Faith, through this cable, moves mountains. This cable is *discipline!***

The words *discipline* and *disciple* come from the same root.
Early Christians were called disciples. That means they became persons so totally and completely committed to the
Christian cause that they were willing to die for it. That, essentially, is the spirit that makes up the word *discipline.*

The person who disciplines his body practices faith,
whether it's through controlling appetite for food or drink, or
any other natural physical appetite.

There are mysterious, intricate, and complex connections
of body, brain, and soul. Persons who discipline their eating,
drinking, and sexual appetites, often experience a mysterious
upsurge of creative powers and a rebirth of spirituality. In contrast, the undisciplined person who "lets himself go" and
doesn't care about proper exercise, physical fitness, or dietary
disciplines finds his faith becoming "flabby." *Undisciplined* is
another word for *disqualified.*

Affirmation: Today I am determined that I am going to
qualify as a disciple of Jesus Christ.

I will be disciplined in the control of my eyes, my ears, my
mouth, my stomach, my hands, and my sexual desires.

I shall bring my body under control.

I shall become a spiritual athlete!

Help me, O God, to succeed in this colossal challenge. Let
my life give evidence, O Lord, of being a disciplined disciple!
Amen.

# Energizing your body

"The zeal of the LORD of hosts shall do this."—
2 KINGS 19:31

You have drawn the mental picture of your dream. You announced your intentions. You're excited about succeeding; now your faith must continue to release enthusiasm so you can perform at your best.

The word *enthusiasm* comes from two Greek words, *entheos*, literally translated "in-God."

**Enthusiasm is the force of God Himself energizing your body.**

So, the zeal of the Lord, the enthusiasm that comes from our God-inspired faith, gives us peak performance power!

Most fatigue is the result of lack of faith. Negative emotions such as worry, frustration, anxiety, fear, indecision, guilt, and depression are weights causing tremendous fatigue of the human spirit. Make room for Jesus Christ. He saves you from all of these negative emotions—and inspires you to set great goals. With Christ, positive emotions replace negative emotions. *Weights become wings!* When our Lord gives us exciting dreams and reassures us of success, we become so energetic that the aging process is transcended by our strength-inducing faith.

Yes, look at some older people move fast, think fast, act fast when they are excited about life's possibilities!

In contrast, young people who have no goals and are not caught up in a consuming project act old. They move in slow motion and are tempted to draw upon chemicals for an unnatural high!

Our Lord comes and calls you to love Him and be His minister of mercy in a suffering and morbid world.

Suddenly you've got exciting goals! You're enthusiastic. His strength flows through you. Your faith is your energy.

Thank You, Father. Amen.

**131**

## Climbing your way up and out

"For the body without the spirit is dead, so
faith without works is dead also."—JAMES 2:26

**132**     We have all seen people who profess to have dynamic faith.
They pray to God. They exercise religious rituals regularly
and faithfully. They even go to religious retreats to seek the
higher spiritual altitudes of emotional experiences. Yet their
faith remains at the same level, and their lives fall far short of
productivity. The fruits of constructive Christian living seem
conspicuously absent. Missing from their faith is human
effort! Faith is climbing your way out and up, and *climbing* is
spelled *w-o-r-k-i-n-g!*

### Faith is not merely believing—it's working!

God's plan is to get you so deeply involved that your total
commitment will be required before you can fulfill your divine destiny.

Many years ago, a wise minister said, "Pray as if it all depends on God, and work as if it all depends on you!"

Show me a person who is giving 110 percent effort to his
work and to prayer, and I'll show you someone who's really
climbing in his walk of faith. For the ultimate test of faith is
this: Are you motivated to get going and *do* the tough jobs you
have been praying about? Jobs that you know God wants you
to do today?

I watched an ant, brushed off a stone bench. Into a jungle of
bric-a-brac, he fell, confused, bewildered, lost. I watched him
madly race through the little passages, never giving up in spite
of the many blind alleys. Finally, he decided to climb up a
vertical cliff! And he found his escape. He surely and successfully climbed his way up and out.

Can you do less than an ant?

## *Checking in before anybody else*

"For God is not unjust to forget your work and labor of love which you have shown toward His name."—HEBREWS 6:10

I've observed that there are strong connections among faith, ambition, and productivity. The person who really believes he is going to succeed goes the extra mile, applies himself, is extremely productive, stands out from everybody else, and understandably wins the promotions.

He's the first one to check in, and the last one to check out. He doesn't watch the clock.

I love the story of a little boy who wanted to be rich when he grew up. He noticed a man who drove a big expensive car, and always stopped at a construction shack next to a high-rise building that was going up downtown.

One day the little boy went up to the rich man and said, "Sir, excuse me, but can you tell me how I can be rich like you when I grow up?"

The man, impressed by the boy's ambitious attitude, said, "Simple, son, buy a red shirt and work like it all depends on you." The man continued, "You see, I am a developer. I buy property, build buildings, and sell them.

"When I started out I decided that if I wanted to get ahead, I'd have to work harder than everybody else. I did a little better job, got to work a little earlier, and stayed a little longer.

"But I also decided my efforts should be noticed. All the workers wore blue shirts with blue overalls. So I bought a red shirt! The boss noticed me. And I was rewarded! That's my advice to you, son."

**God has promised that He will reward the good worker.**

"For God is not unjust to forget your work and labor of love which you have shown toward His name."

**133**

*FAITH IS . . .*
## *Prioritizing your possibilities*

"Let your eyes look straight ahead,/And your
eyelids look right before you./Ponder the path
of your feet,/And let all your ways be
established."—PROVERBS 4:25–26

**134** **The biggest problem you face on your walk of faith is
finding yourself surrounded with more opportunities
than you can handle.**

How do you go about prioritizing all your possibilities?
After all, there are only a limited number of minutes and
hours in the day. Treat each minute of the day as if it were a
gem. Each minute is money that can be invested or wasted!

First, list your daily possibilities on paper. List all of the
things you *could* do today, *should* do today, and *would* like to
do today; review the basic objectives that you want to accomplish.

Now, begin to prioritize the possibilities by giving your best
time to the most important project. The morning hours will
be your most valuable time, while the day is still uncluttered
with uninvited irritations that can easily tarnish your happy
attitude.

**Give your best time to your most important projects.**

Now—if you still lack resources to take advantage of great
opportunities, consider this. Many possibility thinkers lack
the resources to execute all of their dreams. So they carefully
look for other possibility thinkers whom they can approach
with their projects. They'll share their opportunities along
with the potential profit before they abandon the dream for
lack of time or money. In business this is called "setting up
limited partnerships."

To make sure your priorities are in order begin to form and
forge an "unlimited partnership." . . . "Your Lord and you"—
thinking, planning, dreaming together!

Father, thank You for the many opportunities I have to serve
You and others. Help me schedule my time and energy in
order to accomplish all You desire of me. Amen.

[384]

# Chipping away at the block

"He who deals with a slack hand becomes
poor,/but the hand of the diligent makes one
rich."—PROVERBS 10:4

I often define faith in these simple but important D's.      **135**

**Faith is** *deciding.*
**Faith is** *daring.*
**Faith is** *doing* **the job.**
**Faith is** *determination* **and** *dedication.*

The writer of Proverbs tells us that *diligence* produces
wealth.

It is amazing what enormous problems dissipate when a
person's mind is diligently focused on a goal.

The first time I saw Michelangelo's bronze statue of Saint
Peter, in Saint Peter's Cathedral in Rome, there was, as always,
a line of faithful peasants and plutocrats alike waiting to see
this revered statue. It has been a tradition for years for the
faithful to pause at the statue and kiss the bronze toe of Peter,
or rub it softly. Today, that solid bronze toe of Peter is worn
away so it is nothing more than a flat, sharp edge.

If soft and gentle kisses can wear away a bronze toe, what
will daily touches of positive thoughts toward your tough
problem do to that obstacle?

If you've got a project to build or a problem to solve, take
that first crack at it today. You will chip away and before you
know it, the sculptured piece will begin to emerge out of the
marble.

Dear Lord, I need to exercise the six D's of faith today to
keep chipping away. Give me the power to *decide,* the courage
to *dare,* the energy to *do,* the willpower to be *determined,* the
grace to be *dedicated,* and the patience to be *diligent.* Thank
You, Lord. Amen.

*FAITH IS . . .*
## Chiseling away at the mountain

"But you, be strong and do not let your hands
be weak, for your work shall be rewarded!"—
2 CHRONICLES 15:7

**136**    How do you move a mountain? You move a mountain one truckload at a time. You chisel away one chip at a time.

I have stood at the Great Wall of China and marveled at the hundreds of years that were consumed to build this wall over the impossible mountain ranges!

I have walked beside the great pyramids of Egypt and been amazed at these magnificent mountains that were built—one block at a time!

Dallas Anderson was sculpturing a larger-than-life statue of Job out of marble. He invited me to his studio, where I looked up at a ten-foot-tall chunk of white granite marble that weighed many tons.

Dallas said to me, "Job is inside there—and we'll have to bring him out." Then he handed me a sledge hammer that appeared to weigh twenty pounds!

"Take a whack at it; you have to really hammer at it!" With that I swung the sledge hammer with all the power I could muster and saw only a small chunk of white marble chip away. That was many months and tens of thousands of chips ago.

Today, that statue of Job stands in all his inspiring glory.

I learned, once more, how you move a mountain—one truckload at a time. I learned how you take a big rock and turn it into a work of art—one chip at a time. I was reminded again of what faith is all about. We chip and we chisel at life's challenges with confidence and hope until beauty emerges.

Dear God, thank You for giving me this faith. I will chisel away at my challenges one chunk at a time. Amen.

# *Positioning yourself in the marketplace*

"Where no oxen are, the trough is clean;/But much increase comes by the strength of an ox."—PROVERBS 14:4

A contemporary paraphrase of our text today could read, **137** "Where there is no market, the store is empty; but much increase comes by the strength of providing the goods that people need." As you anticipate future growth and struggle with decisions to expand your base, do not abandon your faith to folly.

For example, when the sixties gave way to the seventies, Americans suddenly lost interest in huge automobiles. However, Detroit ignored the pressures of the marketplace and continued to manufacture big cars. By doing so, they plunged the automobile industry into a recession of gigantic proportions. Japan captured Detroit's position.

Success often depends on selling something to someone. Selling is convincing people that you have the answer to their problem and the help they need.

Education sells knowledge.

Universities sell training or professional work.

Hospitals sell health care.

Even churches sell something—spiritual and emotional services—to people whose problems can only be solved through a personal relationship with God and Jesus Christ!

Does the need still exist or is it passé? Who else is filling this need? These are responsible questions you need to ask before you expand your base of service. If there is a need that no one else is meeting, then come up with a program to meet those needs. Position yourself in the marketplace of ideas to provide services that solve problems no one else is really tackling!

**Faith in action is positioning yourself in the marketplace of human effort. I will solve someone's problem in the name of God.**

# Evolving upward

"Be faithful unto death, and I will give you the crown of life."—REVELATION 2:10

**138**   You have a dream, but the solid base you need for a launching pad is not yet established. What do you do?

**You have to let the dream evolve.**

The first level is the *nesting* level. Here you ask the basic question: "Who needs it?"

When you discover that someone can be helped by your forward act of faith, you enter the second level, the *testing* of the dream. Here you ask three basic questions: Will it help people who are hurting? Will it be a great thing for God and for the human family? Is anybody else doing the job? If so, can I do it better and cheaper?

The third level is the *investing* level. This is the level where you invest your resources. Put your money where your mouth is.

The fourth level is *divesting* yourself of negative thinking. Eliminate the fear of failure.

The fifth level is *arresting.* You encounter tough times. God always gives you a great new test before He gives you a great success! This is God's way of making sure He can trust you with success.

The sixth level is the *cresting* level. This is the uppermost level of the evolutionary process of the dream. Faith evolves upward until that moment when the dream is complete! The project is finished!

O Lord, today I shall take time to review each level of evolution my faith has experienced. I shall praise God that He was there all the time. He has not failed me yet. He will not fail me now. Tomorrow will be glorious, for God is there. Thank You, God. Amen.

## Pacing your progress

"To everything there is a season,/A time for
every purpose under heaven . . ./A time to
plant,/And a time to pluck what is planted,
. . ./A time to break down,/And a time to build
up . . ."—ECCLESIASTES 3:1

Doesn't the walk of faith appear to be inflicted with contra-   **139**
dictions or paradoxes? Doesn't it seem like a juggling act in a
possibility-thinking game? Then remember this:

Faith is an art—not a science. Faith advances for a season,
then retreats the next. You are ambitious for a season, then
relaxed; aggressive, then passive; giving, then taking.

As positive and negative wires generate the power of electricity, so in faith, negatives are used with positives to create
mountain-moving energy for the believer.

Faith is pacing your progress. The challenges come in knowing: when to push forward, when to hold back; when to dig in,
when to yield; when to hold on, when to let go; when to plan
alone, when to form a partnership.

Faith paces your progress through life with a rhythmic
steadiness regulated by an all-wise Timekeeper, God Almighty. When you walk the walk of faith, you are assured of
the divine guidance to

**Make the right move, in the right way, at the right
time.**

When you kneel before the throne of the almighty God in
respectful humility and cry out, "I need the wisdom of heaven
to walk this walk of faith," you reach the level of faith where
contradictions become constructive; paradoxes become truth.

So keep trusting God to give you His sense of timing. Pace
yourself. Now you wait. Now you move. Now you race! Now
you rest. Now you leap! Now you walk slowly. Possibility
thinkers don't quit—they change their pace to win the race.

Thank You, God for the exhilaration we experience in the
ebb and flow of faith's pilgrimage. Amen.

# *Triple-checking your position*

"Examine me, O LORD, and prove me;/Try my
mind and my heart."—PSALM 26:2

**140**    Late in the Vietnam conflict I found myself in Tachikawa,
Japan, where the central command headquarters for the entire
medical evacuation of the sick and the wounded was situated.

I was given a personal briefing by the general who was in
charge. It was his job to establish systems and procedures to
care for the patients from the time they fell wounded on the
front line to their final hospitalization in America.

On our tour he said, "Dr. Schuller, we are very proud of the
fact that of the multiplied tens of thousands of casualties we
have seen in the Vietnam conflict to date, we have only wit-
nessed *eleven fatalities in transit."*

Astonished, I asked, "How do you do it?"

He said, "We *check, double-check,* and *recheck!* Before any
wounded person is moved, we take the vital signs. If his vital
signs indicate he can make it, he is loaded onto a helicopter.
Before the chopper takes off, we double-check his vital signs.
If he passes the check, we tell the pilot to prepare to take off.
We wait a minute and triple-check! This triple check often
becomes the key factor in survival!"

Faith is triple-checking the position. Many people succeed
or fail here.

The possibility of suceeding increases drastically if you will
• check
• double-check
• recheck

You ordered it done? You expect a delivery? Somebody
promised? Check, double-check, recheck!

## Narrowing the path

"Enter by the narrow gate; for wide is the gate
and broad is the way that leads to destruction,
and there are many who go in by it. Because
narrow is the gate and difficult is the way
which leads to life, and there are few who find
it."—MATTHEW 7:13–14

**141**

The walk of faith is not the broad path. The truth is, most people choose the wide, safe road, which leads to despair, discouragement, and ultimate lack of self-fulfillment.

**The narrow path is the walk of faith. It leads to excitement, adventure, and discovery, that adds up to *life!***

The exciting path is the narrow road that winds through the mountains. It's the narrow path through the garden that leads to the secluded little spots.

Most people take the wide boulevards. They completely miss the interesting places tucked away in the back streets. They are often like tourists who land at an airport and take the bus down through the main streets of town to see the old monuments and the biggest buildings. They return to the airport, never having felt the heartbeat of the people or the places that throb with charm and mystery.

It is easy to deal in broad strokes, for there is a certain safety in sweeping generalities. Instead, we must refuse to accept mediocrity, and we must keep narrowing the pursuit of excellence.

Philosophy and faith get tough and challenging when you try to apply them to the daily acts of human existence. Your prayers are safer if they deal with the broad platitudes. Dare to be specific today and take a very narrow definition in a dangerous request, and prayer will become exciting. What specific need do you have today? Dare to pray specifically!

God, help me today to narrow my path, to lead a more exciting life of faith. I pray specifically for _____.
Thank You, Lord. Amen.

*FAITH IS . . .*
## Maintaining equilibrium

"Everyone who competes for the prize is
temperate in all things."—1 CORINTHIANS 9:25

**142** In the Christian walk of faith it is so easy to lose one's sense
of balance. It's easy to become religious extremists of either
the right or the left. We've all seen those who believe solely in
prayer and reject all forms of scientific and medical aid on the
assumption that seeking human help would be a lack of faith.

By contrast, there are believers who depend entirely upon
material and medical aid and reject the possibility of supernatural and miraculous intervention by God.

The walk of faith is a narrow walk.

It's a delicate task of remaining equilibristic.

By that, I mean one who maintains equilibrium, that remarkable ability to maintain balance when you walk on two
feet balancing a hundred or two hundred pounds.

Remaining spiritually equilibristic is a tricky task too. I believe in prayer for divine guidance, yet I do not recklessly
plunge ahead as soon as a positive idea comes to my mind.

I test the idea. How?

(1) I use the intelligence God has given me;

(2) I check with positive-thinking experts on the subject;

(3) I make sure it does not violate the moral and spiritual
principles taught in the Holy Bible—God's Word for my life!
And finally,

(4) I ask the question, "What would Jesus do?"

> **Dear God, is there some aspect of my faith that I have
> been neglecting? Today help me to realign the scales
> so that I shall have the poise of a well-balanced artist
> on the walk of faith. To Christ be the glory. Amen.**

*FAITH IS . . .*
## Comparing the values

"How much better it is to get wisdom than
gold!/And to get understanding is to be chosen
rather than silver."—PROVERBS 16:16

On this walk of faith—how do you keep your balance? How **143**
do you maintain equilibrium? You do so by carefully comparing competing values before you make unconditional commitments!

As a possibility thinker, you will spot so many opportunities you will be confronted with innumerable demands
on your time, energy, thoughts, and money!

Here's a word of caution: you will be tempted more often by
the good than by the bad.

The greater dangers on this walk of faith will not be the
temptations to kill, steal, and commit adultery. The greater
temptation will be

- to neglect the higher good for the lower good
- to choose the mediocre instead of the excellent
- to live on the "pretty good" level instead of the "super"
  level, and
- to take the easy goal instead of the impossible challenge.

Every time faith translates into action, what is really happening? Why, some person is making a comparison of values.
Consciously or subconsciously, he or she is making a choice
between alternative values. When people tell me they "lack
faith" I often conclude that they're really confused. They can't
decide between competing options.

Frequently there is a contradiction within their value system.

The spiritual and the carnal compete for control.

The ideal and the practical clash for allegiance.

The call to comfort, luxury, and ease competes with the call
to sacrifice and commitment.

**Decision making is easy if there are no contradictions
in your value system.**

[393]

## Bottom lining

"... seek the kingdom of God, and all these
things shall be added to you."—LUKE 12:31

**144**      Quickly and with great regularity, successful people look to
the bottom line. They review the profit and loss statement. In
the same way, faith asks these basic questions:
- What do I really want to accomplish?
- If I keep going at it the way I am, will I make it?
- If I do, will I be satisfied?
- If I forfeit an opportunity to educate my mind, how will
that benefit me socially, financially?
- At the end of my life, can I face my family, myself, and my
God with pride?
- Or will I be ashamed and find that the victories are hollow
in my hand?
- *What will the bottom line be?*

> **Faith specializes in looking ahead and projecting the
> outcome. Then faith makes the choices that ensure
> the odds that the bottom line will be great.**

Today I shall take the long look. As I calculate the price I'll
have to pay, I'll also anticipate the rewards I shall reap.
- I am asking God for guidance.
- I am promising Him that I will follow His leadership.
- I'm aware that the most important thing in my life is the
welfare of my soul.

O God, don't neglect to take the actions that guarantee the
salvation of my soul. Now I accept You, Jesus Christ, as my
Savior. I ask You to receive my soul, redeem it, guard it against
temptations and sins so that I may be strong and successful!
Amen.

*FAITH IS . . .*
## Maneuvering your way skillfully

"You comprehend my path/and my lying down,/And are acquainted with all my ways."— PSALM 139:3

It's common in most ports for captains of ocean liners to **145** step aside and allow special pilots to come aboard. Every harbor has its own peculiar channels and hidden shoals under the surface.

I remember, on an ocean voyage I took, our ship passed through a narrow and precarious passageway in the Coral Sea, between Australia and New Guinea. The narrow S-shaped crevice that cuts through the coral reef below the water is only about sixty feet wide—just wide enough for an ocean vessel. It requires enormous skill from a captain who knows the passageway.

The voyage of faith is not unlike the passage through the Coral Sea. We need to bring a skillful pilot aboard, one who knows the water and hidden shoals. Our Lord is that special pilot who understands our past and knows us better than we know ourselves.

Faith keeps you moving forward by maneuvering between successes and failures, between accomplishments and setbacks, between victories and defeats.

**Faith is no irresponsible shot in the dark. It is a responsible trust in God, who knows the desires of your hearts, the dreams you are given, and the goals you have set. He will guide your paths right.**

O Lord, give my faith the flexibility to maneuver between the highs and the lows, the ups and the downs, the ins and the outs. I am trusting that under Your skillful patrol my plans are moving in absolutely the best possible way. Thank You, Lord. Amen.

## Buckling your safety belt

"The wise in heart will receive commands."—
PROVERBS 10:8

**146**   As a possibility thinker you buckle your safety belt not out of fear, but because you balance your faith with caution. After all, can there be faith without respect?

By faith you make commitments before you have solid guarantees of success. That is the essence of possibility thinking. You never wait to make the move until all risks are removed. But you do try to cover all bases. Then you use faith to minimize the risks—with a healthy respect for possible dangers.

**You walk the walk of faith—but you still carry liability insurance.**

You walk the walk of faith, but you still lock your doors.

You walk the walk of faith, but you still check credentials and credit references before making a big investment.

Faith is buckling your safety belts—*making a commitment to take the trip without guarantees of successfully arriving.*

You dignify your faith when you separate it from folly.

So keep walking the walk of faith—all the while, watching your step!

One negative thought, carelessly allowed to enter the mind, can undermine the unity of your faith.

Show me the person who buckles his safety belt, and I'll show you one who dares to take a chance,

is not afraid of flying,

and knows there can be accidents on the road.

Doesn't that sound like the kind of faith God will bless?

## Scouting the territory

"If the LORD delights in us, then He will bring us into this land . . . which flows with milk and honey."—NUMBERS 14:8

Entertainers and athletes alike know what we mean when **147** we speak of "scouting the territory." "Scouts" are always on the lookout for new talent waiting to be discovered.

Faith calls out a new greeting to you today!

"Be a good scout! Hey, look around you! There's talent in you waiting to be discovered. Check out the possibilities today."

**Thoughts are like roads; you never know where they will lead you.**

Think through new ideas; discover new formulas. Scout the territory beyond the horizon of your mind; consider the positive potentialities. Ask: where will this opportunity lead me?

As you scout the possibilities, be a good scout! Two persons can scout out the same territory and each come back with a conflicting report. There is a marvelous story in the Old Testament that illustrates the point. Moses sent out twelve scouts to check the promised land of Canaan to see if the territory could be conquered. Ten negative thinkers returned with a despairing report, saying, "There we saw giants . . . and we were like grasshoppers" (Num. 13:33). They saw only the obstacles and recommended that the people of Israel remain in the desert.

Two positive-thinking scouts, Joshua and Caleb, came back bearing gifts of fruit—grapes, pomegranates, and figs. Their report was an enthusiastic one. "Let's take the territory! We are well able to overcome it!"

Faith is scouting the territory and reporting back enthusiastically. Faith is believing that with God's guidance and blessing on your life, you can conquer the territory that flows with milk and honey!

## Creating new products and services

"Behold, the former things have come to pass,
and new things I declare; before they spring
forth I tell you of them."—ISAIAH 42:9

**148**    Faith finally adds up to this: We have to keep creating new
products and new services to meet the changing needs in a
shifting society. Creativity is always the ultimate act of believing.

It takes faith to launch a new idea, for there is always risk
involved. But there are ways to minimize the risk.

Market research may determine in advance whether a new
product will really succeed. Spot testing can predetermine
whether an idea is going to be effective. Field polls conduct
research of public opinion to project which candidate will be
the winner.

But in the final analysis, all creativity entails risk. Many
times the poll is proven wrong on election day; mass distribution didn't succeed as the tests predicted.

The element of the unexpected keeps us on our toes! God
never allows us to become so smart that we can be absolutely
confident our new creations will be successful.

**God does promise He will bless us if we are genuinely
creative and keep moving ahead in faith.**

For unless we keep creating new products or service lines
we will be out of business before we know it. For one thing,
the brightest and best people become bored and drift away
when nothing new, exciting, and challenging is happening.
Lose your best people and you're soon facing a disaster. Stop
all experimentation and life becomes stale!

When was the last time you tried to create something new?

*Today, O God, give me the courage to be creative. Amen.*

## Competing constructively

"In You, O LORD, I put my trust;/Let me never
be put to shame."—PSALM 71:1

Possibility thinkers thrive on competition; impossibility **149**
thinkers quickly and cautiously back away from competition.

What do these impossibility thinkers fear? Are they afraid
they will fail? Surely they don't think they can win if they
never play the game. How will they ever know who they are if
they never enter a competition?

You will never know what your abilities are until you put
yourself to the test.

> **Surrendering to the fear of competition may leave you
> forever in the dark, unaware of hidden strengths you
> possess.**

Begin by competing against yourself. Set a pride-producing
goal to achieve something measurable and worthwhile within
a responsible time frame. Now when that's accomplished,
compete against that achievement; set a larger goal. Faith
calls you to competition!

Compete against the problems of this life by finding a ministry that will help people triumph over their tragedies.

Compete against mediocrity by committing yourself to excellence and inspiring others around you to artistic effort in
their chosen profession and career.

Compete against lethargy by raising your awareness level so
that you challenge social and spiritual sickness with a positive faith.

Compete against negative and sinful persons by living such
a positive and beautiful life that you shall be a "shining light
in a dark world."

As long as you've got the competitive spirit, you are walking the walk of faith and you are alive.

Compete in life today!

# *Tapping the untapped possibilities*

"Launch out into the deep and let down your
nets for a catch."—LUKE 5:4

**150**   So you think you've taken your project as far as you can?
You think you've exhausted the market? You think you know
the answers on philosophy, psychology, and religion? Wait a
minute!

> **When you think you've exhausted all possibilities, re-
> member this—you haven't!**

There is a beautiful story in Luke 5:1–8 about the disciples'
fishing all night. As morning breaks the Lord greets them,
"How's fishing?"

"Master, we've fished all night and caught nothing!" is their
weary reply.

"Go out in the deep and throw out your nets," the Lord
directs.

They have every reason to doubt His advice. After all, they
have been fishing all night. But by faith they throw the net in
once more; and this time there are so many fish they can
hardly pull up the load.

It's a beautiful example of life today! Living is like fishing
on the surface of the sea. Even as schools of fish move from
one place to another, so opportunities are always on the move
around you.

There are untapped possibilities around you now. There are
religious experiences you haven't had yet. Encounters with
God through prayer are possible, even if you haven't experienced them.

There is a distinguishing quality about the possibility
thinker—he goes one step beyond everybody else. That extra
step is called the "mark of faith." It is the "winner's edge."

# Spiraling your way upward

"I will go before you and make the crooked
places straight."—ISAIAH 45:2

Of all the misunderstandings about possibility-thinking **151**
faith, there is one point that must be reviewed again: Faith is
not a wild plunge into dangerous ventures. Faith faces risks
with the wide-awake awareness that success is uncertain.
Nevertheless, faith moves ahead, confident that you can arrive if you keep on keeping on. Faith believes that you can
maneuver your way around the obstacles and dangers.

You may not be able to remove the obstacle and you may
not be able to tunnel through the mountain that lies before
you, but no matter how steep the path may be—it can still be
conquered if you work your way around the obstacle.

Remember: A mountain road is seldom a straight path. The
road will twist, turn, curve, and wind. Not infrequently the
road detours for miles before a "switch-back" can be executed,
and you can start moving in on your destination once more.

The good news is that eventually—after compromising, adjusting, manipulating, and maneuvering—you do succeed!
The crooked place becomes straight. The mountaintop is
reached, and the village with its straight streets lies below.

**Faith calls you to travel ahead in uncharted territory,
exposing yourself to risk. But faith manages the risks
responsibly through wise and cautious maneuvering.**

Affirmation: I shall keep spiraling my way upward. I shall
not fail. My strong spirit of determination is itself a victory
over discouragement! I am a success at this level—anyway!
My willingness to exercise patience is a victory over reckless
impulsiveness. Here, too, I am experiencing a success. Thank
You, Lord!

## Redoubling the effort

"Be steadfast, immovable, always abounding in
the work of the Lord, knowing that your labor
is not in vain."—1 CORINTHIANS 15:58

**152** When someone fails, is it because they've lacked enough
faith? Or was it because they didn't give it enough effort? Is
the problem laziness or is it a lack of faith?

Does effort inspire faith? Does faith inspire effort? Or do
they stimulate and sustain each other?

The answer is yes, they do stimulate and sustain each other,
for actually faith can be defined as "giving it all you've got."

There is no doubt that little effort is put forth without faith.
It is also certain that great faith motivates maximum output
of personal energy and investment.

All of the successful people whom I've met and studied
demonstrate this quality: they give their project everything
they've got. They invest more capital in the business. They
work overtime gladly and cheerfully. No wonder they are promoted!

**When we see someone redoubling his or her effort, we
see an inspiring person demonstrating a strong faith in
action.**

When positive people are faced with temptations, they call
upon God and their inner selves for moral strength beyond
what they have previously tapped in life.

Again and again, spiritual, financial, social, educational, or
professional victory is the result of someone's redoubling the
effort.

Quadruple the output. Calculate the average cost for the
goal that you want to accomplish, then multiply it four times!
Now you join the inspiring team of men and women who
walk the walk of faith.

Today, O God, I'll double, triple, and finally redouble my
efforts! And I'll trust You to bless me. Amen.

## Redoing the job

"Let patience have its perfect work, that you
may be perfect and complete, lacking
nothing."—JAMES 1:4

Faith is redoing a job after you've botched it the first time. **153**
It's removing the wallpaper because the wrinkles couldn't be
smoothed out. It's scraping the new paint job off because it
just didn't come out right. Faith is starting over!

I recall one summer when I was under contract to complete
a book for a publisher. Mrs. Schuller and I were scheduled to
attend a conference in Europe. We spent a beautifully productive week on the island of Madeira where I hand wrote a complete book. Finally, when the entire manuscript was finished, I
proudly put it in the mail in time to meet the publisher's
deadline.

A few weeks later I arrived in New York and telephoned my
editor. He gave me the terrible news: the manuscript had
never arrived! It was lost in the mail never to be found. Since I
had handwritten the manuscript, there was no carbon copy,
only scattered pieces of notes. I had no choice but to start over
again and completely rewrite the entire book.

That took a lot of faith! Faith (a) to find the energy to do it
over; (b) that I could write as well as I had done in a secluded
and creative setting; and (c) that I would still be able to finish
the project in time to meet my publisher's deadline—which
now they had extended a few weeks.

I rewrote the entire manuscript, and I have to admit that the
second writing was considerably better than the first.

**"It's good enough" is an attitude that is not good
enough for the person who is walking the walk of
faith.**

Dear God, give me the faith to do the job over again. There
is a possibility that I can do a better job the second, or the
third, or the fourth time around!

## Staying with it

"Let us hold fast the confession of our hope
without wavering, for He who promised is
faithful."—HEBREWS 10:23

**154** *Stick-to-it-iveness!* That's what faith boils down to, doesn't
it!

I don't know how many rejections I had from a variety of
publishing firms before my first book was published. There
were times in the nearly thirty years of my ministry when I
was tempted to quit! Why didn't I pack up? Because I had
made a commitment! That's another word for f-a-i-t-h!

**Faith is staying with it through thick and thin, believing that eventually you will win.**

For years I kept a saying under the glass top of my desk:
"When things get tough, don't move. People and pressures
shift, but the soil remains the same no matter where you go."
I read these words over and over. Wow! They have really
helped me have stick-to-it-iveness.

Choose today to develop a reputation for being a person of
emotional stability. When you make the decision that you're
going to stay with it, you step up to a higher level of emotional
maturity. In what area of your life do you need stick-to-it-
iveness?

- The goals you know in your heart were given by God—
  like a life-long marriage to one person—cannot be abandoned.
- You're definitely going to continue the program of good
  body care.
- You are not about to give up on life.
- Your commitment to Jesus Christ is stronger than ever.

That's great! You're going to stay with it. That's faith. You'll
never be sorry when you let faith make the move.

## *Forsaking ease and comfort*

"When my father and my mother forsake me,/
Then the LORD will take care of me./Teach me
Your way, O LORD,/And lead me in a smooth
path."—PSALM 27:10–11

I first spotted my wife when she was nineteen years of age. **155**
She was a beautiful, vivacious, energetic, exciting young
farmer's daughter who played the organ on Sundays. I got a
date with Arvella DeHaan, and it was then that I found out
where she lived.

Arvella lived on a remote farm. The only way to get to her
house was by a one-lane driveway, a quarter of a mile long,
leading through a muddy corn field. As long as the driveway
was dry, there was no problem. But when it rained, it turned to
mud. In the wintertime it was often closed with drifts of
snow. No snow plows ever opened this private driveway. But I
wasn't about to let a muddy or snow-filled driveway keep me
from courting my girl! Often I had to forsake the ease and
comfort of my car in order to reach the girl of my dreams.

Such enthusiastic determination has really been the testimony of my life. For every time I've spotted something that
caught my fancy, captured my imagination, and filled me with
passion, it was always something that was seemingly out of
my reach. Or at least the road to get there was tough!

Having a God-given, seemingly impossible dream is rarely a
comfortable spot. So, don't ever think that possibility-
thinking faith is a call to ease and comfort! It is exactly the
opposite. It is a call to a cross. Be willing to deny yourself, take
up the cross, and follow the Lord.

When He gives you a project, it will be tough. Be sure of
that.

**If your project seems impossible, the odds are, the
dream came from God!**

# Paying the high price gladly

> "The kingdom of heaven is like a merchant seeking beautiful pearls, who, when he had found the one pearl of great price, went and sold all that he had and bought it."—MATTHEW 13:45–46

**156**     A supersuccessful multimillionaire in California started his manufacturing and marketing business by selecting a small team of bright men. He shared with them the great opportunities he saw for the business and for them. He promised them a good salary and the opportunity to be very creative. He offered all the benefits on one condition: that they invest all of their money and capital in the company. Why? He wanted their 100 percent investment in the business. One of the men objected and was sure that the founder would compromise. He was mistaken. He was passed by.

All of the others who went along with the president's requirements went on to share in the success of the company that today is known throughout the country. All of them have become multimillionaires.

"I had to have the confidence that they had total faith in the company and what it was designed to accomplish," the founder-president said.

Faith is paying the price—gladly!

**Do you believe in yourself, in your God, and in your God-inspired goals enough to give your all to Him and to His dreams for your life?**

I'm a believer. I'll pay the price. Thank You for giving me this faith, Lord. Amen.

## Striving for excellence

"Whatever your hand finds to do, do it with all
your might."—ECCLESIASTES 9:10

Once you've achieved success, it takes a lot of faith to be- **157**
lieve you can upstage your own accomplishment!

It takes faith for a C student to believe that he can earn B's
or A's!

It takes faith for a straight-A student to believe that she can
do an A+ job in the career world.

Whether you are a low, medium, or high achiever, it takes a
lot of faith to believe that you can do a lot better!

**Striving for excellence is an act of faith.**

God is not honored or glorified by mediocrity.

How can you motivate yourself or others to strive for excellence? If striving for excellence *is* faith, then today's prescription is aimed at building up your confidence so that you will
not fail!

What excellent, superlative, outstanding goals would you
go for if you knew you'd make it?

The strong assurance of a genuine possibility of success remains a major motivating force for excellence.

Motivate yourself today with the assurance that:

I can do it!

I can become a champion if I set my heart on it!

It is my sense of obligation to perform at my best before the
Almighty! Yes, that's what drives me to excellence.

An attitude for opportunity stirs me to noble effort.

Be thankful you're alive! As an expression of your gratitude,
give the Lord the best that you have. In so doing, your work
will be your worship! Your outstanding effort will be your
faith in action, praising God for His goodness.

## Stretching the mileage

"If you walk in My ways . . . to keep My commandments . . . then I will lengthen your days."—1 KINGS 3:14

**158**   Do you suffer from a lack of energy, money, talent, or power?

Before you assume you "don't have enough," learn how to get more mileage out of what you do have.

You stretch mileage much in the same way you use a spoonful of honey. It's hard to measure, much less stop it from going on and on. It drips from the edge of the spoon, becoming a liquid stalagmite, stretching unbroken until it becomes like an exquisite gold thread glistening in the sun.

It's like the trained vocalist who is able to sustain a note, delicate and fragile, yet strong, until finally it fades away. Faith is stretching the mileage.

How do you stretch your assets to get the most mileage from them?

Check out discipline and see the wonders it can do. Believable productivity is achieved by the highly trained and powerfully disciplined person.

In the last years of my mother's life, she lived on an income of only four thousand dollars a year. To many she was living below the poverty level, yet she refused financial help from any of the children. Happily, she managed to live comfortably and still give four hundred dollars a year to her church.

She was an inspiration as she always had a birthday card for each of the grandchildren with a crisp one-dollar bill in it. Plus, she always managed to buy flour and sugar so she could bake homemade cookies as gifts to the neighbors.

My mother stretched the mileage of her faith and her possessions. Her life was as beautiful as a drop of honey, a glistening strand of molten gold.

**Believe that you can do so much more with what you have! You'll delight in the new discoveries that come as you stretch the mileage on this trip of faith.**

## *Phasing in—phasing out—phasing up*

"You have made known to me the ways of life;/
You will make me full of joy in Your
presence."—ACTS 2:28

Perhaps you have already passed through some of life's **159**
phases in your pilgrimage of faith. I've categorized six of them
with rhythmic verbs:

Phase 1 is *sitting:* Faith is to "Be still, and know that I am
God" (Ps. 46:10). Wait until you get God's direction before you
do anything.

Phase 2 is *splitting.* Leave your passive position, break with
inertia and get started.

Phase 3 is *flitting.* There is a certain amount of floundering
in the early days of your pilgrimage. Look at the child who
learns to walk. Consider the novice on the job. Don't give up.

Phase 4 is *gritting.* Decide you are going to settle down. It
may take longer than you hoped, but grit your teeth—and
make the commitment to success.

Phase 5 is *knitting.* Tie the loose ends together. Learn from
mistakes and take steps to improve yourself. Stitch by stitch,
you'll make it.

Phase 6 is *hitting:* You will be a hit! You will score successfully!

### Faith is facing life's many phases positively!

You may find it takes more faith in the final phase than in
the first. Once you arrive, you discover new, unexpected problems. One thing is sure, the walk of faith is never boring.
There are always new challenges. For that be grateful.

**Variety is the spice of life when you make the commit-
ment to live with a positive belief.**

## Moving ahead step by step

> ". . . you would have a walk worthy of God who
> calls you into His own kingdom and glory."—
> 1 THESSALONIANS 2:12

**160**  How would you describe your movement today?

Are you in retreat? Retrenching? Moving backwards?

Are you at a standstill? In neutral? Coasting?

Or are you moving ahead? Are you actively making plans and setting goals to move yourself upward and forward?

The kind of faith that God promises to bless is faith that is expressed in dynamic action.

Meditation must be translated into creative activity.

Creative fantasizing must be transformed into muscle movements.

The actions may be small, but they must be forward movements. "Inch by inch anything's a cinch." Practice these small significant movements. Say aloud:

"I must pick up the telephone."

"I must reach for the pencil or the pen."

"I must do something to move myself forward."

"I must hit the books."

"I must make the contacts and communicate."

"I must sell my ideas, and I must sell myself."

> **You cannot simply wait quietly and piously for God to
> drop miracles out of a cloud.**

What is the biggest problem that you face today?

What can you do about it today?

Answer these questions and get to work. Start by doing the toughest job first.

By the time the day is finished, you'll be able to look back and know that you have made progress.

That's walking the walk of faith.

## Projecting future growth

"A mustard seed which, when it is sown on the
ground, is smaller than all the seeds on earth
. . . grows up and becomes greater than all
herbs, . . . so that the birds of the air may nest
under its shade."—MARK 4:31–32

I must never stop growing—or I will start dying! This is a **161**
law of life. It is evident in nature. In my yard I have a pepper
tree that is one hundred years old. I proudly shared this information with a tree trimmer who had come to prune it. "I'm
sure that it's full grown by now!" I added.

"Oh, but it is still growing," he said. "Trees continue to
grow—until they die."

I said, "Even the giant redwoods that are thousands of years
old—are *they* still growing?"

"Of course they are," he said.

### There is no life without growth.

This is a law of life. Should you decide to grow just for the
sake of growth? Yes, because you must remain youthful and
alive all the days of your life. There are psychological studies
that show that senility may be in part the result of a decision
made by tired old people to stop growing.

Faith is deciding to grow for growth's sake, projecting
growth by carefully considering human needs.

When you believe that the secret of success is to find a need
and fill it, then you must project growth plans to meet authentic market pressures and projections.

I know an old gentleman, keen and alert, over ninety years
of age, who has a huge garden. "And it is bigger than ever this
year," he told me with enthusiasm. "I belong to a little church
through which I contribute fresh vegetables and fruit to people who need the food. It makes me feel so good to give the
food away . . . no one could pay me for the good feeling it gives
me."

*FAITH IS . . .*
## Growing with tomorrow's possibilities

"Mercy, peace, and love be multiplied to
you."—JUDE 1:2

**162** The exercise of faith is the very process of growth! So long as we are growing intellectually, emotionally, and spiritually, we are still alive and youthful.

### Life is growth.

To stifle growth is to initiate the termination of life. The deceptive spirit of decay, decline, and death subtly and seductively enters our human spirit when we gradually or abruptly stop growing. The seed of death is planted in an individual or in an institution when growth is no longer possible.

But growth is always possible for the person who is walking the walk of faith!

You can grow and discover new insights into yourself if you welcome every problem as a possibility, every obstacle as an opportunity, and every age as a new laboratory experience in understanding the path of human existence!

Yes, every phase and condition brings with it a unique possibility for personal growth.

Faith spots positive opportunities. Faith welcomes each tomorrow with its pleasure or pain as an invitation to adventure.

Where are the opportunities and possibilities for my personal growth that I can work on tomorrow? I can become more merciful! It's possible for me to be less judgmental and critical! I'll try—tomorrow. Then I can expect peace and love to really be multiplied in my life—tomorrow!

Thank You, God. Amen.

## Exploring all possible alternatives

"There is nothing hidden which will not be
revealed, nor has anything been kept secret but
that it should come to light."—MARK 4:22

Wouldn't it be exciting to be the first person to discover a **163**
new, previously unknown country filled with exotic birds,
glorious mountains, rushing rivers, and strange but attractive
human beings, previously untouched by civilization?

**Life is never boring to the exploring mind.**

The walk of faith offers this possibility to any person of any
age. The walk of faith is truly an adventure in living. When
you walk by faith you are in the process of becoming an explorer.

Faith is the mental process of exploring all possible alternatives in goal-setting and problem-solving activity.

The shocking thing is, faith honestly does move mountains. Don't deplore your situation; explore it—for hidden
possibilities! When we move forward and assume that a way
will open up to achieve the impossible, then suddenly it happens.

We discover an alternative route through what appeared to
be an impenetrable mountain range.

What appears to be the *end* of the road suddenly turns out
to be a *bend* in the road, leading through a narrow pass.

• A new route to happiness is discovered.
• A new path to prosperity is found.
• A new secret of success is learned.
• A new approach in communication is acquired.
• A new profession is developed.
• A new belief system moves into your thinking.
• A new experience with God is encountered.

Keep exploring and you'll keep discovering the secrets to
exciting success.

God blesses the explorer, for this is faith in action!

## Applying old principles to new situations

"That which has been is what will be,/That which is done/is what will be done,/And there is nothing new under the sun."—ECCLESIASTES 1:9

**164** Is it possible to be really truly creative? If you said yes there would be those who would challenge your creativity. There are those who contend that to create is to come up with something *totally* and *completely* new.

We can, however, be innovative when we apply a proven principle in an area where it has never been contemplated or considered before.

W. Clement Stone said it:

**"The secret of success is learning to observe principles and applying them in new and surprising areas."**

When he said that I took notice, and I realized that he was right. I began to observe marketing principles that were operating in American business and then tried to apply them to our work in the church and to our ministry through television.

By the grace of God we have had a measure of success simply because we applied old principles to new situations.

Now we see how we can use our faith as we apply established principles in areas where they haven't been applied before! You see we need to break from our traditional Western tendency to deal with facts, and start dealing with principles as they do in the Orient.

Begin with this simple principle. The secret of success is to find a need and fill it. When we apply it in marriage, in family, in business, or whether in problem solving or decision making, we know we are on the way to success. Be innovative today. Apply what you know to something new!

*FAITH IS . . .*

# Negotiating your way forward

"By humility and the fear of the LORD/Are
riches and honor and life."—PROVERBS 22:4

How do you sell your ideas successfully? **165**

How do you persuade people that they should accept the
help you want to give?

There's a lot of negotiating that must take place as you walk
the walk of faith. A wife and a husband will not have a happy
marriage for long until they learn how to handle the negotiable values.

There are negotiable and nonnegotiable human values. You
need to sort them out and determine what can be abandoned
without sacrificing your ultimate objective. For example, the
ultimate objective in any marriage should be to live happily
together until death, thereby providing a wonderful harbor of
happiness and hope and emotional health for children.

In our marriage, I have had to negotiate with my wife and
she with me on several occasions. Once, I wanted to vacation
at a certain place—she at another. So, we negotiated, for happiness and harmony is more important than having our own
way.

**"I don't want my own way—I want to be a success."**

This is a principle to live by. If I insist on having my own
way at every turn, I will be foolish; and I may ultimately win
only to find myself with a lonely victory.

Historians talk about a Pyrrhic victory. King Pyrrhus of
Epirus, a small state in Greece, defeated the Romans. They
won the battle, but they lost so many men and ships that they
were never strong again. Their victory defeated them!

Be prepared to negotiate anything—except your moral values and the God-given goal that He has entrusted to your
stewardship!

## *Accommodating yourself to others*

"And whoever compels you to go one mile, go
with him two."—MATTHEW 5:41

**166**  Make the decision today to be accommodating to people
who ask you for a favor. Go the extra mile. Our Lord talked
about this. "When someone asks you to go a mile, go two
miles." It takes faith to go the second mile and to have an
accommodating attitude when your plans are made and your
systems, procedures, and policies are all established.

As difficult as it may be to be accommodating at times, this
attitude of "going the extra mile" can be the key to your success—whether it's in business, marriage, or other personal relationships. We see how important this accommodating
attitude is when we recall how irritating it has been when
we've been faced with an unyielding person or situation.

Is anything more frustrating than a narrow-minded person
who dares not adjust his firm policy to make room for an exception that was not considered or foreseen?

This "policy over people" mentality is the hallmark of total-
itarian systems, such as communism. Anyone who makes a
trip through these countries soon finds out that the lack of
freedom is the nonaccommodating attitude that prevails in
their "policy over people" ideology.

Of course, it is necessary to manage by maintaining control.
Yes, it is important to establish policy, but

**The person who lives by faith lives by the principle of
Jesus Christ: "people over policy."**

This marks a major distinction between Christianity and
communism. Christianity says, "People before policy." Communism says, "Policy before people."

Faith commands us to develop an accommodating attitude
in life, including in business. It is then that we become really
creative, winning new friends and new customers in the process. No wonder faith and prosperity are linked together in
the chain of life.

[416]

## *Sharing the power*

"Two are better than one,/Because they have a good reward for their labor."—ECCLESIASTES 4:9

One of the marks of the truly high achievers is the ability to accomplish much in a short span of time. How do they do it? **167**

They learn the art of delegating authority, responsibility, and power.

**Only the person with a strong self-image is inwardly secure enough to share the power.**

People who suffer from a weak ego jealously hold to the power position without sharing it, because they lack faith in themselves and in others. They cannot bring themselves to share the power and the glory. The result? In trying to do it all themselves, they consequently get very little done. It takes a lot of faith to share power and glory.

"If I don't do it myself, it won't be done right," is a popular illusion that negatively holds a gripping power over the nonbeliever. Replace this negative illusion with the positive fact: "If I share the glory, the power, and the responsibility, I have a greater chance to reach my goals, and know that I have created opportunities for others to grow and to live!

"In the process I'll be rewarded with a mature self-respect! Today I will walk the walk of faith for it is the pathway to spiritual and material prosperity."

People who walk the walk of faith dare to believe that others are as responsible as they are. They have the faith to share responsibility. Yes, mistakes will be made. But you and I have a capacity for error, too.

Better to have something done imperfectly than to have nothing done perfectly.

## FAITH IS . . .
# Teaming up

"Let each of you look out not only for his own
interests, but also for the interests of others."—
PHILIPPIANS 2:4

**168**   The beautiful fringe benefit that comes with this walk of
faith is that it gives us a communal attitude. Possibility thinking that promotes rugged individualism does not reject the
team spirit.

Our faith tells us that divine help will often come in the
form of persons without whose skills and dedication we could
not succeed.

**God can do great things through the person who
doesn't care who gets the credit.**

We must sort through our motives and decide that we
would rather succeed and share the glory than to fail and bear
the blame alone. We must not be ego-involved as much as we
must be success-oriented!

Even the genius has a limited perspective. Multiply your
intelligence and magnify your clever abilities by teaming up
with people who are smarter than you are. I am convinced
that almost any human goal imaginable is possible.

When God trusts you with His dream, it becomes your job
to call together persons with a variety of skills and talents
until, through massive team effort, the mountain is scaled
and the dream succeeds! Success becomes possible the moment you realize you can't do it alone.

**Our Lord and I together are the beginning of a winning
team!**

I'm on my way to a successful life! For I have enough faith
to trust others to work with me and share the great dream
God has given me.

*FAITH IS . . .*
## *Delegating good jobs to others*

"The body is one but has many members. . . .
God composed the body. . . . if one member
suffers, all the members suffer with it; or if one
member is honored, all the members rejoice."—
1 CORINTHIANS 12:14, 24, 26

It's easy to put together a winning team—if you're willing **169**
to delegate the good jobs to others! It takes a lot of faith to
make this move, for it's natural to believe that nobody else
can do the job as well as you can.

Will they drop the ball?

Can they follow through?

Do they understand how important the job is?

Yes, it takes a lot of faith to delegate!

The supersuccessful person trusts others to do the job as
well as he can, if not better.

Years ago I decided to refuse to do something that I could
hire someone else to do. This frees me to do the job that I, and
I alone, can do.

There are those tasks that cannot be delegated to others. I
have learned that I cannot delegate to anybody else the task of
writing my public messages. I cannot delegate the final decisions that reach my desk. But aside from these basic assignments, I have delegated almost all other jobs to other persons.

Until you delegate, you won't have time to plan ahead! If
you don't have enough faith to delegate, you will never be
creative. Great dreamers of great dreams are seldom good at
detail. If they were, they'd be too busy to think creatively. Affirm with me:

**Today I'm going to give up some of the jobs I've always
thought that only I could perform.**

And I shall relish the liberty and freedom to do beautiful
things I've never had time for before!

Thank You for giving me faith, Father. Amen.

## *Assimilating fresh opinions*

"Now we have been delivered from the law, . . .
so that we should serve in the newness of the
Spirit, and not in the oldness of the letter."—
ROMANS 7:6

**170** We all need to learn and to grow. We all need to add freshness to our lives. It is easy to assimilate new facts, but it requires a great deal of faith to assimilate fresh opinions.

Once you dare to relate to others you open yourself to fresh thoughts that replace stale and worn-out opinions. Update your life with current viewpoints, but don't abandon the moral and spiritual guidelines that have brought you safely and successfully to where you are. With that gentle warning, be prepared to exercise faith. Assimilate new thoughts into your old thinking.

Faith believes apparent contradictions can conceivably form a symbiotic relationship.

According to an old Eastern parable, two beggars formed a symbiotic relationship. The blind man was strong enough to carry the legless man on his back. He became the legs for the lame man. In return, the lame man became the eyes for the blind one. Clinging to each other, they both benefited.

We are all weak in some area. But when we broaden our thinking, we are able to assimilate ideas that can bring freshness to our own faith and life.

Without compromising, abandoning, or violating the integrity of your own position, have enough faith to see good in others' opinions. Then draw lessons from them and positively apply them to enrich your faith.

Faith assimiliates fresh opinions!

Dear Lord, give me a fresh experience in my walk with You today. I admit that spiritual staleness has taken over, but now in this movement there is a newness in my spirit. I know it's Your spirit, assimilating mine. Thank You, God.

## FAITH IS . . .
### *Hiring smarter people*

"Thanks be to God, who gives us the victory
through our Lord Jesus Christ."—
1 CORINTHIANS 15:57

**171**

For every problem, there is a profession! Are you sick? There are doctors. Do you have problems selling your product? There are consultants in marketing. You name it, and there is some expert who can help you handle your problem in the smartest way possible.

The other day I discovered that I had locked the keys in my car. Being a possibility thinker, I decided to solve the problem simply and inexpensively with a wire coat hanger. I worked and worked, but I finally concluded that this was not my area of expertise. So I called a locksmith to the rescue. He pressed his nose against the windshield to read the numbers on the keys in the ignition. Then he scratched some numbers on a pad and stepped inside his truck. Two minutes later he opened the lock perfectly. My problem was solved. Expensive? That's not the right reaction. The height of folly is to fail because you didn't want to pay the price to hire expert help.

It takes faith to hire people. Mr. Danforth, the founder of Ralston Purina Company, hired a smart young man to head his company. At the annual corporate meeting the young man's report was so outstanding that a stockholder asked Mr. Danforth, "How does it make you feel to have this young man get all the compliments?" Mr. Danforth confidently replied, "Great! That's a compliment to me! After all, I hired him!"

**The good news is that there is a professional who is skilled in solving your biggest problem—lack of faith! His name is Jesus Christ. He is *able* to save you from sin, negative thinking, and doubt! He wants to fill you with optimism and faith! His fee? His salvation is free!**

## Listening to wise counsel

"Without counsel, plans go awry,/But in the multitude of counselors they are established."—
PROVERBS 15:22

**172** When we walk the walk of faith, does it mean we have so much self-confidence that we never need to seek advice from anyone else?

Is opening yourself to constructive criticism a lack of faith?

Or, on the contrary, is it a demonstration of a remarkably mature faith?

The latter, of course, is the truth.

For it takes a great deal of faith in yourself, in others, and in God to expose yourself and invite others to share their opinion and wise counsel. Faith is the belief that God guides you to success, by giving you some smart suggestions through the wise counsel of others. In the process you win their respect as they share freely their most valued resource: their insightful wisdom.

**You're walking a higher road of faith when you learn to listen.**

Step 1: Listen to compliments and accept them!

Step 2: Listen to constructive criticism and be guided by it!

Step 3: Invite smart people to show you what's wrong with your plan. No one is perfect. Every proposal has its soft spot. No idea is without its problems. There's something wrong with the best idea.

Be smart and find out the points of vulnerability before you go too far.

You can plan to insulate, isolate, eliminate, or sublimate the negative possibilities in the positive proposal. *And you can go on to promote the positive possibilities in the whole scheme.*

That's real maturity in faith! We call it "wise faith!"

FAITH IS . . .
## *Clarifying expectations*

"I will make you an eternal excellence,/A joy of many generations."—ISAIAH 60:15

It is most important you remain steadfast in your expectation that success will be realized.

Faith is clarifying your expectations to insure success.

It is at the expectation level that tremendous things happen—both positively and negatively. It is well established that conflict in interpersonal relationships is usually a result of a confusion of expectations. In counseling, I frequently address two conflicting personalities by asking both of them questions such as:

"What did you expect from him/her?"

"Do you have a right to expect this from him/her?"

"If you revise your expectations, do you believe you'd be able to make your relationship work?"

"How many revisions can you make in your expectations and still survive in your partnership and friendship?"

**Faith is clarifying nonverbalized, confused expectations, thereby setting the stage for success.**

Faith is expecting to succeed. How?
• Clarify your expectations.
• Visualize them clearly in your mind.
• Write them upon your subconscious.
• Hold to them with discipline and determination.
• Nurture them with enthusiasm.
Then expect success!

Dear God, forgive me when I am confused in my expectations of You. You give me all I need to know in order that I can succeed, and You are more than generous with all the blessings You send my way. I will remain faithful in my walk with You today. Thank You for being my Friend. Amen.

**173**

# Removing growth-restricting obstacles

"If the ax is dull,/And one does not sharpen the edge,/Then he must use more strength;/But wisdom brings success."—ECCLESIASTES 10:10

**174**  It is time to remind yourself every day that you have a choice—to walk by doubt, or by faith; to be a believer or a cynic; to be filled with a positive mental attitude or be controlled by a negative mental attitude.

By this time, you have scored some victories; you have realized some successes. You have made progress in your personal life. You have grown!

And you have learned another lesson: When you succeed, you produce a new set of problems.

**Growth always generates a new set of tensions.**

Be careful! Now is the time you are tempted to become negative, and ask the question: "Was it really worth it?" You can easily become cynical about your own success and vote against continued progress.

The most common growth-restricting obstacle is to become stagnant. "I've got enough." "We're big enough." "I know enough." These are all negative reactions to success.

As you keep walking the walk of faith, you must *continue* to press for personal growth. *For when growth stops, death and decay are just around the corner.* Keep on believing in progress.

Today's affirmation: Today I will proceed in an all-out effort to remove any obstacles that would keep me from growing. Failure to do so will be to surrender leadership of my future to a stifling force. I will not allow that to happen.

The obstacles that keep me from growing today are _____

_____.

I will walk the walk of faith and tackle them with determination!

## Following the positive voices

"Whoever hears these sayings of Mine, and does
them, I will liken him to a wise man who built
his house on the rock; and the rain descended,
the floods came, . . . and it did not fall, for it
was founded on the rock."—MATTHEW 7:24–25

Faith is a two-sided power. On one side is the activity of **175**
rejecting negative inputs. On the opposite side is the activity
of following positive voices.

Even an electric cord has both a negative and a positive
wire. So even as you reject the destructive negative stimuli
that enter your brain, also accept and listen to the positive
emotions and incentives that whisper in the back of your
mind.

Seek out friends, acquaintances, literature, books, television programs, and movies that will entertain, amuse, inspire,
uplift, educate, motivate, and challenge you to become a better and more productive person.

> **I know of no positive voice of any living person that is
> more helpful to me on a moment-to-moment basis
> than that of my closest Friend, Jesus Christ!**

How can you follow the positive voice of God?

Constantly ask God questions and wait for His answer in
the hidden corner of your brain. Read what He said, what He
did, and how He lived in the Bible. Seek His advice and expect
Him to answer. The still, small voice will come into the silence of the holy chamber of your subconscious. It is the voice
of your Friend, Jesus Christ.

He nudges you forward. He affirms you can be forgiven of
all sins. He instills new passion to do His good work. He is
speaking to you through this moment of meditation. Simply
listen, then follow. That means you will take action.

## Sorting things out optimistically

"He who follows righteousness and mercy/
Finds life, righteousness and honor."—PROVERBS
21:21

**176**   By now you've discovered that the road of faith isn't always smooth. In fact, it can be downright jarring. The jolts can get to you if you don't watch out.

I've had to ride over some rough roads in my life. One of the most famous—or infamous—is the Hana Road, on the island of Maui in Hawaii. I remember almost bouncing through the roof when I hit a hole in the road. I'm sure that not a few of my readers have driven the same route themselves and likewise found their teeth almost loosened in their jaws. I was terribly tempted to quit and turn around. But I hung in there. And was I ever rewarded!

When I finally reached Hana, I saw the most beautiful waterfall in the world! The serenity at this spot made the torturous trip worthwhile. I'm sure that's the reason Charles Lindbergh chose to be buried there.

You must keep on believing that even the jolts on the rough road of life can have a positive influence on you.

Faith is sorting things out optimistically. That's exactly what happens when you optimistically see the jolts that come your way as the impetus to re-examine your life.

Years ago I told the story of the potato farmer who sorted out the big potatoes from the little ones by riding to town on the rough roads. "Big potatoes ride to the top on rough roads," he said.

My daughter loves to sort out the raisins in her raisin bran cereal and she has discovered that if she shakes her bowl of cereal, the raisins bounce to the top.

**Welcome those rebuffs that can bring out the deeper qualities of life.**

## Reading the good between the lines

"You know in all your hearts and in all your
souls that not one thing has failed of all the
good things which the LORD your God
spoke."—JOSHUA 23:14

"Reading between the lines" is something we all do. It's like **177**
"putting two and two together," a mental activity in which
everyone engages. The difference between the person who's
living by faith and the negative-thinking person is that the
pessimist reads only bad news between the lines where the
optimist reads good news.

Two birds—a vulture and a hummingbird—fly over the
California desert. One sees a rotting carcass; the other, a fra-
grant flower. Each sees what it looks for!

If you are a believer and have received guidance from God
Himself, you don't blind yourself to upcoming problems; but
you do keep your eye on the possibilities! You never allow
problems to overpower the possibilities.

The truth is you can always read either good or bad between
the lines. There is something negative and something positive
in every person, proposal, and project.

The most fantastic idea contains the seeds of problems as
well as the seeds of possibilities!

Both success and failure exist in every project. Your vote
can go either way, but you cast the deciding vote and determine the destiny positively when you choose to read the good
instead of the bad.

Here is a powerful truth: What you see is what you will be.
Our firmly focused imaginations tend to become self-fulfilling
prophecies.

The vulture finds a carcass, while the hummingbird finds
honey in a flower half-hidden in a cactus behind barren roots.

God's Word tells us to believe the best in the worst of times.
Question: Are you practicing positive thinking or negative
thinking today? Here's the test:

**Believe the best! And live with zest!**

*FAITH IS . . .*
## *Resolving conflicts creatively*

"Avoid foolish and ignorant disputes, knowing
that they generate strife. A servant of the Lord
must not quarrel but be gentle to all, able to
reach, patient."—2 TIMOTHY 2:23–24

**178**   Walking the walk of faith will ultimately lead you to a clear-
ing where the sun can shine gloriously upon your well-lived
life! How can you be sure that the walk of faith will lead to
such a happy ending? By its very nature, faith cultivates a
positive mental attitude toward conflicts.

If you anticipate problems and tensions after making a commitment, you are not necessarily guilty of negative thinking.

For the truth is, any time you press forward toward your
goal, you will create conflict.

You can be sure most everyone will agree with you!

Conflicts are inherent in creative accomplishments.

Notice here the difference between the person who has a
positive mental attitude and a negative mental attitude. The
positive person has a creative attitude toward problems,
whereas a negative person has a destructive and complicating
attitude toward conflict.

Negative thinkers become defensive when they face conflicts.

Positive thinkers become peacemakers when they face conflicts.

**When you walk the walk of faith, you discipline your-
self to resolve conflicts.**

Resolving conflicts always starts with a resolution: I will
manage the conflict and not allow the conflict to manage me!

I will not allow the conflict to collide, clash, or collapse the
commitments I have made.

I will be more patient and determined to turn the conflict
around and in the process become healthier and happier than I
was before!

I am resolved to win out over the conflict!

## *Fixing problems*

"My grace is sufficient for you, for My strength is made perfect in weakness."—2 CORINTHIANS 12:9

One of the greatest basketball coaches of all times was John **179** Wooden of UCLA, a fantastic, positive-thinking Christian. One of his great motivating statements to his players was: "Nobody is a real loser—until he starts blaming somebody else!"

Faith believes there is a solution to every problem. Even when the problem defies solutions, faith believes that we can be positive anyway!

Affirm with me:

- Today I shall exercise my faith to seek solutions immediately, instinctively, impulsively, and intelligently.

- I'll look upon this not as a problem, but as an opportunity to grow up and be more effective as a manager of my own life.

- I will categorically reject all arbitrary, negative judgments, and I believe that with the help of God there will be a solution to the problem.

**I'll go to work right now and fix my problem, just as soon as I fix my attitude!**

Dear Lord, I'm aware that the biggest part of any problem is my attitude toward it. I thank You, that You and I together can fix that today. Your strength is my strength, so I'm trusting You. Help me, O God, my Father, to bloom with such faith that I will be surprised, and so will everybody else who watches me go through this trying time. Thank You, Lord. Amen.

## Inventing solutions

". . . always pursue what is good both for
yourselves and for all."—1 THESSALONIANS 5:15

**180** Years ago when my children were yet small, our family
spent summer vacations in Iowa, visiting our relatives. One
summer, as we drove the long road back to California, we
heard an enormous explosion! My left rear tire had blown out!

I stood dejectedly on the shoulder, looking at the tire, now
in shreds. Fortunately, I had a spare tire, jack, and crowbar
readily available. I promptly put the jack under the car and
began to pump it up. Just as the flattened tire rose a few
inches, the jack suddenly started bending as if it were made of
rubber! I couldn't believe my eyes. Never had I seen or heard
of that. The tire slowly settled down again on the hard adobe-
like surface.

What could I do? I had no jack! There was no gas station for
miles and miles! Suddenly I had an idea: "If I can't raise the
tire, why don't I lower the ground?"

I took my only tool, the crowbar, and proceeded to chip
away at the hard ground around the flattened tire. It was hard
work, but after almost an hour, I could remove the bolts, lift
the tire off, and slip the spare tire on!

**The walk of faith can be fun! When something seems
impossible just invent new products or new procedures.**

God gave you the only tool you need—your brain. We can
all be inventors on this walk of faith. We won't necessarily
dream up new gadgets, but we can invent new ideas that will
prove to be the solution to our problem. Faith is inventing
solutions, pursuing "what is good both for yourselves and for
all."

*FAITH IS . . .*
## Negotiating your way around obstacles

"May our Lord Jesus Christ . . . comfort your
hearts and establish you in every good word
and work."—2 THESSALONIANS 2:16–17

Dedicated possibility thinkers stubbornly refuse to accept **181**
defeat. Rather, in the face of apparent catastrophe, they seek
creative solutions. Possibility thinking is a process of creatively negotiating around obstacles.

Begin the process by believing you will not accept defeat.
Hang in there and decide you're going to make it within to the
rules and laws of God and country. Creatively calculate new
and innovative schemes to achieve what appears to be unachievable. Consider all constructive compromises. It may
even require retreat in order to advance later on. Rework, revise, rewrite, reorganize, reschedule, or refinance; and thereby
creatively negotiate your way to ultimate victory. Begin with
these affirmations:
- I am open to new strategies.
- I will review the price.
- I will call for a review of the proposal.
- I will break the stalemate.

After all, I don't want to have my own way; I just want to do
the right thing. For I am a possibility thinker. I exercise faith. I
am a courageous and wise negotiator.

I believe that I will ultimately salvage and save the most
valued part of my life's work.

> **I believe in myself and in my God-given dream. I, and
> only I, have the power to kill my dream. I do that if I'm
> unwilling to negotiate. God has entrusted a dream to
> my care and keeping. I will nurture it carefully. I will
> protect its life at all costs. I will prove faithful, O Lord.**

*FAITH IS . . .*
## Catching the blame

"So then each of us shall give account . . . to God."—ROMANS 14:12

**182** When the finger points at you and criticism falls at your doorstep, when you catch the blame and are held responsible for a mistake, look upon this as a left-handed compliment. You have tried your best; you are willing to be held accountable!

It's hard to find people who are brave enough to accept responsibility. The fear of being held liable for mistakes is enough to frighten many a person from a leadership position.

Faith is "catching the blame." When you walk the walk of faith, you accept responsibility with a tremendously serious attitude. You are able to face the reality that you may make a mistake. But your positive-thinking faith gives you enough confidence in your own abilities to be willing to be held accountable!

**Until you're able to conquer the fear of "catching the blame," you probably will not have enough courage to become the entrepreneurial person you ought to be.**

Do you dare to become an effective manager, a successful supervisor, or an inspiring leader in your church or community? All you need to do is overcome the fear of failure by looking for the positive, exercising optimism, stimulating positive emotions in people, and inspiring and encouraging people.

Today have the faith to believe that these responsibilities of life are steps upward. You are maturing in the walk of faith. You will not be afraid of the blame and criticism that comes with accountability. Criticism won't mean you will get fired—it will mean you'll get inspired—to do and to be better!

Affirm today: "I have the courage to be accountable!"

## *Allowing for error*

"He is able to save to the uttermost those who
come to God through Him, since He ever lives
to make intercession for them."—HEBREWS 7:25

A famous British statesman had his formal portrait done. **183**
When it was finished he took a look at what was a most remarkable likeness. The artist, expecting compliments, instead received this rebuff: "You didn't paint the wart!"

The artist meekly replied, "But, sir, I think you are more
attractive without it. Don't you find this so?"

The politician answered, "Paint me as I am—wart and all!"

Accepting yourself with your imperfections gives evidence
that your faith has achieved a remarkable level of maturity.
Until you and I are able to allow for error in ourselves we will
lack the grace to allow error in others.

Your faith is able to spare you from what psychologists call
"projection"—projecting your feelings toward others. If you
feel good today, you treat people well. If you feel bad, you treat
others badly.

The positive approach does not demand perfection. We have
faith in people, anyway!

When you make a mistake after doing your best, be thankful to God that you're able to perform at all: Have faith that
you are doing a worthwhile job, *anyway!*

Now project this positive attitude toward your family, your
friends, and your business associates.

Allow for error in yourself and others. Until you do, you
will never be able to have a strong relationship with anyone—
including God Almighty.

> **If you can't believe that God accepts you with your
> obvious sins, shortcomings, and errors, you may find
> yourself subconsciously leaning toward agnosticism.**

Faith allows for error. The Lord accepts you anyway!

FAITH IS . . .

## *Hearing what your critics say about you*

"Listen to counsel and receive instruction,/That
you may be wise."—PROVERBS 19:20

**184** I'd rather succeed than have my own way! You agree with
me, don't you?

You are moving strongly forward on this walk of faith. You
have made commitments. The public announcement is out.
It's not secret what you intend to do. Now, for the sake of our
God, you had better make it happen.

In order to do that you need to make sure you have not
forgotten something. You don't know all of the answers. You
can't do everything perfectly. You still are a human being subject to error and fault.

So, if there's something wrong with your project, your
plans, your timetable, or your team, you'd better find out
about it—now!

I learned long ago that if I live by faith, I will listen to what
my critics say. My friends may be blinded to my shortcomings
by their own devotion, loyalty, and affection. In truth, my best
friend may well be my most severe critic. I listen and carefully
evaluate his or her critique.

You are also a person of great faith! If there is something
wrong with a project or performance, it's not too late to correct the problem or compensate creatively for the drawbacks
you may have neglected to notice.

Insecure people are defensive people who refuse to respect
their critics. But you are inwardly secure. You have your calling from God. You are confident.

**You are strong in your faith. You are strong enough to
listen to your critics. For you discover that even they
are sent as friends from God!**

Thank You, Father, that You are protecting me from the
blindness that comes through ego involvement. Thank You
for everything You're doing to guide me to success. Amen.

## Changing your mind

"Put on the new man who is renewed in knowledge according to the image of Him who created him."—COLOSSIANS 3:10

Today's theme sounds like a contradiction, doesn't it? If I change my mind, isn't that instability? And isn't instability a lack of faith?

Think of it this way.

**185**

**People who never change their minds are either perfect—or stubborn.**

One day when I was checking a building under construction on our church campus, I was surprised at how dark and gloomy the room was. "Why isn't there a window over there?" I asked the superintendent.

"That's the way you planned it, Reverend," he replied. I admitted that I had. I looked at the freshly plastered wall; and suddenly I walked over and with a ball-point pen wrote in letters three inches high, "People who never change their minds are either perfect or stubborn." Then I turned around and said to him, "Put a window right there!"

Never surrender to a mistake. Faith, committed to excellence, gladly allows you to change your mind if there's a better way!

How do you avoid the embarrassment that comes with admitting you made a mistake? Simple. Announce you are a human being, and not too proud to do the best possible job. If that means changing course, you'll do it.

It takes a great deal of faith to change your mind.

Dear Lord, I know it's not a mistake when I believe in You. There is no better way to live than to trust You completely with my life. I will dare to "put on the new 'me,'" renewed in Your knowledge. Thank You for creating me in Your image. Amen.

## *Learning from past mistakes*

"Strengthen the weak hands,/And make firm
the feeble knees. Say to those who are fearful-
hearted,/'Be strong . . .'"—ISAIAH 35:3–4

**186** By now you have made more than one mistake on your walk of faith.

Every artist messes up a canvas at one spot or another.

Every accountant uses a pencil with an eraser.

No baseball player ever had a batting average of a thousand, getting a hit every time he was at bat.

Consequently, you cannot allow your mistakes to master your mood and cause you to lose enthusiasm.

Begin to program yourself positively. You cannot surrender leadership to your past failures. You must take a positive attitude toward them for they can prove to be wise teachers.

**The person who never makes a mistake is the person who is a total failure, for that person never tries to do something worthwhile.**

Affirmations for today:
• My mistakes only prove to me that I'm not a total failure.
• I did not fail to try!
• I did not fail to dream!
• I did not fail to decide!
• I did not fail to make a commitment.
• I did not fail in courage.
• I will not fail to learn from my mistakes.
• I will not fail to make corrective changes in my life.
• I will not allow my mistakes to cause me to take my eyes off my goal.

Help me, O God, heavenly Father, to learn from my sins, my shortcomings, and my mistakes. Help me to turn the mistake from a stumbling block into a stepping stone, through the help of Christ. Amen.

## *Congratulating your competitors*

"LORD, You will establish peace for us, for You have also done all our works in us."—ISAIAH 26:12

Congratulating your competitor when he does a better job, **187** when he outpaces you, or when he runs off with the prize is a concrete statement of faith.

> **It shows mountains of faith when you have enough internal pride and self-esteem to give your competition a pat on the back after he has defeated you soundly and squarely.**

In the summer of 1983, at the sixty-fifth PGA Championship in Pacific Palisades, California, Hal Sutton and Jack Nicklaus exercised fantastic faith.

Sutton wanted the world to know that it was possible for him to be a winner. Only two weeks earlier he had had an embarrassing failure at the Anheuser-Busch classic.

Nicklaus, at forty-three years of age, had played poorly all season. Sports writers were declaring he was "over the hill." They were suggesting he pack up his clubs.

As the tournament neared the end the battle was between Nicklaus and Sutton. In the end Sutton won—by one hole! Nicklaus lost by one stroke.

Both proved something terribly important to the world. One proved that he could be a winner. The other proved he still had it! In the process Nicklaus broke his own record.

But Nicklaus had his greatest success when he went up to twenty-five-year-old Hal Sutton, shook hands, and said to him bravely and beautifully, "That will be the first of many for you!"

That's the faith that moves mountains! Mountains of failure, jealousy, resentment, and all other negative emotions disappear when you are confident enough in your own talents to congratulate your competitors.

## Swallowing your hurts

"If I say, 'I will forget my complaint,/I will put
off my sad face and wear a smile.'"—JOB 9:27

**188** Here's some good advice on how to handle the rejections,
defeats, or failures you probably have experienced. You may
have collected enough hurts to keep you from wanting to
press forward. Setbacks can take the joy out of faith if you
don't watch out! Even success—steady, solid, and excep-
tional—can make you the target of criticism from colleagues
who are jealous of your achievement.

Careful! Hidden hurts in the heart can nurture and nourish
negative thinking. Often the most painful wounds are not the
scars that are outwardly seen but the hidden wounds deep in
the heart. Because they are hidden they are often the most
dangerous.

**Swallow your hurts and stimulate a new spirit and
spurt of growth!**

If, in fact, your drive to grow has lost its passionate power, if
the flush of enthusiasm has mysteriously diminished, then
check the accumulation of negative emotions that have attached themselves to you, much like barnacles that attach to
whales.

Along the shoreline in California it is a common sight to
see whales stopping alongside rocks to scrape off barnacles as
they migrate from Alaska to Mexico.

In the walk of faith we too will pick up a collection of personal hurts that will attach themselves to our souls like para-
sites sapping the life and vitality out of us!

Ouch! You can't let these negative emotions get to you!

By faith, learn to swallow hard. Imagine all polluted
thoughts being drained from your mind, body, and spirit.

Lord, with Your help, I swallow the hurts. They will pass on
and out. Thank You. Amen.

## Sensing success in dark times

"We know that all things work together for
good to those who love God."—ROMANS 8:28

How can you describe the experience of faith you have been **189**
experiencing? It's an inner sense that things are going to work
out all right, isn't it? You can almost call it intuition.

Deep down within yourself you know with a solid know-
ingness that the worst times will pass.
- Better days are around the corner.
- The storm is not eternal.
- The clouds have a limited lifespan.
- The mountain has a peak.
- Dark times will give way to bright days. Somehow you
  intuitively sense that the tragedy can turn into a spiritual
  triumph.

No matter how difficult the time may be, remember:

**God has no wastebaskets.**

He makes no mistakes. He never bungles a job. So He will
somehow be able to take the torturing experiences and turn
them into diamonds that will sparkle in the crown of your
life. God will not allow the suffering, the sorrow, the pain, to
be fruitless.

John Greenleaf Whittier put it well, "I know not where the
islands lift their fronded palms in air./I only know I cannot
drift beyond my Master's love and care."

Prayer: O God, thank You for the faith I have today. In spite
of all the suffering, sin, sickness, and unspeakable tragedies
that exist in the human family, I sense deeply and irrevocably
that love will triumph. The sun is stronger than the clouds.
God is more powerful than evil. I shall succeed in spite of dire
predictions, gloomy forecasts, and depressing projections! I
sense success in the dark times. This is my faith operating.
Thank You for giving me this gift. Amen.

## *Marching on—nevertheless*

> "On the seventh day [Joshua] . . . marched around [Jericho] seven times. . . . when the priests blew the trumpets, Joshua said to the people: 'Shout, for the LORD has given you this city!'"—JOSHUA 6:16

**190**

- From thinking—to action!
- From meditation—to marching.
- From the classroom—to the main street.
- From the church—to your daily life and business!
- From reading a book—to living out the principles!

**These are the challenging times of life—when you apply the faith. Life starts when you stop talking and start making it happen!**

David Hartman, the anchor man of "Good Morning, America," always closes his morning program with the challenge: "Make it happen. Make it a great day!"

Almost always when the sun sets and you look back on a well-worn day with the happy review, "It's been a great day," you have to admit—you made it a great day! God blessed you. Unexpected good things happened to you, and you responded positively to the opportunities that hit you unexpectedly!

Some other persons had a similar day, but they came to their sunset discouraged. The only difference is that you made it a great day. You had some tough assignments. You ran into some binding predicaments. But you kept marching on—nevertheless!

When at first you don't succeed, like Joshua you keep marching on! A second time, a third, a fourth, a fifth, a sixth, and then on the seventh try, the walls came tumbling down!

"Shout, for the LORD has given you this city!" Praise God right now! For He is giving you victory today!

## Insulating against the negatives

"The lamp of the body is the eye. If therefore your eye is good, your whole body will be full of light."—MATTHEW 6:22

Once you have declared your intention and entered the contest, be prepared for an attack from negative-thinking people! As much as possible, insulate yourself from their influence on you.

**191**

Insulation is a wonderful thing! We put it in the walls of a house to insulate from the summer heat and the winter cold. How can you insulate yourself from the inevitable negative criticism you can expect, as you move forward, upward, and onward?

"The lamp of the body is the eye." Begin by focusing on the Bible. Go back through this book and find Bible verses that give you courage, confidence, and conviction. Then when negative forces attack, they will bounce off you like sparks off cement, desert sand, or asphalt pavement.

"The lamp of the body is the eye."

**The mind that is filled with a visual eye on God's promises of prosperity and power and peace will see sparks of negativity bounce off! We are insulated!**

(1) Feed your mind with all the positive literature you can read.

(2) Choose as your closest friends and collaborators, dynamic possibility thinkers who will encourage you and keep boosting your spirits!

(3) Attend a positive-thinking house of worship every Sunday.

(4) Program your mind with a possibility-thinking treatment every morning.

Finally, insulate yourself through positive prayer. Affirm today: Thank You, God, that my eyes are focused on my dream which has come from You! As I focus on You, I am insulated from all negativity. Thank You, God. Amen.

## Reversing a negative situation

"Do not be overcome by evil, but overcome evil with good."—ROMANS 12:21

**192**     Faith doesn't immunize you from difficulty. But it does radically alter your attitude. The negative person takes a bad experience and *curses* it. He takes it out on his best friends and innocent people! He *nurses* the affliction and tells people how bad the situation is. He talks up his tough times. He *rehearses* the miserable history that got him into the predicament.

Then there is the believer—the person who looks for positive possibilities. He *disperses* the gloom-and-doom mentality.

He disperses negative thoughts with positive ones: "The sun is stronger than the clouds. And my God within me is more powerful than any depressive mood that surrounds me. Light is stronger than darkness; therefore, the sun will shine again in the new morning!"

The believer waits for the sunrise, with a positive faith he *reverses* the negative situation and turns it into something positive! How do you overcome evil with good? By believing there is good in every situation!

My friend, Denis Waitley, displays on his wall an airline ticket to a flight he missed. By the time he reached the gate, the DC-10 was pulling away. He was terribly dejected! Then it happened! The plane had hardly taken off before it exploded. All passengers on board were killed.

> **Troubles today? Don't curse them, don't nurse them, but disperse them, and even reverse the negative situations into a positive possibility. Trouble is only a blessing in disguise!**

## *Putting up with the disagreeable*

". . . In quietness and confidence shall be your
strength."—ISAIAH 30:15

Today you may encounter disagreeable confrontations with
negative situations. How will you react when you experience
rejection or insult? How will you handle frustrations when
everything seems to go wrong?

**193**

Will you be put out, put off, or will you put up with the
problem? Touchy people will be *put out.* Arrogant people will
be *put off.* Positive people will *put up* with the problem, patiently enduring the unpleasant scene, quietly riding out the
storm.

By faith you can duck a lot of problems, avoiding some of
them and facing sudden cloudbursts the way ducks do. They
simply sit still, waiting patiently, knowing the storm will
pass. The sun will break through again, soon.

Something amusing will happen shortly, and you'll be
laughing again.

Anticipate humorous moods that will replace the time of
tension. This is faith—putting up with the disagreeable. Remind yourself that your reaction can exaggerate, aggravate, or
tolerate the sorry scene. You can make matters better—or
worse.

So faith tolerates the scene patiently. This does not mean
you remain apathetic in the face of injustice or approve of
mediocrity. Instead, you must not allow yourself to be drawn
into troublesome quarrels over petty causes.

Develop the skill of separating the important from the in-
significant before you make a mistake and waste your emotional energy and creative power.

**Don't fret over the frivolous and get tense over the
trivial.**

Faith is putting up with the disagreeable.

## Riding wild horses

"Indeed, we put bits in horses' mouths that
they may obey us, and we turn their whole
body."—JAMES 3:3

**194**    If I were to list ten books that changed my life, I would have
to include, high on the list, a book by the late J. Wallace
Hamilton entitled *Ride the Wild Horses*. Wild horses are
emotional impulses that, at face value, appear to be negative
and destructive.

Is fear negative? Yes, but we have learned how to turn it into
a positive.

Is anger negative? Yes, but take the temper out of steel, and
its strength is gone.

So it is with the ego. We have all seen demonic and destructive forces of egotism. Does that mean we should squeeze
every bit of the ego out of the human being? Not at all! To do
so would kill the drive that can accomplish glorious things for
the human family and for God. The ego is to be redeemed, not
destroyed! When channeled into the drive to do God's good
work, the ego becomes our self-esteem!

What about jealousy? William Shakespeare called this destructive force "the green-eyed monster." But even jealousy
can be a healthy force. Become jealous over the beauty of the
environment and work to protect it. Become jealous over the
beauty of a piece of architecture or a fine garden and work to
preserve it.

**Destructive forces in life—almost all of them—can be
turned into positive values.**

That's what happens when we really want to walk the walk
of faith. Faith is turning negatives into positives. It's deciding
not to shoot the wild horses, nor to break them of their noble,
prancing, virile spirit, but to harness them and ride them
gloriously!

That's possibility thinking! That's practicing the walk of
faith!

## *Gambling God's way*

> "I am the LORD your God, who teaches you to
> profit, who leads you by the way you should
> go."—ISAIAH 48:17

Among the wild horses that need to be bridled is the gam- **195**
bling instinct. The Christian church has long opposed gambling. It has been looked upon purely as a negative impulse.
Its potentially destructive influence has been well studied and
documented.

Gambling is a destructive force when it takes someone's
property without paying for it. Gambling, then, is borderline
theft.

But it is possible to turn this instinct into a controlled and
positive force!

The farmer turns the gambling instinct into a positive force
as he throws the seed on the ground and hopes and prays that
it will return in multiplied numbers.

The researcher working in medical research may invest
millions of dollars gambling on the hope that he or she can
find a cure for cancer. That's turning the gambling instinct
into a constructive force.

The developer who buys property and designs a beautiful
habitat of comfort for humans takes a big gamble as he or she
pledges a great deal of front money.

> **The walk of faith recognizes that the gambling in-
> stinct is a divine quality placed within God's children.**

Challenge the winds!
Scale the heights!
Welcome the gambling instinct. Do not destroy it.
Give God a glorious life.
What an exciting way to live—walking the walk of faith!
Give God the glory of a positive life that dares to live by
faith.

## *Encountering opposition positively*

"Uphold my steps in your paths that my
footsteps may not slip."—PSALM 17:5

**196**   Success often requires clever strategy to maneuver your
way around negative obstructions or negative impossibility
thinkers. And this must be done, for not even the greatest
ideas are unanimously accepted upon the first announcement. Every project I've ever been a part of—building a
church, the Crystal Cathedral, or the television ministry—
has encountered opposition from intelligent people.

Should you abandon your dreams to those who lack the vision?

Should you crudely and callously attack your critics face
on?

Or should you maneuver your way around them?

It's frightfully easy to be intimidated by negative people.
Fearful that you might incur the displeasure of a friend or that
your ideas might not be accepted you quickly become the victim of intimidation. In the process, you slip off the path of
faith. That is not an acceptable option. Obstructions, whether
pressures, person, or property, must never abort your divine
calling.

So the best defense is an offense!

Today go on the offensive in a kind but forceful way. Believe
that your positive dream has the built-in power to attract support and enthusiastic backing.

Do not allow the fear of criticism to stop you. Rather
strengthen your dreams until your project will intimidate the
opposition.

Negative voices will be silenced by your enthusiasm.

Obstructionists will not dare to resist the growing support
that God is sending your way.

Opposing forces will shrink and shrivel in the face of your
God-given success!

The Lord and you are winning today!

*FAITH IS . . .*
## Rejecting negative advice

"Blessed is the man Who walks not in the
counsel of the ungodly."—PSALM 1:1

There are all kinds of negative thinkers who discourage us, **197**
impugn our motives, insinuate that we are insincere, and intimidate us to retreat.

What kind of friends do you have? Are your teachers positive thinkers or negative thinkers? How about the coworkers
and associates with whom you associate?

And what kind of material are you allowing to enter your
brain? Check again the movies you watch, the books you read,
and the voices that penetrate your conscious mind.

### Negative counsel is poison to faith.

The back side of faith is the process of rejecting negative
advice. You walk the walk of faith and exercise dynamic possibility thinking when you sort out and throw away negative
thoughts and emotions from the control positions in your
mind.

No human being can prevent negative stimulations from
attacking his faith-filled mind. You live in a universe that is
saturated with evil and sin. At no point is this more conspicuously clear than when you stop and consider how often your
mind and moods are assaulted with negative forces.

You will be blessed with a blossoming and fruit-bearing
faith as you reject negative advice and separate yourself from
destructive acquaintances. Immunize yourself from the germs
of negativity. It's up to you to keep your faith sanitized and
sterilized. Today, double-check what you allow your mind and
moods to be exposed to.

Begin with this affirmation: I will clean up my mental act,
starting *now!* And I will be blessed appropriately and forthrightly. The very moment I reject a negative thought, I will
immediately sense an inner cleansing invigorating the health
of my soul!

[447]

*FAITH IS . . .*
## Separating yourself from negative pressures

"What part has a believer with an unbeliever?
Come out from among them and be
separate."—2 CORINTHIANS 6:15, 17

**198**    There is such a thing as a divine divorce. By that I mean,
sometimes it is necessary to sever relationships that are mu-
tually self-destructive.

In the culture of Christ's time and locality a husband and
wife promised to hold to each other until death separated
them.

In the Christian church through the centuries it has been
maintained that divorce in marriage is a sinful act. I have
never met anyone who went through a divorce who did not
admit that it was the most self-esteem-shattering experience
they had ever gone through. And I've never met anyone who
bragged about the fact that his or her marriage fell apart. Divorce is always viewed as a failure.

Yet, Jesus indicated that there would be times when even
the divorce of a married couple would be an acceptable course
of action. An adulterous affair by one of the two mates gives
ground for divorce.

The divorce of a married couple is always a shattering experience, but if you are to have a tough-minded faith there are
some persons that you should divorce from your circle of important relationships.

• Never invite a negative-thinking person to the power center of your life.
• Never appoint a dyed-in-the-wool impossibility thinker to
be a member of an important committee.
• Never create a platform for enemies to launch their pro-
posals or projects.

**It takes a lot of faith to say good-by.**

## Utilizing suspicion positively

"Therefore let us pursue the things which make
for peace and the things by which one may
edify another."—ROMANS 14:19

What will you do with that negative emotion—suspicion? **199**
Suspicion is one of the more unreliable forms of mental
activity and one of the more difficult mental habits to uproot
once it has established its malignant tentacles in the mind!

Suspicion is a pregnant demon, giving birth to fear, jealousy,
depression, and anger!

**You *must* check negative suspicion! It can ruin you!**

Suspect that others think negatively about you, and they
will!

If you think people don't love you, you will freeze up, withdraw, and actively sow the seeds of alienation!

Suspicion can easily become a self-generating, self-propagating, self-fulfilling prophecy.

A possibility-thinking faith believes that we can turn negatives into positives! Can we apply this to suspicion?

Yes, faith can turn this negative mental activity, called suspicion, into positive mental activity. Turn paranoia inside out!
Reverse your suspicions! Try practicing positive suspicion.
Here's how:

- I suspect that somebody is going to give me a boost!
- I suspect that people I don't even know are defending me
  behind my back.
- I suspect that people will not condemn me for my faults.
  In fact, they will love me more once they see I'm imperfect just as they are.
- I suspect somebody is going to support me. And faith tells
  me that "somebody" is Jesus Christ.

Yes, turn suspicion, an expression of human imagination,
into a positive mental force. Believe that the best will happen,
not the worst. Before you know it, you will expect a miracle—
and you'll get one!

## FAITH IS ...

# Reacting positively to a negative situation

". . . If God is for us, who can be against us?"—
ROMANS 8:31

**200**

What do you do when the bottom falls out?
When the bubble breaks?
When the market is saturated?
When it looks as if your dreams are turning to ashes in your hands?
Remember this. Keep on believing!

> **You've not lost everything until you've lost your faith!
> And that's a choice . . . never an accident!**

You reserve the right to choose your reaction to whatever happens. You always have the choice to react positively or negatively.
Decide today to react positively . . .

- I'm going to be thankful to God—anyway!
- I will be rejoicing—nevertheless!
- My dreams may be frustrated; nevertheless I will keep standing on my strong feet of faith!
- This could turn out to be my shining hour!
- I can turn a tragedy into a triumph!
- This is my opportunity to build the greatest treasure a person can possess—a fantastic reputation!
- I shall choose to inspire people in my time of suffering.
- I shall achieve respect because of my courage in this enormous difficulty.

Faith is reacting positively to a negative situation.
Thank You, Father, for this gift of faith. Amen.

## Burying old grudges

"'Love your enemies, bless those who curse
you, do good to those who hate you, and pray
for those who spitefully use you and persecute
you.'"—MATTHEW 5:44

Faith is trusting that God will settle the accounts with **201**
those who have been unjust and unfair with you. No one
travels the road of life without being affected by injustice at
one time or another.

But the worst thing that can happen to you is to develop
*victimitis.*

*Victimitis* is carrying your grudge and nursing the hurts.
This only produces a whole new batch of emotional demons
to torment your soul! Resentment, anger, self-pity, and even
vengeance become a mixed-up recipe for messed-up feelings.

But if you walk the walk of faith, you'll recognize that upon
occasion you'll be treated unfairly. You've got the faith that:

**God can handle the injustice a lot better than you can.**

You've got the faith that He'll settle the score in a way that
will be helpful and not hurtful to everyone concerned. So
don't *carry* the grudge, *bury* it.

You can be positive about one thing. God knows the ins and
outs of the entire upsetting situation a lot better than you do.
God knows how to pull weeds without killing the flowers!

He understands your opponents, adversaries, and enemies a
lot better than you do. God knows how to turn an enemy into
a friend, too!

Affirmation: Today I shall drop all resentments, all in-
justices, into the deepest sea of God's power and mercy and
love as I pray that He will settle the matter in the best way!

Thank You, God, for taking over this problem before it does
untold damage to my spirit! Amen.

# Coping creatively

"In all these things we are more than conquerors through Him who loved us."—
ROMANS 8:37

**202** Let's take a look at two different lives: one walks the road of doubt and one walks the road of faith.

Negative people cry, complain, moan, and groan. They look at their losses instead of their victories. They look at what's wrong instead of what's right.

This naturally leads to a state of low self-esteem, which in turn produces an entire new set of problems. As they try to cope with life's hurts, they resort to chemicals, compulsive gambling, or immoral sex.

By contrast, people of faith cope creatively through possibility thinking! This is what Saint Paul did when he confidently wrote the words of our text today.

Positive-thinking people cope creatively by seeing the possibilities, even in the dark times. Instead of becoming pessimistic they start counting their blessings. They see stumbling blocks as stepping stones; obstacles as opportunities. They turn their negative temptations into positive passions.

**Possibility thinkers focus all their efforts toward turning wild impulses into sanctified service.**

What hurt do you need to conquer today? "We are more than conquerors!" Is there a wild passion you need to control? "We are more than conquerors!" What problem do you need to solve? "We are more than conquerors!" What obstacle do you need to move? "We are more than conquerors!"

How do we know we can conquer? The promise is through Christ who loved us!

Faith is coping creatively!

## FAITH IS . . .
# Smiling—anyway

"How beautiful upon the mountains are the feet of him who brings good news, . . . who proclaims salvation."—ISAIAH 52:7

"Dr. Schuller, you smile all the time on television. Are you **203** always that happy?" The answer is no. But when I'm not smiling, I cease to be as helpful as I ought to be.

When I was a student in theological seminary, the professor of practical theology, Dr. Simon Blocker, taught us: "Students, when you get in front of an audience, give them a lift; don't give them a load. Help them with their problems; don't dump yours on top of them! Give them a breath of fresh air! Give them good news, or you're not preaching the gospel!"

Think of all the positive values revealed in the life and faith of our Lord Jesus Christ, and you'll be able to smile—anyway!

To the best of my ability I have tried to live up to that directive. The result is that many people tell me that when they were undergoing stress and crushed with sorrow, my smile was enough to give them hope!

**The talent to smile is given to every living human being.**

Exercise it. Get all the mileage you can out of it! The amazing thing is that if you keep on smiling, you really will feel happy in a little while anyway! Even as the mind affects the body, the reverse is also true. If you *physically* act out the exercise of positive emotion, you can, in fact, awaken those feelings that are within you now. Positive feelings are waiting to be awakened within you. You simply need to exercise them through positive talk and constant smiling.

One dear old soul was credited for bringing many people into the church. Her secret? She simply stood at the entrance of her church each week, "smiling them in and smiling them out!"

[453]

## *Absorbing jolts naturally*

> "What woman, having ten silver coins, if she loses one coin, does not light a lamp, sweep the house, and seek diligently until she finds it?"—
> LUKE 15:8

**204**    "Absorbing" is an important quality of life. People who walk by faith develop the art of absorbing. There are times when we need to be like a sponge—absorbing disappointments, rejections, setbacks. The woman Jesus talks about in today's Bible verse succeeded because she stayed with it. The ability to absorb the initial disappointment gave her come-back-ability. Nine times out of ten:

**Success comes to the person who refuses to give up.**

I remember the time my wife lost her diamond from her engagement ring. One afternoon she looked at her ring and saw an empty setting. The stone was gone! Since she hadn't been outdoors all day, she searched the house high and low, to no avail.

I suggested we might have better luck looking for the diamond in the black of night. With all the lights off, we aimed the flashlight at every corner of the house. Suddenly we saw a flash of color! I reached down and there it was. The light in the darkness had done the trick.

I took it to the jeweler the next day, but he took one look at it and said, "This isn't a diamond; it's only a rhinestone!"

Glass! I was horrified. I said, "But I bought it from a respectable jeweler."

He smiled, "This stone did not come out of this ring. It's almost the right size, but not quite."

We never did find the diamond. My wife learned to take the jolt, absorb it, and go on. Faith is absorbing the jolts.

O God, enable me to keep walking by faith despite life's disappointments. Give me the ability to absorb and then give me the courage to keep going—anyway.

# *Manipulating the rough course*

"I will make each of My mountains a road,/And
My highway shall be elevated."—ISAIAH 49:11

Faith is manipulating your way upward and forward. Manip- **205**
ulation is a negative concept in the minds of people today, but
it does not always mean treating people as puppets for personal pleasure. It does not necessarily suggest using them as
tools to satisfy your needs.

Manipulation can be a positive form of human behavior.
Such is the case when a human being follows the Holy Spirit
down the walk of faith which sometimes twists and turns,
rises and falls, circles and backtracks in its relentless drive to
keep moving upward.

Remember, the walk of faith can be compared to a curved
mountain road which circumnavigates in mysterious twists
and manipulative turns upward to reach the mountain top.

We are managers of responsibilities given to our care by
God. And management is the *positive* manipulation of resources to achieve the impossible!

Faith is *positive* managing and manipulating of ideas and
projects through God's all-wise, all-knowing guidance. God
will guide you until each mountain becomes a road and each
highway is elevated. That's the promise to the people of faith
in the Bible verse today.

God promises that He will make *His* mountain a road; He
will elevate *His* highway. Be sure He is your guide today.

Then possibility thinking really works miracles, for God
will give you the wisdom to know how to use it. Manipulate
the rough course with God's help until you reach the top of
the mountain.

## *Bearing your cross—constructively*

Listen to these words of Jesus Christ: "If
anyone desires to come after Me, let him deny
himself, and take up his cross daily, and follow
Me."—LUKE 9:23

**206**  What did Jesus mean when He made this statement? He
was teaching a fundamental principle for successful living. To
succeed you have to grab hold of God's dreams.

God's dreams will always appear humanly impossible. The
fear of a shameful failure and criticism from colleagues may
be enough to cause you to reject the call of God. If you follow
God's call, you expose yourself to ridicule, criticism, and ha-
rassment in the pursuit of His plan for your life. Yet, in the
process you will experience a constructive crucifixion as you
build cathedrals, establish universities, develop research centers, and launch programs to help people in need.

To fulfill God's dream requires willingness to sacrifice the
comfort of the sheltered life, rather than remaining faithfully
aloof from any possible criticism and rejection by your peers.

Anyone who attempts to do anything positive is going to be
criticized.

That is a price we're called to pay as followers of Jesus
Christ.

The cross is implicit in possibility thinking!

There is no possibility of walking the walk of faith without
being willing to bear a cross.

**The cross is a positive symbol of success, not a nega-
tive reminder of failure.**

The cross is a minus turned into a plus!

It is the biggest plus sign in the world!

Affirmation: If I have enough faith to bear my cross, I shall
leave something wonderful behind me when I'm finally called
to leave this life. That's success!

## Keeping on—anyway

". . . he who endures to the end will be
saved."—MATTHEW 10:22

We are not on the walk of faith long before we encounter **207**
frustrations, obstacles, and obstructions. Then what? Then
it's time to hang on to one powerful, positive word—*endure!*

To endure means: "Inch by inch, anything is a cinch."

To endure means: "There is no gain without pain."

To endure means: "When faced with a mountain, I will not
quit. I will keep on striving until I climb over, find a pass
through, tunnel underneath . . . or simply stay and turn the
mountain into a gold mine, with God's help!"

To endure means: "I have to look at what I have, not at what
I've lost."

So you are unemployed? To endure means you're going to
keep on living a meaningful life anyway.

So you have people problems and are frustrated with regulations and road blocks and negative forces? You are so tired of
fighting you'd like to throw in the towel and quit?

What does it mean to endure? It means to remember that
when you face problems, you keep this point in the forefront
of your mind: people, problems, and pressures are constantly
changing, so don't split. You'll run into the same basic frustrations no matter where you go.

So you are grieving over the loss of your wife? Your husband? To endure means you keep on being positive about
life—anyway!

Never forget this wise warning:

**Never make a negative decision in a down time.**

This is only a phase that you are going through. It will pass.
When it is over, you'll be glad you hung in there!

*FAITH IS . . .*
## *Thanking God always*

"Giving thanks always for all things to God the
Father in the name of our Lord Jesus Christ."—
EPHESIANS 5:20

**208**    Deep in the heart of gratitude is a nugget of tremendous
faith. For the truly grateful person is the one who is walking
the walk of faith. He believes that his prosperity, peace, and
goodness come from forces and sources outside of himself.
Thanksgiving and trust are Siamese twins.

It's amazing how an unbeliever somehow assumes that it
was luck or his own cleverness that caused him to get to
where he is.

In contrast, the believer who thanks God for blessings will
also be able to thank God when the blessings don't come.

I remember visiting a young Chinese Christian in his office
in Hong Kong. Above his desk he had a huge sign made up of
only two words:

**Hallelujah anyway!**

"What does that mean?" I asked.

"Well," he said, "I believe God is blessing me always, and I
must be thankful at all times."

It's amazing how this attitude works miracles. Instead of
complaining when things go wrong, thank God anyway.

Believe that God will turn a tragedy into a triumph.

Once you begin to believe that God can turn an evil event
into a blessing, you will begin to relax. When your attitude
changes, your mood changes. When your mood changes, you
arise above the difficulty. That is the point where the miracle
takes place! Your mountain suddenly turns into a miracle.

Your optimism attracts great and good people! With this
kind of support you can't lose. Be thankful anyway—and expect a miracle!

## *Playing it down*

> "We are hard pressed on every side, yet not crushed; we are perplexed, but not in despair."—2 CORINTHIANS 4:8

**209**

Five years ago, my wife, Arvella, and I were thirty-five thousand feet over the South Pacific flying home from Seoul, Korea. Our hearts were bleeding, and our spirits crushed, knowing that our thirteen-year-old daughter had just had her left leg amputated in a Sioux City, Iowa, hospital.

I called out to God for emotional strength. Into my mind came one of the most beautiful sentences He has ever given me.

**Play it down—and pray it up.**

*Play it down*—I was exaggerating the seriousness of her motorcycle accident. She lost only one leg, not both of them. Her spinal cord was not severed. She had no head injuries, no brain damage. She didn't lose her sight or her hearing. She still has a beautiful face. She has a beautiful figure. She will have an exciting life. She wasn't killed!

*Play it down*—that's faith's counsel in the face of tragedies that can overwhelm you.

- If you surrender to negative thinking, you will *exaggerate* the problem.
- When you exaggerate the problem, you will *aggravate* it.
- You will never *alleviate* the problem until you put it in proper perspective.

Faith is playing it down—and praying it up.

## *Praying it up*

"Blessed be the . . . Father of our Lord Jesus
Christ, the . . . God of all comfort, who
comforts us in all our tribulation, that we may
be able to comfort those who are in any
trouble."—2 CORINTHIANS 1:3–4

**210**    Faith is playing it down—and praying it up. Praying it up
means giving your problems to God. Let Him turn your tears
into pearls.

As soon as my wife and I started praying about Carol's accident, we demonstrated faith again in the providence of God.
We exercised the belief that all things work together for good
when we love God and are faithful to Him.

**Pray it up, and give God a chance to strengthen you in
your sadness, sorrow, and sickness.**

As soon as I surrendered the broken body of my daughter
who was lying in pain thousands of miles away, I left my airline seat and made my way to the lavatory. There, I broke into
loud sobbing.

Compassionately, God met me in the shadows. I felt His
warm arms, like the comforting, gentle hug of a strong father.
I knew we would not only survive but also know His blessing
in the situation. Faith is playing it down and praying it up.

- Is there *sadness*? God can gladden your day.
- Is there *sickness*? He is the Great Physician.
- Is there *sorrow*? Heaven can heal.
- Is there *sin*? Christ alone claims the power to forgive sin.
- Is there *stress*? Christ can touch the nerve center and be-
  stow peace.
- Is there *struggle*? Christ can strengthen you to succeed.
- Is there *scarring*? Christ can turn the scars into stars.
- Is there *scorching*? Christ can heal the searing hurts.

Then *surrender* your brokenness. God is able to pick up the
pieces and mend you again. His strength is all-sufficient!

## Praising God anyway

"Continue earnestly in prayer, being vigilant in it with thanksgiving."—COLOSSIANS 4:2

Our daughter Carol had been in a motorcycle accident. My **211** wife and I were flying to her side from a speaking engagement in Korea, when suddenly I felt grief well up uncontrollably within me.

In the solitary confinement of an airplane lavatory six miles above the Pacific, in the middle of my sobbing, I was moved by a most miraculous positive thought.

The thought came like a clear message from Jesus Christ: *Schuller, if you are going to make a lot of noise, turn it into something positive. Let your lips shape the sounds that are coming.* I found my lips and tongue reshaping the wailing, sobbing sounds and turning them into the word *Alleluia.*

Tears rolled down my face, but the *Alleluia* was repeated. I kept repeating it—"Alleluia, alleluia"—until all of the audible crying sounds were out of my tortured soul.

It was amazing! The last "Alleluias" were offered in a hushed whisper. I found myself looking upward with my hands raised in a gesture that said, "I give this painful event, along with the broken body of my daughter, to You, God, and I praise You.
- I praise You for your comfort,
- I praise You for Your healing,
- I praise You for turning our tears into pearls,
- I praise You for turning her scars into stars."

The next time your life is torn apart from stem to stern, try praying "Alleluia." If you can repeat no other word, keep repeating it again and again.

Then wait for God to come like a sweet dove of peace to bless you. A soft spirit will kiss your tortured soul with tender mercies!

Thank You, Father, for Your faithfulness. Amen.

# Biting the bullet

"Though He slay me, yet will I trust Him."—
JOB 13:15

**212** The phrase "biting the bullet" comes, of course, from the Old West when there were no pain-killers.

I once asked the late actor, John Wayne, a university graduate and a keen student of history and contemporary affairs, about this. He offered this insight: "It's really true, Schuller. People literally put a bullet between their teeth and bit it to help distract them from the pain. It's hard for us to comprehend the pain they had to endure without the benefit of our modern pain-killers."

### Faith is bearing the unbearable by biting the bullet!

I was invited to a home of a shooting victim who had been left a paraplegic. I have never seen a more pathetic person. His mind and eyes were glazed with the drugs to which he had become addicted. All around his wheelchair were evidences of enormous wealth. He lacked nothing that money could buy. But there was an overwhelming spirit of darkness and doubt. He has made a decision to be a cynic, not a believer. He has chosen to publicly reject all belief in God. The Great Soul, the Eternal God, who charismatically sends out vibrations of an indwelling Holy Spirit, simply is not in his life.

Faith bears the unbearable by biting the bullet. That's what Job did when he lost his family and when his friends forsook him. Sitting alone in the ashes of his dreams, He still believed, saying; "Though He slay me, yet will I trust him!" That's inspiring faith!

You can have that kind of faith and so can I. We can bite the bullet, we can accept the disappointment, endure the pain, and in the process we will be an inspiration to all those we meet.

# Turning pain into gain

"When I am weak, then I am strong."—
2 CORINTHIANS 12:10

There is no gain without pain. Everything nice has its price. **213**
Max Cleland, as a soldier in Vietnam, lost both legs and an
arm when a grenade exploded. He could have come back to
the States a broken man, physically and spiritually. But there
was an inextinguishable spark of faith within him that turned
into a flame of burning desire.

Max tells the entire, painful, struggling story in his book
*Strong in the Broken Places.* A strong voice deep within his
spirit called him to greatness! "You can turn your scar into a
star! You can become *Strong in the Broken Places.* This unspeakable tragedy can be profitable to your soul."

Because Max Cleland was moved by faith to take a positive
attitude toward his crushing experience, he was able to look
positively toward his future. His hopes, rather than his hurts,
set his goals.

**Today, let your hopes, not your hurts, set your goals!**

Begin by setting a *reasonable* goal that you can be sure to
realize within the immediate future. With the enthusiasm
that will come with this fresh victory, you will be ready to set
a newer and higher goal.

Remember, anybody can have faith when the sun is shining—but you've got enough faith to be positive even when
you have good reasons to be negative!

You're destined to be above average!

Your courageous response alone will be a tremendous inspiration to yourself and to others. And who can measure the
value of that?

## *Surviving against all odds*

> "For I am persuaded that neither death nor life,
> nor angels nor principalities . . ., nor things
> present nor things to come, . . . nor any other
> created thing, shall be able to separate us from
> the love of God."—ROMANS 8:38–39

**214**  Today I saw something you have probably seen many times—a vibrant, solitary blade of grass standing proud and alert in the crack of a concrete sidewalk. All of the odds were against this blade of grass growing in such an unlikely habitat.

In the same manner, have you not seen a tree growing strong and rugged in a granite cliff? How can this tree survive against all odds and thrive on the side of a stone mountain? Where does it get its water?

**If a blade of grass can grow in a concrete walk and a fir tree in the side of a mountain cliff, a human being empowered with an invincible faith can survive all odds the world can throw against his tortured soul.**

There is an explanation for this marvelous miracle. *God plus one believer is a majority!* With faith in your Lord you can outnumber the enemies that may attack you.

You manage your problems, you don't let them manage you. You choose what kind of an attitude you are going to have.

**One possibility-thinking believer, plus God, equals survival power!**

Dear God, today I imagine my hand with fingers spread wide open. I imagine Your hand approaching mine until our fingers interlock and we grip each other firmly in faith. I will never let You go, and You will never let me go. You are my Lord. We will see this through together. Thank You, God.

So I need never be discouraged.

I'll never let anything get me down.

I am a survivor! Thank You, God!

## Sublimating your sorrow

> "O Death, where is your sting? . . . Thanks be
> to God, who gives us the victory through our
> Lord Jesus Christ."—1 CORINTHIANS 15:55,57

I'm often asked: "Dr. Schuller, do you really believe in this **215** possibility thinking?

"How can you really subscribe to such a positive attitude when the world is in such a tragic mess?"

As a pastor for over thirty years, I bear witness to the truth that sorrow either turns people into sweeter souls or into sour and cynical spirits. The choice is up to the individual. When loss has occurred, you must accept the finality of it. You can either turn sorrow into a living enemy to torment, bedevil, and finally consume you in its poison; or you can make friends with your sorrow.

Sorrow colors a person's life permanently. The hues never fade. Rather, they grow deeper in tone every passing year. However, you can choose the colors. The colors are either rich or they portray emotional impoverishment.

The word *sublimate* comes from the word *sublime*. I have seen great people walk the walk of faith and go through the deepest sorrows you can possibly comprehend. They arose from their grief more compassionate, tenderhearted, and empathetic than ever. They have sublimated their sorrow.

If you walk the walk of faith, there is no doubt you will become divinely different after drinking the cup of tears. When you remember this, it will help you choose how you will react to sorrow. The loss you experience is horrible. Don't compound it by allowing your life to be destroyed, too. How inspiring was the faith of Saint Paul when he said, "Thanks be to God, who gives us the victory . . ."!

Yes, walk the walk of faith; and when sorrow strikes, you'll know that weights can turn into wings!

## *Polishing the silver lining*

> "Can anyone understand the spreading of clouds,/The thunder from His canopy? . . ./God thunders marvelously with His voice;/He does great things which we cannot comprehend."—
> JOB 36:29; 37:5

**216**   People who walk the walk of faith give the world this positive thought: "Every cloud has a silver lining."

Men and women of great faith learn to polish their silver with positive thoughts. They affirm God is bringing good out of evil. They affirm nothing will befall them unless it is a beautiful blessing in disguise. They affirm there is a silver lining to every cloud.

### When it rains—they look for the rainbow!

*Today I will polish the silver lining* of my darkest clouds when the thunder is the loudest, and the waves crash most violently! Today I shall discipline myself to pray a prayer with at least ten sentences, each one beginning with "thank You."

- Thank You, God, that I am alive!
- Thank You that I have friends!
- Thank You that I have the faith to see it through.
- Thank You that there is help available for the problem, even though I see no solution to it today.
- Thank You that there are people who love me and are praying for me!

That's right—keep at it. Make a list of ten thank-you sentences. In the process you will be polishing the silver lining of the dark clouds.

**God can work miracles through His people whose hearts are broken in love.**

# *Waiting for a breakthrough*

"If anyone competes in athletics, he is not crowned unless he competes according to the rules."—2 TIMOTHY 2:5

What distinguishes the person who walks by faith from the person who basically walks the walk of doubt? **217**

**People who walk the walk of faith always expect a breakthrough.**

People of faith anticipate that someone will offer them a "lucky break." When problems produce log jams, those who walk by faith listen for the crack of wood that clears the river for free-floating logs. When experiments fail to produce the magic cure, people who walk by faith keep working on new formulas, intuitively expecting that the big break will come.

Anticipating a breakthrough is enough to keep you going. Persistence ultimately finds the loopholes in an entanglement which threatens to strangle success.

A runner who competes in a race knows that to win he will need to push himself beyond his own limits. He'll need that "second wind," the breakthrough in order to be crowned a winner. He competes expecting a breakthrough!

Beware of crude, complaining voices of cynicism that whisper to you: "Throw in the towel. It's no use. It's never going to happen. Go ahead and quit."

Rather, plant your feet firmly on the high, hard, and holy road of faith. No matter how impossible the project may appear, keep on believing in your "second wind." Tell yourself that a breakthrough is going to happen!

• Wait for it,
  • work for it,
    • and be ready to receive the reward when it comes!

## *Adding up your assets*

> "Bless the LORD, . . ./And forget not all His
> benefits:/Who forgives . . . heals . . . redeems
> . . . crowns . . . satisfies . . . So that your youth
> is renewed like the eagle's."—PSALM 103:1–5

**218** Are frustrations, failures, and fears coming back to depress and fatigue you today?

Faith looks at what you have left, never at what you have lost. Faith adds up the assets. It doesn't surrender leadership to liabilities.

- Consider what you really have going for you.
- Add up your assets.
- Measure your strength.
- Take account of your power.

The psalmist gives us the clue to begin by blessing the Lord. What has the Lord done for you? What can you expect Him to do for you in the future? He forgives. He heals. He redeems. He crowns you with loving kindness. He renews your strength! With a God like that, who can fail?

Now begin to add up the other assets that you may have taken for granted. List your friends, your education, your citizenship.

There is no more helpful therapy for depression or fatigue than the exercise of adding up your assets. Retreat from the hectic style of life. Find a quiet time and place and list on paper everything you have going for you. You will be surprised how rich you are. Your capacity not only to survive your present condition but to succeed is formidable indeed! Now, before you add up the bottom line, reread the Bible verse.

**God promises that when you remember daily what benefits He has sent your way, you will have renewed strength like an eagle!**

## Counting your blessings

"Godliness with contentment is great gain."—
1 TIMOTHY 6:6

It's amazing how many opportunities must have opened up **219**
to you yesterday when you stopped to reevaluate your net
worth:
1. You discovered you had friends whom you did not know
   a year ago.
2. You discovered that the value of your property has in-
   flated and you are richer than you thought you were.
3. You have discovered that you have maneuvered your way
   around a treacherous conflict this past year. Only God
   could have made it possible.

> **As you practice counting your blessings, you will find
> that your faith is being suddenly revitalized.**

Of course! Faith is the practice of counting your blessings!
The cynic exposes bleak and barren stupidity when he feeds
his doubt! No joy ever sprouts from the soil of cynicism!
By contrast, the process of counting your blessings strengthens faith and produces a contentment in the most adverse circumstances.
When our daughter Carol went through the pain of an amputation of a leg, she spent seven months in bed. Yet, she
counted her blessings every day. She thanked God for the
nurse. She thanked God for the bed, for the clean sheets, for
medication, for pain-killing drugs, for shelter from the storm.
What blessings can you thank God for today? List no fewer
than ten: _____

_____

_____

_____

## Coming back after defeat

"Let us not grow weary while doing good, for in
due season we shall reap if we do not lose
heart."—GALATIANS 6:9

**220**    Even saints have their low times! A great Scottish pastor,
Peter Marshall, once said, "There are times when my prayers
never go above the top of my head."

There are seasons of the soul, you know.

There is the wintertime when all the trees appear to be
dead. I remember one winter when my father cut down a dead
tree only to see new sprouts grow from the stump in the
springtime. "Never cut a tree down in the winter," he said to
me. Then he added, "I shouldn't have cut it down. It had more
life in it than I thought."

The principle?

> **Never make an irreversible *negative* decision in the
> dark times. Never set your goals when you are at a low
> ebb. Believe that the springtime will come.**

• This depressing season will pass.
• Positive new feelings will return to you.
• You will come back again.

Yes, your faith will pluck you from the ashes, and you will
be resurrected once more. Youthful enthusiasm will return.

Burned out?

Then refuel.

Take a break.

Seek a retreat.

Find renewal and replenish—you can go on again!

Never make a move from weakness. Always move from
strength.

And the spring will turn to summer and the summer to
harvest time! You will reap successfully simple because you
didn't give up!

## FAITH IS . . .
# Reconstructing after ruin

"Then the nations . . . around you shall know
that I, the LORD, have rebuilt the ruined
places. . . . I, the LORD, have spoken it, and I
will do it."—EZEKIEL 36:36

What happens when life strikes you a blow? What happens **221**
when you "blow it"? When you are too weak to resist temptation?

> **When you stumble, don't crumble. Admit you're
> human. God doesn't expect you to be perfect. He does
> expect you to be dependent on Him.**

Faith is reconstructing after ruin. It probably takes more
faith to rebuild for a second time than to build the first time.

When a tornado completely demolished our farm home, I
saw faith in action as my dad rebuilt the buildings one at a
time, slowly but steadily. And he was in his mid-sixties at the
time.

There's something infectious and inspiring about the in-
domitable human spirit that wades through the flood waters,
rakes through the ashes, and then makes the decision to rebuild.

Faith looks at ruin and says, "This only means that you
have a chance to build something better in its place."

The terrible hurricane that hit the island of Kauai in Hawaii
in 1982 was devastating. The full force of the hurricane lifted
the larger-than-life-size sculptures of Allerton Gardens and,
like torpedos, hurled them through the walls of the owner's
private home. Then flood waters followed, washing out to the
sea a priceless collection of first-edition books from Mr. Allerton's private library. Books—many the only extant copies—
were lost forever. How has he handled the ruin? He has re-
paired his home and planted new trees. He is reconstructing
after ruin.

> **That's how God is with you and me! He is the Master
> Artist, reconstructing beautiful lives from ruin.**

[471]

*FAITH IS . . .*

## Awaiting your turn—especially after crushing disappointments

"The end of a thing is better/than its beginning,/And the patient in spirit is better/than the proud in spirit./Do not hasten in your spirit to be angry,/For anger rests in the bosom of fools."—ECCLESIASTES 7:8–9

**222**

He was passed by for a promotion that he was sure he would receive. His first impulse was anger. He ranted and raved and stomped in the privacy of his home, and decided he'd quit the next day. He said, "Let's see how they get along without me!"

Then he read the Bible verse that we are using today. Faith took over. He thought, *I won't quit. Instead I'll wait my turn. Perhaps I'll get another chance later.*

The person who had been brought in from outside the company to receive the coveted promotion resigned within six months, and the patient person's turn came up. This time he was offered the position. He's doing great today!

**It takes faith to hang in there after you have been hurt, especially if you cannot justify the loss.**

Another friend of mine was an ambitious political candidate with integrity. In the closing days of the campaign, his opponent resorted to smear tactics. And my friend was defeated. The dishonesty made him say, "I'm finished with politics."

I urged him to hang in there. "Voters have a way of being very wise," I advised him. "If I didn't believe that, I wouldn't believe in the democratic system." The story has a happy ending. Three years later he ran for office again. This time he made it.

Faith is waiting your turn.

O God, give me patience in spirit. If I'm tempted to pick up my marbles and run because I did not win the game, I am really too proud. Replace my anger with Your understanding spirit, and save me from the self-destruction that I could bring upon myself by my negative reactions. Thank You, Lord. Amen.

# *Regrouping after a setback*

"Do not remember the former things, nor consider the things of old. Behold, I will do a new thing. . . . I will even make a road in the wilderness."—ISAIAH 43:18,19

**223**

Regrouping may mean little to you, but it is a very meaningful term in military strategy. When the enemy lines collide and the battle (not the war) is over, the side which suffered the apparent defeat does not contemplate surrender, it speaks about "regrouping." They analyze why they lost, calculate the weak spot in the enemy's lines, and develop a new strategy for effective counterattack.

The regrouping strategy is of course mostly known in sports, especially football. The opposing teams are allowed to huddle and regroup to discuss a game plan they hope will surprise and beat their opponent.

Businesses do this when they go through periods of recession. They may permanently discontinue some unprofitable lines they carried at a loss. They may cut overhead, trim their personnel, and regroup their resources.

> **Regrouping is an act of dynamic faith!**
> **It is possibility thinking in action.**
> **Do not dwell on old mistakes; concentrate on new ideas.**

What do you do when you've had
- a nonproductive day?
- a streak of ill luck?
- a poor semester in the classroom?
- a stagnant relationship?

When you face setbacks, don't send up the white flag. Don't throw in the towel. Rather get your best thoughts together. Reorganize, retool, or regroup! Then go back at it again with vengeance!

That's faith, and it moves mountains.

## Redeeming a lost cause

> "Fear not, for I have redeemed you; I have
> called you by your name; you are Mine. . . .
> you were precious in My sight."—ISAIAH 43:1,4

## 224      A "lost cause" simply doesn't exist in God's mind!

And it must not exist in our mentality as possibility thinkers either! Jesus came not to condemn, but to save.

When you see what appears to be a lost cause, instead see a challenge to be miraculously redemptive!

Any act of redemption is a beautiful display of faith. I really admire people who take old automobiles and restore them to the original condition. Or those remarkable artists who have the incredible ability to restore a damaged work of art.

Here is a list of all the lost causes that were redeemed by possibility thinking.

- Eliminating child slavery laws.
- Eliminating segregationist laws in this country.
- Taking a company that was hopelessly bankrupt and turning it around until it turned a profit again.
- The person who was dying from cancer, but is alive today because of medical research.
- That marriage which was threatened, but now is renewed.
- The drug abuser who now is a rising young executive.
- You and I were lost, until Christ redeemed us!

What "lost cause" do you need to turn over to God today? Is there a possibility that you consider yourself to be a "lost cause"? When faith comes into your mind and heart, something wonderful happens. Under the power of your Lord, you are not condemned—you are redeemed! Write your name in the blanks below.

God calls me by name, _____.

I, _____, belong to Him.

I _____, am precious in His sight.

Now—say these affirmations—aloud.

Thank You, Lord, for redeeming us!

## *Bouncing back after failure*

"Every valley shall be exalted,/And every
mountain and hill shall be made low;/The
crooked places shall be made straight,/and the
rough places smooth."—ISAIAH 40:4

*Flexibility.* That's the word that describes this walk of faith. **225**
The pathway of possibility thinking is not flat. The trail of
positive thinking twists and turns, rises and falls.

In a way the walk of faith is like those exciting moving
sidewalks at major airports in the world. I love to walk as fast
as I can on those moving sidewalks! And if I'm the only one
on the horizontal escalator, I will often jog. How fast I can
move! I bounce up and down with every footfall. I almost feel
like I'm flying! What a marvelous feeling!

**The walk of faith is a moving sidewalk! It gives
bounce-back-ability!**

After a defeat, there are the down days and moments of
discouragement; yet you must resist the temptation to give
up on life. Faith finds you bouncing back with new enthusiasm.

Doubt whispers with a devilish voice: "Well, you've learned
your lesson; be smart. Give in. Quit."

But the still, sterling whisper of God nudges and lifts us,
saying, "O.K., learning to walk is learning to bounce back after
you stumble and fall. Step up again. I'll walk with you. Try
again, we'll make it!"

With this definition of faith in mind you can see why the
people who walk the walk of faith are never ultimately defeated. They simply refuse to take up a permanent residence
at a point of failure.

Failure is a juncture in the road. It must never become a
campground. So pack up your tent and move on to greener
pastures. Affirmation: I have an invitation from God to start
over again! Today I have been born again! My new life started
this morning. I have the freedom now to bounce back.

## Saving the broken pieces

"The Spirit of the LORD is upon me. . . . He has sent Me to heal the brokenhearted."—LUKE 4:18

**226** At the Royal Palace of Teheran in Iran, you can see one of the most beautiful mosaic works in the world. The ceilings and walls flash like diamonds in multifaceted reflections.

Originally, when the palace was designed, the architect specified huge sheets of mirrors on the walls. When the first shipment arrived from Paris, they found to their horror that the mirrors were shattered. The contractor threw them in the trash and brought the sad news to the architect.

Amazingly, the architect ordered all of the broken pieces collected, then smashed them into tiny pieces and glued them to the walls to become a mosaic of silvery, shimmering, mirrored bits of glass.

Broken to become beautiful! It's possible to turn your scars into stars. It's possible to be better because of the brokenness. It is extremely rare to find in the great museums of the world objects from antiquity that are unbroken. Indeed, some of the most precious pieces in the world are only fragments that remain a hallowed reminder of a glorious past.

**Never underestimate God's power to repair and restore.**

And when restoration is not in His plan, expect Him to replace what has been destroyed with something even more beautiful. God has ways of filling the empty spots with His love. With God the fragments of our happy memories are like precious gems.

Dear God, mercifully bless me in the broken times, and I shall rise up to praise Your name. And thank You, Father, that through Your love something precious is being salvaged from sorrow, and I shall soar again on eagles' wings. Amen.

## FAITH IS . . .
# *Elevating your hopes*

"I [God] dwell in the high and holy place,/With him who has a contrite and humble spirit,/To revive the spirit of the humble."—ISAIAH 57:15

Do you need a lift today in your walk of faith? Are you in need of a rebirth of hope? Let's consider an elevator of faith and hope to elevate your spirits!

**227**

First, you have to believe there is an elevator. There are those who can't imagine that there's an easier way to the top than climbing each step painfully, slowly. They feel that a great deal of effort is necessary to raise your spirits. Too many people strive at being happy when they could be riding the faith elevator to the top.

Once you believe in an elevator, you've got to have enough faith to step into it. For if you don't step into the elevator, you'll never make it to the top of the skyscraper.

After you are in the elevator, remember to push the button. More than once, I've suddenly realized that I'm in an elevator that is going nowhere, because we all forgot to push the button. Everybody assumed somebody else was pushing it.

Finally, make sure you are in the *right* elevator. High-rise buildings often have elevators that only go to certain floors and bypass the others. Get on the wrong elevator and you'll never get to where you are planning to go.

Faith is elevating your hopes. Don't sell yourself short. Set higher goals, or you'll surrender leadership to your past accomplishments. Who wants to be stuck in an elevator that isn't going anywhere?

> **Press the button and step on an up elevator called F-A-I-T-H.**

Look for the arrow pointing upward, and you will experience a rebirth of hope.

[477]

*FAITH IS . . .*

# *Opening yourself to new opportunities*

"I know your works. See, I have before you an
open door, and no one can shut it."—
REVELATION 3:8

**228**     You know what is so exciting about the walk of faith?
It's knowing that some mistakes can actually be profitable!
Failures and even setbacks may prove to be positive pos-
sibilities in disguise.

My faith sharpens more to spot opportunities in both
failure—and success.

Surely success creates new opportunities.

Success starts a whole cycle of margin successes. The *peak*
to *peek* principle is set in motion. For once you have climbed
a mountain you gain greater self-confidence.

So each new success experience gives your self-image a new
boost.

You are more than you thought you were.

When you conquer a challenging problem you feel like you
are standing on a mountain top! This "peak" experience produces a "peek" experience—you see farther and spot new hori-
zons, and new opportunities.

Now you experience a *"peek"* experience: Your vision ex-
pands; your faith grows! You imagine accomplishing more
than you ever thought you could: "If I could scale this peak—
maybe I could. . .?!"

The higher you climb, the farther you see. From the top of
the hill you can see a valley waiting to be explored. You find
that you are a lot stronger than you were when you started
this walk of faith!

You gain a new sense of self worth! You now have more
money, more friends, more knowledge, more self-confidence,
and more faith than when you started your climb.

O God, open my eyes to see the incredible opportunities
that are before me today and give me enough common sense
never to slam a door shut that you have just opened for me!
Amen.

## Laminating the life for strength

"O God, You are my God. . . ./Because you have
been my help. . . ./My soul follows close behind
You,/Your right hand upholds me."—PSALM
63:1,6–8

When you walk the walk of faith, you experience the "lami- **229**
nating principle." Let me illustrate what I mean.

When we built our first chapel, I discovered how laminated
wood beams are built. A layer of wood about an inch thick is
glued under pressure to another piece of wood of equal thick-
ness. Several other layers are glued under pressure on top of
that. This creates a laminated beam that may be as thick as
three feet and conceivably able to span a width of over one
hundred feet without supporting columns.

Amazingly enough, these beams are stronger than steel and
are virtually fire resistant. Flames lick around the outside but
cannot penetrate, for there are no hollow cores where the
flame can continue to draw oxygen and create a roaring fire.

Steel beams, on the other hand, melt under the heat of a
burning wall, unless they are wrapped in fire-resistant plaster!

> **The kind of faith that moves mountains**
> **doesn't come from one simple religious event**
> **in your life, but through layer upon layer**
> **of experiences, one upon another—**
> **until your walk with God through months and years**
> **becomes an emotional and spiritual**
> **beam that can span the deepest chasm**
> **and the most ghastly gorge**
> **that your path will encounter.**

Thank You, God, for the way You are building my faith
stronger and stronger.

Laminate my life for strength so that I need never fear the
future. Amen.

## Filling the tank

> "The wise took oil in their vessels with their lamps. . . . the bridegroom came, and those who were ready went in with him to the wedding; and the door was shut."—MATTHEW 25:4,10

**230**    Faith is filling the tank—especially when it's a rental car! "Fill 'er up." Now that's faith, isn't it? How do you know you'll take the whole journey and won't change your mind soon after you start out? And if you can't, what a waste it is to have all that gas sitting in the tank. When you return the car, you don't get more for it because there's gas in the tank!

Notice how possibility thinkers fill the tank—before they're sure how long the trip will be. Isn't that what you did when you took that special training course?

"Filling the tank" becomes a key element in success, for it activates an inner commitment. It sets in concrete ways the hopes and dreams you have.

Read carefully the passage from Matthew, chapter 25, verses 1 through 13. The wise women were those who filled their vessels with oil and took extra oil along! There is a warning in this parable: Opportunities will come in unexpected times and places, so be prepared.

Make sure your tank of faith is full of gas so you can be prepared for the unexpected opportunity that wasn't in your plan. Faith is filling the tank so you can be prepared for an unanticipated emergency along the road, helping a lonely wounded person along the road of life.

There's also a promise in this principle. The promise is that God gives great opportunities to those who are prepared.

**Inspiration + preparation + saturation = success.**

Yes, fill the tank. It won't be wasted. Someone will benefit from it!

O God, in a changing world I want to be prepared for the unexpected. Fill my tank of faith today with Your promises and Your wisdom so that I will not miss the opportunities before me. Amen.

## *Bracing yourself against the storms*

"O LORD, You are my God./. . . a strength to
the needy in . . . distress,/A refuge from the
storm."—ISAIAH 25:1,4

Are there stormy forces of sin and doubt that are confront- **231**
ing you today?

Are the waves of cynicism threatening to capsize your ship
of faith?

How will you confront these negative storms?

Is it possible to avoid them?

Not always.

There are the storms of wrong and evil that the believer
must face. There are moral positions you can never compromise without sacrificing your soul.

Sin is still sin! Wrong is still wrong!

Faith is bracing yourself against the storms of doubt, where
lightning may flash, tornados may drop out of the sky, hur-
ricanes may hit the shore, the storms may lash against the
garden of your life. But the faith that God gives stands firm,
bracing you. His voice stills the waves of sin. His hand calms
the wind of wrong.

Practice these positive affirmations today to give you "bracing" power!

• I can brace myself against any storm of doubt, temptation,
sin, and despair, for God is at my side.

• God will not allow me to be defeated.

• God has entrusted me with a holy treasure, a divine idea. I
will guard it with my eternal soul!

• I will not take my eye off the walk of faith.

• This storm shall pass away. The winter season of my soul
will turn to spring with God's help.

• I will not abandon faith in my God, for He will allow the
sun to rise again tomorrow in my faith.

## Focusing on God's power

"O LORD, our Lord,/How excellent is Your
name. . . ./When I consider Your heavens, the
work of Your fingers."—PSALM 8:1,3

**232** Did you ever take a magnifying glass and allow the sun to
shine through it, adjusting it all the while in your hand until
it focused a burning white dot on a piece of cloth or paper or
dry leaf? Do you remember how the magnified rays of the sun
on the dry paper suddenly created a wisp of smoke?

There is tremendous energy generated in the powers that
are created through the "focusing principle."

Is there a malfunctioning in your soul? Is there a source of
disharmony that is upsetting you? Is there an illness in your
body? Is there a negative factor or faith that is disrupting the
normal, happy rhythm that should be characteristic in the life
of a person who is walking by faith?

Then exercise the power of "focusing." Focus on the power
of the God who created the sun. Visualize the incredible immense globe of molten fire that the sun actually is.

Can you begin to comprehend the power of the God of *all*
the ages? Focus all your thinking on His power.

**Allow God's power to magnify your faith until it burns
its healing force into the problem area of your life.**

Continue to focus God's power on the obstructions in your
life, and visualize the sizzling, smoking problem being consumed by the enormous power of God. Nothing can resist His
redeeming forces!

Thank You, Father, for faith in this focusing power of healing that I exercise now in the name of Jesus Christ, my Lord
and my Savior. Amen.

## FAITH IS . . .
### *Connecting with power sources*

"The God of Israel is He who gives strength and power to His people."—PSALM 68:35

"He's very well connected" is a sophisticated statement **233** that analyzes personal power. Powerful people in the world are those who are well connected with power sources, such as faith, freedom, knowledge, opportunity, wealth, and other people around them.

With what power sources are you connected?

> **Today, connect with the power source of the most beautiful and wonderful people alive—the positive-thinking people!**

When you choose to become a believer, you suddenly find yourself moving out of the circle of cynics and into a new company of optimistic people.

When you step out of the society of skeptics and into a circle of trusting souls, an incredible transformation takes over.

Enthusiasm replaces boredom.

Excitement replaces lethargy.

Faith-producing energy replaces doubt-producing fatigue.

Youthfulness replaces weariness.

That's being connected with the *real power people.* Through their minds flows an energy that has its source in positive ideas flowing from the eternal God. That's exciting! That's ultimate living.

Thank You, Father, that You're giving to me today the greatest gift possible—freedom to choose my friends! I am choosing today to connect myself to the most beautiful, positive-thinking people I can meet. I pray that You will lead me. I thank You that I'm connected to You, for You are the ultimate Power Source. You give me the motivation to laugh, love, and lift myself to higher and happier living. Thank You, Lord. Amen.

## *Relaxing under pressure*

"Be still, and know that I am God."—PSALM
46:10

**234**  Imagine a balloon filled with air. You maintain the balloon's
full pressure by tightly pinching the opening closed.

Now separate your fingers to allow the air to rush out. The
balloon completely deflates until it is limp and empty of its
pent-up pressure. It lies lightly in the palm of your hand.

Release the pressure inside you that has blown up like a
balloon ready to explode.

> **Exhale deeply.**
> **Blow out the tension.**
> **Deeply breathe in the presence of God's peace.**
> **Blow out the poison of stressful pressures.**

"Be still, and know that I am God." Can you know God
without being still? Probably not. Tensions can block the freedom of God's flow into your soul. Often in my ministry I have
spiritual experiences high in the mountains. As I relax among
the tall pines I feel God's presence. The secret of dynamic
spiritual power is right here. *First relax!* Defuse those tension
bombs within yourself by blowing out the pressures that have
been pumping up your blood pressure!

Now throw open the sun roof of your mind and let the sun
tranquilize your spirit. Be still—and then you may be able to
hear the voice of God.

I once asked Viktor Frankl the question, "How can you have
a religious experience?" He answered with a question, "How
do you catch a dove?"

The way to catch a dove is to open the palm of the hand and
reach upward with a grain of wheat or a bread crumb in your
hand. If you sit very quietly, the dove will come and rest in the
center of your palm. Be still—and you will catch the faith!
Quiet your spirit, and you will feel God's presence. Relax under pressure, and you'll tap into God's power!

## FAITH IS . . .
### Dissolving anxieties

"Do not worry about tomorrow, for tomorrow
will worry about its own things. Sufficient for
the day is its own trouble."—MATTHEW 6:34

As you walk the walk of faith and discipline yourself to seek **235**
positive possibilities in every situation, you will still face such
realities as sickness, separation from loved ones, and even
death.

**You can't escape the raw realities of life, but you can
shape them!**

You either shape life's realities, or they ravage your mind
until you're devastated with worry.

How can faith help you dissolve life's anxieties?

*Faith faces the worries and anxieties one at a time.* If you
imagined all of the possible painful experiences you might encounter from birth until the end of your life all at once, you
could not handle it. A bridge cannot handle all the traffic that
passes over it at one time. Bridges are designed to handle moving traffic. So faith is designed to handle anxieties, one at a
time. Deal with only your immediate pressures. Let tomorrow's worries wait until then.

*Faith erases anxieties and worries.* By the time you've
spaced your anxieties, you will have erased many of them!
Many anxieties that remain can be erased by transferring
them to a Higher Department. Turn them over to God. He
specializes in problems you are incapable of handling.

*Faith replaces anxieties.* If anxieties and worries still remain after prayer, then faith replaces them. It says: I'll replace
worry with work. I'll replace anxiety with ambition. I'll replace depression with new drive. I'll replace stress with success!

Faith and I together will win. Thank You, Lord.

# *Replacing worry with hope*

"Do not worry about your life. . . . Which of
you by worrying can add one cubit to his
stature? . . . Your heavenly Father knows that
you need all these things!"—MATTHEW 6:25–32

**236**    Our Bible text today is one of the most beautiful prescriptions for the traveler on the road to faith. It comes from our
Lord Jesus Christ. According to His definition, faith is replacing worry with hope.

Somebody said, "worry is like a rocking chair: It gives you
something to do, but it doesn't get you anywhere."

Worry doesn't put a twinkle in your eye, a whistle on your
tongue, or a happy gait to your walk.

> **You are the manager of your moods, with the responsibility and the freedom to manipulate your emotions.
> You can elect to go out today with worry or step forth
> with hope.**

Many Christians have tried this therapeutic experiment:
They write down what they're worried about on their daily
diary. They pray about it and turn it over to God. A year later
they see how beautifully the Lord took care of the situation,
or with the passing of time, discover that it was actually incredibly inconsequential!

Hope is a phenomenon. Faith replaces worry with hope, and
no psychiatrist knows what it is. We only know what it does
to people. It makes gray skin pink, dull eyes sparkle, and releases healing forces in the body itself!

Affirmation: Today I'm going to walk the walk of faith. My
faith will take action as I replace worry with hope.

And what's hope? *Holding on, praying expectantly!*

Good-by, worry! Hello, hope!

## FAITH IS . . .
### *Leaning back with casual confidence*

"Rest in the LORD,/and wait patiently for Him;/
Do not fret."—PSALM 37:7

**237**

Faith takes a tough look at rough spots and asks the responsible question: "Is it my fault? Is this the responsibility of my department?"

Not long ago I missed a flight to Japan because my visa was not in order. This was serious, for I would be a day late, missing the first series of lectures in Tokyo. Not all the positive thinking and talking in the world could get me on that flight. I had no choice but to wire my host in Japan and express my regrets that I would be arriving a day late.

Then I proceeded to lean back, take a casual attitude, and have a great time enjoying this unplanned day of leisure. When I made that decision, my problem was transformed into a joyous experience.

Faith is a wise instructor, counseling you to stop torturing yourself with irritating attitudes. Faith is leaning back with casual confidence, letting positive thoughts stroke the stress away until a mellow spirit comes over you softly, gently, and peacefully.

God is far more concerned about your welfare than you are, for you are His child. He knows how to turn this rough spot into a serendipity, a blessing in disguise. Praise Him for His faithful love and concern for you in this trying condition. He understands it so much better than you do!

Now that you've talked it over with Him, close the door.

**It's time to lean back and let God take over.**

He will handle it in the most responsible way possible. Give yourself a break by believing positively!

# Comparing conditions and choices

"I will sing to the LORD,/Because He has dealt bountifully with me."—PSALM 13:6

**238**     "How do you like your wife?" a Vermont farmer was asked. "Compared to what?" he answered.

Life is made up of values that are relative.

"How do you feel today?" Answer: "Compared to *when?* Compared to *whom?*" Before you answer negatively remember this: You feel great compared to some of the really painful days and times in your life.

Faith is comparing your conditions. Compare your present condition to the conditions of those pitiful human beings in a Siberian labor camp, without any hope of ever getting out. Compared to them you should really feel great!

After all, you have the freedom to make a telephone call.

You have the opportunity to have visitors (even if you are in one of America's prisons)!

You can boost your faith by using this process of comparing conditions. You make your condition better or worse. You aggravate it or sublimate it.

The first condition you face today is a realization that

**You alter your condition by altering your attitude.**

Faith is also the process of comparing choices. What are your options? By exercising possibility faith, list all the positive possibilities that can conceivably come your way if you became positively aggressive!

Affirmation: As I compare choices today, I will make a list of all possible uses of my time and efforts and achievements!

O God, I compare my walk of faith with the walk of doubt that I once experienced—with all of its negative fears, frustrations, and failures. Thank You for releasing me from these negative conditions. I am singing with the psalmist: For You have "dealt bountifully with me." Thank You, Father. Amen.

## *Framing your awards*

"Where your treasure is, there your heart will
be also."—MATTHEW 6:21

Let's review the steps in the process of mountain-moving **239**
faith.
- God sends an idea into your mind.
- He calls you to courageous action.
- He challenges you to attempt the impossible.
- The idea suddenly grips your attention. How does faith
  handle this inspiring possibility?

(1) Faith *forms* the idea carefully in the mind—shaping,
sculpturing, rolling it around like clay in a potter's hand—and
then takes a good look at it to see what it is!

(2) Faith *firms it up.* The idea becomes solid; the potential
appears realistic. The idea has been formed; now it will be
firmed up! You'll make the commitment. You're going to go
for it.

(3) Faith *farms it.* Faith has formed it, firmed it, now it
farms it! This means you give your attention to developing
the new growth to full fruit-bearing maturity!

(4) Finally faith *frames it!* The harvest comes. You are successful. You put the award on the wall and accept the compliments. Do not deprive yourself of the joy of feeling proud over
an achievement made possible by the grace of God! Now you
look forward to greater achievements, greater successes and
greater accomplishments, because you're walking the walk of
faith!

**So long as you keep moving forward in the realm of
this faith you can expect to accumulate more victories, more awards to frame and hang on the wall!**

Thank You, Father, for calling me to such an exciting way of
living! Amen.

## Relying on your source

"And my God shall supply all your need
according to His riches in glory by Christ
Jesus."—PHILIPPIANS 4:19

**240**     She sat at the breakfast table this morning. I don't know her
name. She was obviously blind, but she relied in trust on her
companion, who read the menu to her. Gracefully, politely,
with an elegant charm, her fingers found the utensils and the
napkin. She ate her intricate breakfast without an accident. I
was proud of her!

**Faith is trusting the sources that we will never see.**

We take the doctor's prescription to be filled by the pharma-
cist. Then we take it home and follow the directions, consume the drugs, trusting and relying on the doctor and the
druggist—including those who produced the ingredients before they were mixed and bottled for our consumption.

We listen to a believer in the Christian faith give a testimony. If there is no reason to doubt a sincere confession of
faith, we will believe the witness.

Over five hundred Christians saw the resurrected Christ at
one time! Several others testified to seeing our Lord following
His crucifixion and burial. We believe in the resurrection of
Jesus Christ because we are relying on the sources.

Can we believe the Bible to be the Word of God even
though it has been copied and recopied through the centuries? Yet its marvelous miracle-power of generating and sus-
taining life-transforming faith is obvious. There is power in
the Holy Book. Can we believe that God is morally obligated
to reveal Himself to us? Yes, God owes it to us. He has "put it
in writing"! If not the Bible—then what?

And where does our faith itself come from? Beyond the
Holy Scriptures does it not come from our positive observa-
tion of life around us? Can we not sense that there is a
Source beyond ourselves? Rely on God.

## *Exposing your colors*

"And whoever believes on Him will not be put
to shame."—ROMANS 9:33

Faith isn't faith unless it makes a commitment in the face **241**
of possible ridicule and rejection.

Do you dare to expose your belief?

Is it possible that you have not publicly declared yourself to
be an enthusiastic believer because it might prove embarrassing in your business or social circle? Do you want to be all
things to all people? Are you a fence-straddler? Or is it because you sincerely are afraid of making a mistake? You really
want to make the right move but you can't be sure. What if
faith is all wrong? Is this why some of your friends claim to be
agnostic? Perhaps you are one. Then listen carefully.

When it comes to faith, there are only two choices:

(1) To choose to believe that *there is a God*, that in this
unlimited universe, there is an Intelligence! It is *Good*! It is
*God*!

(2) The other choice is to be an atheist, a believer in
*nothing!*

The third possibility is really not a choice, for an agnostic is
one who *refuses* to choose.

No one can be positive that he is right. But one thing is
sure, either the believer *or* the atheist is right. Certainly the
agnostic is wrong, for he has avoided choice altogether!

> **How do we make right choices? By following the in-
> stinct of faith, not the compulsion to fear.**

The play-it-safe agnostics are not the ones who are leading
the world upward and onward. It is the dreamers who are the
uplifting source of society!

# *Choosing the best option*

"A good name is to be chosen rather than great riches,/loving favor rather than silver and gold."—PROVERBS 22:1

**242**   If I can create a verb to be a synonym for "possibility think-ing," it is the word *optionalizing.* For when you examine all of the possibilities, you actually are listing all of the options. You are "optionalizing"! It starts when you consider your first op-tion: to be a believer or an unbeliever.

Once you and I choose to walk the walk of faith, we will continually encounter those intersections where the road ahead separates, and we need to ask the question: "Which road do I take now?" Then you need to "optionalize." Ask: "Where do I want to go?" and "Which road will take me there?" Be careful what you choose.

The Bible text today gives guidance for choosing the best option: "A good name is to be chosen rather than great riches."

George Beverly Shea was a young man with his heart set on a great career that could bring him fame and fortune. His mother was concerned for him. One day as he went to prac-tice, he found a poem placed by his mother on his piano. The poem was entitled, "I'd rather have Jesus," now a well-known religious song.

After reading the words George Beverly Shea dedicated his talent totally and completely to Jesus Christ. The re-sult? His singing has led untold tens of thousands of people to Jesus Christ.

Today you have many choices to make. Some of them will be small and some may affect your entire future. Choose care-fully. Choose prayerfully.

## Opting for the optimum

"Now may the God of hope fill you with all joy
and peace in believing, that you may abound in
hope by the power of the Holy Spirit."—
ROMANS 15:13

Yesterday we created the word *optionalizing*. Today let's **243**
learn more about *opting*—the beautiful verb that comes from
the same root as the noun *options*. Faith is choosing the best
option. It opts for the optimum. It selects the wisest alternative from a noble value system.

"You mean they are getting married—again—to each
other?" The news sent shock waves through the social circle.
They had divorced nearly three years before and neither had
remarried. Someone commented, "Remarriage after divorce.
That's real faith."

I counseled with them before I reunited them in marriage.
They explained: "We simply didn't have the right foundation
for our relationship. We didn't have a religious faith or value
system. Now both of us are Christians. We have a more mature attitude toward each other and toward life.

"Meanwhile we've considered our options. We've thought
about them very carefully. Neither of us chooses to grow old
without anybody; that's a road that leads to loneliness. We
have chosen the option of genuinely forgiving each other and
loving each other with our mistakes."

Why settle for anything less than the best possible alternative? Faith opts for the optimum. It opts for the very *best* possible alternative, and it believes that the best alternative is
*possible!*

> **Settle for nothing less than best! Philosophically, re-
> ligiously, psychologically, that means you go with
> Jesus Christ. No person that I've ever met claims to
> surpass Him in faith, love, and courage!**

## *Harmonizing your inner self*

> "The LORD your God in your midst, the Mighty
> One, will save; He will rejoice over you with
> gladness, He will quiet you in His love, He will
> rejoice over you with singing."—ZEPHANIAH
> 3:17

**244**   Let's stop to think today about the many different people
who live inside you.
- There is the brave one.
- There is the cautious one.
- There is the dashing, daring adventurer. (Yes, there really
  is—even if you haven't met him or her!)
- There is the saint who would be hcly.
- There is the sinner who would indulge in the lusts of the
  flesh.
- There is a person who would move forward ambitiously.
- And there is another person who would seek the easy way
  out.

We experience wholeness when we achieve harmony within
ourselves. Imagine that several persons that live within each of
us are like spokes in a wheel. A rim and a hub hold the spokes
together. Without them, the spokes would collide and clash.

**Christ is the hub of the wheel. He is the power that
integrates our life until we achieve an inner harmony.
Our Christian faith is the rim.**

Is there a power struggle in your soul today? Between good
and evil? Between the positive and the negative? Between the
Lord and the forces of Satan? Faith is letting Jesus Christ har-
monize your inner self.

Thank You, Jesus Christ, that You are able to take command and settle the internal power struggles within me.
Through Your Spirit now, I feel an inner harmony. And it is
beautiful. Amen.

*FAITH IS . . .*

## Sacrificing your arrogance

"Whoever humbles himself as this little child is
the greatest in the kingdom of heaven."—
MATTHEW 18:4

Humility. What is it? It's the opposite of arrogance. What is **245**
arrogance?

- Arrogance assumes that because you can't imagine how
  something can be done, you can declare without reservation that it's impossible!
- Arrogance does all the talking and none of the listening.
- Arrogance rejects advice, simply because someone else
  said it or because your mind is already made up or you
  don't want anybody else to get the credit.
- Arrogance is refusal to accept help unless you've earned
  it, and inability to accept a compliment when you have
  earned it.
- Arrogance stubbornly refuses to change a mind when it
  knows it is wrong.
- Arrogance is the opposite of faith.
- Arrogance spouts off without reservation: "There is no
  heaven. There is no hell."
- Arrogance is an unwillingness to consider the possibility
  of making the 360-degree turn in your life that will allow
  Jesus Christ to come into your life, converting you into an
  authentic Christian.

**Faith sacrifices your arrogance on the altar of authen-
tic humility.**

What a change it will make in your life! You'll be left with a
confidence that's been purged of cockiness. It's easy to see
why this kind of faith moves mountains and leads to genuine
prosperity.

"Whoever humbles himself as this little child is the greatest
in the kingdom of heaven." That's God's promise to us today!

## Admitting your inadequacies

"Whom have I . . . but You?/. . . My flesh and
my heart fail;/But God is the strength of my
heart and my portion forever."—PSALM 73:25

**246**  Only the people who have a strong faith in themselves, in
their God, and in their best friends dare to admit their shortcomings.

As you continue in the process of positively programming
your mind, and ridding it of conscious and subconscious negative thoughts, it is important to admit your inadequacies.
That is an act of faith, too!

Once you have enough faith to admit your inadequacies you
experience incredible liberation! From that time on, you develop an immunity to hypocrisy.

The word *hypocrisy* is bantered around irresponsibly today.
Hypocrisy is not the human frailty that keeps you from practicing what you preach. Hypocrisy is not the failure to live up
to your own ideals.

Hypocrisy is pretending to be perfect, and in the process,
imposing a sense of judgment and guilt on those around you.
Hypocrisy is giving everybody the verbal assurance that *you*
are living up to your own standards, when you really are not!

**Christians aren't perfect. We know where we must go
for forgiveness!**

Therefore, go to God, on an hourly basis! Your flesh and
heart may fail, but God never gives up on you! That's why you
can dare to be open and honest.

Dear God, I thank You that Your adequacy atones for my
inadequacies. I thank You that Your strength takes over where
my weakness begins. I thank You that Your forgiveness is sufficient for my sins. Thank You, Lord. Amen.

## Waving at a mystery

"How precious also are Your thoughts to me, O God!/How great is the sum of them!/If I should count them, they would be more in number than the sand;/When I awake, I am still with You."—PSALM 139:17–18

The walk of faith is a command to march straight into a mystery! **247**

The Christian faith is based on facts and mysteries. There are several facts upon which our faith is built. It is a fact that Jesus lived. It is a fact that He died. We *accept* His Resurrection as fact. But the Resurrection *remains* a *mystery.* How did it happen? How can it possibly have happened? It's a mystery. Is He alive today? We believe He is.

That's why we call our religion faith, not science. For faith is waving at a mystery!

**Faith assumes that the unknown, the mystery, is not a hostile element but a kind providence!**

"How can you believe in God?" I once asked Viktor Frankl in a long wide-ranging conversation in my office. I'll never forget his answer.

"I see living as being an actor on stage. The house lights are off; since I am blinded by a bright spotlight, I cannot see the audience. Nevertheless, I will give them my best performance. The mysterious darkness keeps me from seeing and fearing what I am facing. Then, when the curtains drops, I hear the applause. The house lights come on and the curtain rises. There they are—my friends!"

So it is with God. He is there, in the darkness, watching me perform. I cannot see Him, yet I know that He is urging me onward and motivating me to do my best.

*FAITH IS . . .*
## Surmising with the soul

"I am the LORD . . . there is no God beside Me.
I will gird you, though you have not known
Me. . . . I am the LORD, and there is no
other."—ISAIAH 45:5–7

**248**  What synonyms can you give for the word *faith?* George
Santayana, the poet and philosopher, used a word I like very
much. It is the word *surmise.*

> O, World, thou choosest not the better part!
> It is not wisdom to be only wise,
> And on the inward vision close the eyes,
> But it is wisdom to believe the heart.
> Columbus found a world, and had no chart,
> Save one that faith deciphered in the skies;
> To trust the soul's invincible surmise
> Was all his science and his only art.*

Faith is applying positive thinking to solve problems, spot
opportunities, and make decisions. Somehow you "surmise"
that there is a universal principle that could unlock the problem you're wrestling with.

It's strange, mysterious, marvelous, yes, miraculous how
faith operates in your daily life. Once you turn your thinking
in the direction of an "invincible surmise," you begin to imagine breakthroughs. You begin to think

- "It might be possible *if . . .*"
- "It could be possible *when . . .*"
- "It might be possible *after . . .*"
- "It might be possible *in conjunction with . . .*"
- "It might be possible *for God . . .*"
- "It might be possible *but . . .*"
- "It might be possible *so* I'll keep on surmising—and I'll
  soon be surprising."

---

*John Bartlett, *Familiar Quotations,* Boston: Little, Brown and Co., "O, World,
Thou Choosest Not" (1894), George Santayana.

## *Preempting the negatives*

"[God] who is in you is greater than he who is
in the world."—1 JOHN 4:4

What does it mean to "preempt"?                                           **249**

Imagine a party happening in a ballroom. Suddenly the
President enters! Every eye turns on him. That's what you
call "preempting the scene"!

Imagine a starry night in the desert. The Milky Way is spectacular. The Big Dipper can be seen clearly. Then, suddenly,
above the horizon comes a full harvest moon! That's called
preempting.

When irritations and frustrations possess you, use your
faith to rise above them! Come up with a bigger idea! That's
called "preempting the negatives."

For example, consider jealousy. Jealous people are people
who never learned how to use their faith to preempt negative
thinking. I cannot recall ever being jealous of anyone in my
life. I was so afraid I would be jealous of pastors with larger
churches that I decided I'd go out and start my own church
and pray that God would make it as large as He wanted it to
be and as effective as He would like it to become.

I didn't realize I was actually using the preempting principle. It has served me well for many years1 I have no problem
delegating important jobs and glamorous assignments to others—simply because I use the preempting principle.

When we spot bigger opportunities and carve out greater
assignments for ourselves, thus meeting our needs for challenges, that's preempting a negative with a positive idea!

When you are tempted toward discouragement, defeat, or
depression, simply think bigger! Upstage the negative thought
with a new and exciting positive thought.

Call for a change of command within yourself. Power is
shifting constantly in this political world. Let there be a power
shift in your life. You call the shots! Replace the negative
thoughts with the positive thoughts.

Here's to you! Your tough-minded faith is making a way!

## *Considering all possible resources*

"In [Christ] are hidden all the treasures of
wisdom and knowlege."—COLOSSIANS 2:3

**250**   Mountain-moving faith is like a magic formula! There are
vital ingredients that make the recipe outstanding. Leave out
a single spiritual chemical, and you diminish the positive results proportionately.

One major ingredient in the walk of faith is *humility.* Big-
thinking people have an amazing capacity for humility. They
are humble enough to listen to advice from anybody who
makes sense!

A chief executive of one of America's top corporations was
approached by a janitor who said, "Sir, I've noticed you seem a
little on edge lately."

"Well, John," the executive replied, "if I am, it's because I'm
carrying an enormous load. Under the circumstances, I think I
have a right to be anxious."

As he turned his back to unlock his door, he heard the janitor say, "But, sir, if you believed in the God I believe in—you'd
be on *top* of the circumstances, not *under* them."

Stopped short by this sentence, but too proud to turn
around and acknowledge it, he walked into his office. He put
his head in his hands and prayed: "God, are You out there? Or
are You here? Have I been missing You all this time?" Then he
called the janitor in and asked him what church he went to.
The next Sunday the janitor took the executive as his guest to
church. And he became a believer!

Faith is willing to accept help from all sources. What pride
and prejudice might be holding you back from developing professionally, personally, or spiritually?

**Be humble enough to take help from anybody. You'll
be surprised what God will open up for you!**

## Repenting the positive way

"Repent therefore and be converted, that your
sins may be blotted out, so that times of
refreshing may come from the presence of the
LORD."—ACTS 3:19

Of the incredible assortment of religions in the world, why **251**
have I chosen Christianity? Because it is true. Because it deals
with the problems of sin, negativity, antisocial behavior, and
psychological aberrations in the most redemptive, positive
way possible! It forthrightly recognizes the reality of sin. It
does not try to explain it away, permitting us to keep indulging in lusts that deprive us or another person of our dignity.

**Positive Christianity has at its heart a God who dem-
onstrates perfect love. He loves us after He has seen us
at our worst. That's forgiveness.**

And forgiveness requires repentance. Repentance obviously
includes regret, remorse, and a genuine sorrow for negative
behavior. But it is not self-condemnation. The word *repentance* is used to translate a Greek word, *metanoia*, meaning to
"turn around." Repentance means to change directions—set
new goals and establish new standards. Pick up on God's
dream for your life! (1.) Positive repentance recognizes doubt
as the real sin. So repentance is a decision to share faith. (2.) To
make daring decisions; to seek to fulfill God's plan for my life
regardless of the price!

Lord, forgive me for not having the faith to live the life I
should have lived. I am now ready to dream Your dreams, to
carry the cross, and to pay the price. I am going to live right,
think right, pray right, and do right! I am trusting You to give
me the power. Together, we shall succeed. Thank You, Lord.
Amen.

# Converting to belief in God

"Most assuredly, I say to you, unless one is born
again, he cannot see the kingdom of God!"—
JOHN 3:3

**252**  It's good to review the realities we've discussed this far on
the walk of faith.

Reality #1: Real faith always leads to commitment.
Reality #2: Commitment always demands and results in
conversion.
Reality #3: Conversion is the process of radical change.
Reality #4: The ultimate experience of faith is the process
of making a commitment to believe in God
and devoting your life to serving Him as He
leads, encourages, and empowers.

**Faith's noblest move prompts a person to convert from
doubt to faith, from immorality to morality, from self-
aggrandizing behavior to unselfish and charitable conduct.**

Is it really possible for human beings to be born again? Does
human nature really change after the age of twenty-one? Is it
possible for a person's character to be turned around 360 degrees? The answer is yes!

Of course it's a miracle. Conversion happens by the grace of
God.

Conversion is the process of making an irreversible, no-
holds-barred commitment to believe in God and to walk according to the light of His Word. Have you been converted?
Let faith call you to make a complete surrender of your life to
the Lord Jesus Christ. Confess your sins to Him. Ask His forgiveness. Accept His cleansing.

Feel the rush of holy life coming into your soul. Do not be
afraid to announce to the world, "I am a Christian. I have been
born again!"

Thank You for the gift of saving faith, O God, my loving
Father. Amen.

## Trusting a stranger

"Because you have seen Me, you have believed.
Blessed are those who have not seen and yet
have believed."—JOHN 20:29

Is it really possible to trust a stranger?                    **253**
Well, that's what happens when two people marry, for you
really don't know your mate until you live together through
years of happiness and tears.

Even then, do you ever really know each other? For you are
constantly changing and growing, aren't you?

I've been happily married to my wife for thirty-three years,
yet I'm constantly amazed at how I have guessed her wrong
many times. It is these surprises that keep our relationship
from growing stale.

When you walk the walk of faith, you need to trust others.
When you trust someone, you bring out the best in him or her.
Even the worst person will manifest good qualities when an-
other person trusts him or her.

But what happens when you try to trust people only to have
them let you down? Guard yourself against the cynical reaction of the negative thinker: "I'll never trust anybody again."
Such a decision is an invitation to a haunting hollowness and
devastating loneliness.

Instead, place your trust in Jesus Christ. Trust Him—even
though you may not understand who He is, where He is, or
what He can do for you. Trust Him—even though He may yet
be a holy Stranger to you.

**Trust Him. He will draw greatness out of you that you
never knew was there.**

Dear Lord, there is so much I don't know about You. But I
do believe You are the reflection of the eternal God and so I
trust You to be my Friend. I ask You to be my closest Companion as I walk the walk of faith.

## Going home after sinning

"My son was dead and is alive again; he was
lost and is found."—LUKE 15:24

**254**    There isn't a single one of us who will not fall short of our
own standards, stumble, and sin.

**A shameful act of sin is made worse by the negative
reaction it can set off within our lives.**

The danger is that we'll be too embarrassed to go back
again. Consider:
—the student who flunks out and never returns to the
classroom!
—the entrepreneur who suffers a business failure and never
starts another business!
—the church member who sins, drops out, and never goes
back to the fellowship again.
—the preacher who fails to practice what he preaches and
leaves the ministry.
—the hometown boy who hasn't made good and doesn't
dare return to his roots.
Think of the damage that happens in the life of a person
who lacks the faith to come home. But once he's returned in
honest confession, he no longer needs to run, hide, and avoid
certain people.
When you demonstrate an immense act of faith through
genuine repentence, you discover again the goodness of God.
Like the father who killed the fatted calf for the feast of his
returning son, so God embraces you with understanding affection!
O God, spare us from the temptation to choose the path of
fear. Give us the faith to face up to You, always believing and
trusting that You will understand, forgive, save, and welcome
us home again! Thank You, Father. Amen.

# Returning to my spiritual homeland

" 'Father, I have sinned against heaven and in
your sight, and am no longer worthy to be
called your son.' But the father said . . . 'Bring
out the best robe.' "—LUKE 15:21–22

We have seen that faith is a mark of mental and emotional
health. We have seen that faith releases creative powers. Ag-
nosticism, atheism, cynicism, and negative thinking are the
abnormal mental activities of the soul that has wandered
away from God.

**255**

Faith, then, is the process of coming home again. It is a
returning to the God who created you in the very beginning,
when the cells creatively collided to cause life to spring forth
in the silent chambers of a woman's womb.

If you have a problem believing, if your faith stumbles and
falters, then you must ask the question: "What is separating
me from a loving friendship with God?"

Begin by checking your private life. Do you have some secret sins? Is there some conscious or subconscious guilt
within your life?

**It only takes a little bit of guilt to produce a large
amount of doubt.**

Doubt is the defense mechanism of a guilty person fabricated by an insecure, subconscious mind to protect itself
from belief in someone or something that could impose a
judgment on him.

Every time I've encountered an atheist or a boastful agnostic I challenged him, "Are you sure there is no sin in your life?
Are you positively sure there is absolutely no guilt within
your soul for deeds done or left undone?"

Faith comes when you return home again like the prodigal
son, begging God's forgiveness. You not only receive forgiveness but also the robe of real faith!

## Confessing your sins

"Search me, O God, and know my heart/. . .
And see if there is any wicked way in me,/And
lead me in the way everlasting."—PSALM 139:23

**256** The choice is so simple: choose to follow the voice of faith or listen to the voice of fear. The path of faith always leads to freedom and peace, whereas the path of fear always leads to oppression and tension.

For example, consider the problem of your own sins and shortcomings. The natural inclination is to hide from failure and try to give the impression that you're perfect. You fear that if your sins are exposed, you will be publicly rejected. The enormous complexities of human behavior that are motivated by a fear of exposure that might reveal imperfections makes an interesting study!
- What mask do you wear?
- What misleading impressions do you try to leave behind you?
- What games do you play?
- How long do you think you can keep up the act?
- What will happen when the curtain is finally lifted?

Until you develop the faith that God forgives you when you confess your sins, you will never be a truly honest, well-integrated personality.

Confession is good for the soul. There's enormous healing that happens in confession.

Alcoholics Anonymous has wisely recommended that healing will never come until a person finds at least one essential friend. Find one person to whom you can confess your sins, to whom you can open up all of your faults. Get the garbage out.

Jesus Christ is that kind of friend to me.

**Confession is an act of faith that begins enormous dividends of incredible peace of soul.**

## *Asking for forgiveness*

"And forgive us our sins, for we also forgive
everyone who is indebted to us."—LUKE 11:4

To ask for forgiveness after you've confessed your sins is an **257**
unsurpassed profession of faith.

You're at the mercy of the judge now.

You are without defense.

Can any act really reflect more faith than open and honest
confession of sin and guilt?

Everything you are or could hope to be is on the line; for
without forgiveness, integrity is impugned.

When you ask for forgiveness, you really ask for people to
trust you again. You encourage them to once more see you as
a wonderful human being.

I'm sure this is why Jesus Christ is so extremely effective
with people around the world. He encourages everyone to
come to Him and ask for forgiveness.

**Jesus Christ has never failed once to forgive anyone
who honestly and sincerely asked for forgiveness.**

Jesus Christ has a 1000 percent record of keeping His word.

One of the classic translations of the petition of the Lord's
Prayer uses the words "forgive us our debts" (Matt. 6:12).

That is what happens when Christ forgives you.

He pays the mortgage off.

He eliminates the moral and spiritual debt you added up
against Him.

Your full line of credit is restored with Him.

Ask Jesus for forgiveness.

He promises to give it to you!

What an unsurpassed blessing!

How wise you were to decide to take this walk of faith!

## FAITH IS . . .
### Wiping the slate clean

"Create in me a clean heart, O God,/And renew a steadfast spirit within me."—PSALM 51:10

**258**    Once you start thinking, living, and moving by faith, you open an almost bottomless well of refreshing water.

Of all the blessings that come from living by faith, none is more valuable than salvation from guilt and sin.

**The peace of soul that comes when you realize you are pardoned by God is the single most priceless gift you will ever receive!**

We are promised in the Bible that "by grace, you have been saved through faith, and that not of yourselves; it is a gift of God." (Eph. 2:8) What could be better news than that?

Human beings sin, make errors, and fall short of *our* standards, to say nothing of the standards of a Holy God, who does not wish for us to perish in our sin.

God wants us to be His happy, helpful servants, spreading love and encouragement in the world. We are of little value as long as we carry a negative self-image. Now faith wipes the slate clean!

Wipe the slate of your own soul clean every night. How? Approach your Lord Jesus Christ with this simple prayer:

*Jesus Christ, You have promised forgiveness of sins. I accept this offer. I can feel you wiping clean the blackboard of my soul. I go to sleep, knowing there is no guilt attached to my record.*

I am exercising my faith by affirming and believing, by the grace of God, that I am declared to be a person made clean in heart and soul. Thank You, Jesus. Help me to be so grateful for my pardon that tomorrow I shall dare to dream great dreams and do a good work for You! Amen.

# *Forgetting your forgiven sins*

"As far as the east is from the west,/So far has
He [God] removed our transgressions from
us."—PSALM 103:12

Faith is a spiritual force—the eternal God, moving in and **259**
through your life. Nothing blocks the fresh flow of God's
spirit more than a sense of guilt. No human being is perfect.
Everyone is infested with sin and exposed to it continuously.
The glorious good news of the Christian faith is that God
waits, moment by moment, to cleanse us of all guilt and to
forgive us of every sin.

**When God forgives, He forgets.**

When God buries the hatchet, He doesn't leave the handle
above the ground.

Sin is any act that robs you of your God-given dignity.
Shame is the first symptom that sin is operating in a life.

When God saves you from your sins, He totally and completely removes all shame and replaces it with a youthful
sense of holiness and righteousness. You feel washed, cleansed
inside and outside! It is now your job to forget the sins that
God has forgiven. How?

No longer repeat self-denigrating confessions of sin. No
longer practice destructive repentance by putting yourself
down as a horrible sinner.

Jesus Christ died on the cross to save me from the
penalty, the power, and the pollution of sin.

**I walk the walk of faith by practicing mountain-
moving faith as I affirm: Christ has forgiven me of
every sin.**

I am spiritually whole. God is flowing through my life with
power again, for I am forgiven. My faith has fresh new power!
Thank You, God.

## Yielding yourself to God

"Do not let sin reign in your mortal body. . . .
but present yourselves to God."—ROMANS
6:12–13

**260**    Faith is crowning Christ as King of your life. It is accepting His imperial command over your thinking. It is acknowledging the lordship of Christ over your life. It is yielding the leadership of your life to the winds of the Holy Spirit—the way tender trees yield to the breeze.

It takes a lot of faith to surrender leadership to someone you have never touched, never talked to—except in prayer. On the twenty-two-acre campus of the Crystal Cathedral we have planted Italian cypress trees and Australian eucalyptus trees. Both were selected because they create a tranquilizing emotion in the landscaping plan.

Landscape architects recognize that there are two basic types of planting—dramatic and tranquilizing. Cactus plants are categorized as dramatic plantings. They stab the air; they rigidly resist the wind. They confront, from an "attack" position, nature around them.

By contrast, the tranquilizing landscape relaxes, yields to space, breeze, and gravity. The weeping willow, the coconut palm, the Italian cypress, and the eucalyptus tree all send out vibrations of tranquility. The tips of the tall eucalyptus and cypress trees reach upward as they sway ever so delicately, sensitive to the slightest breeze. Then they bow gracefully and respectfully, bending to the wind. No wonder they survive storms that destroy rigid, brittle trees.

Yielding is surrendering. Surrendering is the ultimate act of faith. As the tips of the trees bend to the wind, so will you and I respond to the winds of the Spirit of God.

**Faith is yielding yourself to God—to the higher Power, to the loving Presence of our precious Friend, to our loving Lord, to our gracious God.**

## *Overcoming all fears*

"God has not given us a spirit of fear, but of power and of love and of a sound mind."—2 TIMOTHY 1:7

When you and I have yielded ourselves to God, and He has wiped the slate clean, does this mean we will never face fear again? Of course not, but God's promise to the believer is that we *can* overcome all fear through the power of His love and faith. **261**

Where does fear come from? Not from God! But from the source of all universal negativity—the devil. Philosophically we refer to this source as evil.

Neurotic fear that destroys your creative and constructive planning and productivity does not come from God! "God has not given us a spirit of fear" (2 Tim. 1:7); rather God empowers you with a healthy mind.

How do you overcome fear that encircles you? Read today's Bible verse over again and again. Draw close to God in prayer. Ask Him to possess you with His Spirit of

confidence,

courage,

conviction!

Under the leadership and lordship of Jesus Christ, command that negative thought, that destructive emotion, to get out of your life!

**Call upon almighty God to fill your mind and mood with healthy thoughts, loving emotions, and powerful motivations. God will answer your prayer! You will overcome your fears! For God is more powerful than any negative thought.**

Thank You, Father, for being so good to me. Thank You for coming into my life to remove all my fear. Thank You for filling me with this kind of faith.

[511]

## Quieting the storm

"Then He arose and rebuked the wind, and said
to the sea, 'Peace, be still.' And the wind ceased
and there was a great calm."—MARK 4:39

**262**   One of the most beautiful stories ever written is the account of Christ's crossing the Sea of Galilee with His disciples.

Our Lord had gone to sleep in the boat.

Suddenly a storm arose.

The disciples were panic-stricken.

They awoke the Lord.

Christ stood, calmly faced the winds, extended His arms to the troubled sea, and with authority commanded the winds and the waves to subside. "Peace, be still."

Faith assures you that unexpected storms will subside if you take control over them!

Picture yourself standing under the cross of Jesus Christ, where the Savior died for your sins! Here He has paid the price to earn the right to pardon you completely and eternally from all guilt. Beneath the cross of Christ face all guilt within you and affirm, "My sins are forgiven! Peace be still!"

Now, from this position, face the storms of your sin and guilt, and command all negativity and evil to release you from their bondage in the name and by the authority of your Lord. "Peace, be still." Now picture yourself standing before the open tomb on Easter morning. The resurrected Christ, who walked out of the tomb leaving prints of wounded feet in the soft sand, now stands beside you. He promises to be with you always—even unto the end of the world. With Him beside you, you can face the storms of anxiety and worry about today and tomorrow with a quiet confidence. Now, command your fears to leave you with this divine benediction, "Peace, be still."

**Peace of mind—deep, abiding, powerful, and pervasive—is yours when you accept Jesus Christ as your personal Lord and Savior.**

## Bonding a friendship

"I have loved you with an everlasting love;/
Therefore with lovingkindness I have drawn
you."—JEREMIAH 31:3

When my grandson, Christopher, was only ten months old I **263**
traveled so much I had little time to become acquainted with
him. One day, to my surprise, I reached out my arms to him
and he stretched his arms to me. He invited me to pick him
up. He sat on my lap, turned, and looked to me with a most
trusting look.

Then came a beautiful moment when he peacefully rested
his left cheek against my right shoulder as if he was sleeping
in his own bed.

Suddenly he lifted his head, and looked up to see who was
holding him. His big wide eyes searched my face, with an "I
know-who-you-are" look.

He realized who I was! His mother interpreted and explained his look: "Dad, you know I edit and review the 'Hour
of Power' television program before it is aired across the country. Christopher often sits beside me as I work. He knows
yours is the face he has seen on television every day for most
of his life."

The child recognized me as someone familiar. In that moment a bonding was formed between a grandfather and grandson. It was wonderful.

**Faith brings you to a moment when suddenly you real-
ize you are on solid and safe ground with a Friend!**

Faith is bonding a friendship with Jesus Christ! Let this be
the day when you rest your eternal soul on His heart. He will
encircle you with His love and embrace you to give you eternal spiritual security. That's faith! That will make a difference—always and forever!

## Ruling out disqualification

> "My sheep hear My voice, and I know them,
> and they follow Me. And I give them eternal
> life, and they shall never perish; neither shall
> anyone snatch them out of My hand."—JOHN
> 10:27–28

**264**   When we walk the walk of faith we rule out the possibility of ever being declared disqualified in the spiritual race of successful living.

My daughter Carol is determined to become an award-winning skier in national competition even though she has had her left leg amputated. It is nothing short of divine inspiration to see how she disciplines her body to qualify for the competitions sponsored each year by the National Handicapped Sports and Recreation Association.

It took Carol two years to meet the rigid standards to qualify. I will never forget watching her participate at the Twelfth Annual National Ski Championships in Squaw Valley, California. We watched her win a gold medal in the downhill race and a silver in the giant slalom. Then the slalom race was announced. We were waiting for her to come down the hill when the announcement was made: "We have a DNF ('Did not finish') at the top of the hill: Carol Schuller." She did not qualify! There is enormous disappointment when you are disqualified.

When we are saved by faith, Christ redeems us. He doesn't put a short-term lease on our spiritual welfare! Christ saves us—forever!

He doesn't select us for His team only to disqualify us if, and when, we fail to live up to His holy standards. He has written our names in heaven's Book—in indelible ink! He has adopted us as His children—not just accepted us as "foster children" for a season!

He holds us and never lets us go! We may be tempted to let go of Him, but He will not let us ever be disqualified from the family of God!

Dear God, today I commit my life and soul to Jesus Christ. Forever and forever! Amen.

## Trading off anxiety for peace

"Peace I leave with you, My peace I give to you;
not as the world gives do I give to you. Let not
your heart be troubled, neither let it be
afraid."—JOHN 14:27

Life is made of trade-offs.                                    **265**
When you started this pilgrimage called "the walk of faith,"
you traded off safety and security for stimulation and success.
When you accepted God's gift of salvation by grace through
faith, you traded off arrogance for faith.
When you made a commitment in marriage to love, honor,
and respect your husband or wife, you traded off freedom for
friendship.
When you decided to believe in the promises of God, you
traded off anxiety for peace.

**Worry doesn't bring happiness. Stress only brings ill
health, and anxiety robs us of peace of mind.**

So today let's trade off anxiety for peace. Give yourself a
therapeutic meditation.
Picture yourself on a lonely and isolated island.
A long stretch of beach rolls out before you like silver car-
pet.
Now you see the only other living person on this island.
He is walking toward you.
Suddenly you recognize who He is! He is Jesus Christ.
He walks with strong, swift strides toward you.
He is opening His arms, throwing His head back, His hair
blowing in the wind.
His suntanned face breaks into a wide welcoming smile.
His greeting is strong.
"Peace I leave with you, My peace I give to you; not as the
world gives do I give to you. Let not your heart be troubled,
neither let it be afraid."
You respond to His appealing and attractive greeting.
You embrace as friends forever!
You have just made one of life's wisest trades:
His peace—for your anxiety.

## *Displaying the flag*

"For I am not ashamed of the gospel of Christ,
for it is the power of God to salvation for
everyone who believes." —ROMANS 1:16

**266**  I saw a little fellow in the grocery store, who proudly wore a Los Angeles Dodgers baseball cap. At the time, the Dodgers were on a miserable losing streak. I went up to the little fellow and said, "So you're a Dodger fan, right?"

He smiled back and said, "You bet! And they're going to win the pennant!"

It doesn't take much faith to wear the cap and publicly declare yourself a strong supporter of the winning team. But when they have one setback after another, then it is a beautiful demonstration of confidence to stand in the limelight and reaffirm your trust in them.

I've always admired a certain courage in the political activist who is the first to fly the flag and flash the bumper sticker of the candidate whose campaign is just being launched.

Can we begin to imagine what it meant for those first twelve apostles to publicly declare their love and loyalty for that young, unknown religious leader called Jesus of Nazareth? When Christ was betrayed, and marched off carrying His own cross to a public execution, the apostles were nowhere to be found.

It was not until after our Lord was raised from the dead that this itinerant band of apostles became inflamed with an all-consuming faith in the divine Person and mission of our Lord.

Can you find any person who offers more than Jesus does?

**To the lonely, He is a Friend; to the sinful, a Savior; to the dying, the promised Guide across the troubled waters; to the enslaved, the Power to be free again.**

Offer your life to Jesus Christ today. Volunteer your services to the campaign headquarters. Dare to be known as one of His friends. Display the flag of belief.

# Going out without looking in a mirror

". . . glorify God in your body and in your spirit, which are God's."—CORINTHIANS 6:20

What well-dressed person dares to step out into the public **267** limelight without checking himself in the mirror? Have you ever been in a position where you had to do that? I have. I blindly fingered my tie: "Is it adjusted correctly?" With that, I marched onto the center of the stage into the spotlight to deliver the lecture.

What do I really mean when I say, "Faith is going out without looking in a mirror"? To begin with I'm not condoning the crude, unclean lifestyle of socially rebellious persons. There are those anti-social reactionaries who dress to attract attention, "make a statement," or provoke an argument. The person who takes the attitude, "I don't care what people think," is surely not making a constructive Christian statement! Certainly he's headed for failure and trouble.

What does matter profoundly, however, is an awareness that my success and self-esteem are rooted in my positive attitude more than in my style of dress. My hope for social acceptance and personal success depends more on the moral and spiritual values my life style reflects than upon the "label" clothing I wear.

In the final analysis you must believe that you will be judged by character, more than clothing or connections. And that self-confidence will make you a very persuasive personality on the road to success.

**For when you walk by faith you develop profound moral integrity which is reflected in your face.**

I can go out today without checking the mirror if my heart is right, for I am following the lordship and leadership of Christ Jesus.

## FAITH IS . . .
## *Sustaining your self-esteem*

"Cast your burden on the LORD,/And He shall
sustain you;/He shall never permit the
righteous to be moved."—PSALM 55:22

**268**   Wouldn't it be wonderful if you were perfect! How do you
judge between the better and the best? How do you keep the
lesser human value from taking priority over the higher
human value?

Faith moves in to act as referee, blowing the whistle and
calling you to attention with the command: "You can do better
than that! Start over again and be great!"

When you drop the ball, lose the game, and head for the
locker room with humiliation, then faith becomes your
coach, who slaps you on the back, turns you around, and
barks out tough encouragement, "Come on, now. You can't
win them all! You're great—anyway! Don't be so hard on
yourself!"

Faith is the referee; faith is the coach, and faith has become
your best friend who goads you on when you want to take the
easy way.

Now you know why the walk of faith is so beautiful and
effective. It's a lifestyle that sustains your own self-respect.
You are learning to say yes to challenges that lift your dignity,
and no to negative involvements that degrade yourself and
others.

Today's affirmations:

I have become a more beautiful person because I have
chosen to live by faith. Through the positive attitude that my
faith gives me, I find it easier to make friends. I am not as
lonely as I used to be. Through my belief in a beautiful God, I
am opening up like a flower. Because of my positive self-esteem, I am attracted to good people and good people are attracted to me. As faith sustains my self-esteem, I become a
wonderful person.

Jesus Christ, I have to thank You for being at the heart of
my faith. Faith has become a friend with a face; it is the face
of my Lord, and I love You. Amen.

## *Broadcasting good news*

"Behold, I bring you good tidings of great joy
which will be to all people."—LUKE 2:10

The secret of happy living is to give yourself all the good **269**
news you can, as often as you can! Start the day by reporting
all of the positive events that have happened since you awoke.

Faith is broadcasting good news to yourself: *I am alive!* I
survived the night. I did not die in my sleep. I have been
given—free of charge—the gift of another day, fresh and clean.
It affords me wonderful and marvelous opportunities to think,
plan, execute, advance, build, love, and enjoy.

Tune your mental dial into radio station TGNT.

There's **G**ood **N**ews **T**oday!

Scan the papers for good news. Believe it or not, you might
have to begin on the sports page, the women's page, or the
entertainment section.

If you can't report good news, then make your own good
news. That's called "living" the gospel. For the word *gospel*
literally means "good news."

The good news you, as a Christian, can report is that God
lives!

- He came to this world in the person of Jesus to tell us that
  He loves us.
- He died on a cross to save us from our sins.
- He promises to live in our hearts through the Holy Spirit.
- He will do this by giving us ideas, dreams, and oppor-
  tunities.

> **Give yourself this good news—right now—"God has a
> plan for my life today!" I'm going to be open to won-
> derful things that are about to happen. I will be op-
> timistic, pleasant, cheerful, and hopeful today!**

## *Forming a partnership*

"Abide in Me, and I in you. As the branch
cannot bear fruit of itself . . . neither can you,
unless you abide in Me."—JOHN 15:4

**270**    What happens when we become Christians? We have
formed a holy partnership. You will now live a more productive life. In the final analysis God wants us to choose the path
of faith that will maximize our productivity.

Who has more faith— the person who is confident he can
make it all by himself or the person who shares the power, the
credit, the risks, and the rewards with a partner?

Both avenues require great faith.

### Life requires different styles for different miles.

On part of the road you may be challenged and tempted to
travel alone—challenged, because you can't find the help you
need; or tempted, because you enjoy and relish the freedom of
operating as an independent entrepreneur.

Forming a partnership will restrict your freedom—to some
degree. To trade off greater productivity for more privacy may
be tempting, but it's a bad deal!

There is an interesting story in the New Testament where
Jesus Christ noticed the solitary fig tree, resplendent in lux-
uriant leaves. There was no fruit—only leaves. And our Lord
cursed the tree.

What's the point of it all? Style without substance is shallow, show without service is sinful; freedom without fruitful-
ness is folly.

In a world where so many people are hungry there's no excuse for luxuriating in selfish solitude.

It gets down to this: "Can I accomplish a great deal more in
my lifetime if I am willing to limit my freedom, restrict my
privacy, swallow some pride, and take on a partner?" Yes, certainly, if the partner is my Lord Jesus Christ.

## *Linking up with winners*

> " 'If you abide in Me, and My words abide in
> you, you will ask what you desire, and it shall
> be done for you.' "—JOHN 15:7

Faith links up with winners. Doubt links up with losers. **271**
What trumpet do you respond to? What drum do you follow?

**Faith links up with a Winner—Jesus Christ.**

What is *your* relationship with Him? Do you link up with
Him in prayer? Through the Bible? Through His Holy Spirit,
who can give you high and holy thoughts?

Faith links up with other *winners*—positive people who
walk the walk of faith with you.

A family I know moved, in desperation, to California from
New Jersey because their sixteen-year-old daughter was being
influenced by the wrong kind of friends in school. No sooner
did they reach California than she found the same kind of
friends there. Why? Because she had such a negative self-image that she was attracted to losers. She felt successful according to their standards.

The family began attending our church, and we joyously
watched this young teen-ager accept Jesus Christ as her Savior. When that happened, her new Christian friends became
her closest friends. Most of them were diligent in school and
had high moral and spiritual standards. Now that she was in a
new circle and had a new faith, she found that the new linkage
changed everything!

I can't recommend anything stronger to you today than
this:

Link up with a good church.

Visit the churches in your community until you find a fellowship of believers that feeds your faith.

Join the only club that is committed to sharing the love of
Jesus Christ for the building up of human character.

# Aligning yourself with positive people

". . . that I may be encouraged together with
you by the mutual faith."—ROMANS 1:12

**272** Faith is fantastic! The positive fruits and by-products that
will spring up in our lives as we walk this walk of faith are too
numerous to count. Yet, let's examine just one of the assets of
this risky business called faith. When you make the decision
to become a believer, you put yourself in the company of brave
people, the possibility thinkers. That carries an immediate reward. Every time you make a new commitment, you meet
new friends. You have the joy of the company of people who
laugh, sing, pray, and are generally enthusiastic.

### Faith is aligning yourself with the up-and-comers.

The believer is drawn into the circle of eagles when the
doubter is siding with the lame-duck crowd. The insecure person who hesitates to make the plunge finds himself in the
company of shrinking violets and withering flowers. The price
he pays for his security is a creeping awareness that life is
passing him by.

Today reaffirm your commitment to be a believer! Don't
miss the chance at excitement in life.

There is a train pulling out of the station. On it I see people
who are laughing, excited, and enthusiastic. I'm going to jump
on board with them—now! I'm joining the crowd of positive
people who are going places and doing great things.

I choose to be a believer. I am parting company with the
losers. Thank You for leading the way, Jesus Christ. I am align-
ing myself with the up-and-comers. I feel an aliveness with
me now. Is this Your presence, Lord? This keen and energizing
vibrancy within me? Thank You, Lord!

FAITH IS . . .
## Combining contradictions creatively

"According to your faith, let it be to you."—
MATTHEW 9:29

Possibility thinkers who walk this walk of faith are success- **273**
ful because they have learned yet another principle:

**Contradictions that creatively clash often open a treasure box of undiscovered values.**

Designers, architects, musicians, and chefs sometimes combine contradictions creatively. They creatively use colors and materials that at first seem to clash to bring about amazing beauty. Chefs do this with sweet and sour sauce.

On our church grounds we have a statue of Jesus. The right hand is open, inviting, offering food to hungry sheep, making a statement of tenderness! The left hand and the strong, muscular forearm hold a staff: a statement of toughness. Tough and tender—contradictions? Yes, but combined creatively they are beautifully harmonious.

How often have we heard the questions asked about a couple: "What can those two have in common? What holds their relationship together?"

In many ways the personalities and lifestyles of a couple can seem to contradict each other. Yet their relationship combines the contradictions creatively and the combination works!

Take a look at a church and you will find a judge and an ex-convict, a sinner and a saint, rich and poor, working and worshiping together creatively.

Can God bring good out of evil? Can He combine tragedy and triumph and produce something inspiring? Of course, He can!

Finally, take a look at your own life. Everybody has some internalized contradictions. When we walk the walk of faith and give Christ lordship over our life, He is able to take these contradictions and combine them creatively.

# *Drinking from new wells*

"If anyone thirsts, let him come to Me and drink."—JOHN 7:37

**274** Jesus Christ promises in this Bible verse that, when you connect with Him and become an authentic Christian, your faith will never suffer from thirst.

**Your faith may falter and grow faint, but it shall never fail unless you refuse to replenish it with a refreshing drink from the Source, the Lord Jesus Christ.**

One Sunday morning I was in a strange city. I was spiritually thirsty. I waited expectantly for my own television program to come on the air. I knew I could relax, enjoy the music, see familiar faces, and join in worship. I expected a blessing. But when the program came on and I began listening, I became self-critical. I thought, *Schuller, you can do better than that!* When the program was over, I was disappointed.

Another religious television program with which I was unfamiliar came on. The style of worship was completely opposite to mine. Yet I found myself lifted to God in a spiritually satisfying experience. God used the voice of an unknown minister to meet my spiritual need.

Still another religious television program followed, and again the voice and the personality were most dissimilar to my own. Within a few moments, two Bible verses were quoted that gave me the upward thrust my faith needed that morning.

I prayed, "God, what are You trying to tell me?" I waited and listened. Within my being this truth came as a message from my heavenly Father: "Schuller, you will never be alone; you will never be thirsty, *if you are willing to drink from new wells.*"

Thank You, Father. I now know I have a faith that will never die.

# *Perceiving the worlds around you*

"The appearance . . . as it were, a wheel in the middle of a wheel."—EZEKIEL 1:16

It is important to be lifted by your faith to a level of self-reliance where you will be able to recognize, observe, and appreciate the varied worlds around you this very moment.

**275**

Today's Bible text tells that the prophet Ezekiel looked up and saw wheels within wheels. We need only to read the newspaper to be aware of wheels within wheels and worlds within our world: the sports world, the entertainment world, the business world, the women's world.

New York City points up the worlds within the world. There are people on the East Side of New York who never get to the West Side!

Do you know how many worlds are around you?

Do you dare to explore, to become an adventurer, to take a trip to a foreign country, or to even get into a taxi and check out your own neighborhood? It takes a lot of faith to choose to become perceptive!

> **Dare to step out of your own small world to see how the other side lives.**

At the same time begin a wonderful ministry of Christian charity, leaving behind a witness to another world—somebody cared enough to pay a visit!

That's what Jesus did when He left one world—heaven—and came to another—earth. Jesus knows a lot more heaven and earth than you or I. He specifically came to earth to tell us about the world called heaven. Someday you will want to go there, too. Have the faith to step into that world by affirming Christ today.

# Adapting yourself to the unfamiliar

"May the Lord make you increase and abound
in love to one another and to all."—1
THESSALONIANS 3:12

**276** It is a natural experience for everyone to suffer from an inferiority complex during certain times or circumstances of life. Our goal is to have an adequate supply of faith in ourselves and in our ability to meet any situation in life. Each of us may feel very secure in our own home or community, but when we suddenly are put into unfamiliar surroundings, we can easily become frightened.

Faith is adapting yourself to the unfamiliar, even when the cultural environment is dramatically different—clothes, language, skin color, food. Faith says you are adaptable!

It is remarkable to see how the Christian faith bridges cultural gaps. Long before international jet-setters arrived on the scene, missionaries crossed oceans to step ashore on strange continents. They had the faith to leap into an unfamiliar and sometimes hostile culture. Through the eyes of our Lord, they saw deeper than the skin. They looked upon every person as a precious, priceless immortal soul, redeemable by God.

If we ever become afraid and threatened by the unfamiliar, we can be sure we are facing an area of life where our faith is proving inadequate. It simply means this is an opportunity to grow!

Christ Jesus, thank You for helping me to see every person as a soul for whom You died on the cross. Give me the faith today to adapt myself to the unfamiliar, so that I can be Your hands and Your heart, loving them. Amen.

# Relating respectfully to "foreigners"

"One God and Father of all, who is above all,
and through all, and in you all."—EPHESIANS 4:6

Faith is relating respectfully to those whose skin is a different color, whose eyes are shaped differently, and whose language and dress are different. Faith respects all people, for God's family transcends race, language, and culture. In Christ there is no east or west.

How do you relate to "foreigners" with whom you make contact—such foreigners as a foreign idea; contrary ideology; or an unheard-of concept? Are you so set in your ways that you refuse to listen to peculiar ideas?

Faith believes you grow intellectually when you understand and respect someone else's position.

Possibility-thinking people are people who achieve enough emotional maturity to view objectively foreign

- persons
- ideas
- races
- foods
- dress
- music
- religion
- language

They are secure enough in their belief system to listen to a contrary presentation without becoming frightened or furious.

## It takes a lot of faith to relate.

Dear God, give me enough security in my faith to relate to all people without being disrespectful, unkind, or frightened by what may seem foreign. I thank You that through faith I have confidence to communicate Your love with those who don't share our faith. I thank You that I belong to Your family, where there are no boundaries and no foreigners. In You we are all one. By the way, Lord, I'm enjoying our relationship on this walk of faith. Thank You for planning it that way. Amen.

**277**

# *Discriminating against prejudices*

"[Love] does not rejoice in iniquity, but rejoices
in the truth!"—1 CORINTHIANS 13:6

**278**    Think of this: People who are prejudiced display a lack of
faith. Somehow they cannot believe that persons of another
faith, race, or ethnic group really are as good as they are. Prejudice, such as racism, provokes enormous hatred. And what is
hate? It is the fruit of fear. Angry people are persons who feel
threatened. And people who are insecure or easily threatened
are people who lack faith in themselves and others.

You are really walking the walk of faith, when you discriminate against prejudice. Discrimination can be a positive mental attitude when it focuses on the elimination of negatives
from life.

Learn to sort the good from the bad,
   the positives from the negatives,
      the enobling from the shameful,
         the excellent from the mediocre,
            the right from wrong!
   the beautiful from the ugly,
      the kind acts from the unfair,
         the Christ-like from the crude.

**Discriminate against prejudice. This is the most intel-
ligent choice, for prejudice ignores the pursuit of
truth.**

The person who walks the walk of faith will ultimately succeed, for he not only dares to face truth, he seeks truth.

God's promise is that faith will move mountains. So, as
faith discriminates, eliminates, and eradicates presumptuous
judgments of issues and individuals, it throws open the door
for illumination of new insights and new truths. In the process, growth occurs, and you are on the way to moving mountains.

# Disengaging yourself from destructive prejudices

"For there is no partiality with God."—ROMANS 2:11

Is any person really free from destructive prejudices? I don't **279** believe I am. I'm doing some real soul-searching as I write these words.

Prejudice is always destructive, for it blocks my capacity to understand another person's position. It keeps me imprisoned in a distortion of the truth.

Today, let us all honestly ask ourselves: Is there any active or latent racial prejudice in my life today? Am I guilty of religious prejudice? Am I prejudiced against those who are financially superior or inferior to me?

How can you be freed from the prison of prejudice? First of all, believe that God wants to build bridges—not throw up barriers! He is interested in creating a sense of family among us human beings on planet earth. A spirit of community must replace the spirit of conflict.

If I ask God to heal me of my prejudices, He will surely do it, "for there is no partiality with God." He does not see the differences that you and I see.

God does not see people as rich or poor. He does not see the color of our skin! He is not impressed with our academic credentials.

**At the feet of God, we are all the same—sinners saved by grace, potential saints in the making!**

God's saving grace alone can break the chains of prejudice that bind us.

Thank You, Father, that You are disengaging me now, releasing me this very moment, liberating me in this time of prayer from prejudices, known and unknown. Thank You, God. Amen.

## *Tearing down the walls*

"The rich and poor have this in common, the
LORD is the maker of them all."—PROVERBS
22:2

**280**   "All my life I was told I couldn't do it," the letter read. She
went on, "My father was never successful. My mother was
poor. We never had money for anything other than the basic
necessities of bread and food. Even then, we only had a meal
with meat probably once a week.

" 'You've just got to remember that we're poor. We can't do
it. The answer is no. You just have to learn to accept your
place in life.' These were the responses I heard each time I
wanted to do something different or new.

"When I wanted to go to college, again my folks said to me,
'We don't have the money. Where do you think you're going to
get the money?' Then, a scolding voice, 'Get out and work. It's
time to buy your own clothes. College is for rich kids.'

"I kind of felt like I was herded into a negative box that was
put inside a small backyard where the walls were so high I was
never allowed to dream my dreams.

"Then I started listening to the 'Hour of Power.' I heard the
minister talk about possibility thinking.

"I heard him say that every human being has the same
right—to dream great dreams! I heard the minister say that
nobody has a money problem. It is always an idea problem. I
heard that possibility thinking teaches that we can get out of
our own prison of self-imposed limitations.

"I felt free for the first time in my life! I realized that God
made me just as good as the rich kids.

"Dr. Schuller," the letter went on, "I want you to know that I
got the faith five years ago, and today I got my college degree!
I'm going to become a school teacher and inspire kids in poor
communities to dream big! They can do anything they want
to do!"

Possibility-thinking faith tears down the walls! Impossibility thinking builds the walls.

## Inquiring into scientific reality

"For You will light my lamp;/The LORD my
God will enlighten my darkness."—PSALM
18:28

**281**

Of all of the prejudices that Christians need to attack, none
is more important than the prejudice against scientific inquiry. On the other hand, scientific inquiry also requires discrimination against prejudice.

Unquestionably there are scientists who prejudge religious
truth negatively and approach their scientific research with a
presumption that there is no spiritual reality. In the process
they flaunt truth in the name of brilliant analysis. What a
contradiction!

It is to the credit of Christianity that we have great universities. Scientific inquiry has found tremendous support from
the Christian religion. Our compassion for suffering souls has
motivated Christians to support research into the cures for
many major diseases.

Great universities like Princeton, Harvard, Yale, Stanford,
and the University of Southern California—to name a few—
are universities that were started by Christians committed to
the pursuit of truth.

Science and religion should not be viewed in an adversarial
relationship.

> **Science and religion are Siamese twins; opposite sides
> of the same coin—the coin of truth.**

True religion is a pursuit of truth, for real truth liberates. So
positive religion educates, and education sets persons free
from ignorance, superstition, and prejudice.

It takes strong faith to pursue knowledge! Insecure people
fear free inquiry.

People of faith never fear truth! No wonder so many brilliant scientists are also positive believers.

## Liberating people

"If you abide in My word, you are My disciples indeed. And you shall know the truth, and the truth shall make you free."—JOHN 8:31

**282**  Jesus was not interested in slaves, but in servants. He did not attempt to build an empire so that He could become master over slaves. Rather, His idea was to become an inspiring Lord who can motivate people to develop their possibilities. In the process we become helpful servants, not oppressed slaves.

If religion enslaves people, one can challenge the morality of that faith! One of the legitimate criticisms that is leveled against a great deal of institutional religion in all of the major faiths—Christianity, Judaism, Islam, Hinduism, Buddhism— is that it indoctrinates. Religion, under the management of insecure leaders or insecure theological positions, can indoctrinate people until they are no longer capable of hearing or understanding any viewpoint other than what was crammed into their minds.

> **True Christianity seeks not to indoctrinate, but to educate. For when we indoctrinate, we enslave; but when we educate, we liberate.**

In all of our enthusiasm, let us be guided by this noble ethic:

> **The dignity of every person is a nonnegotiable value.**

Any time we fail to use our efforts to liberate people, we violate their right to the kind of dignity that only comes through freedom.

What, after all, is the purpose of truth, but to set us free? That was the teaching of the Founder of our faith, Jesus Christ.

Help me, O God, my Father, so to live that I shall not oppress people, but liberate them. Amen.

## *Gazing into the eyes of a stranger*

"By this all will know that you are My
disciples, if you have love for one another."—
JOHN 13:35

Love starts with a look. Faith uses the power of a gaze to **283**
establish creative communication and redemptive relationships.

**Communication is looking into somebody's eyes with
the goal of establishing a friendship.**

I remember when I visited the primitive people of the high-
lands of New Guinea. Our tiny plane landed on a small clear-
ing in the jungle, where we were transported first by Jeep and
then on foot through the tall tropical forest. My missionary
guide said to me, "You cannot see them but they are all
around us. They are watching us. Just keep smiling! Keep your
hands stretched out with your palms open so they will know
you can be trusted. They will look at your eyes! And they can
tell if you are afraid."

Suddenly, the woods opened and out leaped a naked,
painted "savage." His eyes searched mine suspiciously. But I
returned the gaze confidently, smiling all the while, praying
hard. Then with a wave of his spear, he summoned the others
to greet me. Our communication was almost entirely limited
to looks, so I sincerely prayed that God's love would shine
through my eyes.

Faith is gazing at a stranger with the love of Christ shining
through your smile.

What jungle do you need to enter today?

Hold your head high and dare to look everyone in the eye,
all the while sparkling with the reflection of Christ's love
within you.

# Countering the negative with a positive

"Love suffers long and is kind."—1
CORINTHIANS 13:4

**284**   You? A negative reactionary? Me, too? Yes, by nature every human being is a negative reactionary.

The natural response to a negative situation is a negative reaction.

When someone is angry at us, we get angry at him.

When someone insults us, we insult him back.

When a threat comes our way, we are defensive.

When we are afraid, we become hateful.

This human tendency to negative reaction is infectious throughout the human family.

What we are witnessing in society today—nationally and internationally—is a negative chain reaction! So our society has become violence prone!

We all worry about a nuclear war, the chain reaction, and the nuclear fallout. But we should also worry about a danger that is present now! It is the *negative* chain reaction of *negative* thinking and the *negative* emotional fallout that is bombarding the human family. I call this widespread infection of negativity *sin!*

In the Christian religion there is a doctrine that teaches that every person is conceived and born in sin. Does this mean that every newborn baby is "sinful?" If by *sin* we mean "something negative or evil *that we do,*" the answer must be no. A newborn baby is innocent of any wrong*doing.* But if by *sin* we mean "a negative condition," or something that I *am* then the answer is "yes." For every child is born nontrusting, *a negative reactionary in the making.*

But when we are born again, we are converted from doubt to faith! Jesus turns us from negative reactionaries to positive reactionaries!

**Through the love of Christ within us, we are able to react to negative stimuli with positive responses.**

## Bridging the gap

"And you shall be called the Repairer of the
Breach, the Restorer of Streets to Dwell In."—
ISAIAH 58:12

People who live by faith bridge the gaps. They trust others **285**
enough to believe that reconciliation can take place between
two alienated persons. People with faith are by their very nature looking for the best outcome. Therefore, they see redemption, not condemnation, as the positive solution to be
pursued.

No wonder the early believers were called "Repairer of the
Breach" and "Restorer of Streets to Dwell In."

On the morning that I was ordained to the Christian ministry, I read my Bible and I claimed today's text as the theme for
my ministry. I made a commitment never to make public critical, judgmental statements about other Christians or their
ministries. This can only create chasms, generate divisions,
nurture conflict, and invite suspicion among good people.

> **The person who is really living by faith does not crit-
> icize or condemn. Instead, he constructs a bridge of
> understanding and an avenue where interchange of
> opinions can be pursued.**

Remember, God has promised you prosperity if you walk
the walk of faith! Here, then, is one of the real blessings: You
feel good and your self-esteem is nourished when you devote
your energies to building bridges between peoples in the
world.

The next time you see a bridge, think of what it symbolizes!
Two divided areas are joined by one bridge! You can be a bridge
between conflicting persons. You can be the reconciling influence between groups that suspect each other and distrust each
other.

You can become the solution! God will bless you for believing that!

## *Respecting persons after you know them*

"Honor all people. Love the brotherhood. Fear
God. Honor the king."—1 PETER 2:17

**286**  Wow! Talk about a challenge. Is it possible to know and
respect *all* people? That would take a mountain of faith!

Is it possible to honor crude and cruel persons who destroy
life and love? Yes. We do not condone their behavior, but we
recognize that they are still souls for whom Christ died on the
cross. And we can still pause to pray, "God have mercy on
their souls."

On a far more practical level, the challenge you and I have is
to respect the people with whom we live, work, and closely
relate. Can we respect them after we've seen them at their
worst? Can we honor them as beautiful human beings even
after their weaknesses have been grossly exposed? The answer
must be a resounding YES.

How can our faith perform this miracle? Quite simply. Our
faith reminds us that we too are imperfect human beings.

**Our faith reminds us that God loves us even though
He knows us better than anybody else! And if God
loves in spite of what we are, He will give us the grace
to pass that charitable spirit along!**

I thank You today, O God my Father, for honoring me even
after I have disappointed You, for treating me like a noble person even after I have been guilty of disgraceful behavior in
Your sight. Help me now to treat my fellow human beings
with no less respect than You have shown me.

Thank You, Father, for this faith. It's working miracles.
Amen.

# Hugging in-laws

". . . love one another fervently with a pure
heart."—1 PETER 1:22

The anthropologists have long noted that human beings **287**
tend to gravitate to their own kind.

Human societies tend to be suspicious of ethnic groups that
are racially, religiously, or culturally different.

**It takes a great deal of faith to build a level of trust and
affection with persons who have been outsiders but
who suddenly move into your social circle.**

An in-law can be one who has become a part of your family
through marriage. You did not choose the person to be included in your family reunions, but you have no choice.

But an in-law can be anyone who enters, without invitation, your circle of relationships.

An in-law may be someone who works in the same company as you; or it may be another member of your club,
church, or community. You cannot avoid some of these people—like them or not. What do you do?

There will always be the uninvited people who step inside
your circle. To resent or to resist them will set off a cycle of
negative vibrations that inevitably will be counter-productive
to your welfare.

By contrast, you can learn something from them. If you embrace an in-law with a positive attitude, you will see and appreciate his value as a special person God has created.

In the process, in-laws become beautiful friends, enriching
your life. You will be blessed because you are walking the
walk of faith.

## *Forgiving yourself and others*

"Though I have all faith, so I could remove mountains, but have not love, I am nothing."—
1 CORINTHIANS 13:2

**288**   It's exciting in our walk of faith to see how God is able to do fantastic things through imperfect people when they receive forgiveness from God. Today let's take another step of faith—that step of forgiving ourselves. For many people who call themselves believers find it difficult to forgive *themselves* for their sins and shortcomings. The act of forgiveness is an affirmation of faith that your sins are forgiven! Your mistakes are being handled by the grace of God.

When you forgive yourself, you declare that you believe that you are still a wonderful and a worthwhile person.

When you forgive yourself, you tell the world—beginning with the God who made you—that you have not lost faith in your ability to make a distinctive contribution by sharing beauty and love with those around you.

The act of forgiveness is also an affirmation that we must forgive others. When you forgive someone who has offended you, you declare that you believe that there is so much good in them that you must forgive them, even as you desire more than anything else that God forgive you. In the process of forgiving you exercise faith and love!

**Forgiveness is the sublime act of faith. Unless I forgive I do not love.**

Affirmations: Today I shall forgive myself and in the process love what God loves . . . myself.

Today I shall forgive someone who has offended me, believing that faith can move this mountain.

I am walking the walk of faith today, for I am experiencing love.

*FAITH IS . . .*
## *Questioning respectfully*

"Be of the same mind toward one another. Do not set your mind on high things, but associate with the humble. Do not be wise in your own opinion."—ROMANS 12:16

**289**

This Bible verse gives a clue to the secret of dynamic success in business, religion, and interpersonal relationships: learning to question respectfully. Switch from the accusatory approach to the inquisitive approach.

You demonstrate great respect toward your colleague, friend, colaborer, or family when you ask questions rather than level charges.

Because of training, conditioning, and human nature, most people impulsively react negatively when they spot an activity that appears to be offensive. They immediately pass judgment, express disagreement, and thereby promptly provoke an argument.

Faith does not react in such an irresponsible and unstudied way.

**Rather, faith motivates us to use the interrogative approach!**

We need to ask questions—questions that do not intimidate, but sincerely try to understand: "Am I understanding you correctly?" "Can you help me understand the reason you have done this?"

Questioning respectfully is faith in action.

Learn the art of positive communication.

Learn to develop the skill of asking questions that are success oriented—questions that will buy time, questions that will disarm an adversary, questions that will protect you from polarization.

Father, forgive me for passing judgment irresponsibly when I should have been questioning wisely, for accusing unjustly when I should have been inquiring sincerely. Forgive me for preaching sermons when I should have been listening. Amen.

*FAITH IS . . .*
## *Anticipating the best*

"For Your lovingkindness is before my eyes."—
PSALM 26:3

**290** My wife and I recently attended a religious conference in Europe. After checking into a London hotel, we discovered that one of our bags was missing. Expecting the worst, I telephoned the unclaimed baggage office. A pleasant voice answered, "Lost and Found. May I help you?"

The enthusiasm of the sincere offer to help caught me off guard. I was shocked by the helpful spirit. After I gave him the number and description of the missing bag, he asked me, "Do you live in Los Angeles?" I affirmed that I live near there.

"Oh, I go to California quite often. It's such a beautiful place," he answered.

I said, "Then you must have seen the Crystal Cathedral."

He said, "Of course! It's beautiful!"

His pleasant manners and happy conversation were unexpected blessings—and scoldings at the same time. I suddenly felt tremendous guilt for my subtle negative attitude. I had anticipated the worst when I should have believed that the best would happen.

**Faith calls us to believe in the best. If you believe the best will happen and it doesn't, you lose nothing! For you have the joy of anticipating something wonderful! The happiness that comes through positive anticipation pays out dividends instantaneously. Each smile, every happy heartbeat, every elegant thought is an immediate reward.**

Lord, forgive me for being negative. Pardon me, Father, for not believing that I will be helped properly, cheerfully, and efficiently. Help me to have enough faith to believe that the best will happen, for You have only good planned for us. Thank You, Father. Amen.

## *Loving the unlovable*

"Beloved, let us love one another, for love is of
God; and everyone who loves is born of God
and knows God. He who does not love does not
know God, for God is love."—1 JOHN 4:7–8

**291**

What do you do when your roommate or coworker is un-
likable, and unlovable? Then remember who you are!

You are a person of faith! Believe that it is possible to see
some good in the most unlovable person. Practice possibility
thinking and believe that it's possible that the unsolicited
companion may turn out to be a friend in need.

Remember also that the walk of faith is meant to be a
growth experience. You are not an only child. You are part of a
family. God does not intend to treat you like a solitary child.
He intends to put you in positions where you experience
working and living with uncomfortable personalities.

What can you learn in these awkward circumstances? Patience? Yes. The ability to be charming? Perhaps. There is
something else to learn.

**There is something beautiful in every person. If you
can't see it or find it or feel it then you have a problem.**

For somehow you are lacking the sensitivity or skill to
motivate, inspire, or mold him into the kind of person in
whom some goodness glows.

The walk of faith does not permit you to be crude, rude, and
abusive to the unlovely person. You cannot stoop to that lower
level. Instead be calm and demonstrate an enormous amount
of faith that things will work out somehow.

Make me into the kind of a person who loves the unlovable,
O God. And when my patience reaches an end, then I'll get
out of your way. For it is *not impossible* for You to love the
unlovable person. Love them through me if you want to. Take
over and do the job that's too big for me. Thank You, Father.
Amen.

## *Pleasing God*

"Without faith it is impossible to please
Him. . . ."—HEBREWS 11:6

**292**    In this text we see that faith ultimately is a nonnegotiable
human value. By that I mean

> **It is impossible to have satisfying interpersonal rela-
> tionships with others or with God without faith.**

God is not pleased until we walk the walk of faith. If I give
Him all the money I have but do not trust Him, He remains
displeased.

It's the same way in all of our personal relationships. If I
give attractive gifts of immense value to my wife but do not
trust her, our marriage will never last. Relationships can never
grow and thrive without mutual trust. Oftentimes I meet sincere but negative Christians who are pious and proud of pleasing God, but who fail to aid in constructive contributions
such as:

- launching positive helpful programs in their church or
  community.
- promoting projects to build a better society.
- joining in ventures proven to support the great causes that
  could build a better and more beautiful world.

The bottom line of pleasing God is right here:

> **No holiness of life, no extreme generosity of giving of
> oneself and substance, can compensate for the failure
> to demonstrate great faith in God's promises and
> power. When God calls, respond in faith!**

Today there is something God wants you to do. Respond in
faith; for without faith, you will never please Him, nor will
you be happy with yourself. Life leads to pleasure and happiness for God and for His people who trust Him enough to
respond in faith to His call.

# *Centering yourself in God's love*

"All things are possible for You. Take this cup
away from Me; nevertheless, not what I will,
but what you will."—MARK 14:36

The whole purpose behind the walk of faith is that through **293**
personal commitment and self-development, you are able to
fulfill the plan that God has for your life! Therefore, the central aspect of your walk of faith must be to center your life on
the will of God. Remember, God's will for your life is always
born and bathed in divine Love!

To walk the walk of faith is to be the love of God in human
form and function.

> **You are truly successful when you are a healthy chan-
> nel through whom God's living love can flow like
> fresh water to thirsty souls.**

How can you keep from being distracted from this one goal?

Obviously, persons who have an objective for personal
achievement are already spared from distraction. The athlete
in training, the scholar pursuing an academic degree, the professional climbing up the ladder, all have their eye on a goal
that consumes their complete dedication and commitment.

As you walk the walk of faith, picture today in your mind a
bull's-eye target—the kind of target used for dart games or
archery contests. Now let the center dot of the target be the
focus of your whole panorama of life—the love of God. Focus
your faith on this target.

That's what Jesus Christ did in the Garden of Gethsemane.
He easily could have been distracted from paying the price of
the cross. Like Jesus, you need to keep your eye on the number one purpose of life—to be the love of God to a hurting
world.

O God, I center my faith on Your love today. I concentrate
on the faith and face of Christ. I ask You to give me His face;
and may it turn me into a beautiful human being, enabling me
to accomplish great things for You. Amen.

## *Finding a need and filling it*

"Though I bestow all my goods to feed the poor
. . . but have not love, it profits me nothing."—
1 CORINTHIANS 13:3

**294**     We begin to understand now, why the promise that God
attaches to faith is the promise of success.

### Faith is love in action.

Love is finding a need and filling it;
I believe I can help someone in need.
Love is finding a hurt and healing it;
I believe I can comfort someone in pain.
Love is finding a problem and solving it;
I think I can come up with solutions.
Love is feeling someone's grief and consoling them;
I believe I can soothe the troubled mind.
Love is seeing the chasm and bridging it;
I believe I can be a reconciling, unifying spirit!

### Real love is my deciding to make your problem, my problem.

In that definition of love, I do not give help to people in
order to exploit them. I love them simply because when
someone hurts, I hurt. When love is nonmanipulative, non-
judgmental, nonself-serving, then it's real love.

Have you noticed? That kind of love is nothing less than
faith in action!

It takes a lot of faith to love. The fear of having your love
rejected, the anxiety of "getting involved," the worry about
not being appreciated, are only a few of the negative thoughts
that keep people from loving people. Did you notice? All of
the above excuses by the noncaring persons really are reflections of a lack of faith!

Insecure people dare not care! They feel too empty of love to
give it and too unworthy to accept it. So they become truly
incapable of giving or receiving love until they develop a
powerful inner faith.

## Channeling Christ's love

"I am the vine, you are the branches. He who abides in Me, and I in him, bears much fruit; for without Me you can do nothing."—JOHN 15:5

Faith allows you to open up and be yourself! It is connecting yourself, with spiritual integrity, in a relationship with Jesus Christ. When that happens you can work wonders in helping other people. Happiness, self-esteem, and self-worth will be natural byproducts!

What is a Christian anyway? A Christian is a mind through which Christ thinks, a heart through which Christ loves, an eye through which Christ looks, a face through which Christ smiles and encourages people, a hand through which Christ touches, and a voice through which Christ offers hope. Can I be a Christian?

**You can do it if you are willing to be a conduit.**

Recently a friend shared with me, "Your possibility thinking really helps me. I was having real problems with my son. One day I was out in my garden. When I looked at the water pipe, I thought to myself, *Christ wants me to be a conduit. He wants to flow through me. I simply have to let Him do it.*

"Then," she said, "the phrase hit me: '*I can do it* if I will be a *con-du-it.*'"

That's what a branch is to a tree—a conduit for the sap to flow upward to bear fruit.

That's what an electrical wire is—a conduit for energy to flow from the source to the place of need. That's what you and I are in this life—conduits for Christ carrying love. Through us, Christ can turn on lights in dark minds!

**295**

## Touching someone you don't know

> " 'Which of these . . . was neighbor to him who
> fell among the thieves?' . . . 'He who showed
> mercy on him.' Then Jesus said . . . 'Go and do
> likewise.' "—LUKE 10:36–37

**296** Today's Bible text is from the story of the Good Samaritan. A man was attacked by thieves, was wounded and left half dead. A priest and a Levite saw him and passed by. A Samaritan had compassion on him, bandaged his wounds, and helped him. Jesus asked his disciples, "Which of these . . . was neighbor to him who fell among the thieves?" They answered, "He who showed mercy on him." Then Jesus said, "Go and do likewise."

Here's where the walk of faith becomes exciting! Living out Christian love is intensely personal and practical as we reach out and touch someone. It's always risky to touch the life of a stranger. It takes courage to risk "getting involved!"

**It takes faith to touch somebody you don't know.**

In the story of the Good Samaritan, our Lord's challenge was directed not only toward physical poverty, but also toward the emotional starvation that destroys human lives today in all societies of the world.

What hunger for love, acceptance, and understanding exists in the hearts of people around you today?

There is tremendous healing power in a touch. A psychiatrist told me confidentially, "About all I can do for many of my patients is to give them a look, a word, and a touch. It's amazing how the *touching* becomes such a healing!"

In a world where many people hurt, there is no excuse for our not touching with healing love. If we don't have the courage to touch them, who will?

Our first motive should be a desire to get involved! When God sent Jesus Christ into this world, to His cross, He reached down and touched us at our worst to save and to heal us! We should be willing to do no less than Christ has done for us.

## FAITH IS . . .
# *Bailing out a friend*

"But there is a friend who sticks closer than a brother."—PROVERBS 18:24

There are very successful bail bond businesses which bail **297** total strangers out of jail. By contrast, many people find it amazingly difficult to lend money to a friend.

My own father advised me, rightly or wrongly, "Loan money to an acquaintance, but never to a dear friend. If he is a friend, *give* him the money!

"When you loan a friend money, you expect him to pay you back. If he can't, your friendship will be strained. You'll not only lose the money, but a friend as well."

**For Christ, "bailing out a friend" meant dying for you and me on the cross.**

In ways that God understands better than any of us, Jesus atoned for our sins. He died upon the cross of Calvary to save us from all of our sins and guilts. Can you imagine what faith that took? He ran the risk of giving everything He had—including His life—to save His friends, who might not appreciate it!

Faith is "bailing out a friend." It is defending your friends behind their backs when they are being criticized, only to find out later they were probably guilty! Yes, it is risky. It takes faith to bail out a friend!

However, if you make a mistake, you're making it on the side of faith! If you sin, let it be on the side of love. If you err, let it be on the side of mercy. And that's always the wisest decision for one who is trying to live the life of Christ today!

# Soliciting help for a great cause

"... comfort the fainthearted, uphold the weak,
be patient with all."—1 THESSALONIANS 5:14

**298** Don't you marvel at the person who has the courage to go out and ring doorbells, sell tickets to a charity, or ask for volunteers?

What if someone asks you today to volunteer to solicit help for a great cause or to give witness to your faith? Is your faith ready to face these tests? Or would you rather cop out and offer a contribution in money or the excuse, "I really don't have the talent to testify to people about what the Lord has done."

Welcome every challenge that appears to be something impossible for you to perform. If every vital Christian was willing to be a solicitor in positive, enthusiastic, and energetic terms for Jesus Christ, we could see this world being converted to a society dominated by the love of God in short order.

**God calls us to be responsive to His calling. It's God's responsibility to enable us to be effective.**

The next time the church or community organization asks for volunteers, speak up! Give it a try. Believe that you can be effective!

I'm asking you today to be a solicitor for a great cause. The cause? The Christian religion! Plan to invite someone to attend church with you this coming Sunday. Plan to invite others to participate with you in exposure to the sources and forces of positive good that are available. You can be somebody's answer to prayer. You can be the saving influence in turning a life around! Simply be willing to solicit in the name of Christ and lead some soul to the faith that has saved you.

# *Priming the pump*

> "Whoever drinks of the water that I shall give
> him will never thirst. But . . . will become in
> him a fountain of water springing up into
> everlasting life."—JOHN 4:14

At a remote road stop in the desert stood a deserted gasoline **299**
station. Alongside was a well with an old-fashioned pump.

A traveler, dying of thirst, stumbled into the outpost. He ran
to the well, and there he saw a cup filled with water! But under the cup was a note.

> Dear Traveler:
> There's loads of water deep down in this well. Use this cup to
> prime the pump. Then drink all you want from the bottom of the
> well. When you've had all you want, fill the cup again for the next
> person who comes thirsting down the road.
> Whatever you do, *don't drink from this cup* or there'll be no water
> to prime the pump—ever again.

The thirsty traveler read the note and looked at the cup of
water. Unable to heed the warning, he brought the cup to his
lips. Then he hesitated for a moment, and, in a sublime act of
faith, followed the instructions.

He poured the water down the dry pump, worked the handle as fast as he could, and suddenly out of the mouth of the
pump poured forth cold water from the depths.

Delighted, he drank. When he'd had all he could enjoy, he
filled the cup and left it on the well with the note.

> **You prime the pump when you spend your last ounce
> of energy on the hope that your energy will be re-
> newed.**

Invest seed money. Call it venture capital. Because someone, somewhere helped you get started, pray that your success
will help someone else down the road of faith.

With that kind of faith, and that kind of attitude, you'll
never run dry!

# Filling someone else's cup

"For I was hungry and you gave Me food; I was
thirsty and you gave Me drink. . . . inasmuch as
you did it to one of the least of these . . . you
did it to Me."—MATTHEW 25:35,40

**300** What will keep you going and growing?

What can protect you from the perils of success?

What force can keep motivating you all the days of your
life?

Where can you tap into a power source that will sustain and
feed an unending compulsion to creativity and productivity?

I know of only one answer.

Focus on human need rather than on selfish pleasures.

Look at lost souls rather than on selfish comfort.

When the farmer sees hungry people devouring with relish
the fruit of his labor, he knows that unless he gets back to
work to produce a new crop, the next year there will be hungry people and starving children. That is his motivation for
continued productivity!

"Why don't you retire?" I said to my financially secure
farmer brother. "People still have to eat!" he answered. He is
still at it.

Faith is filling someone else's cup. Self-serving and self-
seeking is ultimately self-defeating. That's a fundamental
principle of life.

Commitment to the service of others is the satisfying life-
style. It is the only pathway to spiritual prosperity.

**The walk of faith leaves you no choice but to focus on
filling someone else's cup. In the process you are
spared from the haunting hollowness of life that only
God can satisfy.**

O God, as long as I live help me to look for someone who is
hungry for encouragement. Help me to fill that cup! Amen.

# Casting your bread upon the waters

"Cast your bread upon the waters,/For you will find it after many days."—ECCLESIASTES 11:1–2

Possibility thinkers are people who look for the impossible! **301** That's the age-old principle we deal with today.

It's this paradox:

> **It's impossible to give anything away. It always comes back to you.**

- Give love and love will return.
- Show affection and people will be inclined to respond in a kind way.
- Be cold and frigid and people will give you a chilly reception.

When he drops an offering in the collection plate at church, the impossibility thinker says, "There it goes. I'll never see it again." Wrong! The money comes back to you faster than you'd ever imagine, from sources least expected. I'm speaking from the vantage point of practicing this principle for over forty years. It has not failed me yet!

It's impossible to throw bread on the waters—it does return. Try standing at the ocean's edge and throwing something in. The retreating wave will carry it out to sea, but the next wave will move it back until it's deposited again on the shore.

Naturally, it takes courage to make that first move. But, after all, what are your choices? Possibility thinkers are not controlled by fear, but by faith!

Affirmation: Today I shall make the commitment to walk the walk of faith because I'm going to throw some bread on the waters. "There it goes! It's going to be fun seeing how God gives back what I try to give away."

## *Lighting one candle*

"You are the light of the world. . . . let your
light so shine before men, that they may see
your good works and glorify your Father in
heaven."—MATTHEW 5:14, 16

**302** "Better to light a candle, than curse the darkness" was a
favorite quotation of Eleanor Roosevelt's.

You can't save the whole starving world from famine, but
you *can* save one child's life by feeding him.

You can't reverse immoral trends that threaten to take society down a cesspool of spiritual self-destruction, but you *can*
lead one person to God.

**You can choose today to be part of the solution, not
part of the problem.**

You can choose to be part of the uplifting force, rather than
contributing to the downward movement.

You can choose to be a dreamer, rather than a despairer.
Dreamers of great dreams create the real uplifting movements
in society and in the world. More often than not their dreams
materialize! But even when their dreams do not reach frui-
tion, they make a contribution in their day. They lift people
above despair and bring laughter, love, and joy to human lives.
And because of their dream, they are creative, constructive,
and helpful human beings.

Affirmation:

I will light a candle today rather than curse the darkness.

I will feed a child today.

I will lead someone to God today.

I will give someone the gift of hope today.

Dear Lord, I am deciding today to be part of the solution,
not part of the problem. I will light one candle. I will be Your
light in my home, at work, and in Your world. Keep shining
through me. Amen.

## *Applauding the positive projects*

"Do not withhold good from those to whom it
is due,/When it is in the power of your hand to
do so."—PROVERBS 3:27

- Have you wondered what good you can do with your life?
- Do you sometimes feel that you really aren't doing any-
thing significant?
- Are you tempted to look at others with their accomplish-
ments and rate yourself as not too effective?
- Do you ever think, *I'm just a little person?*

Now hear this:

**303**

**You become as great as the projects you support.**

The little people are the negative-thinking critics of positive-thinking persons who try to do something great. You lift
yourself or lower yourself, depending upon which side you
take.

Remember that you are walking the walk of faith!

Applaud positive people who try to accomplish positive
projects. Encourage them. Speak well of them. Defend them
behind their backs. They need all the help they can get!
They'll never be able to succeed without the support of a lot of
good people.

Vote for the brave ones! Share in their victories! Participate
in the joys of their success!

You can be sure you'll never enjoy the enthusiasm that
comes through success until you connect yourself with dynamic causes.

Affirmation: Today I will applaud the people who are attempting the impossible and who need my encouragement
and support.

When you come to the end of your life, you'll know that
you participated as a partner in a good work. You'll be as big as
the person or cause you support!

*FAITH IS . . .*

## Adjusting your attitude toward the community

"Do not forget to entertain strangers, for by so doing some have unwittingly entertained angels."—HEBREWS 13:2

**304** You are ready now to see how this mountain-moving faith inspires you to "entertain strangers," who might be angels in disguise.

Your faith is challenged as you adjust your attitudes toward the community. As you support positive projects, you will become a part of the creative community of people who work with you and for you. How do you criticize those who fail to perform up to your expectations of them?

(1) Praise and thank them for all the good they have already done.

(2) Then ask questions. Formulate respectful questions that will reveal why they have done what they have done, and why they have failed to do what you had expected them to do.

(3) Give them the opportunity to explain their position without losing their self-esteem. "I'm sure you had a good reason. Would you mind explaining it to me?"

You will probably discover that in the pursuit of their assignment they have uncovered problems or opportunities that you are unaware of.

Where do you need to do some adjusting today?

As a parent, do you need to adjust your attitude toward your children today?

As a child, do you need to adjust your attitude toward your parents today?

As mates, do you need to adjust your attitude toward your husband or wife?

They are angels God has sent your way.

Faith is adjusting your attitude toward your community.

**Faith believes you are entertaining angels oftentimes posing as strangers.**

# *Winning friends and influencing people*

"A friend loves at all times."—PROVERBS 17:17

You are really blossoming! The walk of faith is transforming **305** you. You are winning friends and influencing people! That means that you can be a successful evangelist, missionary, or communicator. You're succeeding in your social life because Christ has turned you into a person who cares about others. We succeed when we find a hurt and heal it. And everybody who is hurting is searching for someone who is able to help and who really cares.

You can be *the* person in their life!

T—the
 H—hearing
  E—ear

You can be **The Hearing Ear!**

Where can hurting people go to find a listening ear? Is this one of the reasons why local bars are so popular? Is the bartender the only one who has a listening ear?

### Anybody can be a somebody to someone!

Christ is calling you to live His life through you today. Are you willing to become a listening ear, a bearer of others' burdens? With your silence and assurance, you can encourage others to *bare* their souls to you. Then you can *bear* their burdens with them!

You begin the process of becoming a creative communicator with a look—your eyes meet their eyes; a word—you respond with a kind hello; a touch—your hand touches their shoulder.

You are on your way.

Faith is winning friends and influencing people—"I will be an effective channel for Jesus Christ." God bless you.

# Socializing with a purpose

"Here am I! Send me."—ISAIAH 6:8

**306**  It takes a lot of courage for many people to socialize in circles that they consider above their own class. But you have worked on releasing yourself from your prejudices. You have learned to adjust your attitude to strangers. The walk of faith has given you the self-assurance to win friends. Now you are ready for the new adventures you can experience if you feel free and self-assured in any social circle.

You can do it!

Here's the secret. It starts in a prayer of faith which I use often. It has never failed me.

> **Lord, show me the person to whom You want to speak through my life today.**

Begin each day with that prayer.

Be open and sensitive to every opportunity to communicate with another person. It may be the salesperson in the store, a solicitor at the door or on the telephone, or a hostess at a social event.

Move through society with a mission. Socialize—with a high and holy purpose.

Every day there is some person to whom God wants to speak through your life.

Remember, it's God's responsibility to do the talking; you simply have to be available. He may want you to silently respond with a kind look, or to listen with a caring ear. He only needs an honest love that you will emit and transmit from your soul!

Live with this prayer.

Try it every day for thirty days. That's faith in action.

# Mending the broken fences

"How often shall my brother sin against me,
and I forgive him. . . . Jesus said to him, . . . "up
to seventy times seven."—MATTHEW 18:21-22

I was born and grew up on an Iowa farm. What did we do **307**
when we were not planting seeds or harvesting the crops? We
were mending fences constantly!

As you know, the carefully surveyed borders on the Iowa
farmlands are always marked by fences to keep cattle confined to each farmer's property. Broken fences are seriously
viewed and promptly mended, for broken fences soon rupture
relationships between good neighbors. Therefore the wise
farmer accepts the fact that fence mending is an important
part of farming.

Faith *expects* that fences will need to be mended! It assumes that relationships will be strained, perhaps ruptured. It
doesn't discard the friendship because of a deep disagreement.
That is simply a fence that needs to be mended.

You don't sell a farm because the fences keep breaking
down. You don't sell a car because the tires keep wearing out.
You don't discard a marriage because you keep having dis-
agreements. You don't throw out clothes when they're dirty.

Yesterday, an architect friend of mine said to me, "We've
been married thirty-six years. My wife and I cook together, eat
together, play tennis together, make love together, and disagree together." How his eyes twinkled!

**Mending broken fences—repairing broken relation-
ships—is God's specialty.**

How often He comes back to us to forgive us. When the
disciples asked Jesus, "How often shall my brother sin against
me, and I forgive him . . . seven times?" (Matt. 18:21). Jesus
answered, "I do not say to you, up to seven times, but up to
seventy times seven." (Matt. 18:22). That's how faith works—
mending broken fences!

## Explaining your position diplomatically

"The Spirit of the Lord GOD is upon Me,/
Because the LORD has anointed Me to preach
good tidings."—ISAIAH 61:1

**308** You are now ready on the walk of faith to be a diplomat for God. Your faith has matured to the level that you express your convictions with confidence and kindness. You dare to disagree agreeably—that's diplomacy!

What are the distinguishing marks of a diplomat? The first mark of the diplomat is that he is always *friendly*. This respectful attitude is a must in diplomatic relationships, for it allows your adversary to accept your frank disagreement without becoming hostile to you.

The second characteristic of the Christian diplomat is that he seeks to be *fair* in all communication and relationships. When someone holds a different viewpoint, be fair in your judgment of him, even though you cannot agree.

The third characteristic is to learn how to be *frank*. Dare to say such things as, "I see it from a different perspective," or "I want to agree with you, but in good conscience I really can't."

Fourth, and finally, the diplomat is *firm*. Resist pressures to violate your values.

**Faith is explaining your position through *friendliness*, *fairness*, *frankness*, and *firmness*.**

Today you have become, through faith, a successful diplomat for Jesus Christ. Congratulations! You have really matured in your faith.

You have learned the four principles for effective communication. They will work in all of your interpresonal relationships. You will no longer be manipulated and intimidated. You will be positively, politely, diplomatically aggressive. You sense a tremendous feeling of liberation in and by the power of your Lord.

## *Communicating effectively*

"Therefore we are ambassadors for Christ."—2
CORINTHIANS 5:20

Let's think some more about how you and I can be successful communicators. Faith changes our attitudes toward people; and when our attitudes are positive, effective communication is already established! Inner thoughts soon show
through our communication, verbally or nonverbally. Depending on our attitudes we will be either restrained or recep-
tive to the first sensitive word, smile, look, or touch.

When we walk the walk of faith, our self-esteem gives us
the self-confidence to mix and mingle in any circle with confidence.

**309**

**Our Lord allows us to be ambassadors. He wants us to
be His official messengers, instruments through
whom His attentive caring can be communicated.**

How can we be effective communicators or ambassadors?
My wife is a beautiful illustration of how this works. Arvella
was a beautiful farmer's daughter from Iowa. Years later she
found herself sitting at the head tables with famous people.
*How can I possibly carry on a conversation and be an inter-
esting dinner companion to them?* she asked herself. She
knew nothing about their background, other than that they
were famous and powerful.

In her quiet time the Lord gave her this wise counsel: The
next time she found herself in an elevated social setting, she
spoke little, asked questions, and sincerely listened. When the
evening was finished, the gentleman with whom we had dinner turned to me and said, "What a wonderful wife you have.
She is such a wonderful conversationalist."

We all can be good conversationalists if we will love the
person next to us enough just to listen.

Today I shall be an ambassador for my Lord. I shall begin by
making sure my attitude is positive. Thank You, God. Amen.

## Cleaning up our environment

"For God did not call us to uncleanliness, but in holiness."—1 THESSALONIANS 4:7

**310** "Why bother to pick it up?" I overheard one person say to someone who picked up a piece of litter. "Somebody is going to drop something in the next ten minutes anyway!" Every homemaker has said: "I no sooner get the house clean than it's dirty again."

What are the options? Certainly we can't let dirt build up and live in filth. We can't let it go from bad to worse!

I was inspired by the story of a citizen who bought a small portable sandblasting machine to use on his neighborhood's cinderblock walls that had been defaced with obscenities and pornographic graffiti.

"Why bother?" he was asked. "They'll just mess it up again!"

His answer was, "For the same reason I take a bath every night!" His positive approach became infectious. Today it's a clean neighborhood.

> **Service offers an immediate payoff—the instantaneous gratification that comes when you know you have done something right!**

Affirmation: Today I will ask myself, "How can I help clean up my environment? After all, I have to live in it!"

Lord, help me to begin with the environment of my mind. Help me to clean up the litter of negative thoughts, and recurring sinful impulses. Thank You, Father, for cleaning up the same old graffiti again and again! You never give up on me. Is it because You've chosen to live within me?

## Quilting the scraps

"Then [Ruth] went and gleaned in the field after
the reapers. . . . So Boaz took Ruth and she
became his wife . . . and she bore a son."—
RUTH 2:3; 4:13

Our Lord didn't believe in waste; possibility thinkers don't **311**
believe in waste. One company's waste product is another
company's opportunity!

Faith is quilting the scraps! It creates beauty from throwa-
ways.

In America's early days frontier people could not afford to
throw anything away. Empty tin cans were cut and flattened
to be used for patching holes in the grain wagons. All clothing
was homemade. Scraps were carefully kept to be sewn together in a multicolored collage and stuffed with cotton to
create a quilt. To break the boredom of sewing, it was not
uncommon to have quilting parties. ("Possibilitizing" creates
a party out of a boring chore.)

We hear a great deal today about the shortage of energy.
There is no shortage of anything—unless it's possibility
thinking!

Our real problem is waste. We waste money, we waste food,
we waste energy, and we waste ideas.

One day my wife agreed to pick me up at noon at a specific
location. She was fifteen minutes late, and during that time I
composed one of these devotionals, recording it on a little tape
recorder. I couldn't afford to waste those fiffteen minutes. I
quilted the scraps of time until it all came together to make
this book.

**Look for possibilities in wastebaskets.**

Remember how Ruth went gleaning in fields after the harvest was over. Faithfully she gathered the scraps. Read how
she was blessed in the lineage of our Lord.

## FAITH IS . . .
# Pyramiding your success

"He who had received five talents . . . brought
five other talents . . . His Lord said to him,
'Well done . . . I will make you ruler over many
things.' For to everyone who has, more will be
given."—MATTHEW 25:20–21

**312**     Here is a principle that will help you understand why successful people usually succeed more than ever. It's called the pyramid principle. When you're walking this walk of faith, take a little and invest it with all the faith you've got! The little divides and multiplies. Carefully invest the new earnings and the returns multiply again.

A person begins the walk of faith by risking what he has, expecting to multiply it. As you keep investing, you pyramid your success.

Read today's text again. Doesn't it mean that if you choose to play it safe by storing all your assets in a vault to protect them from theft or loss, you are sure to lose them all? Of course! It's just a matter of time before inflation alone will consume the uninvested dollar.

**If you try to keep what little you have, you will lose it.**

The only way to keep what you have is to keep moving ahead. Faith is pyramiding your success.

When I started the Crystal Cathedral congregation, I began with one member—my wife. It was hard work to gather up the first hundred members. After several years we had a thousand members. Then, the growth really skyrocketed. Why? Because by that time the one thousand members all were inviting their friends to come to church! The pyramid principle began to work!

If you're willing to start with one solid step, take a second, then expand slowly but effectively, you can build your pyramid of success, too! That's exercising the power of your faith! You are on the right road. Stick with it!

Thank You, God, for challenging me to keep moving ahead, step by step, setting the goals higher. Amen.

# Painting yourself into a corner

"A desire accomplished is sweet to the soul."—
PROVERBS 13:19

I've painted myself into a corner many times. Foolish? Not **313** really. "A desire accomplished is sweet to the soul." That means we all need the good feeling that comes when we have accomplished a project we've dreamed about. When we make commitments to deliver—before we know how we are going to produce—then we paint ourselves into a corner. In the process we put ourselves under pressure to achieve. Every possibility-thinking person does this—often!

Perhaps you have sent out the invitations to the party. You have invited people to an open house. You have volunteered to host the next meeting at your house. You have agreed to serve as chairman of the committee. What are you doing?

You're painting yourself into a corner! Then how do you get out of the corner? Here is where faith comes in. Extraordinary resources of thought and energy automatically come to your rescue. You never knew you had it in you to finish the job, to accomplish your desire.

I have been a jogger for nearly fifteen years. One morning I decided I would run over four miles. I didn't feel like it, so I deliberately ran two miles from my home. Once I had done that I had passed the point of no return. Now there was no way I could quit. I had painted myself into a corner. The decision was made for me. I simply turned around, running and puffing back home, adding up to four miles!

> **Do you dare to paint yourself into a corner? It works every time! You discover resources within you you never knew you had.**

## Splitting the diamond

". . . which have been given to us exceedingly great and precious promises."—2 PETER 1:4

**314**   I have had the exciting opportunity of seeing the most beautiful diamonds in the world—the crown jewels of the czars of Russia in the Hermitage Museum in the Soviet Union, and the collection of imperial gems of Persia in a bank in Teheran—but the largest and most beautiful diamonds are in the crown jewels in the Tower of London in England.

The largest diamond ever found is in that collection. When it was discovered, it was almost the size of two chicken eggs. It was determined that the gem would have to be split in order to bring out the potential beauty within. Studies were made. Then came the decisive moment when the blow would have to fall. There was the risk that the stone would be permanently ruined. Today the masterful results are there for you to see. Two diamonds—each nearly the size of a chicken egg—dazzle the eye.

Faith takes you to the point of no return, where there is no looking back. Win or lose, the decision must be made.

When Hannibal crossed the Rubicon on his massive military journey to conquer Rome, he watched until the last of his troops was safely across the river. Then he ordered the bridges burned! Hence the phrase, "burning bridges behind you." He wanted no opportunity for his troops to retreat. It was his way of exacting total commitment to a venture that had to succeed. It is no wonder that he won!

Are you facing such a moment today? Make sure that your move is a positive one!

**Strike a blow that will deepen your commitment to your God-given goal. Run the risk of a loss. There is no success without taking a chance!**

FAITH IS . . .

## *Giving before receiving*

"Give, and it shall be given to you: good
measure, pressed down, shaken together, and
running over . . . For with the same measure
that you use, it will be measured back to
you."—LUKE 6:38

It is easy to see why people who take the walk of faith live **315**
joyous and prosperous lives. Faith gives before it receives.
Flash a smile and people are friendly to you. But act shy, and
worried about rejection, and the sparkle of magnetic charm
will be frozen under the mask of apprehension. If you wait for
others to smile first, your walk of faith will be disappointing!
Give and you shall receive. The farmer knows this. He plants
the seed, giving it away, before he can expect a harvest.

**Life's satisfying experiences rush to the person who
gives before there is any guarantee of return.**

The successful entrepreneur understands this principle. He
prepares to spend "front money" for promotional literature
and preliminary architectural drawings, before he has any assurance of support for the project. He is walking the walk of
faith.

Do I want my life to be filled with singing and sunshine?
Then I need enough faith to give it out before I can expect to
take it in. What gifts can I give to God today? A positive lift to
encourage someone who is down? A happy word to someone
who needs a new drink from the fountain of joy? I'll take the
walk of faith today and step out to give of myself to someone
else.

But what if nothing comes back and I lose what I've given?
Well! I have already received something—the assurance that I
am walking the walk of faith! I'll win some; I'll lose some. But
of this I am sure: Life will start drying up; my youthful personality will become wrinkled and arthritic; and a slow, insidious decay will infect my heart, when I cautiously wait to give
until I receive. So long as I give before I receive, I remain vital
and truly alive!

[565]

*FAITH IS . . .*
## Pledging support

"God loves a cheerful giver."—2 CORINTHIANS
9:7

**316**   I have a great deal of admiration for people who pledge financial support to worthy causes. They sign pledge cards and make commitments before they are positive they can deliver the money on schedule. Oddly enough, commitment usually opens the way to possibility!

**Commitments are keys that unlock doors to great opportunities.**

Faith is trusting God to enable you to do what He asks.

It's exciting to me on life's walk to make pledges long before I have any idea how they can be fulfilled. Invariably doors open that I don't expect; my prosperity is at a higher level than I anticipate.

I truly believe God knows what's going on! And He is pleased by the signatures of courageous people that appear on financial pledges for His work.

- If you have the faith—God's got the power!
- If you make the commitment—God opens the way!
- If you make the pledge—God gives you the winning edge!

The next time you hear somebody ask for help, think twice before you say no. Doing so may be failing God's test of your faith!

Pledge your support. Pass the test.

And see how He will promote you to a higher level.

Do you have the vision to imagine something that seems just beyond your reach? How can you get hold of it? Does it seem so close, yet so far? Are you on the sidewalk looking into the store window? And the door is locked? Life's dreams are all there—but not for you? Wrong! Make the commitment! That's the key to unlock the possibility!

[566]

## *Tithing your income*

"Bring all the tithes into the storehouse. . . ./
And prove me now in this, . . ./If I will
not. . . ./pour out for you such blessing/That
there will not be room enough to receive it."—
MALACHI 3:10

In the Old Testament God commanded His people to im- **317**
mediately set aside a tenth of their income to be returned to
the work of the Lord. This is called tithing. They were told
they could keep nine-tenths of the harvest, but the first one-
tenth was to be given back to God for His good work. Understandably there were those who felt they couldn't possible live
on nine-tenths. They felt they needed the entire harvest.

I'll never forget how scary it was when I first started tithing.
I didn't think I could possibly feed my family on the balance
of my small fixed salary. Then I was forced to be honest and
face the challenge God put directly before me. "Prove Me,"
were His words. He was saying, "Schuller, I dare you to practice your faith. Either you believe in Me, or you don't. You are
either living by faith, or you have surrendered to doubt."

If I list the most important decisions in my life, I have to say
my most important decision was to give my life to Jesus
Christ and to His service in ministry.

My second greatest decision was to marry Arvella. The
third most important and positive decision was to take 10
percent off the top of every salary check I received, and give it
back to God.

**A tithe is not a debt we owe, it is a fertile seed we sow.**

I dare you to start tithing today! You will find another reason why God blesses the men and women of great faith!

Plant the seed—and the harvest will astound you! For
tithing will make a believer out of you! God will have a measurable opportunity to prove to you life's most important lesson: nothing is ever achieved until somebody has believed!
Yes, tithing made a possibility thinker out of me! It transformed my life, my destiny! Try it!

*FAITH IS . . .*
## *Merging to make miracles*

"Whoever desires to become great among you
shall be your servant. And whoever of you
desires to be the first shall be slave of all."—
MARK 10:43–44

**318**     It takes two to make a miracle. When a believing human
being merges his will with God's powers, miracles happen.
Miracles require faith—and faith is often spelled *w-o-r-k*.

There is a great misconception today that faith is simply a
matter of asking God to perform a miracle, sitting back, and
waiting for it to happen. Don't be misled! Prosperous, wealthy
Christian people don't become great by manipulating, perhaps
dishonestly, to get to the top of the ladder. They work for it
after they've prayed through their plans!

Jesus Himself encourages the pursuit of greatness. But our
Lord makes it clear that the pathway to success is the path of
service.

**If you want to be great—be prepared to be a servant.**

This works in the business world, too. In a free economy,
people buy only the products and services that meet their
needs. The professional person who becomes ego-involved instead of human-service-oriented, soon finds himself in trouble.

Great things happen when we follow our prayer with hard
work. Work means serving; and serving involves thinking
about others' needs and meeting them at their level.

Today, ask yourself: Have I been sitting back just waiting for
God to pour out blessings in my life without making an effort
myself? Am I willing to merge with God to make a miracle? I
believe it will happen as I become a servant.

## *Wading into deeper water*

"When you pass through the waters,/I will be
with you,/And through the rivers,/they shall
not overflow you. . . . Thus says the LORD,/who
makes a way in the sea/And a path through the
mighty waters."—ISAIAH 43:2, 16

Miracles happen when you practice the faith of deep water. **319**
Your first acts of faith were like approaching the water on
the beach with a timid toe, suspecting an unpleasant chill.
You continue to move cautiously, deeper and deeper into the
water. Soon the water reaches your waist, then your chest.
Now your arms reach out to fan and skim the surface. You are
leaving the solid bottom. By faith you swim to the deeper waters.

Faith always calls you forward. It never allows you to settle
back and be satisfied. Faith compels you to wade deeper, go
the extra distance.

Faith keeps you from giving up. Faiths calls you again, echo-
ing and reechoing that solitary word, "More!"

**It takes faith to wade into deep waters—especially
when you don't know where the bottom is.**

You do not know what the future holds, but you know who
holds the future.

God is your Captain, and He knows the waters well. He
keeps calling you onward and forward. God is committed to
leading us always onward to new life. God knows that something dies within us when we are so safe and secure we no
longer need daring and courageous faith. He is not satisfied if
He sees you become stagnant. For stagnation quickly leads to
swamps.

God, give me the courage to swim in the strong stream, to
wade into the deeper water, to move into an area where it will
be impossible to succeed without Your help! Only then will I
know I live by faith. Thank You, Lord. Amen.

## *Striking water in the desert*

". . . waters shall burst forth in the wilderness,/
And streams in the desert."—ISAIAH 35:6

**320**  The shepherd walks with his sheep even today, across blazing desert sands until he comes to a rock. There at the foot of Mount Sinai, he will do what Moses did. Moses satisfied his thirst by striking the rock in the desert. And water gushed out of the rock.

Unbelievable? Impossible? The truth is it still happens today. My son-in-law, Paul David Dunn, observed this himself when he traveled with a Bedouin to Sinai. The rocks in Sinai are granite, but have soft, porous limestone veins running through them. These limestone veins trap and hold rainfall in the rainy season. The water seeps down through invisible arteries inside the rocks collecting like little natural cisterns.

The Bedouin's staff only has to crack the side of a dry rock for water to gush out!

Faith is striking the rock that will gush with water to save the thirsty traveler.

You strike rock when you maintain and hold an unswerving positive attitude toward your predicament.

**Strike the rocky experiences of life with faith and good will emerge.**

Dear Father in heaven, thank You for causing deserts to spring forth with refreshing water . . .

for turning mountains into gold mines . . .

for turning upsetting experiences into unbelievable blessings.

Thank You, Father, for giving me the faith to dig for wells in the desert. Amen.

# Walking on the water

> "Peter . . . walked on the water. . . . But . . . he was afraid; and beginning to sink he cried out, 'Lord, save me!' . . . Jesus . . . caught him, and said to him, 'O you of little faith, why did you doubt?'"—MATTHEW 14:29–31

By now I'm sure you understand that the walk of faith is really a call to walk on water!

**321**

What happened? Was Peter suddenly defying the law of gravity? Is there some law known only to God that can override this law? The entire miraculous event is meant to teach this principle: we have to move ahead even when it seems impossible!

**Until you attempt the impossible—until you're willing to walk on the water—you're not walking the path of faith.**

Every mountain has its peak. Every river has its deepest point. Every trouble has a life span. Every recession has its low point. Tough times turn around when you do—when you turn from doubt to faith.

God knows the altitude of the Alps and the depths of the seas. He will not call you beyond His ability to see you safely to the other side. As a father urges a creeping infant to take those first faltering steps, attempting awesome impossibilities; so God always calls you beyond your abilities.

It may seem that God is calling you to do the impossible. It may seem that God is telling you to defy the law of gravity.

It may seem that God is telling you to walk on water. Believe! For the walk of faith says, "It's possible."

O God, I want Your blessing on my life. I need Your divine blessing in my heart and mind and soul. And I know You will not give it to me until I give myself to You and take those first fearful steps. I'm trusting You, Father, as I move forward in faith. Amen.

# *Hypnotizing yourself positively*

"Call to Me, and I will answer you, and show
you great and mighty things, which you do not
know."—JEREMIAH 33:3

**322**    Christian medical practitioners have come to appreciate
this Bible verse, as they utilize the God-given powers of
"depth relaxation," or hypnosis. Mrs. Schuller gave birth to
our fourth child, Carol, with the help of a medical doctor who
specialized in hypnosis, or depth relaxation. Her first three
children came after long, painful experiences in childbirth.
When she became pregnant with our fourth, a Christian
friend, Robert Zimmerman, now a practicing psychiatrist in
New York City, recommended the hypnosis approach. After
several months of conditioning, she became suggestible and
responsive to the positive thoughts the doctor was applying to
her mind, such as:

**You and God are partners in the act of creation. Relax
and let God take over.**

Part of the preparation included pinpricks. The doctor said,
"I'm going to take a piece of metal and touch your skin. You
will feel the cells move as they separate, allowing the metal to
enter their domain."

The process was slow, but very effective. "It is not pain unless you call it pain. It is the fear of being hurt." Positive
thought after positive thought was poured into her mind.
When Carol was delivered, Arvella was transcended above
pain. She was overwhelmed by an unforgettable experience of
the presence of God. She was living in another dimension. She
was using the power of faith that God has created within all of
us! It is available to you.

How do you go about tapping this transcendent power of
faith? Begin by deprogramming yourself from all that is negative . . . now allow positive thought after positive thought
after positive thought to pour into your mind.

## Transcending the present plane

"For indeed, the kingdom of God is within you."—LUKE 17:21

"Great dreams and great dreamers are never fulfilled—they are always transcended." Alfred North Whitehead said it. It's really true. The pyramiding principle and the laminating principle, which we studied earlier, are examples on the materialistic plane. On a spiritual level, faith does give us the power to transcend our present plane. It is possible to lose all awareness of the physical body when we are totally immersed in thought. A good illustration is fear. Many times people have been cut and bleeding but never noticed it until they felt the wetness of flowing blood. **323**

In a different way, when I'm in the process of writing, I become so absorbed in thought that I become like the absent-minded professor, completely unaware of activities happening around me.

There are several "planes" of scientific reality. Many remain undiscovered. We think in terms of first, second, and third dimensions (length, height, and breadth). How about a fourth? And a fifth? What powers does a mind possess? What are the limits of the powers within you?

"The kingdom of God is within you," Jesus said. What are the ultimate dimensions implicit in this statement?

### Miracles do happen!

Cases have been documented where cancer has spread throughout the body—and then the cancer miraculously disappeared. What forces are operating? What mysteries are at work? Considering all of the unknown realities that do exist in the known and the unknown universe, it is audacious, arrogant, and stupid to deny the possibility of a wonderful God working in all of us! Yes,

**Faith says it is possible to transcend time and space!**

# Swimming upstream

"Now this is the confidence that we have in
Him, that if we ask anything according to His
will, He hears us."—1 JOHN 5:14

**324** It doesn't take much faith to float down a river: "Even a
dead fish can float downstream." But it takes a lot of faith to
row upstream or swim against the current. Making a new
mold, starting a new trend, forming a fresh fashion, resisting
the popular wave, does require faith. It takes a great deal of
self-reliance and self-assurance to break out of the mold and
break new ground.

Watch the people who are rowing upstream. Chances are,
they're not doing it to be popular or to follow the herd. They
must believe in what they are doing, because they are bound
to be criticized.

> **What does it take to row upstream? It takes a belief in
> your own brilliance, the confidence that you are abso-
> lutely as smart as any others who are succeeding!**

Come alive.
- Preserve your God-given invitation to rugged individu-
  ality.
- Discover your uniqueness.
- Maintain your separate identity.
- Resist the temptation to become a sheep that simply runs
  blindly with the flock.

Who knows how far you can go and what new discoveries
you'll make when you decide to become an explorer? Do your
own thing, and start rowing upstream.

Make sure of one thing: be led by God. When He calls, grab
the oars and jump into the boat.

## *Confessing openly your inner convictions*

"For there is nothing covered that will not be
revealed, nor hidden that will not be known."—
LUKE 12:2

"Dare to say no," Charles Spurgeon once advised young **325** seminarians, adding, "It can be worth more to you than a knowledge of all the foreign languages."

It takes courage to say no. That's why the development of your faith is all-important. Until your faith is strong enough for you to verbalize your inner convictions, you will cease to be a moral influence for goodness and righteousness in our society.

A wise man made this observation years ago: "All that is required for evil to conquer is for good people to do nothing."

Adolf Hitler rose to power because good people lacked courage to confess their convictions and protest the evil of his ways.

> **Powerful negative forces in our world must be offset by the strong voices of men and women with inner convictions and the faith to speak up!**

By now your faith is becoming strong enough to turn you from a person who has been easily intimidated to a person who is quickly motivated to a leadership position! Jesus said, "You are the salt of the earth; but if the salt loses its flavor, . . . it is then good for nothing . . . You are the light of the world. . . ."

Congratulations! I applaud you! Sure it takes a lot of faith! But you've got it. Now use it.

## Teaching someone to think

"Do not neglect the gift that is in you."—
2 TIMOTHY 4:14

**326** Does anybody have more faith in human nature than professional educators—who teach others to *think*?

You liberate people when you educate them. You dare to trust them with the freedom to make their own decisions. There have been periods in church history when the religious establishment discouraged people from reading the Bible for fear they might come up with interpretations that would conflict with the official theological position. Insecure people indoctrinate. Secure people educate.

More than one dictator has hesitated to wipe out illiteracy for fear of the power of the printed page. However, when Mao Tse-tung conquered China, he decided to indoctrinate the people in order to unify the country. This meant he had to wipe out illiteracy.

Until the advent of communism, 90 percent of the Chinese people were illiterate. Fourteen thousand characters made up the alphabet, and only a few people could read. By dictatorial fiat, Mao Tse-tung substituted a new and simplified alphabet for the ancient Chinese characters. This opened the possibility of teaching the peasants to read.

Christians saw this as a great opportunity to teach the Bible to millions of Chinese who had never been able to read. Bibles were printed in the new alphabet, and today the good news is penetrating the villages of China.

**Imagine how much faith God has in you! He gave you the ability to think! He put you in a position where you have learned to read. He has given you incredible liberties. He trusts you!**

O God, thank You for letting me go! I welcome my freedom to think and to believe. I will not disappoint You, Father. I will keep the faith. Amen.

## *Seasoning life around you*

"Salt is good, but if the salt loses its flavor, how will you season it? Have salt in yourselves, and have peace with one another."—MARK 9:50

Christ says it so clearly. He expects His disciples and followers who walk the walk of faith to be the salt in the society. **327**

What precisely does this mean? Let me illustrate: Can you imagine how bland food is without salt? That's precisely what happens in an institution—whether it's a club, church, or legislative body—without new ideas and creative opportunities.

A community, state, country, or life becomes very matter-of-fact until a possibility thinker steps in. When he dreams great dreams, he seasons life. He creates

• beauty where there was drabness.
• excellence where there was mediocrity.
• excitement where there were only ho-hum attitudes.

Watch out, world, wherever there is a possibility thinker, life is never going to be the same again!

When possibilities begin to bounce around and big ideas produce big projects, a sleepy little town starts awakening! This is the exciting challenge!

Put some energy and enthusiasm in the lives of people around you!

Dynamic leaders who season the world with fulfilling plans can liven things up in a hurry!

Dear God, may I never lose my saltiness.

May I never stop dreaming dreams that can put excitement in my life. May I never surrender to the great "yawn," the boredom that comes through impossibility thinking.

Today, I am going to get things moving! I will be the seasoning in the feast of life. Thank You, Lord. Amen.

## Inching ahead

"If you have faith as a mustard seed, you will say to this mountain, 'move . . .' and nothing will be impossible for you."—MATTHEW 17:20

**328**     One of the elements that makes faith powerful is its requirement to believe in the might of the miniature. A tiny seed—but what a mighty plant can emerge!

A small thought passing through the mind inconspicuously, without fanfare, can be easily overlooked. There are latent possibilities in the small thought, the little act, and the commonplace functions of life. I telephoned two friends today. One was hospitalized. I encouraged him and prayed a positive prayer for him. When I finished, his voice was broken with emotion as he thanked me. It was such a small thought. It took only a minute.

The other call was to an attorney friend who is experiencing business difficulties. I assured him that whatever happens I recognize him as a person of unquestionable integrity. By reassuring him of my respect, I gave him a lift! Again, it was such a little thing to do.

A telephone call, a positive reinforcement—these encouraging words to a troubled person can make the difference between life and death! A simple act of thoughtfulness may appear to be such a little thing. But it can turn the mood from depression to hope, and in so doing move a mighty mountain!

> **Today, move a mountain with a little thought. Pick up a telephone, write a letter, or make a hospital call; simply be positive and optimistic. Build the spirits of someone who needs a lift!**

Thank You, God, that I have been given the gift of encouraging people around me! I'll make every day beautiful by some small act of love and kindness. Amen.

## FAITH IS . . .
# Steering a steady course

".. . and He [Jesus] steadfastly set His face to go to Jerusalem."—LUKE 9:51

When you are a believer in yourself and your dream, you become believable to others. Stay steady on the course, never taking your eye off your ultimate objective.

**329**

**You may compromise your position or accommodate your strategies, but never take your eye off the ultimate goal.**

Do not be rattled by setbacks. Don't allow panic to grip you when projections fall short and cash flow produces a crunch, for faith steers a steady course.

My friend who is a pilot once told me about the time when he was making a bombing dive over enemy waters during World War II. "I was just at the end of my descent and ready to level off when I was hit." He said, "Instantly I recalled what was drilled into us at pilot school. 'When you are in real trouble, don't do a thing! Just *think!*' So I never touched the controls. My first impulse was to grab the controls, but at that precise moment that was the worst thing to do. The controls were already set. And my plane leveled off. Had I touched the controls, I would have nose-dived into the bay!"*

When you take a potentially fatal hit, just *think!* And *think positively!* You'll make it.

You know, Jesus Christ steered a steady course. He announced that He was going to be our Savior. He predicted that it would mean death on a cross. He never backed away from His cross. He "steadfastly set His face" to pursue His God-given goal.

---

*Robert H. Schuller, *Tough Times Never Last, But Tough People Do* (Nashville: Thomas Nelson, 1983), pp. 101–103.

## Soldiering the battle

"Take up the whole armor of God, . . . having girded your waist with truth, having put on the breastplate of righteousness, . . . above all, taking the shield of faith . . . the helmet of salvation and the sword of the Spirit . . ."—
EPHESIANS 6:13–17

**330**    Why does this walk of faith involve so many difficulties?

If God loves me, why do I have so many troubles? If God is so good, why does the road have to be so rough?

It's important to remember that the walk of faith is designed to serve God's cause in His kingdom.

**We are invited to be soldiers in God's army—not tourists on an around-the-world trip.**

I have written some of these pages in Europe, where, as a tourist, I stayed in fine hotels, slept in beds between white sheets, and ate from tables with white linen!

My brother covered the same territory a few decades back when he served the American Armed Forces as a medical litter-bearer during World War II. It was his job to run to the front lines, pick up the wounded and the dying, and race them back for emergency treatment.

My brother traveled as a soldier. I traveled as a tourist.

At no point does the Bible invite us to go on a worldwide luxury tour with Jesus Christ as our guide.

Rather we are commissioned to be God's soldiers in a rough battle to conquer the enemy and liberate the land for the glory and the good of the human family!

Affirmation: Faith is soldiering for battle. I can expect tough times. Therefore, I will put on the helmet of salvation and the shield of faith. I shall carry the sword of the spirit. I shall wear the breastplate of righteousness! I expect to win!

Thank You, Father for reminding me today that I am called to be a soldier, not a tourist. Thank You for setting my faith straight again today. Amen.

## Undergoing to be an overcomer

"This is the victory that has overcome the
world—our faith."—1 JOHN 5:4

**331**

Anybody who is going anywhere is going to be undergoing
something! And anybody can be an overcomer if he has
enough faith. Endurable optimism is what gives you the
power to succeed. To put it another way: the undergoers become overcomers! Let me teach you a prayer today that I believe will give you the extra faith to be victorious and to
overcome.

Almighty God, You know what I am undergoing. Help me
to overcome. Don't let me become a pessimist. Preserve my
optimistic outlook. I may lose many things, Father, but let me
never lose my faith.

- Lord, You were the Undergoer who became the Over-
  comer!
- You died on the cross;
- You rose on Easter.

Today hundreds of millions of people around the world
know You, love You, respect You, admire You, draw inspiration and life from You!

You promise to be my Friend. You promise that if I keep
believing I will win. You promise: "This is the victory that has
overcome the world—our faith." Give me the courage to overcome the negative feelings that may depress my spirit, deflate
my hopes, and defuse my enthusiasm.

> **My faith tells me that I have Your power within me
> now, because You are standing beside me, encouraging
> me all the way with Your promise, "Victory will be
> yours, My friend."**

Thank You, Jesus Christ. Amen.

## Following through—anyway

"Love . . . bears all things."—1 CORINTHIANS
13:7

**332** Love and faith are two faces of a single coin. Can there be love without faith? Can there be faith without love? Read today's text this way: "Faith bears all things." What do you do when you trust someone, and they let you down? Faith follows through on your part of the bargain—anyway. Did someone leave you stranded, not sharing part of the burden? Faith carries on—without them!

When you made a commitment in happier times you never expected that the scene would shift into such a negative situation. Now that the tide has turned, what do you do? Do you use the present difficulty as an excuse to get out, or does your strong sense of honesty and integrity compel you to live by the commitment you made in good faith?

> **Faith is the positive attitude that if you are faithful to the contract you will be able to hold your head high. You will be a believable and trustworthy person.**

Such perserverance sustained and strengthened by your integrity will win you a reputation that will command great support the next time you prepare to move into new possibilities.

Our Lord Jesus Christ gave a great illustration of this. He experienced the agony of hell on the cross. Even though His heavenly Father was silent, Jesus kept the faith! He went on about His positive work of redemption. Faith keeps on believing through the difficult times in a God who is still kind, compassionate, and good. That's precisely when you need God most!

## Laughing up a storm

"A merry heart does good, like medicine,/But a broken spirit dries the bones."—PROVERBS 17:22

To the best of our knowledge, the human being is the only **333** creature that has the capacity for humor.

Humor after all is impossible without faith.

People who lack faith are easily irritated and agitated! Uptight and touchy, they are easily provoked to anger and are slow to see amusement in life's negative experiences.

Only a self-confident, self-assured person has enough faith to laugh at himself and his critics.

Yes, humor is one of the most beautiful reflections of faith in a human being. Positive-thinking believers become the kind of people who smile through their tears and laugh despite tragedy.

Humor, as we now know, is part of the healing process. It's now well accepted that humor releases endorphines, chemicals in the brain that are stimulated by positive emotions. We have always known thoughts stimulate the body glands to produce secretions. Researchers at UCLA Medical School have proven that the brain is, in effect, a gland that produces chemical secretions when stimulated by the positive emotion of humor.

Is it irreverent to welcome comedy in the middle of tragedy? Not at all! It is God's design to relax the tension of grief. Humor in times of horrific hurt will contribute to the healing and comfort so desperately needed in the tortured community.

Affirm today: I will resolve to bring laughter to life. I can always purchase some balloons, blow them up, and watch children laugh as I release the balloons to sail off or float down to the little hands of a child!

Today, I'll prove to the world I'm a believer—I'll laugh a lot!

Today, I will laugh up a storm—in the middle of one.

## *Compromising on trivialities*

"Turn away my eyes from looking at worthless things,/And revive me in Your way."—PSALM 119:37

**334** Walking along the beach in Hawaii, I noticed two native Hawaiians in the shallow surf. They held a little screen between them, which they were shaking back and forth. I walked over to them and inquired, "What are you looking for?" They named a little ocean creature that I had never heard of.

I watched them pick a little beetle off the screen and put it in a can with several others. Then they casually discarded several attractive seashells.

"You threw away some pretty shells!" I exclaimed.

They looked at me incredulously, but answered respectfully, "You can't catch fish with shells. With these little beetles, we catch big fish, food for our family!"

Faith is the fine art of compromising wisely. Shells are *trivial*—they are pretty but not life-supporting. Fish is *basic*—it is food to sustain health and strength.

There is always the present danger of being distracted from the basics by being attracted to the trivial.

You have to turn this business of compromising into a fine art.

**Faith compromises the alluring, veneer values in favor of the intrinsic values.**

Thank You, Father. You are guiding me and giving me Your wisdom.

I won't make the mistake of losing a dollar by trying to save a dime.

I will not sacrifice my marriage for some cheap relationship.

I will not give up my godly faith for some passing pleasure.

I make this commitment now—to give up the trivial in favor of the really valuable.

Help me, Lord. Amen.

## *Knowing it can be done*

"I can do all things through Christ who strengthens me."—PHILIPPIANS 4:13

Faith is an inner conviction.

**335**

It is an unshakeable assurance.

It is the profound "knowing" that comes before reality confirms it.

Faith is a sense of destiny: "It's possible." "It's going to happen."

Faith is knowing that you can do it.

**The person who walks the walk of faith knows he can solve his problem!**

He *knows* that he can detach himself from that awful habit.

He *knows* he can extricate himself from his negative enslavements.

The person who walks the walk of faith faces his projects, affirming:

I *know* I can do it—*if* God will help me. And I'm sure God wants to help me!

I know I can do it *when* I'm totally dedicated to Him, which I really am!

I know I can do it *after* everything is in readiness. And I am trusting God to help me get my act together!

I know I can do it *only* with the help of my Lord. He is my best friend. He wants me to succeed.

I can do all things *through* Christ who strengthens me! I know it's possible after all.

Deep down in your heart, you know it will work out. An unquenchable confidence keeps fueling your feelings that you're going to make it.

Again and again the person who succeeds did so because he or she didn't know it was impossible!

## Renting with option to buy

"My people will dwell in a peaceful habitation,/
In secure dwellings, and in quiet resting
places."—ISAIAH 32:18

**336**    It is not uncommon to sense tension in residential communities between homeowners and people who rent nearby
apartments and houses. It is assumed—not always correctly—that people who are buying a home and investing in
real estate have a far greater vested interest in the community
institutions: local government, public schools, and social services.

Now, for people who would love to buy but can't afford to,
the sellers of new homes in California have established a practice of allowing people to rent their homes with an option to
buy.

Remember? There are degrees of faith! There are those with
faith so strong they simply plunge into the purchase agreement, as it were. They put up a heavy chunk of earnest money,
which they are prepared to forfeit if the transaction is not executed. They are willing to risk thousands of dollars to secure
their purchase position in the market.

But what about those sincere people with faith that toddles
on childish feet! God gives them the chance to build their
faith. He makes it easier for them to take the first faltering
steps, encouraging them to try. Let them simply rent the
house but apply the rental fees to the purchase price, if they
will make a firm commitment within a reasonable period of
time. We should not criticize those with feeble faith but
rather applaud them for their first steps of faith, however faltering they may be!

At least people who want to believe put themselves in a
position where they can maneuver themselves into a stronger
corner and step up at a later date. They're getting their foot in
the door.

If you don't have the faith to make the total commitment,
at least take that first step.

## Analyzing the obstructions

"If any of you lacks wisdom, let him ask of
God, who gives to all liberally and without
reproach. . . . But let him ask in faith . . . for he
who doubts is like a wave in the sea driven and
tossed by the wind."—JAMES 1:5–6

I had an experience last week that illustrates today's theme
dramatically. I made a trip to Fort Wayne, Indiana, for a special
speaking engagement. My schedule was really tight. The
plane landed only thirty-five minutes before I had to walk into
the black-tie event. I was rushed downtown to the coliseum,
then backstage to a dressing room where a rented tuxedo was
waiting for me. "You have only ten minutes, Dr. Schuller. The
governor is waiting for you. So hurry." These were my instructions.

I tried on the coat. Perfect fit. I then slipped on the trousers.
Perfect fit. I checked the shoes, socks, cummerbund, black tie.
Everything was there. I slipped on the white shirt. The neck
was perfect, the sleeve length was perfect, but it was a tapered
shirt. Much more tapered than I. At that point, there was a
knock on the door. "Are you ready, Dr. Schuller?" I said, "Not
quite!" A button at my wasit—now, I'm not exaggerating—
was ten inches from the hole. I took one look at that shirt and
noticed it had a seam on both sides. I had only two seconds to
solve my problem. I ripped the shirt seams open, creating so
much space that I closed the buttons neatly. I pulled the cummerbund
on and then the coat. Naturally I kept the coat buttoned,
and during the entire speech I never waved my arms.

Of course, at the end of the evening I told my friend to send
me a bill for the shirt. It's amazing how easily we can be intimidated
or manipulated by material things. They can take
control and take charge unless you and I have the faith to
analyze the obstruction and begin to take action.

**337**

## Daring to fail

"He [God] will not allow your foot to be
moved,/He who keeps you will not slumber.
. . . The Lord shall preserve your going out and
your coming in . . . forevermore."—PSALM
121:3,8

**338**   For over thirty years as a pastor, I have counseled untold
hundreds of persons face-to-face, and tens of thousands by
mail. Beyond a shadow of a doubt, the vast majority of these
persons who profess to walk the walk of faith and who claim
they are living by faith, are, in fact, missing the mark.

Mountain-moving faith is something they have never truly
experienced. Why? Where did their faith get bogged down?

What hidden sandbar grounded the ship?

What rubble under the water snagged the hook?

What obstacle in the road blew out the tire?

What impurity in the fuel caused the engine to fail?

What infectious germ entered the body of faith to produce a
debilitating sickness?

In one single phrase, the problem can be easily summed up:
"fear of failure."

I determine to succeed in the walk of faith by making one
simple decision, one powerful affirmation:

**I will dare to fail.**

I will not be afraid of failure, for God has promised that He
will be my help. He will not allow me to stumble or fall.

He will plant my feet firmly one step at a time. And with
each upward step, I shall climb without a fall!

Then I shall pause and turn around.

I'll be shocked at how high I have climbed, and how successful I have been!

Great goals are never reached until you decide to dare to
fail!

*FAITH IS . . .*
## *Advertising your abilities*

"Let your light so shine before men, that they
may see your good works and glorify your
Father in heaven."—MATTHEW 5:16

Yes! Let the world know you believe—in yourself! "You    **339**
mean toot my own horn?" you ask.

I answer, "Yes, unless you can find someone else to blow it
better."

"Isn't that dangerous self-congratulation?" you ask.

I answer, "Depends on how you do it. Just don't be a shrinking violet."

When you advertise your ability, you are bragging—about
*the goodness and greatness of God* in your life! Tell the world
what God can do! Let everybody know the difference faith
makes in your life! Share with people how you've been able to
conquer problems through walking the walk of faith.

Expose, without modesty, in word and in deed, the good
things God has done in your life. Let your light shine!

Don't be afraid to sell yourself!

After all, who created you?

After all, who redeemed you from evil and failure and sin?

After all, who gave you your abilities and talents?

After all, who gave you the motivation that drives you upward and forward!

After all, who gave you the integrity and enthusiasm that
makes you the kind of worker the average employer would
love to hire? It is, of course, God and His Son, Jesus Christ.

When you advertise your abilities, you are bearing witness
to the power of faith in your life!

Get on with it. Advertise—today—without fear. Don't
worry about becoming proud or arrogant. The easiest job in
the world for God is to humble a human being.

**God's biggest job is to keep you believing, minute by
minute and day by day, how good you really are once
His Spirit has moved into your life!**

## *Hammering the nails*

"As for me, You uphold me in my integrity,/And set me before Your face forever."—PSALM 41:12

**340**    Faith—like a driven nail—aims at connecting separated elements, binding them into a stronger, more effective union.

The process of faith, too, is not unlike the hammering of the nail. Carefully select the right nail for the right job. Select the correct length. Too short, and it will fail to hold. (Do I have enough faith? Is it too weak? Do I need more patience?)

Too long—and it will go all the way through, doing more harm than good. (Am I being too patient? Neglecting treatment? Avoiding the painful and inevitable extraction? Hurting myself and others by delaying the costly decision?)

Faith is making the move, now. It is hammering the nail once I have selected the right one!

I take that nail and hold it cautiously, steadily, between two fingers. I raise the hammer. I tap the nail gently. I repeat the tapping. A bit harder. The nail stands on its own now, precariously, but steady and unmoving. The next tap of the hammer is crucial. I don't want to dislodge it, and send it flying. I need to drive it a bit deeper. Another whack. A hard one now! It's halfway in the wood. I can't even wiggle it. Now I can drive it full force. It is almost all the way in. I can just get the claws under it to extract it if I want to. I don't ever want it to come out! A final all-out blow. There, the head of the nail is below the surface of the wood. I can see the indented print of the hammer head. It will never come out!

That's the process of building a strong faith!

Each new adventure with God is another blow driving your faith deeper.

Each moment you spend in positive prayer makes your faith more solid.

Each positive affirmation of faith contributes to the self-confidence and power God gives you as you move forward on your walk of faith.

## Standing up to be counted

"He who walks with integrity/walks
securely."—PROVERBS 10:9

The challenge to "stand up and be counted" comes to every **341**
person more often than he might choose.

Faith becomes the force that puts us on our feet!

Fear might keep us sitting on the sidelines.

Worry about possible conflict we may encounter through
sharing our commitment might seal our lips.

The fear of offending someone when standing firm on our
convictions, might urge us to maintain neutrality.

But faith commands integrity, and integrity forces us to
confront the issue.

Ultimately your character and mine will be evaluated by
our integrity.

Have we been honest, reliable, and responsible? Faith, more
than any other single factor, causes us to develop and to maintain a character branded with the hallmark of integrity!

The faith that calls for integrity will actually be strengthened in the process.

> **Internal peace of mind comes to a person who *knows*
> *that he did the right things*.**

Consider the anxiety-prone, over-cautious person. He is so
security minded that he doesn't want to take sides! He lacks
the courage to stand up for his own convictions. Does he secure his position when he loses his integrity? Does he become
a braver, more self-confident person through this duplicity? Is
this the strategy for personal security?

On the contrary, by remaining evasive he loses the respect
and the support of his most powerful and important friends.
In the process one actually loses the base of his security!

How wise was the writer of Proverbs when he wrote these
words: "He who walks with integrity/walks securely."

## Embracing God's grace

> "For by grace you have been saved through
> faith, and that not of yourselves; it is the gift of
> God, not of works, lest anyone should boast."—
> EPHESIANS 2:8

**342**  What's the best gift that faith can deliver to your life?

It is the gift of salvation from sin.

It is the peace of mind that comes from knowing that Christ died for your sins on the cross.

It is the serenity of spirit that comes over you when you know God has pardoned you.

It is the mental health you experience when old guilt is gone.

How can you earn this salvation?

You can't. A gift is something you can only accept. If you earn it then it becomes a salary—not a gift!

> **You are pardoned, forgiven, and saved by the grace of God. And what is grace? It is God's love in action for those who don't deserve it.**

*Grace* is the most beautiful word in the English language. Nothing is more valuable than a gift that is given when you don't deserve it—

- love before you've earned it.
- credit when it is not justified.

The hardest task in the world is for an honorable person to accept something he has not earned. This explains why people are extremely reticent and resistant to accepting the gospel of Jesus Christ, salvation by the grace of God.

Today make one of the greatest leaps of faith that is possible! Embrace God's grace. Accept His understanding and forgiveness. Trust Him not only to cleanse you of sin and negativity but to inspire you to treat other persons the same way.

You suddenly realize that you are *forgiven not through the good works you do, but to do good works!*

## *Glorifying God with great victories*

"Now to Him who is able to do exceedingly
abundantly above all that we ask or think,
according to the power that works in us, to
Him be glory. . . . Amen."—EPHESIANS 3:20–21

Does possibility thinking sound arrogant? Can this walk of **343** faith become a vain venture? Is there the danger that you're really glorifying yourself? Are you in it for yourself more than for your Lord?

The answers to all of these questions are abundantly clear.

**God is glorified by the great victories of His people.**

And what is victory? Any God-given idea that, with His help, has turned into an actual achievement!

If God started the project with an idea planted in your brain, and God stimulated the success by motivating you to plunge ahead and run the risk of failure and criticism, and if God will finally see you through to an ultimate success, who really is glorified? Both you and your Lord. God wants you to be honored. He wants you to experience a wonderful sense of humble pride in accomplishment! After all, you are His child.

All parents love to see their children enjoy a proud accomplishment. But who really gets the credit? Of course the glory goes to our Lord! You do not need to piously announce in every breath, "I'm doing this for the glory of God." The achievements of those who believe carry with them the unmistakable label that God has been at work.

How then can you best glorify God? By committing yourself to the great ideas God has entrusted to your stewardship, which He expects you to return to Him as human achievements worthy of being offered as gifts on the altar of my God.

O God, I will attempt to glorify You, not simply through pious prayer, but through great achievements! Amen.

## Pressing the wrinkles

> "O God, You have taught me from my youth;
> . . . /Now also when I am old and gray-headed,
> O God, do not forsake me,/Until I declare Your
> strength to this generation."—PSALM 71:17–18

**344**  "Oh, I don't think I should wear this dress, it'll get too wrinkled," I heard my wife say.

"Of course it will," I reminded her, "but you can press out the wrinkles."

Faith is wearing a suit—even if it does wrinkle! It's taking the shiny car out—even if it is raining. It's deciding to live the Christian life—even if I can't live it perfectly and sinlessly.

Faith believes that cars can be washed again; sins can be forgiven one more time; mistakes can be corrected. Or they can turn us into wiser, wealthier, or more wonderful persons; and wrinkles can be pressed out!

Faith presses out the negative wrinkles! You have to do that all the time.

Do you see the universal principle here? Every time you forgive others and give them another chance, you press out a negative wrinkle.

We do it in our marriage too, don't we? "I'm sorry I hurt you." That's pressing out a negative wrinkle.

But faith also presses *in* the *positive* wrinkles. Since some wrinkles can't be pressed out like wrinkles around the eyes, then it's very important how you choose the wrinkles! I know people who live positively, year after year. By the time they become old and gray they have what I call "twinkle wrinkles."

No wonder they're more beautiful the older they get! The "twinkle wrinkles" are actually attractive lines pressed into their face by a lifetime of positive thinking.

All the while a positive mental attitude presses out the wrinkles and lines left by life's troubles, trials, and tribulations.

Meditation: Imagine your mind like a wrinkled garment. Imagine your faith as a steam iron erasing the wrinkles! Imagine the hand of Jesus on the iron! Amen.

## Sculpting your spirit

"Let this mind be in you which was also in
Christ Jesus."—PHILIPPIANS 2:5

"I don't like the looks of that man," Abraham Lincoln is **345**
reported to have said to an aide.

"A person can't help what he looks like, Mr. President," the
aide replied.

"Oh, yes, he can," Mr. Lincoln answered.

Negative-thinking people develop faces that become hard,
or hostile, or unfriendly. Skepticism sketches scars on the face
of a cynic, creating wrinkles that carve deeply into the face. It
bears repeating again and again: beauty is mind deep.

Each thought, like a drop of water on a marble statue, will
leave an effect, however indelible or invisible it may appear,
on the shape and sculpture of your soul. Today, resolve that by
the grace of Jesus Christ, you can and will become a beautiful
human being. Here's an affirmation beauty treatment:

• I shall believe in a God of goodness and generosity. This
will reflect a hopeful sparkle in my eye.

• I shall believe the best about people.

• I shall have peaceful attitudes toward my fellow human
beings; which will cast a beauty across my face.

• I shall never become a mean-looking person!

• I shall believe that hardship and pain, trouble and sickness
will all shape my appearance with a look of kindness and
compassion. For I believe God will bless my sufferings. This
belief will shape my face into a serene and sweet-looking face.
People will meet me and leave remarking how beautiful I
looked. I shall walk upright, shoulders back, chin high, well-
postured, proclaiming to the world that I am self-confident,
for I am walking with Jesus Christ. He is my Savior; He is my
guide; He is my inspirer. He is my *number-one encourager*. I
am living and walking with Him day by day. I am becoming
more and more conformed to His likeness. I am becoming
beautiful. Thank You, Lord.

## *Grandfathering my hopes*

"The mercy of the LORD is from everlasting to
everlasting . . ./And His righteousness to
children's children . . ./And to those who
remember His commandments to do them."—
PSALM 103:17–18

**346**  There was a time when the word *grandfather* was known
only as a noun. Today in governmental circles it has become a
verb. Politicians use the word *grandfather* to mean passing off
liabilities that we incur today to future generations. This is a
negative use of the word. I want to use it positively.

Remember the gas in the tank that you probably won't use?
If you don't use it yourself, you can grandfather it. Somebody
who comes down the road can benefit from it.

**Faith believes that when you take positive action,
great good will result. You may not personally benefit
from it, but somebody will.**

I'll never forget the tornado that raged across our Iowa farm
home destroying all of the nine buildings, most of the livestock, and virtually all of our personal possessions. Not the
least of the damage was to the orchard. Yet my arthritic, crippled father, cane in hand, walked through the demolished orchard and said, "We'll plant an apple tree here," as he left a
scratch in the tortured ground. Then he made another X in
the scarred earth and said, "We'll plant another apple tree
here."

I looked at him and said, "But, Dad, you're an old man. Do
you expect to live to eat the fruit of these trees?"

To my surprise he retorted swiftly, "The fruit I eat is from
trees somebody else planted! I have to plant trees for others
who will follow me."

Grandfathering! What a beautiful philosophy of life! Today I
want to think of investments that will outlast and outlive me!
Can I plant a tree? Can I share a treasured recipe? In some way,
I can pass on the knowledge of my walk of faith to my grandchildren yet unborn.

## *Surrendering to love*

"There is no fear in love; but perfect love casts out fear."—1 JOHN 4:18

On the walk of faith, faith is the most important value in human life—except for its Siamese twin, love. The two cannot be severed through any form of spiritual surgery without killing both.

**347**

One thing is certain: When you surrender to love, you can't be making a big mistake.

When you are in doubt, do the most loving thing.

If you ever face a situation where faith and love are in adversarial positions, let love win out. Faith will follow.

> **Faith has enough trust in mercy that it can dare to surrender to love! Love without faith is weakness. Faith without love is dangerous.**

It is well to remember this when you face times when you are compelled to ask yourself:

- Is this the time for me to step down and retire?
- Should I stop fighting this cancer?
- Should I continue to battle for my viewpoint? Or is there a time and place when I should surrender?
- Are there times when giving in might actually be a greater move of faith than stubbornly hanging in there?

As a pastor, I once offered this prayer for one of my people, and I share it again today for your benefit.

*Lord, give me the guidance to know when to hold on and when to let go, and the grace to make the right decision with dignity. Amen.*

## Singing a new song

"Oh, sing to the LORD a new song. . . .
Proclaim the good news of His salvation from
day to day. . . . His wonders among all
peoples."—PSALM 96:1–3

**348**  There are four levels of prayer. The first level of prayer is *petition*. Go to God and ask Him for help.

The second level of prayer is *intercession*. Don't ask for anything for yourself; instead, pray for someone else who really needs God's help.

The third level of prayer is *praise*. Go to God and thank Him for all the blessings you enjoy today.

The fourth level of prayer is "two-way" prayer. Simply go to God and ask Him questions; then let Him answer. "Dear God, is there anything that I should praise You for today? Is there any reason why I should be thankful?" Now *listen!* Listen for God's answer, "Yes, be thankful that I am here. Be thankful that you are alive, and can talk to Me!"

After suffering heart failure and undergoing major surgery, Jerry Lewis said, "Every morning I know that I am a winner, for I have survived! Everybody who wakes up in the morning is a success!"

You can choose today to sing a song in discordant melodies of gloom and doom. That's an old song; it's a worn-out record.

Try singing a new song!

**God is alive. Sing a song of praise to Him. He has spared you from more problems, pains, and perils than you will ever know! Start singing!**

Dear God, I am a believer. I'm going to sing a new song today. My mood is changing. That's a miracle! It's going to be a great day, Lord! Thank You for turning me around. Amen.

# *Retiring from retirement*

"Take heed to the ministry which you have
received in the Lord, that you may fulfill it."—
COLOSSIANS 4:17

"I'm retiring from retirement—too risky," the bright, twin-  **349**
kling senior citizen chuckled. Then he became very serious. "I
really mean it. This business of retirement is downright dangerous. It is putting strains on my marriage. I'm so bored. I'm
grumbling too much. I'm turning into a crotchety old man,
and I'm not going to let that happen."

"What do you plan to do?" I asked.

"I've decided to drive a cab!" I was amused and amazed,
since he has a professional degree and an impressive resumé.
"I've been a passenger in cabs all over the world," he explained, "and I've observed that taxicab drivers are in the
unique position of being able to talk to people. I expect to be
able to share my faith in my country and in our system of
politics and economics, and to say a good word for Jesus
Christ!"

Faith is *fulfilling* your calling, not retiring from it. What
calling must you fulfill today?

Let's step out of retirement today and do the ministry that
Christ has entrusted to us.

- Today I will be an encourager to someone who is discouraged.
- I will give someone a sincere compliment today.
- I shall believe that my positive faith will help someone
  become a believer in themselves and in God.

I feel the presence of Christ within me. It's a wonderful feeling, letting a beautiful God live within me and love people
through me. Wow. There is a good work waiting for me to do
today! I'm getting out of retirement and into the stream of life
again.

## *Looking forward with hope*

"Hope in God;/For I shall yet praise Him, The
help of my countenance and my God."—PSALM
43:5

**350**     Are you really walking the walk of faith? Ask yourself these
questions: Am I looking ahead with hope or am I looking back
with disappointment? Do I tend to count my strike-outs or do
I tend to count the hits?

If you keep score of your mistakes, setbacks, and disappointments you undermine your faith as surely as a raging,
flooded stream undermines the foundations of a building.

Charles Spurgeon, the famous English clergyman, once
faced a great disappointment. He went to visit a farmer who
was a devoted elder in his church. The farmer said, "Pastor,
what is that cow doing?"

Spurgeon looked and answered, "Well, she's looking over
the wall."

The farmer said, "Yes, she is looking *over* the wall because
she can't see *through* it."

In the walk of faith there will be times when you face walls
that you can't see through. But you can look over them! When
you look *beyond, around,* and *over* the obstacles, fanciful or
factual, an amazing thing happens: You visualize yourself
with the obstacle behind you! When you can imagine success,
then an inner energy is generated that can best be described in
one short word: *"Hope"!*

Hope is the difference between ultimate success or failure;
between life or death.

> **I choose to live and succeed by continuing to look for-
> ward with hope.**

In the process I know that I am exercising the mountain-
moving faith which God promises to bless!

## Spotting the hidden potential

"Love . . . believes all things."—1 CORINTHIANS 13:7

Have you noticed how some people spot opportunities while they are still opportunities, and others never recognize opportunities until they have become accomplishments?

**351**

> **Possibility thinking is the mental process that intuitively sifts and spots opportunities while they are still fresh and potentially viable.**

"Love believes all things." So possibility thinkers have the capacity to believe in *all things*, which means that:

- You see opportunities in obstacles.
- You believe that a stumbling block can become a stepping stone.
- You believe that frustrations can become meaningful forces to guide you along the right path.
- You believe that God uses both the good and bad experiences to mold, motivate, and educate you.

More than once in my life, when facing an enormous setback, I have prayed aloud to God, "Now, Lord—it's going to be very interesting to see what you will make out of this mess!" Believe me, He has always surprised me with His creativity!

The Lord does not lack the imagination to build something beautiful out of that which has been broken.

The heavenly Father is no failure! His goals are to turn you and me into wonderful people. Through sunlight and storm He is sculpting your soul. You need only to keep on believing that something beautiful is going to emerge out of all of this. Choose to believe in this wonderful, sovereign, sensitive God—today!

## Living without insurance

"Heaven and earth will pass away, but My
words will by no means pass away."—LUKE
21:33

**352**    The most valued possessions of life cannot be covered by
insurance! The challenge of faith is to live life abundantly and
adventurously—even without insurance!

Who can insure you against cancer?

against car and plane crashes?

against loss of a loved one?

against an untimely death?

against painful divorce or personal relationships?

Yes, careful observance of natural laws of providence can
reduce risks in these categories.

Yes, dynamic philosophy of life can minimize the chances
of pain in the human heart.

But the reality is this: Life without risk is impossible. So
there is no alternative to faith! Faith is our only option!

In *Alice in Wonderland*, the white knight, as he prepared
for a journey, anticipated all the possible problems that could
befall him. To withstand attacks from lions, he covered his
horse with sheets of steel. To protect his horse from alligators,
the knight attached knives to the legs of his horse. By the time
the horse and rider were protected against all of the fantasized
dangers, the horse collapsed under the weight!

**As you walk the walk of faith you live without insur-
ance, but your faith is your assurance.**

Christians trust God's Word, and God's promises of eternal
life! They are convinced that heaven and earth may pass away,
but the words of God will never pass away!

Thank You, God, that You are calling me to march forward.
You beckon me to holy adventures in the journey of life.
Thank You for the insurance I do have: the insurance of Your
promise that You will never leave me nor forsake me. Thank
You, God. Amen.

## *Abandoning all fears*

"Who shall separate us from the love of Christ?
Shall tribulation, or distress, or persecution, or
famine, or nakedness, or peril, or sword? . . . In
all these things we are more than conquerors
through Him who loved us."—ROMANS 8:35, 37

I admit I was once a chain smoker, indulging in what I now **353**
know to be a very physically destructive and hence a negative
and sinful habit. But addiction to cigarette smoking was a difficult habit to break. It was fear of lung cancer that finally
caused me to quit. But it was a positive desire to live more
than a fear of dying that made me break the habit.

How does faith conquer all fears? A psychiatrist once said,
"The fear of death is the mother of all fears." If you conquer
the fear of dying, you really conquer all other fears as well.

How does faith conquer the fear of death? Faith believes
there is a God who made this world and is alive today. He
came to this world in the form of a human being—Jesus
Christ. Jesus died on a cross to save you and me from our sins.
Through Him, we have forgiveness of sins and a solid assurance of pardon, which removes all guilt and all fear of judgment.

I know that if I die tonight, I need not fear divine judgment;
for Jesus Christ will be my lawyer to represent me before the
Great Judge. He will plead my case, and I shall be admitted to
the presence of the Eternal One with joy and gladness!

Have you accepted Jesus as your Friend, your Savior?

> **Jesus Christ, I accept You now as my Savior. I open my
> mind and life for Your refreshing love to flow in me
> and through me. I rejoice with tears of gladness in the
> salvation which You give me now. I need fear nothing
> anymore!**

*FAITH IS . . .*
## Enduring all the way

"Love . . . endures all things."—1 CORINTHIANS
13:7

**354** Faith can be compared to a battery. Some people have faith with a short life span, while others have super staying power.

Staying power is what you need today. Your faith will become so strong that you will have the power of endurance adequate for whatever your life encounters.

### God gives endurance to match encounters.

My dear friend, the late Corrie ten Boom, often told the story of how she expressed her anxieties to her father when she was a child. "Daddy, I wish I had the faith to face tragedies with a cheerful spirit."

Her father answered her: "Corrie, the Lord will give you the faith when you need it! Just keep trusting Him."

Then he went on to explain, "Corrie, when I send you to the store, I don't give you the money to carry in your pockets while you are playing. I give you the money when you are ready to go to the market."

Corrie learned the lesson well. Years later she was arrested by the Nazis and placed in a concentration camp. She found that she had unbelievable faith to face the worst possible human tragedies without collapsing internally.

Have you really committed your life 100 percent to Jesus Christ? Have you accepted Him as your Living Friend? Your personal Savior? Your ultimate authority? Your private Lord? If so, I guarantee that God will not allow you to be deprived of your most needed resource at the most critical time. He will provide faith when you need it the most, and you will endure to the end!

## Compromising before quitting

"Love . . . hopes all things."—1 CORINTHIANS
13:7

Faith produces success *when it is strong enough to compro-* **355**
*mise before quitting.*

Compromise can be kingly! It takes an inwardly secure person to back down, back off, settle for less, and still make a go of it.

Retreating is sometimes the wisest way to advance. Compromise today; make up for it tomorrow Give a little now. Regain it—and more—down the road.

Mao Tse-tung used this principle of success very cleverly. "One step back, two steps forward." It was a major element in his success. It is a clever device that has been used by other Communist powers worldwide.

"I'm going to blow my brains out, Reverend." The man was desperate. Life was too much for him to handle.

"Before you quit on living," I urged, "why don't you quit doubting and give faith a chance."

He was a proud man who wanted to run his life without any interference from an almighty God. But the result was alcoholism and now attempted suicide.

"Why don't you compromise a bit?" I asked. "Why don't you give in to God? He's there. You've just been too stubborn to give yourself a chance to become a believer!" The good news is this man compromised—before quitting. He turned his life over to God and became a believer.

**Compromise is the gateway to the great way.**

What compromise do you need to make today? If you're facing tough times, don't quit. Compromise!

## Bowing out gracefully

"Lord, now You are letting Your servant depart in peace . . . for my eyes have seen Your salvation."—LUKE 2:29–30

**356** One of the beautiful old men in the Bible is Simeon. Talk about faith. He dared to pray that he might live to see the birth of the Messiah. The day finally came when Joseph and Mary brought their newborn baby boy to be circumcised. With a deep conviction that came from God, Simeon knew this baby was the Promised One. This Jesus would be the fulfillment of the Old Testament prophesies.

Simeon's prayer was answered. And so he added a charming affirmation: "Lord, now You are letting Your servant depart in peace."

What more could we hope for as we come to the end of the year? The time comes to close the book, to turn in the report, to offer your resignation, or to accept retirement from the company.

It takes a lot of faith to climb a mountain! But it takes just as much faith to climb down.

Can your walk of faith carry you through your golden years, down the sunset trail, to the very end, with joy in your spirit? Yes, it is possible with Christ as your guide.

Jesus knew how to bow out gracefully. After paying the price, making the sacrifice, and shedding His redemptive life's blood on the cross, He left His earthly life with the words, "It is finished" (John 19:30). He had completed the job He was sent to do.

**Simeon's words are a promise to all who never yield to the temptation to wrestle their destiny out of the hands of the sovereign and merciful God. You and I, like Simeon, will come to the end of life with pride behind us, love around us, and hope ahead of us. That is bowing out gracefully.**

## FAITH IS . . .
### *Facing death unafraid*

"For God so loved the world that He gave His
only begotten Son, that whoever believes in
Him should not perish but have everlasting
life."—JOHN 3:16

**357**

Can you handle the prospect of thinking about your own
death? Does your mortality depress you or frighten you? Then
deal with this fear forthrightly and deal with it now. For the
fear of death is the mother of all other fears.

Once you have destroyed the fear of death, you have slain
the ultimate dragon that would devour your soul of its peace
and the power that comes from a peaceful mind.

What is death anyway? It is a transition. Every person lives
three lives. The first life is nine months long. Then we die.
Yes, birth is a process of dying to a world we've known for
nine months. But it's also the process of being born.

When we live our second life, the soul is prepared within
the womb of the body to be born out of this body into eternity! And eternity is life where consciousness surpasses the
consciousness of this earthly plane in the same way that consciousness in my life today transcends my consciousness
while I was still in my mother's womb!

So death is a transition. Death does not have to be anything
to fear. The only thing to fear is hell. And God offers to every
person the promise of heaven if we will only accept His Son,
Christ Jesus, to be our guide across the chasm between time
and eternity.

> **Why am I so sure that when I die I will step, not into a
> thunderstorm, but into the sunlight? Because Jesus
> Christ is my Savior and my Friend.**

Today I ask you to take the greatest leap of faith confronting
the prospect of your death. Accept God's promise of salvation.

## Immortalizing yourself—forever

"I am the resurrection and the life. He who
believes in Me, though he may die, he shall
live."—JOHN 11:25

**358**   Human beings of all ages and all cultures have gone to all
lengths to try to achieve immortality.

For instance, I recently visited an apartment building where
there was a bronze plaque in the entrance bearing the title:
First President of the Homeowners Association.

Don't misunderstand me. The desire to want to be immortal should not be condemned! For when a person says, "I don't
care if anybody remembers me," more often than not he or
she suffers from a negative self-image. It is normal, natural,
and basically healthy for a person to want to be immortalized.

The inclination to achieve immortality is honorable. The
universal instinctive hunger for immortality is God—im-
planted! Respect and respond to this human hunger. The problem is, how do we go about achieving immortality?

**Our faith holds the perfect pathway to immortality.**

It tells us that we shall achieve immortality in the imper-
ishableness of this human soul. Go back and read John 3:16.
Reread again and again the Bible verse of today.

**We are told that if we believe in Jesus Christ, though
we may die, we shall live!**

I believe that! Because I believe that Jesus Christ arose from
the dead. He is alive today. He has experienced the transition
from mortality to immortality! And He wants to bestow that
same incomparable treasure to you, today!

Thank You, God, for giving me the gift of immortality! I
accept Your promise of eternal life. I know You will keep Your
promises. Amen.

## Parting company hopefully

"Go therefore and make disciples of all the
nations. . . ; and lo, I am with you always."—
MATTHEW 28:19–20

Negative thinking is so widespread in our society that our **359**
entire vocabulary is permeated with negative-thinking clichés.

Today, replace a negative-thinking farewell phrase with a
positive send-off!

This past year I've been trying to change a very popular
phrase that appears harmless enough, but in reality is far too
negative. It is the parting comment, "Take care!"

Can you imagine the mental climate that is created when
tens of millions of people repeat over and over again, many
times a day, the words "Take care"?

After all, the subconscious mind doesn't make judgments.
Rather, it accepts the recorded negative directive as an order to
be fulfilled! Little by little, those words subtly take over our
thinking.

Programmed to be cautious, and avoid risk, we reticently
approach the next opportunity subconsciously programmed
for *caution*, rather than *courage*.

Here is the truth:

**People who take care never go anywhere.**

When positive-thinking people part company, they *don't*
say, "Take care"; they say, "Take a chance and take charge!"

Can you imagine God's saying to Christ before He was sent
from heaven to earth on His saving mission, "Take care, My
Son"?

Can you imagine God's saying to you as you catch His
dream, "Take care, My child"?

Our Lord's final farewell was not a cautious, tender good-by.
It was a courageous challenge to go into all the world and
make disciples "of all the nations," and then a promise, "I am
with you always."

## *Impressing others*

"Let all that you do be done with love."—
1 CORINTHIANS 16:14

**360** A quarrelsome, crotchety woman made an awful scene on a city bus. As she stepped off the bus, she threw a parting insult to the driver. Just before he closed the door, he called out to her, "Lady, you left something behind!"

She stopped abruptly on the sidewalk, turned around, and asked, "Oh, what?"

"A very bad impression!" the driver said, as he closed the door.

Longfellow's words impressed me when I was a little boy in school.

> *Lives of good men all remind us*
> *that we can make our lives sublime*
> *and in departing leave behind us*
> *footprints on the sands of time.*

What the world needs today is a good impression of the human family. What unbelieving people need is a good impression of Christians! What negative-thinking people need is a good impression of positive thinkers.

**Faith puts our life on a path that guarantees us we can leave a good impression behind! And that is important. In the process we inspire others to live life on a loftier level!**

That means that you and I have a fantastic opportunity today to be cheerful, optimistic, encouraging, hopeful, thoughtful, and beautiful human beings! In the process we'll leave a wonderful impression behind. Let's be wonderful walking advertisements for Jesus Christ!

And people will admit, "If that is what Christianity is, I want it!"

## *Preparing to live to be one hundred*

"Indeed, You have made my days as
handbreadths,/And my age is as nothing before
You."—PSALM 39:5

If you are walking the walk of faith, you should be planning to live to one hundred years of age! I am! I'm planning and hoping to live to be one hundred. Then what? Then I'll write a book entitled *How to Set Your Goals When You Are One Hundred Years Old.*

At the time of the writing of this book, there are over thirty thousand centenarians in America.

Meanwhile, good physical exercise, proper nutrition, vitamins, a wise diet, coupled with the power of positive faith—to say nothing of continued medical developments—all add up to the very real possibility that you may live to be one hundred!

"I don't want to live that long," one negative thinker said to me. "And spend the last 5-10-or 15 years feeble, senile, and a burden on others."

"Shame on you!" I scolded. "Think possibilities! You can—if you live, eat, exercise, pray and think right. Be peppy, bright, keen, until the end. My grandfather was—and he lived into his ninety-seventh year! Don't cheat yourself on years of life—or life in those years!"

**Not being prepared to live to be one hundred is to be controlled by a lack of faith!**

Doubt tells you that you are getting old and you ought to give up and simply die. If you are eighty years old, get excited about your future. When you are one hundred years old you'll look back and say, "I wish I had realized how young I was when I was eighty years of age. If only I had known I had a fifth of a century still ahead of me!"

If you are walking the walk of faith today, you will indeed prepare yourself to live to be one hundred! What goals do you have today? What good do you still want to accomplish? Imagine yourself being alive, awake, active, alert, and enthusiastic until the end—and your faith will make it so!

**361**

## *Renewing your strength*

"Those who wait on the LORD shall renew their strength;/They shall mount up with wings like eagles."—ISAIAH 40:31

**362**   Are you bored? Tired of life? Do you feel burned out? Today's walk of faith gives four steps to renew your strength and fly high naturally through God-given dreams that generate energy, excitement, and enthusiasm. The steps are:

1. Don't **sigh.** If today is difficult, don't feel sorry for yourself, sighing, "Why me?" Sighing only saps strength. Rather, ask the right question: "Why not me?" Why do you think you should be exempt from the trying human experiences that challenge you to be tough and courageous?

2. Do **try.** Yes, you can make it anyway! You are loaded with mental powers! You can go anywhere from where you are today, when you T-R-Y!

T—*Trust God.* He will give you an idea that will appear absolutely impossible. That's probably a sure sign that it comes from Him.

R—*Reach out to Him.* He will give guidance to you and to others for support.

Y—*Yield your life to God's Holy Spirit.* He will give you the power to move surely and successfully.

3. Do **buy.** Buy the idea that you can be a successful person just as well as anybody else. Don't let this challenge pass you by. Grab it. Pay the price. Look for no shortcuts. Seek no easy solutions to your problems.

4. You will **FLY!** You will be renewed. You can mount up with wings like an eagle. You will fly high over disappointments that normally ground you. Faith is flying high—God's way—with dreams, not drugs.

This is God's minute. Pause to pray. Open your mind. Ask Him for a dream. He will renew your strength.

**Decide to do something positive today, and you will mount up on wings of faith!**

# Shielding, fielding, and wielding

"'Surely God is in you,/And there is no other;/
There is no other God.'"—ISAIAH 45:14

What triumphant power there is in faith! Look what a **363**
tough-minded faith you have!

1. Faith provides *shielding power.* Shield your mind from
the negative thoughts by affirming:

• I have broken free from the tyranny of past mistakes, sins,
and errors.

• I no longer react to great ideas with the "impossibility
complex."

• I am in love with myself, with life, with the Lord, and
with other human beings.

• I find that this perfect love casts out all fear.

2. Faith provides *fielding power.* Now use this faith-power
to field the opportunities around you. Affirm:

• I gather the opportunities. When I was a child, I had
dreams of finding lots of nickles and dimes on the ground or
in the grass. That childhood dream has become a reality!

• I search for opportunities to grow, to study, to develop possibilities all around me!

3. Faith provides *wielding power.* Wow! How wonderful
this possibility-thinking faith works! You are *shielded* from
the negative thoughts that tell you it won't work. Immediately you begin to *field* the opportunities, and now you
*wield leadership.*

Take command!

Set goals!

4. Faith provides *yielding power.* Faith gives you the freedom to take control. Affirm:

• I will *not yield* to any negative persons the right to make
the decisions that affect my future.

• I yield my life to the lordship of Jesus Christ, the greatest
possibility thinker of all time!

# Starting—and then starting over and over again

"Love never fails"—1 CORINTHIANS 13:8

**364**  Yes, faith gives you the power to conquer your biggest problem: getting started!

The hardest part of any project is beginning. The gravitational pull of negative emotions is a powerful force to keep us from launching out.

Did you remember this lesson in our earlier writings? *The person who starts can never be a total failure.* At least he succeeded in overcoming his inertia. He did not fail to try!

Faith gets you started because it assures you that this is the one battle you cannot lose. Starting is winning now! Your job today is to get started, today—at least—you will be a success! For you will win over the fear of beginning!

Which means you have conquered your fear of trying. You have overcome your fear of failing. You have exercised initiative and have taken leadership over your own destiny. You have broken free from mental chains that have bound you. You have snapped the handcuffs that the enemy of negative thinking has clamped around you. So getting started guarantees you success *today!* Will you succeed every day?

And when you don't succeed? Then what do you do? You start over again! My first book, "Move Ahead with Possibility Thinking" was rejected by several publishers, but I didn't lose faith! Finally, it was picked up, and my writing career was launched.

It's exciting to think of this thrilling freedom that is yours! You have the freedom to start over again right after you have had a failure! Have you had a failure in your educational program? In personal relationships? In your walk with the Lord? Have you slipped and stumbled on this path of faith! Faith simply tells us that we can start—and start over again!

That's why we can declare: Faith never fails!

## Admiring what works

"Now thanks be to God who always leads us in triumph in Christ."—2 CORINTHIANS 2:14

I saw a fantastic saying on a bumper sticker: "If it works, don't fix it." Yes, if it works, don't tamper with it. Don't re-organize a successful operation just to "make your own mark." Don't reject a great tradition just because you want "something new." Be sure of this—if anything lived long enough to become a tradition there must be something good in it. Does it work? If so *mind it, don't mend it.* For you might do more meddling than mending.

There is always the danger that our ego will get involved. We will be tempted to redesign a workable plan to fit our style only to find out it doesn't work as well.

Admire good ideas that work—even if you didn't think of it first. Don't be too proud to imitate somebody who is doing a better job than you are. After all it has been said that imita-tion is the most sincere compliment you can give.

- Hitch your wagon to a star.
- Follow a leader.
- Listen to the winner.

Faith is admiring what works. This gives you the clue as to how faith liberates you from ego involvement in your judg-ment of other persons, projects, procedures, and positions. Faith saves you from rejecting ideas simply because *you* didn't think of them!

**People who walk the walk of faith never suffer from a lack of inner spiritual resources. They have enough faith to look honestly at what's happening, to admire what works.**

Compliment the achiever—even if he's your competitor. You will be walking the walk of faith on a higher elevation than most people ever dream of reaching.

**365**

## *Leaping into the unknown*

"So he, leaping up, stood and walked and
entered the temple with them—walking,
leaping, and praising God."—ACTS 3:8

**366**    Faith is often called a "leap." How appropriate! How else
could you possibly move from one point to another when
there is no direct link?

How do you cross over a crevice when there is no bridge?
Faith is leaping across gaps that exist between
>    the known and the unknown
>    the proven and the unproven
>    the actual and the possible
>    the grasp and the reach
>    the "I've got it" and the "I want it"
>    the knowledge and the mystery
>    the material reality and the spiritual reality
>    the truth exposed and the truth undiscovered
>    the goals achieved and the goals still pursued
>    youth and maturity
>    sickness and health
>    sin and forgiveness
>    life and death
>    time and eternity.

Yes, there is always a chasm between today and tomorrow. I
cannot be sure I can cope with tomorrow. But by a running
leap I will jump into tomorrow with expectancy! There is always a chasm between my present achievements and my unfulfilled hopes and dreams. By faith I make the leap—and
grow!

There is always a chasm between where I'm at and where
I'm going—by faith I make the leap forward!

What lies ahead? Tomorrow? Next week? Next month?
Next year? Beyond this life?

I believe in faith! I believe in believers! I believe in God! I
believe in Jesus Christ! I believe in tomorrow! I'm going to
take the leap of faith!